COMMUNION OF LOVE

COMMUNION OF LOVE

WILLIAM DEWBERRY

authorHOUSE®

AuthorHouse™ LLC
1663 Liberty Drive
Bloomington, IN 47403
www.authorhouse.com
Phone: 1-800-839-8640

Published by AuthorHouse   07/30/2014

ISBN: 978-1-4969-2872-6 (sc)
ISBN: 978-1-4969-2873-3 (e)

Any people depicted in stock imagery provided by Thinkstock are models,
and such images are being used for illustrative purposes only.
Certain stock imagery © Thinkstock.

This book is printed on acid-free paper.

Because of the dynamic nature of the Internet, any web addresses or links contained in this book may have changed
since publication and may no longer be valid. The views expressed in this work are solely those of the author and do
not necessarily reflect the views of the publisher, and the publisher hereby disclaims any responsibility for them.

Scripture taken from the New King James Version
Copyright 1982 by Thomas Nelson, Inc.
Used by permission. All rights reserved.

Scripture is taken from the NKJV Study Bible and may be used in magazines, articles, newsletters, bulletins, and reviews without
the written permission of the publisher. Each such use must be accompanied by the following credit line: From the NKJV Study
Bible, Copyright 1997, 2007 by Thomas Nelson, Inc. Used by permission. Scriptures used with the consent of Thomas Nelson Inc.

Contents

Authors Preface

The author of this book believes in the God of creation and in the authenticity of the Bible. The Bible is an international book that contains the most important information that is available to the people of the world and is presented in this commentary in a way and language that is easy for the reader to understand who God is and learn about God's incredible plan of grace for the people He created. Knowing God is a lifelong adventure that never ends even with death. This book is an explanation of the story of redemption written by a Layman in simple every day terms.

Introduction

The source of information for this story is based on the Bible, which is a book about God and the people he created in the beginning of time. Communion means the act of sharing; a having in common, an exchange of thoughts and feeling in a spiritual relationship. God exists outside the sphere of time and is the creator of all things. He is eternal and the ultimate first cause of all life and matter. There is a communion of love between God and the people He created. True love is a matter of the will, not emotion. The Bible says God is love. Every thing God does in regards to people is motivated by love.

Love is a positive emotion that seeks to best for anyone that is loved and love can be known to exist only by the action that it prompts. 1st John 4–Let us love one another for love is of God: and everyone that loves is born of God and knows God. He who does not love does not know God, for God is love. God sits above the circle of the earth, and its inhabitants are like grasshoppers who stretches out the heavens like a curtain, and spreads them out like a tent to dwell in." The Bible records the history of the people God created from the beginning of time to the end of time when the faithful followers of God's Son enter heaven. People realize their existence must have come from a superior intelligence and power much greater than any person but they do not find the God of creation until someone teaches them about God or they read about Him in the Bible. That is why God inspired people to write the Bible so that everyone could find the only real God.

The first words in the Bible are–In the beginning God created the heavens and the earth. In the 'beginning' means the act or fact of rising or springing from a particular source – such as from God. In my own experience in life I found God when I as a young man who did not believe or disbelieve in God because I had never experienced God or thought seriously about Him. I was about eighteen years old when I first read the Bible and what I read convinced me that God was real and I needed to find out more about God and the people who attended church meetings. Soon after that I continued to read and think more about God and Jesus and decided I needed to know more so I attended a church meeting and obeyed the gospel of Christ. God's Word in the inspired Bible worked on my heart convincing me that God is real and He wants me t love Him. The Bible tells the story of the creation and the history of God's interaction with people in the process of the salvation of mankind. It answers questions about the creation and all other questions that pertain to the life of people on earth and their eternal destiny, including life after death. The Bible welcomes all people to have a relationship with God. There are 66 separate books in the Bible and each book reveals a part of the entire story of the creation and the history of God's plan of redemption. The Bible was in the process of being written for more than one thousand years.

The Bible consists of the Old and New Testaments which record the plan of redemption from the creation at the beginning of time to the end of time. The Holy Spirit of God inspired the men who wrote the Bible. The forty men who had a part in writing the Bible lived in different time periods yet they all wrote a significant part of the Bible that tells a part of the same story.

The Bible contains some events that began to be written soon after the creation and were not completed until the first century A.D. What may be known about the glory of God can be seen and understood by the things He made when He created the universe and they are explained in the Bible. The Bible was completed nearly 2,000 years ago and its authenticity has been carefully preserved. The Holy Spirit inspired the men who wrote the Bible. The Bible begins with the first days of the creation story and moves from there to the history of God's dealings with man from the beginning of time to the end of time. The Bible explains that God cannot be worshiped with men's hands people must worship God with their heart. The entire story of the Bible is a self-revelation of God's love for the people He created. John 3:16–For God so loved the people of the world that He gave His only Son to die, that whoever believes in Him will not perish.

The Bible is the inspired Word of God–All scripture is the inspired word of God and is to be used for doctrine, reproof, correction and for instruction in righteousness. 2nd Timothy. 2nd Peter 1–No prophecy of the scriptures is for private interpretation only. God does not need people but they need Him and they need a knowledge of His word because God made the universe for his own glory and the creation of the universe and all the things needed for human life. God loves people and He wants a personal relationship with people like a Father to His children because He is our heavenly Father. The Bible speaks of God the Father about 250 times. Jesus spoke of God as His Father and He referred to God as your father when He was speaking to the disciples. 1st John 3–What manner of love the Father has given to us that we are called the children God. God desires His children to be like Him insofar as that is possible. The gracious character of God is described in Exodus 34 when He descended in a cloud to describe his nature.

The Lord passed before Moses and said– "The Lord, the Lord God is merciful and gracious, longsuffering, and abounding in goodness and truth, keeping mercy for thousands, forgiving iniquity and transgression and sin." God makes Himself known to us in ways that our senses tell us. God can have a dramatic impact on the spirit of people - Spirit to spirit. God chose to communicate with people so they would accept Him and obey Him. All knowledge of God is limited by the intelligence of the people God created.

The Bible reveals God's message to the people He created. The Bible was originally written in the Hebrew, Aramaic and Greek languages. There is overwhelming evidence today that the Bible people depend on is the genuine Word of God. There were thousands of copies of the original writings. Many of the original 5900 Greek manuscripts of the New Testament still exists. By the year A.D. 200 the Bible had been translated into several languages. People all over the world depend on the Bible for the authentic Word of God and the Bible is the main source for their faith in God and Jesus Christ.

Deuteronomy 4:32–For ask now concerning the days that are past, which were before you, since the day that God created man on the earth, and ask from one end of heaven to the other, whether any great thing like this has happened, or anything like it has been heard. Exodus 4:11–So the Lord said to him, "Who has made man's mouth? Or who makes the mute, the deaf, the seeing, or the blind? Have not I, the Lord?" Christians base their knowledge and understanding of the mysteries of the universe and the existence of living moral, intelligent human beings with their gifts of inductive and deductive reason, on faith and logical reasoning. The Bible allows people to understand what they are, who they are, and their responsibility to obey the only true and living God that created them. Christians can actually feel the effects of God's Spirit on their spirit when they read and meditate on the Holy Scriptures.

The writing in the Bible is called scripture and the scriptures have been preserved through the ages as the Word of God. The Bible is a story about eternal life involving sin, redemption, faith, hope and love. The writers of the Bible included kings, fishermen, priests, government officials, farmers, shepherds and doctors.

Even with this diversity there is perfect unity in the story of redemption in the Bible. The writings in the Bible are called scriptures, and the scriptures have been preserved through the ages as the Word of God. These scriptures came by way of revelation, defined as a work of God in which He communicated divine truth to men who otherwise would not know God's word. The original languages of the Bible were Hebrew and Greek. Each book of the Bible is a supernatural work of God in which He communicated divine truth to men who were inspired by the Holy Spirit. The Bible is the world's all-time best-selling book. Millions of copies of the Bible have been printed and distributed. People do not have an excuse to fail to learn about God and obey Him. The Bible is a story about eternal life, sin, redemption, faith, hope and love. Prophecy is a prediction of future events made known by a revelation of God's Word.

Prophecies, written in the Bible never failed and were believed by faithful people. Old Testament books of the Bible were written between 1450 BC and 430 BC and they contain hundreds of prophecies about the coming of God's Son, who would come to redeem people from sin. Each Holy Spirit inspired author, added God's Word to the story of redemption. The Bible answers the questions that people cannot find the answer to outside of the Bible. The bible is divided into two main parts called the Old Testament and the New Testament. God's word was breathed out in words and thoughts, God literally put the words into the mind of the people He inspired to preach, teach and write the Bible. The Bible has survived for many ages and is available all over the world today. The Old Testament begins with the creation including people and the founding and preservation of the Hebrew nation. Moses wrote Genesis the first book even though he was not born until many years later when the children of Israel were in Egypt. Moses wrote with the inspired direction of the Holy Spirit. The prophecies in the Old Testament about God's Son were written about Him in the Bible many years before His birth.

2nd Timothy 3:16 "All scripture is given by inspiration of God, and is profitable for doctrine, for reproof, for correction. For instruction in righteousness, that the man of God may be complete, thoroughly equipped for every good work."

There were numerous prophets, such as Moses, and many other men chosen by God to write the Bible and every one of those men were inspired by God. The word of God in the Bible is known as scripture. The Bible consists of 66 individual books divided into groups. The major division is between the Old Testament and the New Testament. Both testaments record the ministries of the prophets. The Bible of 66 books is a complete book revealing the righteousness and salvation of God. The New Testament is the best commentary on the teachings of the Old Testament and the Old Testament is the best commentary on the teachings of the New Testament. If the interpretation of any prophecy in the Old Testament is not in accordance with New

Testament teaching, then that interpretation is wrong. The Bible does not contradict itself but sometimes is misunderstood.

The Bible is a marvelous gift from God and it demonstrates His great love and concern for all of the people He created. God's Word can have a dramatic impact on the spirit and lives of people who read the Bible containing God's word - Spirit to spirit. God chose to communicate with people so they would accept Him and obey Him. God has always existed and will always exist. God is not subject to scientific proof. God is known and taken for granted on a basis of reasoning and faith. All people were made for a purpose they may not realize until they think about the origin and purpose of life and learn about God. The Bible is the only book with the authority to instruct people how to obey and worship God. The Spirit of God inspired the men who wrote. During the 1380's John Wycliffe and many faithful scribes translated the Bible into the English language from the Latin. Johan Gutenberg invented the printing press in the 1450's and a Bible in the Latin version was printed. Archaeology, and a great number of ancient manuscripts such as 5,300 Greek manuscripts, 10,000 Latin Vulgate manuscripts, the Samaritan Pentateuch manuscripts 400 B.C., the Septuagint Greek manuscripts 280 B.C. and 9,300 various manuscripts. Copies of the manuscripts make it possible to reconstruct the original documents with almost complete accuracy. Psalm 145:18 "The Lord is near to all who call on Him in truth." The entire story of the Bible is a self-revelation of God's love for the people He created. John 3:16–For God so loved the people of the world that He gave His only Son to die, that whoever believes in Him will not perish.

Most people believe in the God who created the universe and everything else but there are still those who refuse to accept Him. With the invention of the printing press the Bible could be reproduced in large quantities. In 1496 John Colet translated the Greek version of the New Testament into English. William Tyndale printed the New Testament in the English language. The process of translating the entire Bible into English continued for many years and today there are millions of Bibles containing God's word in most if not all places in the world. In one year alone 627,000,000 copies of the Bible were distributed by the (United Bible Societies, 1999).

The Bible convicts people of sin when they fail to obey God's revealed law, which has been assigned. The consequence of disobedience is known as sin and sin leads to spiritual death, which is defined as being separated from the grace of God. Sinners, we all, must obtain God's forgiveness for sin or be punished with eternal death. The first five books of the Bible are called the Pentateuch (the books of the law). Since the Word of God has been written people have no excuse for failing to obey God's law for every particular age.

Christians use the advantage of the Holy Bible to learn more about God from day to day. Each book in the Bible tells a part of the entire story, and each of the 66 books compliments the other books in telling one complete story. God's Word can have a dramatic impact on the spirit and lives of people who read the Bible and experience God's word - Spirit to spirit. God chose to communicate with people so they would accept Him and obey Him. God has always existed and will always exist. God is not subject to scientific proof. God is known and taken for granted on a basis of reasoning and faith. All people were made for a purpose they may not realize until they think about the origin and purpose of life and learn about God. Each book of the Bible is a supernatural work of God in which He communicated divine truth to men who were inspired by the Holy Spirit. The Old Testament begins with the creation and the founding and preservation of the Hebrew nation. God's Son Jesus and the Holy Spirit were with God during the creation and they had a part in the creation.

Colossians 1:15-17– God's Son Jesus is the image of the invisible God, the firstborn over all creation. For by Him all things were created that are in heaven and that are on earth, visible and invisible, whether thrones or dominions or principalities or powers.

All things were created through Him and for Him. And he is before all things, and in Him all things consist." No matter where you go on earth or in its atmosphere or in space and beyond, the evidence of God's creation and His glory can be seen. Isaiah 40:21-22 "Have you not known? Have you not heard? Has it not been told you from the beginning? Have you not understood from the foundations of the earth? God sits above the circle of the earth, and its inhabitants are like grasshoppers who stretches out the heavens like a curtain, and spreads them out like a tent to dwell in."

God is not motivated by or cognizant of time or place, because He is everywhere at the same time. The Bible has survived for many ages and is available all over the world today. The Bible answers the questions that pertain to the life of people on earth and their eternal destiny including life after death. There are 66 separate books in the Bible. Each of the 66 books reveals a part of the entire story of the creation and the history of God's plan of redemption. The Bible is the world's all-time best-selling book. Millions of copies of the Bible have been printed and distributed. Old Testament books of the Bible were written between 1450 BC and 430 BC and they contain hundreds of prophecies about the coming of God's Son, who came to redeem people. Prophecies about God's Son Jesus were written in the Old Testament many years before the birth of Jesus. 2nd Timothy 3:16 "All scripture is given by inspiration of God, and is profitable for doctrine, for reproof, for correction. For instruction in righteousness, that the man of God may be complete, thoroughly equipped for every good work." There were numerous prophets, such as Moses, and many other men chosen by God to write the Bible. There is evidence in the Bible, that God is the creator of the universe in its entirety.

Most people believe that God created the universe and everything else but there are still those who refuse to accept Him. Christians conclude their understanding with a belief in an Omniscient, Omnipotent, Glorious Creator we call God, the Holy Spirit and the Son of God. Paul a man who knew the only real, true God had experienced the awesome power of God explained to the people in the city of Athens that there was only One God and He was responsible for the creation and for life. In Acts 17– Paul was in Athens and he spoke to some very religious people but they did not know about the only real living God of creation and they were worshiping and serving idols as their God.

The people made an inscription to the unknown God. The people worshiped idols they could see and touch. Paul told them they were very religious in every way. Religious means they realized there must be a superior being, a God that created all things and they owed Him reverence and obedience. Paul taught about the only real God that created everything a God they knew nothing about. Paul an Apostle that knew God very well and found faith in Jesus because He had experienced God personally.

Paul stated—the real God is the God that made the world and He is the Lord of heaven and earth, and He has no need for material things since He is the one who created life and death and everything. God began human life with one person, Adam, and one woman Eve, and everyone else is an off-spring. Since God is the Creator He owns all people and He has the right to bless them or to punish them. People cannot blame God for sin, evil, misfortune or punishment, because He has provided His Holy Word in the Bible as a guide for people to learn what God expects of them. God even made provision for the forgiveness of sins by sending his own Son to earth to die as a sacrifice for their sins in order that people can be forgiven and regain their righteousness. People who remain in fellowship with God can expect to be blessed with eternal life. Christians believe in God as the Creator who sustains life. Without any evidence to the contrary, the most reasonable belief is what the Bible teaches about God. People can know God by His Self-Revelation in the creation and in His Word recorded in the Bible. God has a triune nature consisting of God the Father, the Son and the Holy Spirit and the Bible reveals the nature of all three. God is known as a personal God by His own revelation through his word in the Bible. God is sovereign and exercises His will according to His supreme intelligence, holiness and attributes of love, compassion and wisdom. There is evidence in the Bible that God is the creator of the universe in its entirety. Christians base their knowledge and understanding of the mysteries of the universe and the existence of living moral, intelligent humans on God. Human beings have God's gifts of inductive and deductive reasoning and they develop faith in God with logical reasoning in an effort to understand who we are, what we are and where we came from. Forty men inspired by God's Holy Spirit had a part in writing the Bible.

The authors of the Bible lived in different time periods yet they all wrote a significant part of the Bible that tells a part of the same story. The words inspire and inspiration in 2ⁿᵈ Timothy 3"16 means God breathed. God actually through the agency of the Holy Spirit put His words and understanding into the minds of the people who wrote the Bible and preached and taught His Word. When the Bible says, "in the beginning," it is referring to the beginning of the creation when time on earth began.

Any effort to find the source for the existence of the universe besides God is purely hypothetical and all effort to find a way of creation besides God has been fruitless. Scientists have difficulty, because they conduct their research on the belief that nothing exists beyond what can be seen, measured or felt. The Bible states that God is the creator of all matter and of the first humans to live on the earth, who began multiplying and filled the earth with humanity. God's Word teaches all people how to live and please Him. God created matter first and then converted that matter into the things that exist, including all life. God spoke directly to the first people created and later He revealed Himself in other ways including direct inspiration. The Bible will guide people through life if they are faithful to be obedient to God's Word. Moses wrote the first five books of the Bible called the books of law, and Jews and Christians both accept the Bible as the word of God who through the action of the Holy Spirit, put the scriptures into the mind of Moses, supplying the words for him to write. God communicated divine truth to people who otherwise would not know, or could know, about what God expected from them. The Bible contains some events that began to be written soon after the creation was completed.

God inspired men to write the Bible so that people could know God, acquire faith in God, love for God and have hope for eternal salvation. Christians developed their knowledge and understanding of the mysteries of the universe and the existence of living moral, intelligent human beings on the Bible. 2nd Timothy 3:16-17 "All scripture is given by the inspiration of God, and is profitable for doctrine, for reproof, for correction, for instruction in righteousness, that the man of God may be complete, thoroughly equipped for every good work."

1st Timothy 3:14-17–You must continue in the things which you learned and were assured of, knowing from whom you learned them. From childhood you have known the Holy Scriptures, which are able to make you wise for salvation through faith, which is in Christ Jesus. The answer to the questions of knowing where we came from and why we are here is the only way a person can have a meaningful purpose driven life. God is rational, personal, self-determining and supreme and He is Holy in every way. Since God is personal, He has a personal relationship with His Son, the Holy Spirit, the angels and the people he created. God desires a personal relationship with people like a Father to His children. The laws that have come from research and investigation all support the belief that the universe could not have created itself, and without a constant source of energy the universe would have run down a long time ago. The universe does exist, therefore it had a beginning, and it must have a cause and some entity to keep it in existence.

God graciously created the earth as a place for the existence and support of human life. There is some controversy about the creation of all matter and scientists look for some reason other than God. Popular arguments for the existence of God and His creation are the cosmological, the ontological and the argument for the intelligent design of created things. The cosmological argument proves God's existence by observing the orderly and harmonious creation. The Bible states that God created the heavens and the earth. Genesis 1:1-2 "In the beginning God created the heavens and the earth. The earth was without form, and void; and darkness was on the face of the deep. And the Spirit of God was hovering over the face of the waters." Then God said let there be light. And God saw the light that it was good; and God divided the light from the darkness. God called the light day, and the darkness He called night. So the evening and the morning were the first day. God created everything just right for the support of human life. There are many arguments that point to God as The Supreme Being that created all things. Scientists endeavor to find an answer to the creation by depending on scientific knowledge and investigation. After countless hour of investigation and spending billions of dollars for research, scientists are no closer to bridging the connection between matter and life or of proving the theory of evolution.

The laws that have come from research and investigation all support the belief that the universe could not have created itself, and without a constant source of energy the universe would have run down a long time ago. The universe has existed for many years and is being sustained by an energy source that Christians believe is God. God is self-existing and the creation is dependent on Him. In His nature God is Spirit and is represented as the Great Spirit that created all things. God limited the creation to time and place, and the creation is under His control. God is omnipresent, omniscient and omnipotent and completely holy in every way. God is known as a triune being consisting of God the Father, Jesus Christ His Son, and the Holy Spirit. God has a personal relationship with His Son, the Holy Spirit, the angels, and He desires a relationship with the people He created. God is personal, He can enter into a personal relationship with His Son, the Holy Spirit, the angels and the people he created. God's glory is revealed by His Own attributes of holiness.

The people God created are created in God's image and are intelligent beings that have creative ability and qualities that are invisible, but they can be seen through visible manifestations. There is no plausible explanation for human intelligence that enables people to learn and make choices except for the fact that God made man in His own likeness (image). I believe in the God of creation, because God revealed Himself to me as I read the Bible and I realized God is the only rational answer for the existence of the intelligence, faith, hope, love and desires of people. Freedom of expression and action come from a person's own will and is desirable but unfortunately all people sin by failing to obey God's laws and God withdraws or separates them from His promises. It is without reason to believe or even imagine that anyone else besides an omnipresent omniscient and omnipotent God could have created the universe and all things including people.

The big bang theory concocted by scientists agrees that the creation took place all at once from a source that is more powerful than our minds can comprehend. This seems to be correct if we realize that it was the power of the creator that Christians believe is God Who created the universe with an effect similar to the big bang theory. God is known and taken for granted on a basis of reasoning and faith.

People are the only creatures who are conscious of time, and they govern and understand everything by time: seconds, minutes, days, weeks, months, and years, the past, present and the future. The bible portrays God as pure Spirit and the creator of the Universe including all forms of life that exists now or have ever existed. A complete knowledge of God goes beyond the power of human intelligence but His existence is evident by the nature of His creation and self- revelation. God is rational, self-conscious and self-determining. He is the source of all rational knowledge, and as the Creator He is the supreme authority and sovereign over the entire creation. God exercises His will according to His supreme intelligence, and Holiness. One evidence for God is the existence of the invisible spirit in people. The spirit is the sentient element of people that enables them to perceive, reflect feel and desire, which are also attributes of God. God is infinite, eternal, holy, unchanging, omnipotent, omni present, all knowing, self-sufficient, gracious, merciful, loving and sovereign. The first five books of the Bible are called the Pentateuch (the book of the law). God had the oversight of what was written in the Bible.

God directed the minds of men Through the Holy Spirit teaching them what to write in the Bible. God can see and knows all things, in all places at all times. He is the same today tomorrow and forever. God specifically chose the men to write the Bible. Psalms 8 and 9–"O Lord our lord, how excellent is your name in all the earth. Who have set Your glory above the heavens! O Lord our Lord, I will praise You with my whole heart; I will tell of all Your marvelous works. '"I will be glad and rejoice in You; I will sing praise to your name, O Most High. When my enemies turn back, they shall fall and perish at Your presence."

Without inspiration from God the men who wrote the Bible could not have known, about the things they wrote about, such as the human senses, emotions, attitudes and intelligence that were given to them by God. God wants the people He created and provided for to love Him and obey Him so they could continue to live forever but soon after the creation people transgressed God's commandments, a violation of God's law was called sin.

All sin has its beginning in the mind and heart, then when acted on it becomes sin. The definition of sin is not, arbitrary, dos and don'ts, the Bible teaches us the way God wants us to have faith in Him, love Him and live, in peace and harmony with Him and our fellow man. God, Christ, the Holy Spirit and angels existed in heaven before people were created. The angels witnessed God creating the universe and the other works of God. God created the Arch- angels and the regular angels. God created a great host of angels including powerful angels known as Archangels. Angels are spirit beings that live in heaven and serve God. Job 38:4-7– The angels were present when God created the earth. Angels are celestial beings that can travel back and forth from heaven to the earth and they can appear as men and speak as men. Angels serve as God's messengers. The Angels were all created together in a countless number as God's ministering spirits. Angels can defy the forces of gravity and move swiftly through space with little resistance. They can travel at least near the speed of light (186,000 miles per second) and possibly faster by exerting more of their energy to propel them. Angels are mentioned in the Bible 273 times. Angels could appear on the earth in disguise and the Bible refers to them as sons of God cherubs or cherubim. Angels have a free will and can choose to disobey or rebel against God even though they are subject to strict obedience. Archangels are much greater in power than the other angels. God made at least two great Archangels greater in power and glory than the other angels. Gabriel and Michael are archangels. The description of the power and the activities of Satan suggest that he is very powerful angel and is known as the devil, an adversary an accuser the red dragon and the prince of evil. The Bible speaks about good angels and bad angels among a countless numbers of angels who were created to serve God. The Angels that serve as messengers can also carry out the various acts that God sends them to do. The Psalmist described angels as the mighty servants of God who do His will. When Jesus returns to earth at the end of time His mighty angels will come with Him in flaming fire and will take vengeance on the people who do not acknowledge God.

Satan is a powerful angel who rebelled against the authority of God and tempted people to sin. Satan is one of the most powerful beings created by God and at some time after he was created he rebelled against God and one third of the angels followed him. Satan wanted to be in the position of God and control the angels and the people God created. In the Garden of Eden where God put the first man and woman Satan tempted Adam and Eve to disobey God. Satan and those angels who follow him are called demons and they work against the people God created in an effort to separate people from the fellowship of God. Satan will work against God and His people until the end of time when God destroys him. During your journey through God's redeeming plan you will become acquainted with Satan's evil designs and his destruction.

The phrase in the beginning means when time first began to be counted in regards to the creation of the earth. People measure almost everything by time, but God is eternal, and there is no measure of time with God. Psalms 90:2–Before the mountains were brought forth, or ever you had formed the earth and the world, even from everlasting to everlasting, you are God. Genesis means beginning, and Genesis 1:1 through Genesis 3 gives a brief summary of the chief points of the creation; explaining and enlarging on that part of creation that relates to mankind. In the beginning of God created the heavens, the sun and moon, the earth, dry land and the waters. God separated the waters from the land and created grass, herbs and trees including fruit trees.

God created the creatures that live in water and the birds that fly. God created cattle and other land animals and He was pleased with what He had created. Then God created people, called them man and woman and they were named Adam and Eve. Man and woman was made in some ways like God because God put an intelligent, invisible spirit in the man and woman. The spirit God puts in people is the sentient element in by, which they can perceive, reflect, feel and desire. With the spirit people can feel love, anger, joy, happiness and grief. The people God created were equipped to accumulate knowledge to think, like or dislike and make their own decisions about their activities and actions. The people God created were capable of choosing between good and evil and they have free will to obey or disobey God's commandments, therefore they are responsible for their thoughts and actions.

Adam and Eve were personally responsible for their own decisions and actions. People are responsible individuals, but they can be misled, lied to and deceived and that is what Satan does. God is the benefactor of people because He loves people and he created everything for their benefit. God planted a beautiful Garden on earth for Adam and Eve and He put everything in the garden that is needed to sustain their life. Since Adam and Eve were made by God they belonged to Him and were obligated to obey Him.

Their life was good, they had everything they needed. God gave them one commandment, do not eat from the tree in the middle of the garden, if you do you will die. Among, the animal life God created there was a serpent (snake) and Satan caused the snake to lie to Adam and Eve by telling them they could eat of the tree that God said not to and they would not die. Adam and Eve obeyed the snake (Satan) and ate the forbidden fruit. They disobeyed God and they were afraid because they knew they were wrong to disobey. This is the account of the first sin. God cursed the snake and He punished Adam and Eve. From that time on Adam the man were responsible for working and providing food and the other necessities of life. The punishment of Adam set a precedent for all people that would exist after them. All people would sin and become separated from the fellowship of God and there was no provision for forgiveness of disobedience to God's law in the beginning. In the story of the Communion of Love, which is an overview of the story of redemption we will learn about the consequences of sin and God's gracious plan to redeem people from sin and death which is a consequence of sin.

The Bible reveals the objective of Satan who decided to uses lies and deception to make the people God created rebel against the authority of God by disobeying the law God gave people to obey. During the life of the creation all people will sin and be separated from the fellowship of God. The people who find redemption for their sin, will according to God and His Word in the Bible inherit a new place for God's faithful people to live eternally. Revelation 21—And I heard a loud voice from heaven saying, "Behold, the dwelling place of God is with man. He will dwell with them, and they will be his people, and God Himself will be with them as their God.

God will wipe away every tear from their eyes, and death shall be no more, neither shall there be mourning, nor crying, nor pain anymore, for the former things have passed away." Satan will be destroyed at the end of time when Jesus returns to take His kingdom to heaven. When Satan rebelled against God and exalted himself above God. Satan led other angels to rebel against the authority of God and enslave people in sin. Satan made an attempt to rule over people and cause them to sin against God. Satan is still alive and near the end of time He will lead a crusade to enslave all people in sin. Satan continued to lie and use deceit during the history of God's people that is recorded in the Old Testament and one third of God's angels chose to follow Satan instead of God and they willingly obeyed Satan the Devil. The angels that chose to follow Satan were called demons. In the book of Job we find that there was a continuous struggle in heaven between God and Satan for the souls of people. Satan and his demons harassed God's people before and after the birth of Jesus and Satan is still an enemy of God people today but his power has been limited. Before the end of time Satan will regain his ability to cause great tribulation on earth.

The Bible gives us a vivid picture of the character of Satan. He is a powerful celestial being that does not respect God and is an adversary of Christ and all people. Satan was capable of going back and forth between heaven and earth to tempt God's people to sin. At the end of time God will destroy Satan. John 8:44 Jesus said that Satan the devil was a murderer from the beginning of the creation. 1st John 3:8–He who sins is of the devil, for the devil has sinned from the beginning.

For this purpose the Son of God (Jesus) came to earth to destroy the works of the Satan. Ephesians 6:10-12–Be strong in the Lord and in the power of His might. Put on the whole armor of God that you may be able to stand against the deception of the devil. We do not struggle against flesh and blood but against the principalities, against powers, against the rulers of the darkness of this age, against spiritual hosts of wickedness in the heavenly places. Therefore take up the whole armor of God that you may be able to withstand in the evil day. James 1:4– James tells us that each person is tempted to sin when he is lured and enticed by his own evil desires. The devil and demons tempted people to sin and each person is accountable for their own sin.

The promises of redemption and salvation can be accomplished at any time through faith in Jesus but will not be fully realized until the end of time. God promised to be with His people, in Spirit forever. God will utterly destroy the earth because of the sin of the people but He will make all things new Revelations 21:1-4 –Now I saw a new heaven and a new earth, for the first heaven and the first earth had passed away. Also there was no more sea. Then I John saw the holy city, New Jerusalem, coming down out of heaven from God, prepared as a bride adorned for her husband.

The Holy Spirit

The concept of God in the Bible is that God exists in three personalities, the Father, the Son and the Holy Spirit and all three took part in the creation and in God's plan of redemption. The Holy Spirit is a personal invisible being being under the authority of God and He leads, guides and helps the people God created. The Spirit has personal characteristics like God and great power. The Holy Spirit is set apart and devoted to God's service. The Greek word for the Holy Spirit is pneuma and identifies the Holy Spirit as the third person of the Trinity–Father, Son and Holy Spirit. The Hebrew word ruah means breath, wind or spirit in the Old Testament meaning he is invisible but his power is overwhelming. The Holy Spirit was and still is involved in the life of God's people. The Holy Spirit is a personal being like the Father God and the Son Jesus. The Spirit possesses intelligence, emotion and a will dedicated to carrying out God's commands. Romans 8:26-27– The Spirit helps in our weaknesses. For we do not know what we should pray for as we ought, but the Spirit Himself makes intercession for us with groaning's which cannot be uttered.

1st Corinthians 12:13–for by one Spirit we were all baptized into one body–whether Jews or Greeks, whether slaves or free. First Corinthians chapter three–Christians are called the temple of God, not an edifice of any kind, the very human being that has become a Christian by obedience to the commands of Jesus. "Don't you know the Spirit of God lives in you?" The spirit of people can be influenced by the Holy Spirit. Mk 12:36–David spoke by the inspiration of the Holy Spirit. After Jesus ascension to heaven Jesus Disciples were inspired by the Holy Spirit giving them the ability to preach and teach.

John 14:26– But the Helper the Holy Spirit, whom the Father will send in My name, He will teach you all things, and will bring to your remembrance all things that I said to you. John 15:26– When the Helper comes, whom I shall send to you from the Father, the Spirit of truth who proceeds from the Father, He will testify of Me. The Spirit of truth will guide you into all truth for He will not speak on His own authority, but whatever he hears He will speak; and He will tell you things to come. The Holy Spirit had a part in the creation, and a vital part in God's plan of redemption. The Holy Spirit spoke by the authority of God through the men that wrote the Bible and the prophets that proclaimed the word of God to His people. The Holy Spirit indwells Gods' people to help them spiritually. Without inspiration of the Holy Spirit it would be impossible for humans to write the Bible. God intended for man's spirit to be influenced by God's Holy Spirit so He could communicate with them, allowing people a free will to read the Bible and decide whether to or not to choose a life according to obedience to the Word of God.

Holy Spirit inspired men throughout the story of redemption could influence peoples thinking, affections and decisions, them about love, joy, peace, patience, kindness, sorrow, grief, and anger. Holy Spirit inspiration was necessary because people have a sinful nature that ignores the will of God but if taught they can repent and have a desire to do those things that please God. People who worship God, worship must worship with their spirit in truth, not in ritual expressions of the flesh. Romans 8, says that God did not make mankind to live according to the sinful nature of the flesh but with their spirit. Through the influence of the Holy Spirit, people can be adopted as children of God. Romans 8:27–He who searches our hearts knows the mind of the Spirit, because the Spirit intercedes for the saints in accordance with God's will. The Holy Spirit works closely with God's people and intercedes with God on behalf of God's people. After Jesus resurrection, before His ascension He told the Apostles to remain in Jerusalem until they received power from the Holy Spirit. The power of the Holy Spirit is active in the miraculous power and works of God, Christ and the Disciples of Christ. God's people who have been redeemed have an indwelling of the Holy Spirit to help them withstand the temptation to sin but each individual personally must choose whether to sin or not.

The Bible warns Christians about Satan and his evil ways. James wrote, saying resist the Devil, Paul said do not give the Devil an opportunity to deceive you but take up the Word of God which is the shield of faith. Peter told Christians to be alert because the Devil is like a roaring lion that prowls around looking for someone to devour. The Word of God, which furnishes people with all of the knowledge they need to be faithful to God and His word in the Bible. The Bible tells us Satan will continue to rebel against God and tempt God's people until he is destroyed at the end of time. The Bible warns God's people to avoid the temptations of the Devil. 1st Peter 1: 5-9– Because your adversary the devil walks about like a roaring lion, looking for someone he might cause to sin. Resist him in faith, knowing that the same sufferings are experienced by your brother-hood in the world."

James 4–Submit to God, resist the Devil and he will run from you, draw near to God and He will draw near to you. All People continually face a spiritual battle led by Satan but God gave us a defense against the deception of Satan. 1st John 3–Whoever sins, is guilty of lawlessness. The people God created are free of sin when they are born but as they age they are face with all kinds of temptation to sin. People cannot escape temptation but if they are strong in faith in Christ they can resist the temptation to sin. When people reach an age when they are accountable to God for sin they become unrighteous if they sin and are in need of redemption. Before the ministry and death of God's Son Jesus there were no provisions for the forgiveness of sin and unrighteous people were condemned. God promised to send his son to earth to become a sacrifice for the guilt of sin. The removal of the guilt of sin is called redemption.

Romans 3:21-26–The righteousness of God was revealed and witnessed by the prophets, even the righteousness of God, through faith in Jesus Christ, to all and on all who believe (have faith). All people sin and fall short of the glory of God. God knew people would sin and because of His love, He provided them a way to be forgiven of their sins and be justified by His grace through the redemption in Jesus–whom God set forth as a sacrifice by His blood through faith to demonstrate His righteousness. God passed over the sins that were committed by His people during the time of the history of the Old Testament, sins that were committed before He sent His Son.

Jesus the Son of God demonstrated His own righteousness by willingly becoming a sacrifice for sin when He died on the cross. God's Word has been made known in every time period from the beginning. God cannot be worshiped with physical elements or with people's hands. God must be worshiped with the spirit heart and will of people. People are created with a body and a spirit and the combination of the two is the soul. The human spirit gives people the ability to have an intimate relationship with God. God is an invisible, all wise and almighty Spirit, and the effects of his creation are all around us but the Bible claims that God can be known by anyone as a personal God. People can individually or in a group approach God in humility and let the desires of their heart be known. God cares about each individual person like a father who cares for his son. If a father's son disobeys him, the father may be disappointed even angry but he does not disown him. God has made it possible for any individual to come to Jesus in repentance and prayer seeking redemption.

Colossians 1:15-17 "He is the image of the invisible God, the firstborn over all creation. For by Him all things were created that are in heaven and that are on earth, visible and invisible, whether thrones or dominions or principalities or powers. The question of what or who was responsible for life and the creation is a question that has enters the minds of people even from the beginning of time. People realize their existence must have come from a superior intelligence and power and those people who did not know the true God of creation invented their own false gods and worshiped them because it seemed reasonable that a super intelligence and power did exist and was responsible for the creation.

The God of the Bible is infinite, eternal, holy, unchanging, omnipotent, omni present, all knowing, self-sufficient, gracious, merciful, loving and sovereign. Col 3–Let the words of Christ live in you in wisdom and teach you to admonish one another with songs, hymns and spiritual songs in your heart to the Lord. Whatever you do in word or deed, do all in the name of the Lord Jesus, giving thanks to God the Father through Him. Romans 10:17 "Paul said faith comes by hearing the word of God. During the time period of the Old Testament the people could not see Jesus or even any evidence of Jesus but they had faith in God's promise of redemption.

God's promise is revealed in the book of Genesis and by prophecy throughout the rest of the Old Testament. God's promise to send His Son was finally, fulfilled in the time of the New Testament when God's Son was born in the first century A.D. Romans 10:8-11–The Word of God is near your mouth and heart, the word of faith that is preached. If you confess the Lord Jesus with your mouth and believe in your heart that God raised Him from the dead you will be saved, for with the heart one believes, has faith in Jesus to gain righteousness.

Faith Hope and Love Equals Redemption

Redemption means deliverance from paying a debt you owe in order to free you from that debt. Sin separates a person from God meaning the sinful person is condemned and will be punished but people can receive forgiveness through faith in Jesus. God knows all things all of the time and He knows the spirit of all people, whether they or guilty or innocent. Sin make a person unrighteous. God has requires that all people be righteous or become righteous through faith in His Son. God sent Jesus to earth to become a sacrifice for the guilt of sin so that anyone could be redeemed-forgiven of their debt by obeying God's plan of redemption in the New Testament to become righteous. To understand God's plan of redemption people need to read the Bible and practice the requirements for redemption to understand the meaning of faith, hope and love.

Faith is an attitude of confidence and trust in the Word of God and in Jesus Christ. By faith believers accept the fact that God created the universe and made all things from things that cannot be seen. The people that obeyed God from the beginning of time did so because of their faith in a God they could not see. The eleventh chapter of Hebrews explains that the people who lived during the period covered by the Old Testament could obtain righteousness through faith because the redeeming power of Christ is retroactive. Spiritual death began with one man Adam, the gift of God through grace came through one man Jesus Christ the Son of God. Romans 5–For is by one person's offense death came to all people, those who receive the grace of God will live through Jesus Christ.

Faith in God is more involved than simple belief that there is a God but faith begins with a belief in a God that will forgive people of their sins if they have faith in God's Son. Several Old Testament scriptures use the word faith in the sense of trusting. Ps 37–Trust in the Lord, and do good. Understanding life involves learning about faith, hope, love and righteousness and the greatest source of knowledge about faith, hope and love is the word of God in the Bible. The word faith in the Bible is translated from the Greek language and means being firmly persuaded by what you believe to the point of obedience. Faith is more than a mental acceptance it means an unquestioning, without doubt belief. The word, believe is used with the accusative to mean to be convinced. Faith then is an attitude of complete, unquestioning confidence and trust in God and in Jesus Christ. Hebrews 11:1– People hope for many things, even things they have never seen and they believe in the reality of those things. "Faith is the substance of things hoped for, the evidence of things not seen." If we have faith in God we understand that He exists and He will reward us according to the things He has promised if we obey what He tells us to do according to the scriptures in the Bible. People with faith in God also have hope which is a confident expectation of receiving what God has promised. The word faith in the New Testament occurs 20 times and always means a voluntary firm persuasion and trust by the believer. The book of Hebrews defines and illustrates the meaning of faith in God that was displayed by some of the faithful believers in God. Romans 10:17–Paul said faith comes by hearing the word of God. The word of God came through the word of the prophets and other inspired men who wrote the Bible and was passed on to the millions of people who read the Bible. Romans 8:24-25–People with genuine faith, hope and love in God and Christ are redeemed. Faith is a belief without being able to see what is hoped for. Hope that is seen is not hope because people do not hope for what they already have. Because of Enoch's faith he did not see death because God took him. During the Old Testament time people could not see Jesus or even any evidence of Jesus except through the promises of God but they had faith and hope in God's promise of redemption through the death of Jesus and they obeyed what God told them to do.

God's promises of redemption are revealed in the first book of the Bible and by prophecy in the rest of the Old Testament. The promise of the coming of Jesus Christ was fulfilled in the time of the New Testament. God's Son was born in the first century A.D. Romans 3:21-26—But now the righteousness of God apart from the law is revealed, by the Law and the Prophets, even the righteousness of God, through faith in Jesus Christ, to all and on all who believe. God asks people to have faith–in things they cannot see and have no evidence of except for God's word stated in the Bible. God wants people to be convinced by his Word in the Bible that He will keep His promise of redemption and He will never change His mind. God confirmed His promise with an oath. Hebrews 6:17-20–God, determined to show the heirs of promise the immutability of His counsel, confirmed it with an oath, that by two immutable things, in which it is impossible for God to lie.

Love

The Bible explains and defines the loving nature of God. Love is a positive feeling of goodwill towards those we love and a willingness to help them. God's love for people has been demonstrated in every way. Romans 8, 37-39–In all things we are more than conquerors through Him who loved us. Not death, or life, angels, rulers or anything will be able to separate us from the love of God for those in Christ Jesus. The dictionary defines love as a strong or passionate affection. In the Greek text the word love describe God's attitude toward His Son and the people God created.

1st Corinthians 13:–Love suffers long and is kind; love does not envy; love does not parade itself, is not puffed up; does not behave rudely, does not seek its own, is not provoked, thinks no evil; does not rejoice in iniquity, but rejoices in the truth, believes all things, hopes all things, endures all things" The three greatest Christian virtues are faith, hope and love; but the greatest is love." The word love describes the essential nature of God to save sinful people that deserve destruction but receive grace if they will obey Him. Love is demonstrated by the actions that it prompts. John 3:16 "For God so loved the world that He gave His only begotten Son, that whoever believes in Him should not perish but have everlasting life.

The Bible describes agape love in the book of 1st Corinthians chapter 13. The interaction between people that love one another is described, Love is patient, kind, truthful, unselfish, trusting, believing, hopeful and enduring. Love is not jealous, boastful, arrogant, rude, selfish, or angry. Agape love is the kind of love God has for people. God's love for the people of the world was so great that He gave His only Son as a sacrifice, that whoever believes in Him should not perish, but have eternal life. Love is measured by the way people feel about each other and the way they treat other people. God's love is unconditional He loves people even though they sin. His love prompted God to sacrifice His Son so sinners can be saved through faith in His Son Jesus. Galatians 5:16 "Walk in the Spirit and you shall not fulfill the lust of the flesh." To walk in the Spirit means to live in the way the Holy Spirit inspired scriptures in the Bible teaches people to live to please God. The only escape from obeying the lust of the flesh and the other temptations is to be led by the Spirit of God. Romans 8:14 – As many as are led by the Spirit of God, these are sons of God, for people walk by faith not by sight. The New Testament encourages Christians to love one another fervently from the heart. 1st Peter 1:22 "Since you have purified your souls in obeying the truth through the Spirit, in sincere love of the brethren, love one another fervently with a pure heart." Matthew 5:43-48 "You have heard that it was said, 'You shall love your neighbor and hate your enemy.' But I say to you, love you're your enemies, bless those who curse you, do good to those who hate you and pray for those who spitefully use you and persecute you the sons of your Father in heaven.

God makes His sun rise on the evil and the good, and sends rain on the just and on the unjust therefore people who are evil and unrighteous will exist among the righteous until the end of time. The Bible lists love as the greatest gift of all virtues that God, Jesus, the Holy Spirit and people can possess and without love people are classified as nothing, of no worth to God or to other people. God's righteousness has been known and proclaimed in every generation since the creation.

People did not want to learn the truth about God and they suppressed the truth and practiced unrighteousness–Romans 1 and 2. There are many ways people can sin and become unrighteous.

The sins God hates are sexual immorality, wickedness, covetousness, maliciousness; envy, murder, strife, deceit, evil-mindedness, whisperers, backbiters, haters of God, violent, proud, boasters, inventors of evil things disobedient to parents, undiscerning, untrustworthy, unloving, unforgiving, unmerciful; who knowing the righteous judgment of God are worthy of death. When a person sins they become alienated from God and His promises of eternal life in a place of paradise no longer applies to them unless they receive God's forgiveness for the guilt of their sin. All people become guilty of sin and the simplest definition of sin means a transgression of God' law.

All lawlessness is sin and all people sin and separate themselves from God, Christ and from His blessing of redemption. Therefore all people are unrighteous and worthy of death if they are old enough to know the difference between right and wrong, righteousness and unrighteousness. Removing the guilt of sin is called redemption and denotes paying the price to buy forgiveness for sin thereby restoring righteousness. God's Son Jesus Christ died to pay the price to redeem people from the guilt of sin and became the Redeemer. God's Word instructs people how to live to please God, and His word convicts people when they fail to obey. The consequence of disobedience to the word of God leads to spiritual death, which is defined as being separated from the grace of God and needing to be reconciled. Sinners must obtain God's forgiveness for sin or they will be punished with eternal death. God set the mark high because by the grace of God people can be redeemed by faith in God's Son. Ephesians 1:7–In Christ we have redemption for our sin through His blood. Redemption of sin is a gift of God's grace. The blood of Christ represents Christ's death on the cross, which was a gift from God. God is gracious, loving and faithful, and He promised to send His Son to earth to die as a sacrifice to provide a way of redemption for sins so people could be reconciled to God's favor. The word sin means a person's voluntary act of violating God's will by missing the mark God set for righteousness. The simplest definition of righteousness is the character or quality of being right and it signifies justice. God's standard of righteousness for people is to obey the revealed will of God as explained in the Bible. Any disobedience to God's word is sin. God gave people a conscience to help govern their behavior.

The conscience serves as a warning sign to avoid sin. When people know what is right and wrong and deliberately fail to do right, it is sin and they become aware of the sin because of their conscience. The Holy Spirit of God helps people live in a way that they will recognize sin and avoid it.

Romans 8:10-11– When you are in Christ you do not obey the sins of the mind and body. The Spirit of God is life and if He lives in you, you are righteous. "He who raised Christ from the dead will also give life to your mortal body through His Spirit who lives in you." Sin separates a person from the fellowship of God and they are considered to be unrighteous. The people God created deserved to die if they are guilty of sin. God must be worshiped with the heart, the seat of physical life, and of the nature of our inner spirit, the spirit and the soul that lives in people. People's spirit learns the will of God, and it guides them through life if they are faithful to be obedient to God's Word in the Bible.

Any unfaithfulness is sin. God's Word instructs people how to live to please God and His word convicts people when they sin. Hebrews 4:12–The word of God is living and powerful, and sharper than a two-edged sword, piercing even to the division of soul and spirit, and of joints and marrow, and is a discerner of the thoughts and intentions of the heart. God does not control the choices and decisions made by people, but He does make His indisputable will known and warns mankind not to disobey, because there are consequences for disobedience. The story of Adam and Eve's sin in the beginning is an example of the way people actually respond to God's Law. The spirit God put in people at birth is made in God's image and that spirit is a free will spirit capable of making choices but the decisions made by people are always subject to God's judgment, approval or disapproval.

In the first 10 chapters of the book of Genesis, the need for redemption is obvious. Even though God's law was made known, the people of the earth soon became involved in sin. It is also obvious that without God's intervention the people on earth would continue to sin and be destroyed without any hope of being saved for eternal life. God always holds the future of everyone and everything, in His hand.

The Bible Story of God's Communion of Love

All people at some time in their life choose to sin. God's first law is in Genesis 2:17 "But of the tree of the knowledge of good and evil you shall not eat, for in the day that you eat of it you shall surely die. Do not eat was a simple command for Adam and Eve the first people and the consequences of disobedience was death unless they were reconciled with God. In the beginning there was no provision for the redemption of sin. God provided the only way for redemption many years later through the sacrifice of His own Son because of His love for the people He created. The Bible is the story about people becoming reconciled to God by faith, hope and love. God's way of forgiveness of sin is explained in the story the, Communion of Love.

God created the heavens and the earth in the beginning of time. The earth was without form and empty. There was darkness that covered deep waters. And the Spirit of God, hovered over the surface of the waters. God said, let there be light and the light appeared and the light was good. God then separated light from darkness and God said the light was day and the darkness was night, which was the first day. God put a space to separate the waters on earth from the waters of heaven. The space between heaven and earth was the sky. God separated the waters above from the waters on dry ground, which is land and the waters were called seas.

God created all kinds of vegetation. God said the creation was good because it provided a suitable environment for people God would create. God created two great lights in the sky the sun and moon to separate day and night to mark off the seasons, days and years. God created fish and other life to live in the waters He created. He created birds of every kind to fly in the sky and great sea creatures and all of the fish and birds to multiply.

The evening and morning came marking the fifth day. God created every kind of animal to live on the earth and produce offspring. Then God said to His Son and the Holy Spirit, let's create humans in our image to be like us. The lord God made the first man Adam, from the dust of the ground and breathed the breath of life into him and he became a living soul.

The spirit is the sentient part of a person that perceives, reflects, feels and desires including the seat of will and purpose and is the eternal part of people. The Lord God planted a garden, made a tree of life and put it in the middle of the garden. The Lord said it was not good for the man to be alone and while Adam was in a deep sleep God took one of Adam's ribs and made a woman He named Eve and Eve became, living soul's endowed with a body similar to man and a spirit in the image of God. God intended for the man and woman to live together as mates have children and fill the earth with people. Chapter 2 of Genesis Lord God made every tree grow that is pleasant to the sight and for food. In the next verse, the tree of life was in the midst of the garden. It is obvious that the tree of life is not like the other trees it represents a figurative tree not a literal tree. Genesis 2:4-25 gives a brief summary of the chief points of the creation; explaining and enlarging on that part of creation that relates to mankind. God looked at everything He made and declared that it was good. God blessed the seventh day and ceased from creating.

Genesis 2: 15-17 –Then the Lord God took the man and put him in the Garden of Eden to take care of it. God said the people were to have authority over the fish, birds, livestock and all the wild animals. God blessed people and gave them plants, trees, fish and animals for food. He also created the food for the animals and birds. Genesis 3:1-7–The serpent (snake) was more cunning than any beast of the field, which the Lord God had made. Satan inhabited the serpent and he said to Eve, "Has God indeed said, you shall not eat of every tree of the garden?" And Eve said to the serpent. "We may eat the fruit of the trees in the garden; but of the fruit of the tree which is in the midst of the garden, God has said you shall not eat, nor shall you touch it, lest you die"

The serpent said to Eve, "You will not surely die. When the woman saw that the tree was good for food, that it was pleasant to the eyes, and a tree desirable to make one wise, she took its fruit and ate." Eve gave some to her husband and he ate. Adam and Eve disobeyed God's law, then both of them realized they had disobeyed the Lord. God had given them a positive command not to eat the fruit for the tree because if they did they would surely die. They would die spiritually. Spiritual death is a separation of the spirit from the fellowship of God.

Adam and Eve became dead spiritually because they failed to have faith in God and disobeyed Him. The bodies of people were not made to live forever and the death of the body is inevitable but the spirit God gave people was made for eternal life. The death of Adam and Eve was a spiritual death. God intended for the spirit of people to commune with Him as spirit to spirit but spiritual death is a separation of God's Spirit from the fellowship of a person's spirit. Adam and Eve died spiritually as soon as they disobeyed God but they continued to live physically. This first example of sin and spiritual separation from God is the beginning point of the need for God's grace that restores spiritual life to the sinner. The Bible records the history of God's people waiting for Jesus Christ birth and life so they could be reconciled to God. God. From that time forward the population of the earth would consist of people that obeyed God and those who obeyed Satan the Devil. From the creation of Adam and Eve to the end of time people, will of their own mind sin and need God's forgiveness and that is why Jesus was born and died so through faith in Jesus sinful people could be reconciled to God.

Adam and Eve were banished from the garden and from the tree of life. God gives mankind obligations, and He intends for man to be responsible and obey Him. God told man to take care of the garden, and He allowed him to eat the fruit of the other trees in the garden. Knowledge of good comes from God and the knowledge of evil comes from Satan. The expression 'good and evil' implies that there was evil as well as good in the world after Adam and Eve transgressed God's law. The term evil has a broad meaning, such as what is morally or ethically wrong, and is inclusive of thoughts and actions. Goodness is the opposite of evil, and good is beneficial, morally honorable, ethical, kind, honest, and compassionate and these attitudes are pleasing to God.

In the beginning God looked at all of His creation and said, "It is very good." God made everything perfect, but Satan and mankind spoiled it. In the Bible, the words righteousness and unrighteousness identify that which is good and that which is evil. Righteousness is the quality of being right or just, and it is used as an attribute of God. Unrighteousness is the opposite of righteousness and can be identified as evil, originating with Satan.

Evil originates in the mind of people when they are tempted by Satan or by their own lust, evil desires, and act in an evil way. When Adam and Eve sinned, they became unrighteous without any way to regain righteousness by their own will. God's answer to the just penalty for sin was to sacrifice a sinless life to cover the transgressions of all men. Romans 5–Through one man sin entered the world and death through sin, and death spread to all men, because all sinned." 1st Corinthians 15:20-26–Christ is risen from the dead, and has become the first fruits of those who have died. For death came by man by the man Jesus Christ came the resurrection of the dead. All people die, in Christ all shall be made alive. The body will die but the spirit that is redeemed by the blood of Christ will live forever. After Adam and Eve's transgression, the Lord called out to them, and they hid from God, because they realized they were naked. After their fall from grace, Adam and Eve had knowledge of both good and evil, and they realized that it was wrong for anyone to see their nakedness. In Adam and Eve we see a common characteristic of human nature. Eve blamed the serpent for her sin, and Adam blamed Eve. The Lord God drove Adam and Eve out of the Garden of Eden and shut the entrance so no one could enter.

God punished Adam and Eve by placing them outside the paradise of the Garden of Eden and they no longer had access to the tree of life. Eve's punishment was to suffer pain in childbirth to remind her of her transgression. Adam's punishment was he had to work all of his life in order to supply the necessities of life. God still provided sunshine and the essentials of life, but Adam and Eve had to make an effort to take care of each other. Adam and Eve had to protect themselves from the elements of nature, from dangers associated with other people, from animals and other dangers they might encounter. They had to labor to provide food and shelter and the other material needs for their existence. God punished the serpent that had a part in Satan's deceit by putting enmity between the serpent and man and making the serpent forever crawl on his belly.

Genesis 4:1-5–Now Adam knew his wife, and she conceived and bore Cain, and she said, "I have acquired a man from the Lord." Then she bore again, this time his brother Abel. Now Abel was a keeper of sheep, but Cain was a tiller of the ground."

When people first began to work to supply food for nourishment, each one did what pleased them. Adam and Eve and their sons, Cain and Abel, knew God, and they served God by offering sacrifices. The Bible doesn't mention a commandment from God to offer sacrifices until much later in the history of mankind, but from the story of Cain and Abel we learn that God would at that time accept sacrifices if they were offered with the proper attitude of the heart. Cain and Abel both offered sacrifices to God. Abel offered his sacrifice because he had faith in God and God was pleased with Abel's offering, but He was not pleased with Cain's offering because he did not offer from faith, so Cain became angry. We must read between the lines and assume that God had revealed what He wanted them to offer. The brothers offered God what they had to offer. Abel had faith in God and he offered an acceptable sacrifice but Cain did not have faith and God punished Abel. The story of Cain and Abel sets an example of the behavior of people from that time forward. Abel obeyed God because of faith and Cain did not obey.

The Lord said, "If you do well, you will be accepted, but if you do not do right, sin lies at your door." God wants people to offer sacrifices from the heart. Hebrews 11:4 "By faith Abel offered to God a more excellent sacrifice than Cain, through which he obtained witness that he was righteous, God testifying of his gifts; and through it he, being dead, still speaks." God punished Cain for murdering Abel and his crops didn't produce, so he became a restless person and a wanderer. In the very beginning pages of the Bible, we learn what is important to God and what God wants from people. God expects people to have faith in Him and obey Him. People on earth continued to multiply but most of them like Cain ignored God. Cain lived in Nod east of Eden and fathered a son named Enoch. Cain built a city and named it after his son Enoch. Adam and Eve had another son named Seth and he was like Adam. Adam lived for 800 years and fathered sons and daughters. When Adam died he was 930 years old. Adams descendants beginning with Seth also lived a long time before their death.

Enoch was of the 7th generation from Adam and he was a man who had faith in, and fellowship with God. Enoch prophesied about God's Son Christ several thousand years before the birth of Christ. He also prophesied of the future coming of the end of time and about God's Son Jesus coming with thousands of angels to punish un-godly sinners.

Enoch was faithful to God all of the years he lived. The Bible says God took him implying that God took Enoch's spirit to live in heaven. Hebrews 11:5-6–Because of his faith Enoch was taken so that he did not see death, and was not found because God had taken him; for before he was taken he pleased God. Without faith it is impossible to please God, for people who come to God must believe that He is, and that He rewards those who diligently seek Him. Genesis chapters 6-10–From the time of Adam and Eve, God's presence and law (not the Law of Moses) was made known to people but the morality of the people continued to decline until all were unrighteous except for one man and his family. The sons of God the people who were born took as many wives they chose and the population on earth grew. And the Lord said My Spirit "shall not Genesis 6:1-3–when men began to multiply on the face of the earth, and daughters were born to them, the sons of God saw the daughters of strive with man forever, for he is indeed flesh; yet his days shall be one hundred and twenty years.

The sons of God are people and they are called sons because God created them. God had been patient as He observed the behavior of people but the people were engaging in evil conduct. Because of the evil of the people God threatened to withdraw His Spirit and destroy those who were evil. The result of God's threat led to a great flood that covered the whole earth drowning most of the people. God was grieved in his heart. So He said–I will destroy people whom I have created from the face of the earth, both people and beast, creeping things and birds of the air, for I am sorry that I have made them." A man named Noah who was a descendant of Seth. Noah was 500 years old and he had three sons Shem, Ham and Japheth. The earth was filled with violence and the people were sinful.

Genesis 6:9-12– Noah had faith, he was a righteous person and he was a just person, perfect in his generations. Noah was the father of three sons Shem, Ham and Japheth. People were sinful and the earth was filled with violence for all people had corrupted their way. God accepted Noah and his family because they were righteous. Hebrews 11:7– Noah was warned by God that He was going to destroy life on earth with a great flood because the wickedness of the people had become very great. Noah was moved with godly fear and he built an ark (large boat) to save his family and the land animals from flood.

God gave Noah instructions how to build the ark, so Noah built a huge boat with three decks to house his family and the animals he was to take into the ark. Genesis 6–God said, I am bringing flood waters upon the earth, to destroy people and other creatures all flesh in which is the breath of life; everything that is on the earth shall die. And of every living thing of all flesh you shall bring, two of every kind to keep them alive with you; they shall be male and female. Of the birds after their kind, of animals after their kind, and of every creeping thing of the earth after its kind will come to you to keep them alive. And you shall take for yourself of all food that is eaten, and you shall gather it to yourself; and it shall be food for you and for them. The waters prevailed and greatly increased on the earth, and the ark moved about on the surface of the waters and all the high hills were covered.

The waters rose fifteen cubits upward, and the mountains were covered and all flesh died that moved on the earth: birds and cattle and beasts and every creeping thing that creeps on the earth, and every man. Genesis 7:17-24 "Now the flood was on the earth forty days." The waters destroyed all living things, which were on the face of the ground: man and cattle, creeping thing and bird of the air. They were destroyed from the earth. Noah his wife and three sons and their wives and the animals on the ark were saved. And the waters were on the earth one hundred and fifty days." After the floodwaters receded every living thing in the ark came out on dry ground and Noah built an altar and offered the flesh of clean animals to God as a sacrifice, and God was pleased with Noah's sacrifice. After the flood Shem, Ham and Japheth, and their wives began to repopulate the earth.

God promised Noah and his sons that He would never again destroy all life on earth with a flood, so God created the rainbow as a sign that He would keep His word. The rainbow today still reminds us of God's promise. Noah lived three hundred and fifty years after the flood. He was six hundred years old at the time of the flood, so he lived a total of 950 years. All the people after the flood spoke the same language, and they traveled to other places on earth. God wanted the earth to be filled with people that would have a relationship with Him. The people began to ignore God and depend on their own wisdom.

People began to make their own lifeless gods and to worship them and they depended on them instead of the true God, so God confused their language and scattered them all over the earth. They still practiced evil after they were scattered, but they were no longer united in their evil ways. The people of God's creation were a great disappointment to Him, because they loved evil. Most people lost any interest in the True God of creation.

God Calls Abraham (2235 B.C.)

Genesis 9:18-19–The sons of Noah that went out of the ark were Shem, Ham and Japheth and the earth was re-populated from their descendants. God's Son was born through Shem's descendants. The Bible records the history of God's plan of redemption but the history of Noah's descendants is mostly obscure in world history from the time of the flood to the time of a man named Abram whose name was changed to Abraham. Abraham became one of the most important people in God's plan to bring Jesus Christ into the world. For that reason the Bible follows the life of Abraham from the time of his introduction until his death.

God had not forgotten the descendants of Noah and his sons but most people had become exceedingly wicked and evil again. There was only one language spoken by the people who were descended from Noah and his sons. God decided to select one man He could depend on and work through him and his descendants to promote His plan of redemption by a people through whom His Son could be born and become the Savior of all people who would have faith in Him. Two years after the flood, Shem was one hundred years old, and he was the father of Arphaxad who is in the birth line of Jesus. Shem lived for five hundred years after the birth of Arphaxad. He settled in Mesopotamia and was the ancestor of the Semitic peoples, including the Hebrews, Arabs and Syrians. Shem's descendants spoke Semitic languages. Several nations, languages and peoples emerged from the three sons of Noah including a man named Abram. Abram's name was changed to Abraham because God was going to bless him and he would become an ancestor of God's own Son Jesus.

Genesis 17–God said to Abram "No longer shall your name be called Abram, but your name shall be Abraham; for I have made you a father of many nations.

When Abram was 99 years old, the Lord appeared to him and said, "I am Almighty God; walk before Me and be blameless. And I will make My covenant between you and will multiply you exceedingly." God then told Abram he would the father of many nations of people and the Lord changed his name to Abraham.

Story of Abraham

The Lord told Abraham to leave his home and go to the land He would show him and He would make him into a great nation, bless him and make his name great. God promised to bless those who blessed Abraham and curse those who cursed him. God said all of the families on earth would be blessed by Abraham. The blessing would come through the descendants of Abraham and would be fulfilled by Jesus the Son of God who would be born from Abraham's descendants. The, ultimate fulfillment of the blessing would not be until the first century A.D. when Jesus was born. From the time of God's promise to bless all people to the birth of Christ would not take place until approximately 2,000 years. Jesus would be sacrificed to redeem all people who had faith in Him.

During the intervening years the history of God's redeeming plan was taking place and being written in the Bible. When Abraham left his home he went to Haran, settled there, and Terah his father died there at the age of two hundred and five years. Abraham moved on from Haran to Palestine near Bethel in the land of Canaan. Abraham set up an altar for offering sacrifices to God everywhere he lived and he became a wealthy man with servants. Abraham lived in peace among the other people in the surrounding area. In the culture of Mesopotamia where Abraham's ancestors lived, many false God's were worshiped. At the time of Abram's birth, there is no mention of any culture that was worshipping the God of creation. Noah and his sons are the last mention of faithful believers in God before Abram. The Bible doesn't say when Abram first became a believer in God but Abram obeyed God when he was called by God to leave Mesopotamia and go to Canaan.

Joshua 24:2-3 – Joshua said to all the people, "Thus says the Lord God of Israel: Your fathers including Terah, the father of Abraham and the father of Nahor, dwelt on the other side of the River in old times; and they served other god's. Then I took your father Abraham from the other side of the River, led him throughout the land of Canaan, and multiplied his descendants and gave him Isaac." The land of Canaan became the land of Abraham and his descendants by the will of God. After Terah died the Lord talked to Abram and told him to leave his father's house and go to a land that He would show him, and Abram obeyed. When God made a covenant with Abram, God changed Abram's name to Abraham which, means 'father of nations.' God changed Sarai, Abram's wife's name to Sarah, which means 'mother of nations.'

Genesis 12:1-3– The Lord had said to him: Get out of your country, from your family and from your father's house, to a land that I will show you. I will make you a great nation; I will bless you and make your name great; and you shall be a blessing. I will bless those who bless you, and I will curse him who curses you; and in you all the families of the earth shall be blessed." All the families of the earth includes all people who would have faith like Abraham. Abraham did everything God asked him to do. God considered Abraham righteous because Abraham obeyed Him. Abraham did not question God or hesitate to obey Him.

The Old Testament clearly shows that the descendants of Abraham were Hebrews and Israelites who were a nomadic, pastoral people. They were exposed to harsh desert conditions and moved often from one location to another to provide food and water for their animals. They had few material possessions and lived in tents. The early Hebrews and Israelites were shepherds and keepers of animals, which they depended on for their food and other needs. Several nations would come from the descendants of Abraham and his wife Sarah. Jesus God's Son would be a descendant of Abraham. Abraham was chosen because of his great faith in God. Abraham was the most faithful man on earth at that time, and his faith became a model for the kind of faith God wants every person to have even today. Redemption is based on the individual faith of each person, not on a religious organization or national affiliation.

Abraham was twenty generations removed from Adam, and through faith, Abraham became the father of all of the people of faith. God credited Abraham with righteousness because of his faith. God had great plans for Abraham and his descendants that plan included forming a great nation from Abraham's descendants. God blessed Abraham and promised him that God's plan to redeem the people of the earth would come through his descendants. God communed with Abraham through visions and by angels. Galatians 3:26-29 "For you are, all sons of God through <u>faith</u> in Christ Jesus. For as many of you as were baptized into Christ have put on Christ. There is neither Jew nor Greek, there is neither slave nor free, there is neither male nor female; for you are all one in Christ Jesus. And if you are Christ's, then you are Abraham's seed, and heirs according to the promise."

Jesus the Son of God, was a descendant of Abraham. Galatians 3:6-9–Abraham believed God and it was accounted to him for righteousness. Therefore only those who are of faith are sons of Abraham. And the Scripture, foreseeing that God would justify the Gentiles by faith, preached the gospel to Abraham beforehand, saying, "In you all the nations shall be blessed." So then those who are of faith are blessed with believing Abraham." Jesus Christ the redeemer of sinners came from the seed of God but His human ancestry came through the birth-line of people who were faithful to God and were descendants of Abraham. Galatians 3:16 "Now to Abraham and his seed were the promises made. He does not say, "And to seeds," as of many, but as of one, "And to your Seed, who is Christ." The process of salvation from Abraham to Christ would take approximately 2000 years and would involve the descendants of Abraham, Isaac, and Jacob whose name was changed to Israel. From the time of Abraham to the time of Christ, the story of God's redeeming plan follows the events of the lives of Abraham, Isaac and Jacob. When Abram was ninety nine years old, the Lord appeared to Him and identified Himself as the Lord and He told Abraham to be blameless. I will make My covenant with you and Me and I will God's Covenant With Abraham Genesis Genesis 17:And I will mMy covenant between Me and you multiply you exceedingly. Then Abram fell on his face, and God talked with him saying, "As for Me, behold My covenant is with you, and you shall be a father of many nations. No longer shall your name be called Abram but your name shall be Abraham; for I have made you a father of many nations.

I will make you exceedingly fruitful; and I will make nations of you, and kings shall come from you. And I will establish My covenant between Me and your descendants after you in their generations, for an everlasting covenant, to be God to you and your descendants after you. Also I give to you and your descendants after you the land in which you are a stranger all the land of Canaan, as an everlasting possession; and I will be their God." A covenant is a solemn agreement (standing contract) between two or more parties, however in order for a covenant to remain in force, both parties of the covenant must obey the terms of the covenant. If Abraham or his descendants after him did not keep their part of the covenant the covenant would be broken and no longer binding on either party.

The first agreement God made with Abraham depended on Abraham leaving his home and family and going to a place that God would show him. If Abraham fulfilled his part of the agreement, God promised to make him into a great nation and bless him. God promised to bless all people on earth through Abraham. Abraham believed that God would keep his promises, and it was that faith in God's word that saved faithful Abraham and motivated him to continue to do what Abraham agreed to go to the land of Canaan, and God promised to give that land to Abraham's descendants.

Galatians 3:6-9–Abraham believed God, and He was considered righteous. "Therefore know that only those who are of faith are sons of Abraham. And the Scripture, foreseeing that God would justify the Gentiles by faith, preached the gospel to Abraham beforehand, saying in you all the nations shall be blessed. So then those who are of faith are blessed with believing Abraham." God made several other covenants with Abraham before he died. He told Abraham that he would bless him, and his descendants would be as numerous as the stars in heaven, and Abraham believed God even though as yet he had no son with his wife Sarah who was barren and Abraham was very old and had no descendant to fulfill his part of the covenant.

God's plan of redemption would continue through the descendants of Abraham until the time for the birth of Jesus. Abraham asked for a sign to help him believe God's promise. God instructed Abraham to bring animals for an offering.

Abraham arranged the animals for sacrifice just as God told him to do, and then he fell into a deep sleep. God spoke with Abraham as he slept and told him that his people would become slaves in a foreign land, and they would be mistreated for four hundred years. He also promised that He would punish the foreign nation that would make slaves of His people and they would leave that land with great wealth.

The foreign land in which the Israelites would be slaves was the land of Egypt. That same day God made a covenant with Abraham and promised that the land from the river of Egypt to the Euphrates River would belong to Abraham's descendants. Sarah had an Egyptian servant named Hagar. Sarah told Abraham that since she was barren, Abraham should have children with Hagar. This was not an unusual request from Sarah according to the custom of that time. Later Hagar and Abraham had a son named Ishmael. Ishmael was both Hebrew and Egyptian and was not the son of promise. After Ishmael was born, Sarah became very jealous of Hagar and despised her, so she dealt harshly with Hagar and sent her and her son Ishmael away into the wilderness. Because Ishmael was Abraham's son, God sent an angel to the wilderness area and rescued Ishmael and Hagar. The angel told Hagar to return to Abraham's house and serve Sarah. The angel also told Sarah that Ishmael's descendants would be multiplied and that Ishmael would be a wild man who would be against every man. Hagar and Ishmael returned to Abraham's house. Ishmael survived and married an Egyptian, became an archer, and fathered twelve princes.

Genesis 18:1-5–The Lord appeared to Abraham in Mamre between Jerusalem and Beersheba in the land of Canaan. Abraham was sitting in the tent door in the heat of the day. He saw three men (angels) and he ran from the tent door to meet them and bowed himself to the ground, and said my Lord, if I have now favor in your sight, do not pass on by Your servant. Please let a little water be brought and wash your feet, and rest yourselves under the tree. And I will bring you a morsel of bread, that you may refresh your hearts.

After that you may pass by, inasmuch as you have come to your servant. They said, "Do as you have said." Abraham addressed one of his visitors as Lord. In the 19th chapter of Genesis, two of the men who came to Abraham's tent were identified as angels. The other man was called the Lord. He may have been an Arch Angel, or as some believe, he may have been Christ. Regardless of their identity, the three came representing God and His authority. Angels have the ability to appear as humans and did so in several Biblical examples. The one Abraham called Lord told Abraham He would return to him in time, and Sarah would have a son. Only someone with authority from God could make that promise. Sarah laughed silently, because Sarah and Abraham were both too old to have children.

The angels were on their way to the city of Sodom to destroy it, and they told Abraham where they were going. They said there was a great outcry against Sodom and Gomorrah because of the sin in those cities. Abraham's nephew Lot lived in Sodom, so Abraham was concerned about the safety of Lot and his family. Abraham bargained with the two angels and the Lord about not destroying the city in case there may have been some righteous people in the cities. At the end of Abraham's bargaining with the Lord, the Lord said they would not destroy the cities if at least ten righteous people were found there. As they left the Lord rained fire and brimstone on the cities of the plain destroying them. The two angels came to Sodom in the evening, and they found that the only righteous people left in the cities were Lot, his wife, and his two daughters. Before the Lord destroyed the cities, the angels left, and the Lord rained brimstone and fire on the cities of the plain, destroying them. However, Lot's wife hesitated and looked back, and she was turned into a pillar of salt, because she disobeyed God.

Abraham's Faith Is Confirmed (Genesis 22)

When Isaac was a boy, God decided to test Abraham's faith. Abraham had always obeyed God, but God was about to test Abraham in an extreme way. God told Abraham to take Isaac to Mt Moriah and offer him as a burnt offering. This would mean that Abraham would have to kill Isaac and offer him like an animal on an altar.

Abraham didn't argue or plead with the Lord. He rose early the next morning and took firewood, Isaac, and two young men and left to go to the mountain. It was a three-day journey, and Abraham had time to think about what God told him to do, but he didn't hesitate to obey. Isaac thought they were going to Mt Moriah to offer a sacrifice, and he knew they took no animal for the sacrifice, so he asked his father, where is the lamb for the sacrifice. Abraham said, "My son, God will provide for Himself the lamb for a burnt offering." Abraham had faith that God would provide the sacrifice for the offering and spare his son Isaac. When they reached the place for the sacrifice, Abraham built an altar, tied up Isaac and laid him on the altar. Then he took a knife and was about to kill Isaac, but the Angel of the Lord spoke to Abraham and said, "Do not lay a hand on the lad, or do anything to him; for now I know that you fear God, since you have not withheld your son, your only son, from Me." (vs.12)

Hebrews 11– By faith Abraham obeyed when he was called to go out to the place, which he would receive as an inheritance. And he went out, not knowing where he was going. By faith he dwelt in the land of promise as in a foreign country, dwelling in tents with Isaac and Jacob, the heirs with him of the same promise for he waited for the city, which has foundations, whose builder and maker is God. Abraham believed there was a place called heaven where people of faith will live with God. Faith motivates people to do what God commands. The Bible stresses faith first, because faith is the first step of doing what God tells you to do to obtain God's approval. The Bible follows the life of Abraham from the time of his introduction until his death. From the time of the birth of Abraham to 2235 BC, Abraham and his descendants were assigned a great and very essential part in God's plan of redemption, Genesis 17 through the rest of the Old Testament they were involved in God's plan.

Genesis 18:17-19 "And the Lord said shall I hide from Abraham what I am doing, since Abraham shall surely become a great and mighty nation, and all the nations of the earth shall be blessed in him.' Abraham's descendants would become a great nation called Israel. Genesis 12– God told Abraham "In you all the families of the earth shall be blessed." Because of Abraham's great faith, God made a promise to bless the people on earth through his descendants.

For there is no difference; for all have sinned and fall short of the glory of God, being justified freely by His grace through the redemption that is in Christ Jesus, whom God set forth as a propitiation by His blood through faith to demonstrate his righteousness, because in His forbearance God had passed over the sins that were previously committed to demonstrate at the present time His righteousness, that He might be just and the justifier of the one who has faith.

According to God' promise God's Son would be born from the birth line of Abraham's descendants and they would live in the land of Canaan. Abraham became known as a Hebrew when he crossed over from Mesopotamia into Canaan. Hebrew means 'one who crosses over.' God blessed Abraham and promised him that that all people on earth would be blessed through him. Genesis 12:"Now the Lord had said to Abram: "Get out of your country, from your family and from your father's house, to a land that I will show you. I will make you a great nation; I will bless you. And make your name great; and you shall be a blessing. I will bless those who bless you, and I will curse him who curses you; and in you all the families of the earth shall be blessed." During the years leading up to the birth of Jesus Christ God did bless Abraham, his family and his descendants and they eventually became the nation of Israel. Galatians 3:6-9 "Just as Abraham believed God and it was accounted to him for righteousness. Therefore know that only those who are of faith are sons of Abraham. And the Scripture, foreseeing that God would justify the Gentiles by faith, preached the gospel to Abraham beforehand, saying, "In you all the nations shall be blessed." So then those who are of faith are blessed with believing Abraham."

Galatians 3:26-29 "For you are, all sons of God through faith in Christ Jesus. For as many of you as were baptized into Christ have put on Christ. There is neither Jew nor Greek, there is neither slave nor free, there is neither male nor female; for you are all one in Christ Jesus. And if you are Christ's, then you are Abraham's seed, and heirs according to the promise." The story of God's redeeming plan follows Abraham's descendants beginning with Isaac and Isaac's son Jacob. Genesis 17:1-8–Abram was ninety-nine years old when the Lord appeared to him and said, "I am almighty God; walk before me and be blameless, and I will make a covenant between you and Me and will multiply your descendants. God told Abraham the covenant would be between them, and Abraham's descendants after him in their generations.

God said to Abraham "I will be a God to you and your descendants after you. Also I give to you and your descendants after you the land in which you are a stranger, all the land of Canaan, as an everlasting possession; and I will be their God." Abraham had no children, Sarah was barren and Abraham wondered how he could become the father of many nations without an heir. Sarah offered her Egyptian handmaid Hagar to Abraham to produce a son for Abraham. Sarah then became Jealous of Hagar and she made Hagar leave and Hagar left but an angel of the lord appeared to Hagar and told her to return to Abraham and she returned and bore Abraham a son and he was named Ishmael. Ishmael's descendants later were known as the Muslims of Islam. Ishmael was not the descendant through whom God would bless the people on earth. Sarah Abraham'sd

The angel prophesied about Ishmael saying he would be a wild donkey of a man and his hand would be against everyone and everyone's hand against him. He would have hostility toward all his brothers. When Abraham was ninety years old God appeared to him and said I am God Almighty and He told Abraham if he obey Him, He would make a covenant with Abraham. God said He would bless Abraham and his descendants forever and give them the land of Canaan. The sign of the covenant between God and Abraham was, every male of his descendants must be circumcised at the age of eight days. God told Abraham and Sarah that she was going to have a baby and Sarah laughed because she was barren and did not believe that she would have a child.

One day Abraham was sitting in the doorway of his tent and he saw three strangers and he ran to meet them and bowed himself before them. Abraham addresses one of the men as Lord and sought his favor. The strangers were angels that were sent to deliver a message about Sarah's son and to destroy the evil cities of Sodom and Gomorrah where Abraham's nephew Lot lived. One of the three angels told Abraham that he would return next year and Sarah would have a son. The son Sarah gave birth to would be the son through whom God would bless the people on earth.

Abraham was one hundred years old when Sarah, became pregnant, she had a son, and they named him Isaac. According to the covenant when Abraham died Isaac would inherit the promises and the responsibilities God had given Abraham. Hagar and Ishmael left Abraham's house. Genesis 21 describes the time Hagar and Ishmael survived in the wilderness because God took care of them. Ishmael married an Egyptian woman and she bore him 12 sons and they settled from the border of Egypt to Arabia.

Abraham and the three angels walked over to a peak that overlooked the cities of the plain and they discussed the fate of Sodom and Gomorrah. The Lord was going to destroy the two cities because of the gross immorality of the people that lived in the cities Genesis 19:29 "And it came to pass, when God destroyed the cities of the plain, that God remembered Abraham, and sent Lot out of the midst of the overthrow, when He overthrew the cities of Sodom and Gomorrah because of their evil ways. Lot was Abraham's nephew and he was a righteous man and God spared his life, but Abraham looked toward the cities from a distance and he saw the smoke rising from the land like smoke from a furnace.

Abraham left Mamre and settled in Gerar between Kadesh and Shur in the land occupied by the Philistines. While he was living in Gerar he claimed that Sarah was his sister and Abimelech the king had Sarah brought to him for a wife but God warned him in a dream that he would die if he laid a hand on Sarah. Abimelech was afraid and sent Sarah back to Abraham and gifted Abraham with sheep, oxen and servants and he told Abraham he could live anywhere he wanted to. Abraham planted a grove in Beersheba and worshiped God. Sarah became pregnant and bore Abraham a son, and he was named Isaac. Ishmael was thirteen years old at the time of Isaac's birth and Abraham gave Hagar and Ishmael bread and water and sent them away and they wandered in the wilderness of Beersheba. They ran out of water and were in complete despair in the desert but an angel of God came to them and told Hagar that Ishmael would also become a great nation. A well of water miraculously appeared and their life was saved.

Genesis chapter 22–when Isaac was still young Abraham was commanded by God to offer Isaac as a sacrifice on an altar. Becoming a sacrifice would mean death to Isaac but Abraham was always faithful to obey God. Everything was made ready for the sacrifice but God prevented the death of Isaac by sending the angel of the Lord with a sacrifice in the place of Isaac. God tested Abraham and Abraham proved to be faithful, so God provided a ram for the sacrifice. Because of Abraham's faith God promised to continue to bless him and to multiply his descendants as the stars in heaven and the sand on the seashore. Besides the physical descendants of Abraham all Christians are spiritual descendants of the promise God made to Abraham. One of Abraham's faithful descendants would eventually give birth to God's Son, Jesus Christ the (Messiah) and fulfill God's promise to Abraham.

Isaac the son of Abraham inherited the promises God made to Abraham and his descendants. Isaac was the son of Sarah the Son God had promised Abraham. When Isaac was forty years old he married Rebecca and she was not able to have children. Isaac pleaded with the Lord God for his wife to give him children and the Lord answered his prayer and she became pregnant with twin sons. The babies struggled inside her and she didn't understand what was going on so she asked the Lord about it, and the Lord told her that there were two nations in her womb. He said, "Two people shall be separated from your body; one people shall be stronger than the other, and the older shall serve the younger." When Isaac died, the promises and blessings that God had made to Abraham and to Isaac would be passed to one of Isaac's two sons. God knows the heart of every individual from birth to death and God was the one to choose between the twin sons of Isaac. Isaac lived in the land of Canaan. The oldest son of Isaac would normally be the one in line to inherit the promises God had made to Abraham. However God knows all about people before they are born and God knew Jacob would be the one who would inherit the promises. Isaac's sons, Jacob and Esau, were born at the same time, but Esau was the first one from the womb, making him the oldest. There was an ancient birthright custom that gave the firstborn son of a family special honor and privileges. When a father died, his oldest son would receive twice as much inheritance as the other male siblings and he would become the head of the family.

The birthright was rightfully Esau's according to human tradition but God knows best and He chose Jacob over Esau. Esau was not as wise as Jacob and Esau sold his birthright to Jacob. It was God's will that the promises made to Abraham would continue through Jacob and his descendants because God knew Esau would was a profane person. Jacob was the son chosen by God to be the son through whom the birth line of Jesus Christ would come.

Romans 9:10-13–Rebecca conceived by one man, Isaac and she bore twin boys and God knew everything about the two boys before and after they were born and He determined that Jacob the youngest boy would inherit the promises God made to Abraham instead of Esau. Esau the oldest was not chosen because God knew he would not be the right one for the responsibility. Jacob the younger boy was chosen by God. The plan of redemption would progress through Abraham's descendants to Jacob and his descendants to Judah. For this is the word of the promise; at this time I will come and Sarah shall have a son. And not only this, but when Rebecca conceived by our father Isaac (for the children not yet being born, nor having done any good or evil, that the purpose of God according to election might stand, not of works but of Him who calls), it was said to her, the older shall serve the younger, As it is written, "Jacob I have loved, but Esau I have hated." Hated means that God loved Esau less than He did Jacob.

Rebecca remembered what the Lord told her about the older boy serving the younger. Jacob was to be the blessed one instead of Esau, and Isaac blessed Jacob with these words, "May God Almighty bless you, and make you fruitful and multiply you. And give the blessing of Abraham, to you and your descendants with you, that you may inherit the land in which you are a stranger, which God gave Abraham. The promises that God gave Abraham were passed on from Abraham and Isaac to Jacob and his descendants. Jacob received a dream from the Lord. When Jacob was young and single he left his father's house in Beersheba and went toward Haran where his uncle lived. Jacob stopped somewhere along the way and laid down to sleep. As he slept, he had a very strange dream; a dream from the Lord. In his dream, Jacob saw a ladder reaching from the earth all the way to heaven with the angels of God ascending and descending on the ladder.

The Lord stood at the top of the ladder and said, "I am the Lord God of Abraham your father and the God of Isaac; the land on which you lie I will give to you and your descendants. Also your descendants shall be as the dust of the earth; you shall spread abroad to the west and the east, to the north and the south; and in you and in your seed all the families of the earth shall be blessed." God confirmed the decision He made to bless Jacob.

Behold, I am with you and will keep you wherever you go, and will bring you back to this land; for I will not leave you until I have done what I have spoken to you." (Genesis 28: 13-15) God's promise to send His Son was drawing nearer but it would be a long time before Jesus was born. Jacob's dream was his first personal encounter with the Lord God of Abraham and it made a lasting impression on Jacob. The dream of the ladder established a link between God in heaven and Jacob and his descendants on earth. The dream of the angels ascending and descending was a message meaning that God would be with Jacob and his descendants and by the intervention of the angels God would protect and take care of him and his family.

Jacob inherited the promises God made to his father Isaac and grandfather, Abraham. All people of the earth would be blessed through Jacob and his descendants and Jesus the Son of God would be a descendant of Jacob. When Jacob woke up from his dream, he declared that God was in that place, and he called the place 'The house of God,' and it became known as the city of Bethel. Jacob went on his way to his uncle Laban's house to find a wife. He met a girl named Rachel, the daughter of Laban his mother's brother and a descendant of Abraham's brother.

Jacob wanted Rachel to be his wife, but Laban would not give Rachel to Jacob unless he first married Leah Rachel's older sister. Jacob married both Leah and Rachel, and together they bore him twelve sons. Later the twelve tribes of Israel would be the descendants of Jacob. Jesus would be born from the birth line of Jacob. After many years of working for his uncle, Jacob took his wives and children and left Laban's home to go back to his homeland. Jacob wanted to win the favor of his brother Esau.

The last time Jacob saw his brother Esau, Esau hated him and wanted to kill him because he had stolen his birthright. Jacob thought Esau might attack him. Jacob was afraid of Esau. Esau was a hunter and a warrior but Jacob had a gentle nature. Jacob was near his homeland and Esau got word that he was on his way home. Esau left to meet Jacob with four hundred armed men. Jacob prayed to God for deliverance from Esau thinking that Esau might attack him.

When they came to the River Jabbok, Jacob crossed the river and bowed before Esau seven times, expressing sorrow for the way he had treated Esau. Esau ran to him, fell on his neck and kissed him, and they wept and they were glad to see each other. Genesis 32 Jacob left that night with his two wives two female servants, and his eleven sons. They crossed over the brook of Jabbok then Jacob was left alone. That night an angel wrestled with Jacob until the breaking of day. Now when the angel saw that he could not prevail against him, He touched the socket of Jacob's hip; and the socket of his hip came out of joint. Jacob said, "Let me go, for the day breaks." But he said 'I will not let you go unless you bless me! So He said to him, what is your name?" He said

Jacob. And the angel said your name, shall no longer be called Jacob, but Israel; for you have struggled with God and with men, and have prevailed."

This event in the life of Jacob was a sign that the descendants of Jacob (Israelites) would struggle with God through the many years the people of Israel waited for God's Son to be born. Jacob again asked, tell me your name and He said why is it that you ask my name. Jacob said tell me your name again. The angel did not give a name but he blessed Jacob. Jacob called that place Peniel, which means the face of God. The man who wrestled with Jacob most likely an angel whom God sent for that purpose. Jacob held on to the angel and would not let him go unless the angel promised to bless him. The nation Israel would become the name of the tribe of Israel. The New Testament reveals that the Gentiles would receive God's blessings through the gospel of Christ, Gentiles were to be brought into the blessings of Israel by promise, and all believers in God and Christ are Abraham's spiritual descendants.

Ephesians 3:1-7–According to the grace of God the Gentile should be Heirs of the same body. God chose the Israelites for His people with the intentions to make all people of faith come into the Kingdom of God through faith in Christ, who was an Israelite that died as a sacrifice on a cross for all people of faith, Jews and gentiles. When Jacob wrestled with the angel he was in effect wrestling with God. Jacob failed to have faith in God's word at that time. For a reminder of Jacob's lack of faith Jacob walked with a limp to remind him of his encounter with God. The name Israel means 'God strives.' God struggled with Jacob in order to make him obey Him.

Jacob lived with his sons in the land of Canaan. He returned to Bethel, and God appeared to Him again and blessed him. Genesis 35:10-15 "God said to him, "Your name is Jacob; your name shall not be called Jacob anymore, Israel shall be your name." So he called his name Israel. And God said to him, "I am God Almighty. Be fruitful and multiply; a nation and a company of nations shall proceed from you, and kings shall come from your body. The land, which I gave Abraham and Isaac I give to you; and to your descendants after you I give this land." So Jacob set up a pillar in the place where God talked with him, a pillar of stone; and he poured a drink offering on it, and then he poured oil on it. And Jacob called the name of the place where God spoke with him, Bethel, the house of God. The nation of Israel were the people of God's promises but they often rebelled against the commandments of the Lord before they finally took possession of Canaan, the land God promised them. The fulfillment of God's promises (covenants) depended on the willingness and faithfulness of the people of Israel to remain faithful to obey God.

When the Israelites forsook God He would chastise them and when they were faithful God blessed them. Jacob lived with his sons in the land of Canaan, the land God promised Abraham and Isaac. Abraham's descendants from then on were known as the Israelites. Jacob returned to Bethel, and God appeared to Him again and blessed him. Genesis 35:10-15 "God said to him, "Your name is Jacob; your name shall not be called Jacob anymore, But Israel shall be your name."

So he called his name Israel. And God said to him, "I am God Almighty. Be fruitful and multiply; a nation and a company of nations shall proceed from you, and kings shall come from your body. The story of redemption continues through Jacob and his descendants. The land, which I gave Abraham and Isaac I give to you; and to your descendants after you, I give this land. The land was Canaan. So Jacob set up a pillar in the place where he talked with him, a pillar of stone; and he poured a drink offering on it, and then he poured oil on it. And Jacob called the name of the place where God spoke with him, Bethel, which means 'God strives,' and He struggled with the nation of Israel. Jacob's name was changed to Israel and Jacob's people became the nation of Israel. Jacob had twelve sons whose names were: Reuben, Simeon, Levi, Judah, Dan, Naphtali, Gad, Asher, Issachar, Zebulun, Joseph and Benjamin. These sons would eventually become the twelve tribes of the nation of Israel and possess the promised land of Canaan. That happened after many years of hardship and struggles.

The people of Israel, all lived during the patriarchal era. Abraham, Isaac and Jacob were patriarchs, the rulers of a family or tribe. The patriarchal age covers the lifespan of Abraham, Isaac and Jacob all leaders of the families the inherited the promises God made to Abraham. The promises eventually passed to Jacob's son Judah. Judah the patriarch was chosen by God to inherit the covenant. Genesis 49: 8-10 "Judah you are he whom your brothers shall praise; your hand shall be on the neck of your enemies; your father's children shall bow down before you. Judah is a lion's whelp;' "From the prey my son you have gone up" He bows down he lies down like a lion; and as a lion, who shall rouse him? The scepter shall not part from Judah, nor a lawgiver from between his feet, Until Shiloh comes; and to Him shall be the obedience of the people. Binding his donkey to the vine."

The blessing from Jacob to his sons was prophetic and it forecast the future history of the nation of Israel. The emblem of a lion is a symbol of the strength of the leaders of the tribes of Israel and Judah. They would be strong like a lion the king of beasts. Judah would eventually receive the national leadership of Israel.

Shiloh makes reference to Jesus who would be the last in the line of the kings of Israel and Jesus became the King of Kings over all the people of faith. Jacob and his family lived in the land of Canaan but they were destined by the will of God to become slaves in Egypt where they would grow into a large nation of people. The people of Israel were God's chosen people through whom the Jewish Messiah, the Son of God, Jesus of Nazareth would be born in the first century A.D. Jesus the Son of God became the last King in the line of kings. After the death of Jacob the destiny and future of Judah, was important in God's plan of redemption and his descendants would become kings of Israel. King David and King Solomon were two descendants of Judah.

God's People Leave Canaan and go to Egypt

God told his people the descendants of Abraham they would be strangers in Egypt and then He would judge Egypt, and Abraham's descendants would leave that land with great possessions and return to Canaan. Gen 37 through 50. Jacob had a son in his old age and named him Joseph. Jacob had 12 sons but Joseph was his favorite and his brothers were jealous of Joseph because Jacob favored him. Jacob made Joseph a beautiful coat of many colors and his brothers resented him more. Joseph in a prophetic way dreamed of becoming famous and his brothers were jealous.

Abraham, Isaac and Jacob were patriarchs, the rulers of a family or tribe. The patriarchal age covers the lifespan of Abraham, Isaac and Jacob all leaders of the families the inherited the promises God made to Abraham. The promises eventually passed to Jacob's son Judah. Judah the patriarch was chosen by God to inherit the covenant. Genesis 49: 8-10 "Judah you are he whom your brothers shall praise; your hand shall be on the neck of your enemies; your father's children shall bow down before you. Judah is a lion's whelp;' "From the prey my son you have gone up" He bows down he lies down like a lion; and as a lion, who shall rouse him? The scepter shall not part from Judah, nor a lawgiver from between his feet, Until Shiloh comes; and to Him shall be the obedience of the people. Binding his donkey to the vine."

The blessing from Jacob to his sons was prophetic and it forecast the future history of the nation of Israel. The emblem of a lion is a symbol of the strength of the leaders of the tribes of Israel and Judah. They would be strong like a lion the king of beasts. Judah would eventually receive the national leadership of Israel. Shiloh makes reference to Jesus who would be the last in the line of the kings of Israel and Jesus became the King of Kings over all the people of faith. Jacob and his family lived in the land of Canaan but they were destined by the will of God to become slaves in Egypt where they would grow into a large nation of people. The people of Israel were God's chosen people through whom the Jewish Messiah, the Son of God, Jesus of Nazareth would be born in the first century A.D. Jesus became the last King in the line of kings, the King of kings and He provided redemption for sin to everyone with faith in Him. After the death of Jacob the destiny and future of Judah, was important in God's plan of redemption and his descendants would become kings of Israel. King David and King Solomon were two descendants of Judah who became kings of Israel.

God's People Leave Canaan and go to Egypt

God told his people the descendants of Abraham they would be strangers in Egypt and then He would judge Egypt, and Abraham's descendants would leave that land with great possessions and return to Canaan. Gen 37 through 50. Jacob had a son in his old age and named him Joseph. Jacob had 12 sons but Joseph was his favorite and his brothers were jealous of Joseph because Jacob favored him. Jacob made Joseph a beautiful coat of many colors and his brothers resented him more. Joseph in a prophetic way dreamed of becoming famous and his brothers would bow down to him. Joseph's older brothers were tending their father's flocks in the fields and Joseph was sent by Jacob to check on his brothers. When Joseph approached them from a distance his brothers saw him coming and they took Joseph's coat and called Joseph a dreamer and decided to kill him, but instead they threw him into a pit. Later Joseph's brothers put blood on Joseph's coat and they deceived their father Jacob who thought Joseph was killed by a wild animal. Some descendants of Ishmael came near and Joseph's brothers sold Joseph.

When Joseph's brothers went home they lied to their father saying Joseph was dead and Jacob mourned the death of Joseph for a long time. Joseph was taken to Egypt and sold to an Egyptian named Potiphar an officer of the Pharaoh of Egypt. The Lord God favored Joseph in Egypt and he became very successful. The Egyptians trusted Joseph and he was given a position of authority. God was blessing Joseph, giving him the ability to interpret prophetic dreams so he would know what would happen in the future and would be able to help his family. Joseph learned there was going to be a great drought in the land and Joseph advised the Pharaoh to store up grain to feed the people, then Pharaoh gave Joseph even greater authority–Genesis 41:42-44 "Then Pharaoh took his signet ring off his hand and put it on Joseph's hand; and he clothed him in garments of fine linen and put a gold chain around his neck. And he had him ride in the second chariot, which, he had; and they cried out before him, Bow the Knee!" God prepared Joseph to have influence in Egypt to help his people who were destined to come to Egypt because of the famine.

The famine came and Jacob decided to send his sons, Joseph's brothers to Egypt to buy food then return home. Jacob's sons took Benjamin their youngest brother with them because Joseph had never seen Benjamin before. The Pharaoh invited Jacob and his family to come to Egypt and the whole family left Canaan went to Egypt and settled in the part of Egypt called the land of Goshen because the people in Goshen were keepers of livestock. Joseph had been in Egypt for a long time when Jacob and his family arrived in Egypt.

The Last Words of Jacob to His Sons

Jacob called his sons to him and blessed them. God would inform Jacob of the blessings. The order of the blessings begins with the firstborn Reuben, he would be strong but he would not be in the line of Israel's kings. Jacob blessed his other sons and told Joseph he was dying, and God would have his body taken to the land of Canaan. Jacob gave Joseph a larger portion of land than his brothers. The greatest blessing was given to Judah. Judah would be the one in the birth line of God's Son Jesus Christ who would be born in the first century A.D. The descendants of Jacob (Israel) were known as Israelites.

The history of the Israelites through the line of Judah will be the next subject in the story of the Communion of Love. Genesis 49:8-12–Judah you are the one who your brothers shall praise– Your hand shall be on the neck of your enemies; your father's children will bow down before you. Judah is a lion's whelp; from the prey, my son, you have gone up. He bows down he lies down as a lion; and as a lion, who shall rouse him? The scepter shall not depart from Judah, or a lawgiver from between his feet, Until Shiloh comes. And to Him shall be the obedience of the people. Binding his donkey to the vine, and his donkey's colt to the choice vine. He washed his garments in wine, his clothes in the blood of grapes. His eyes are darker than wine, and his teeth whiter than milk. Jacob gave his sons instructions to bury him near his ancestors, in a cave in the land of Canaan. Abraham had previously purchased a field, there. Joseph lived for one hundred and ten years and when he was near death. He told his brothers and their families that God would take them out of Egypt. The Israelites would remain in Egypt for 430 years Exodus 12:40 "Now the sojourn of the children of Israel who lived in Egypt was four hundred and thirty years"

The twelve sons would become the heads of the twelve tribes of Israel but only one son and his descendants would be chosen by God to have the major responsibility and the lead in God's plan of redemption. Joseph was Jacob's favorite son and Reuben was the firstborn but they were not chosen. The descendants of Judah were chosen. Jacob met with his sons before his death to tell them about their future. Reuben was the firstborn and the strength of Jacob with dignity and power but he was unstable. Simeon and Levi were cruel. Judah was the one chosen and Jacob said he would receive praise.

Genesis 49–Your hand shall be on the neck of your enemies. Your brothers will bow down before you. Judah is a lion's whelp he bows down and lies down as a lion. The scepter shall not depart from Judah or a lawgiver from between his feet until Shiloh comes; and to Him shall be the obedience of the people. Judah's descendants would be leaders and kings in Israel and Jesus would be born from a descendant of Judah. The term Shiloh is a reference to the peaceful one, which is Jesus.

The Book of Exodus–Moses

The Israelites were still in Egypt when a new Pharaoh over Egypt decided to make slaves of the Israelites and set Egyptians over them. The Egyptians made them work and treated them harshly. The Hebrew's multiplied very fast and the Egyptians became afraid their number would become too great and told the midwives to kill all of the male babies of the Hebrews. They were given orders to drown the newborn babies in the river. A man and woman of the tribe of Levi had a newborn son and the daughter of the Pharaoh wanted him for her son because he was a beautiful child and he was saved from drowning and became the son of Pharaoh's daughter. He was named Moses because he was taken out of the water and not drowned. Moses was saved by God to become the next leader of the Israelites. God chose him to take his people out of Egypt and back to the promised land of Canaan. Hebrews 11-23-24–Moses, was hidden for three months by his parents of the tribe of Levi when he was born because they saw he was a beautiful child; and they were not afraid of the King's command.

Pharaoh's daughter, an Egyptian saw Moses and she took him for her son and raised Moses. Pharaoh's daughter hired Moses sister to nurse Moses in her home. Moses lived in his sister's home an undetermined period as he grew older. One can assume that while Moses was in his sister's home he learned the history of his people and he chose to suffer affliction with his own people the people of God, than to enjoy the pleasures of Egypt. Pharaoh's daughter had felt sorry for Moses even though he was a Hebrew baby but when he was grown he refused to be called the son of Pharaoh's daughter. Moses knew who he was. Because of the promises God made to Abraham and his descendant it was necessary for the Israelites to return to the promised land of Canaan where the Son of God would be born and Moses would become a great leader of God's people and by God's will he would be instrumental in leading the Israelites out of Egypt. When Moses was grown he killed an Egyptian and became afraid and left Egypt and went to the land of Midian to escape punishment. The Midianites were Arabian people descended from Midian a son of Abraham who lived east of the Red Sea.

The Egyptians worshiped many idols-false gods but the Midianites at that time worshiped the God of Abraham. Moses arrived in the land of the Midianites went to a water well and he met seven young women there watering t animals. The women had come to water their father's sheep, but some shepherds would not let them. Moses rescued the women from the shepherds and he watered their sheep for them. The women were daughters of Reuel (Jethro) the priest of Midian. When the women told their father what Moses had done for them, Jethro invited Moses to eat with his family. Moses stayed with Jethro's family and married Zipporah, one of Reuel's daughters. Moses and Zipporah had a son whom they named Gershom. At first Moses, was not willing to obey God, he was forty years old and he had not experienced the presence of the Lord God before.

God introduced Himself to Moses in a miraculous way so Moses would have faith in Him. Acts 7:30-34–When Moses was forty years old an angel of the Lord appeared to him in flames of fire from a burning bush. Moses was in the wilderness of Mount Sinai tending sheep when he saw a bush on fire but the bush did not burn up. God spoke to Moses out of the flames of the bush and said Moses. Moses said, "Here I am." The Lord told him to remove his sandals, because he was standing on holy ground. The ground was holy because the presence of the Lord was there. The Lord identified Himself as the God of Abraham, Isaac and Jacob. Moses covered his face because he was afraid to look at God. Exodus 3:7-15 The Lord was concerned about the oppression of His people in Egypt. The Lord said "I have come to deliver them out of the hand of the Egyptians, and to bring them up from that land to a good and large land flowing with milk and honey, to the place of the Canaanites and the Hittites, and Amorites and the Perizzites and the Hivites and the Jebusites." God was going to help His people return to the land of Canaan. The Lord God told Moses He would send Moses to Pharaoh and say to pharaoh let my people go. Moses said to God, "Who am I that I should go to Pharaoh, and that I should bring the children of Israel out of Egypt?" Moses was afraid to go back to Egypt because he had killed an Egyptian. The Lord said to Moses, "I will certainly be with you. And this shall be a sign to you that I have sent you.

When you have brought the people out of Egypt, you shall serve God on this Mountain." The mountain was Sinai. God would make His presence known on the mountain. God told Moses He knew about the oppression of His people in Egypt and He was going to bring them out and take them the land of Canaan. He told Moses He was sending him to the Pharaoh to tell him to let God's people leave Egypt. Moses was reluctant to go and he said who am I to tell Pharaoh to let my people go? God promised Moses that He would be with him. Moses asked God what he could say to the people, when they ask him, what is God's name? God told Moses to say I Am Who I Am sent me to you. The descendants of Abraham the people where Moses would had known God for years and they knew the God they had been acquainted with all of their life. God said to Moses, Say to the children of Israel: The Lord God of your fathers, the God of Abraham, the God of Isaac, and the God of Jacob, has sent me to you. This is my name forever and this is my memorial to all generations. If the Israelites in Egypt believed Moses He would become their leader and spokesman for God. God is the same today as He was yesterday the day before and forever. God is self-existing and pure spirit without physical form or parts. God is personal and He was the God of the Israelites. I Am Who I Am was not another name but the inner meaning of the God of Abraham, Isaac and Jacob and it is His name forever.

Moses was told to go to the older men of Israel and tell them I appeared to you and I have seen what was done to you in Egypt and I will bring you back to the land of Canaan. God told Moses He knew the Egyptians would refuse to let the Israelites leave. The lord God said He would strike Egypt with all kinds of miracles then the Egyptians would let the people leave Egypt. Moses was not fully convinced that the Egyptians would believe him. God's purpose was to bring His people out of Egypt and lead them to the land of Canaan, the land He promised to Abraham and his descendants. Moses did not want to return to Egypt even after God revealed Himself to him. Moses was afraid the Israelites would not accept him. The Lord told Moses He would convince the people that Moses was a spokesman for the God of Israel. The Lord also told Moses that He would perform mighty miracles to convince the Pharaoh of Egypt to let the Israelites leave.

It was inevitable that the Israelites leave Egypt and go to the land of Canaan, because of God's promise to the descendants of Abraham, Isaac and Jacob forever. Moses said, "Suppose they will not believe me or listen to me? Suppose they say, 'The Lord has not appeared to you.'" Moses had a staff in his hand and the Lord told him to throw it on the ground. When Moses threw his staff down, it became a snake. Then the Lord told him to pick up the snake by its tail. When Moses reached down and picked it up, it became his staff again. The Lord showed Moses a few more things that would convince the Israelites that God was with Moses. Moses was still afraid to go back to Egypt, and he thought of reasons why he should not go. He said the people wouldn't listen to him, because he was not a good speaker, and he didn't know what to tell the people. The Lord told Moses that He had the power to help him speak, and He would tell him what to say.

Exodus 4:11-17 "So the Lord said to him. Who made man's mouth? Or who makes the mute, the deaf, the seeing or the blind? Have not I the Lord?" God became angry with Moses for doubting Him. God told Moses that his brother Aaron was a good speaker, and Aaron could speak for him. Moses was told to speak to Aaron and put the words in him and He the lord would put the words in His mouth and teach him what to say. God gave Moses a rod to hold in his hand to perform miracles to convince the Pharaoh to let the people of Israel leave Egypt. God then told Aaron to go into the wilderness and meet Moses on the mountain. When they met, Moses told Aaron all that God had said to him, and Aaron agreed to speak for Moses. So Moses, along with his family and his brother Aaron, left the land of the Midianites and returned to Egypt. Moses had been in the land of the Midianites for forty years when the Lord told him to return to Egypt and He was then eighty years old and his brother Aaron was eighty-three years old. Moses and Aaron gathered the elders of the children of Israel, and Aaron told them everything that God had said to Moses. Then they did miracles before the people, which the Lord told them to do. The people of Israel were convinced that God had sent Moses, and when they heard that the Lord was concerned about their oppression, they bowed down and worshipped the Lord. The Egyptians continued to oppress and afflict the Israelites.

God heard the groaning of the children of Israel in Egypt, and God told them He would redeem them with an outstretched arm and with great judgments. He said, "You will be my people and I will be your God. You shall know that I am the Lord your God who brings you out from under the burdens of the Egyptians." God promised Moses and all of the people of Israel that He would make the Egyptians let them leave, and the Israelites would be a nation of people belonging to the Lord, and the Lord would help them go to the promised land of Canaan.

God Would cause great plagues against the Egyptians to convince Pharaoh to let the Israelites leave. The plagues would be so severe that The Pharaoh would beg the Israelites to leave. The Lord said to Moses, "Now you will see what I will do to Pharaoh with a strong hand and he will be so glad to let them go, that he will drive them out of his land." God told Moses what to say. "I am the Lord. I appeared to Abraham, to Isaac, and to Jacob, as God Almighty. I have also established my covenant with them, to give them the land of Canaan." God told Moses to go to Pharaoh and demand that he free the Israelites, tell him the Lord said, "Let My people go. The Pharaoh refused to let the Israelites leave Egypt and God told Moses that Pharaoh's heart was hard meaning he was very stubborn, so God began to send plagues on the Egyptians to convince them to let the Israelites leave.

Exodus Chapters 7-11–God performed great miracles and signs to convince Pharaoh, but each time Pharaoh was stubborn, and he would not let the people of Israel leave. Each time

Pharaoh's magicians duplicated the same signs with their magic. God sent ten great plagues on the Egyptian people. (The story of the plagues begins in Exodus 7:14 and ends in chapter 11. The first plague God sent was, turning all the fresh water in Egypt into blood. That was followed by nine other plagues: plague of frogs, lice, flies, livestock, disease, a plague of boils, hail, locusts, and darkness. The last plague was the death of all the firstborn of people and animals would die. Each time after a plague stopped, God sent another plague.

God shielded the Israelites from harm during the plagues. Each time Pharaoh stubbornly hardened his heart and refused to let the Israelites leave. Before God struck the Egyptians with the last plague God told Moses to speak to the Israelites and tell them to ask their neighbors for articles of silver and gold. God wanted the Israelites to leave Egypt with great wealth and articles to use later in the construction of the tabernacle, a place where the Israelites could worship God. The Lord caused the Israelites to have favor with the Egyptians and the Egyptian people gave the Israelites the treasures they asked for. These things they would take with them when they left Egypt.

The Feast of Unleavened Bread, also called the Passover Feast, was a feast the Israelites were told to observe before they left Egypt and they have continued to observe the Passover Feast every year since that time. The Passover was instituted to remind the Israelites of God's grace and kindness toward them when He delivered them from Egypt. The last plague, the death plague of the firstborn of Egypt, literally means to pass over in the sense of sparing the life of the firstborn of Israel on the night that all of the firstborn of the people and animals in Egypt would die.

The Lord said to Moses, "I will bring one more plague on Pharaoh and on Egypt. Afterward he will let you go from here. When he lets you go he will surely drive all of you out of Egypt." The death of the firstborn would be the last and the worst plague. Each family lost their first-born even the first-born son of Pharaoh. After the ninth plague, Moses and Aaron appeared before the Pharaoh and he said, Get away from me! Take heed to yourself and see my face no more! For in the day you see my face you shall die! So Moses said, you have spoken I will never see your face again. The Lord acted with great violence against the Egyptians because of the stubbornness of Pharaoh. All of Egypt's firstborn died. God demonstrated His great power and Glory for all the Egyptians and the Israelites to see. Exodus 11: (Vs 4-7)–Moses said, "Thus says the Lord: about midnight I will go out in the midst of Egypt; and all the firstborn in the land of Egypt shall die from the firstborn of Pharaoh who sits on his throne even to the firstborn of the female servant who is behind the hand mill, and all the firstborn of the animals."

There was a great cry, weeping and wailing throughout the land of Egypt, such as was not like it before, nor shall be like it again. But against the children of Israel not even a dog moved its tongue, against man or beast so that the Israelites would know that the Lord does make a difference between the Egyptians and Israel." Exodus 12:29-30– At midnight the Lord killed all the firstborn in the land of Egypt' from the firstborn of Pharaoh who sat on his throne to the firstborn of all of the captives who was in the dungeon, and all of the first born of livestock. Pharaoh and his servants got up and all the Egyptians. There was great crying in Egypt, for there was not a house where there was not one dead.

Pharaoh sent for Moses and Aaron and told them that all of the Israelites could leave Egypt with their children, animals and all of their possessions and go into the wilderness to serve the Lord. The Israelites left Egypt with great wealth, of gold, silver and other things they received from the Egyptians, plus all of their livestock. And they went toward the wilderness of the desert of Sinai. Hebrews 11:28-29–By faith Moses kept the Passover and the sprinkling of blood, so God would not destroy the firstborn of the Israelites. By faith they believed God and they passed through the Red Sea as if on dry land, but the Egyptians who attempted to do so, drowned. The Lord led them through the Red Sea and they camped in a place called Etham that was at the edge of the wilderness between Egypt and the Jordan River. The Lord went ahead of them with the presence of an angel. He led them by a cloud during the day and a pillar of fire at night.

Exodus 13:18-22–God led the people through the wilderness of the Red Sea. And the children of Israel went up in orderly fashion out of the land of Egypt. And Moses took the bones of Joseph with him, for he had placed the children of Israel under solemn oath, saying, God will visit you, and you shall carry my bones with you. There were more than two million Israelites that left Egypt and headed for the wilderness. Pharaoh went back on his word and made his chariot ready and took his troops with him and attempted to catch up to the Israelites. He took 600 choice chariots, and all the chariots of Egypt with captains over every one of them.

The Egyptians chased the children of Israel but the children of Israel continued to run from the Egyptians and the Lord protected them. Moses told to the people, not to fear, stand still and see the salvation of the Lord which He will accomplish for them. The Egyptians you see today, but you shall never see again forever, the Lord will fight for you and you shall hold your peace. The Israelites set up their camp at Migdol near the Red Sea. Pharaoh led an army of charioteers after them and the Israelites were trapped between the Egyptians and the waters of the sea." The Israelites became frightened because Pharaoh's army was closing in on them from behind and the Red Sea was in front of them. They began to cry out to God and to Moses. The children of Israel stood on the shore of the Red Sea the angel of God and the pillar of cloud moved behind them so the Egyptian army couldn't see them and come close to them. Moses lifted up his staff over the sea, and a pathway opened up through the waters, and Moses and the people walked across the Red Sea and came out on dry land. The Egyptians came after God's people on the dry path through the sea, but the Lord caused their chariot wheels to become stuck in the mud to slow them down. The Egyptians became afraid and turned around to go back. Moses stretched out his arms over the sea and walls of water on each side of the pathway came down on the Egyptians and drowned them. Because of this miracle the people of Israel began to have more faith in the Lord.

Exodus 14:30-31 "So the Lord saved Israel that day out of the hand of the Egyptians, and Israel saw the Egyptians dead on the seashore. Thus Israel saw the great work which the Lord had done in Egypt; so the people feared the Lord, and believed the Lord and his servant Moses." Moses and the people of Israel celebrated and sang to the Lord. Miriam the sister of Moses and Aaron led them in song. They continued their journey from Succoth and camped in Etham at the edge of the wilderness. And the Lord continued to go before them by day in a pillar of cloud to lead the way, and by night in a pillar of fire to give them light. While the Israelites were in the wilderness of Sinai God told the people of Israel that He was sending an angel to go before them and guard them through the wilderness. The people were warned to listen to the angel and follow his instructions.

God told Moses that the name they were to use when speaking of God was Yahweh meaning the Lord. The children of Israel numbered an estimated two million people. The wilderness was a barren place, a desert, sand dunes and rock with no vegetation and very little water. The people tried the Lord's patience with their complaining and lack of faith in the Lord. God tried the faith of the Israelites by bringing them out of a land of plenty into a desert wilderness where there was little water and not enough food. At one time both the Lord and Moses disowned the whole nation. God said to Moses they are your people, but Moses said, Lord they are your people. However, the Lord and Moses continued to help them. God wanted the people of Israel to have faith in Him. God planned for them to become a great nation of people. A people prepared for the Messiah their last king who would be the Savior of all people. The Lord sent the Israelites food from heaven, a substance that looked like bread fell from heaven every morning and they called it manna. The word manna means 'what is it.' the Israelites had never seen anything like it before.

The Lord also sent them quails for meat, the quails covered their camp every evening and everyone had enough to eat. The Lord established the seventh day of every week as a holy day, and a Sabbath day because God created everything in six days and on the seventh day He ceased. The word Sabbath means to cease or to come to the end of all activity. The Sabbath was a day of much needed rest for the Israelites. The Lord provided for the daily needs of the people but they were not satisfied and were not grateful. Hebrews 3:7-11 "Therefore as the Holy Spirit says: "Today if you will hear His voice, Do not harden your hearts as in the rebellion, in the days of trial in the wilderness, where your fathers tested Me, tried Me and saw My works forty years. Therefore I was angry with that generation, and I said, "They always go astray in their heart. And they have not known My ways.' So I swore in My wrath, they shall not enter My rest." Many of the Israelites that started the journey through the wilderness on their way to the land of Canaan never made it all of the way. Many would die because they refused to trust the Lord and obey Him. When the people had walked all of the way to a place called Rephidim, there was no water to drink. The people became angry and argued with Moses, and Moses told them they were temping the Lord.

The people were not trusting in the Lord to provide for them even though He had always done so. Moses was angry with the people and he asked God what he should do with the people. Moses was ready to leave, but the Lord told him to stay with them. The Lord told Moses to take some of the elder men of Israel with him to Horeb and strike a certain rock with his staff and water would come out of the rock. When they came to Horeb, Moses found the rock, and when he struck it, water flowed from the rock. (Exodus 17:7)

The place was called Massah and Meribah, because the people argued with the Lord and tempted the Lord saying, "Is the Lord among us or not?" Moses chose men with the ability to lead and made them leaders over the people. The problems of the people that were too hard too difficult to judge they sent to Moses. The Israelites continued to walk through the desert, and on the third month after leaving Egypt, they came to the Sinai wilderness near Mt Sinai where they set up camp at the base of MT Sinai (Mt Horeb). Jethro the priest of Midian was Moses father in-law and Jethro came to Moses with Moses sons when they were at Mt Sinai. The Lord at Mt Sinai

Sinai is sometimes called Horeb and the Israelites arrived there in the third month after leaving Egypt and they camped at the base of the mountain on a plain where the top of the mountain was visible. The Lord revealed himself to Moses on the mountain and gave him the Ten Commandments. God made a covenant with the people of Israel. When Moses went part of the way up the mountain the Lord spoke to him and gave him instructions for the people. The Lord reminded Moses of how He had protected the Israelites from the Egyptians by carrying them on Eagles wings - a metaphor concerning God's protection of them like an eagle that protects their young.

Moses went up the mountain and the Lord called to him saying—You shall say to the house of Jacob, and tell the children of Israel: You have seen what I did to the Egyptians, and how I bore you on eagles wings and brought you to Myself. Now if you will indeed obey Me and keep My covenant, you will be a special people to Me above all people, for all the earth is Mine. And you shall be a kingdom of priests and a holy nation."

When Moses came down the mountain, he called the elders of the people and told them what the Lord said. The people agreed to do everything the Lord commanded, so Moses returned to the Lord to tell Him what the people said. The Lord told Moses that He would come before the people in a thick cloud. (The Lord covered Himself with the cloud so no one could see the Lord's face. The Lord said He would speak with Moses. The people could not see but they could hear the Lord then the people would trust Moses. The people were told to consecrate themselves by cleaning their bodies and their clothes so they could come near to the Lord. Moses had three days to prepare the people, and on the third day the Lord came down on the mountain while the people watched. Moses was told to mark boundaries all of the way around the mountain so that the people would not be able to touch the mountain. If anyone touched the mountain when the Lord was on the mountain, they would be put to death, stoned or shot with an arrow. The people were not to go up to the mountain until they heard a loud blast from a ram's horn. Rams horns were used like trumpets to signal the people.

Exodus 19:16-20—On the third day, in the morning that there was thunder, lightning and a thick cloud on the mountain; and the sound of the trumpet was very loud, and all the people who were in the camp trembled. Moses brought the people out of the camp to meet with God, and they stood at the foot of the mountain. Mt Sinai was completely covered with smoke, because the Lord descended on it in fire. The smoke went up like the smoke of a furnace, and the whole mountain quaked. The blast from the trumpet sounded and became louder and louder, Moses spoke and the Lord answered him by voice. Then the Lord came down to the top of Mt Sinai. And the Lord called to Moses and Moses went up to the top of the mountain. The Lord told Moses to go down the mountain, warn the people not to try to break through the cloud and see the Lord. He then told Moses to come back up the mountain and bring his brother Aaron with him. When Moses and Aaron went up the mountain, God gave Moses the Ten Commandments plus a very detailed and lengthy law containing rules and regulations the people were to observe.

Moses received the Law that was known as the Law of Moses and he taught the Law to the people of Israel. The Law of Moses and would remain in effect until the Messiah (Jesus) came in the first century. Moses received the Law and wrote down the law and taught it to the people.

Aaron became the first high priest of the Israelites. A priest is one that offers sacrifices to the Lord for the people priests administer gifts and sacrifices for sin. Sacrifices before Christ were made while the first tabernacle also called the tent of meeting was a small portable meeting place for God to meet the people. They took the tabernacle with them as they moved from place to place on their journey to the Land of Canaan. When the Israelites camped in a new place the tabernacle was set up in the middle of the camp. The tribe of Levi was responsible for transporting the tabernacle and its furnishings when the people moved. Many years later when the nation of Israel was back in the land of Canaan the people of Israel would build a glorious temple to worship God in. Moses would enter the tabernacle first.

The worship and tabernacle service was symbolic for that time and could not make the people who performed the service perfect in regard to the conscience. Their sins were not forgiven. The Israelites were obligated to offer to the Lord a service consisting of fleshly ordinances. This type of worship could not free a person from the guilt of their sin and give them a clear conscience but it would satisfy the Lord at that time if the people were faithful to obey the law. That type of worship would last until Jesus came and died for the redemption of people's sin. All Christians are priests that offer spiritual sacrifices from their heart. If the people under the old covenant given at Sinai remained faithful to God according to the ordinances of worship, the sacrifice of Christ would be retroactive in forgiving their sins. The priesthood continued until the time of Christ then Christ became the only High Priest by offering himself as a sacrifice for sin. Hebrews chapter 4–Today God's people have a High Priest, Jesus the Son of God, who can sympathize with our weaknesses because he was tempted in every way like we are, therefore we can come to the throne of God's grace and obtain mercy.

Speaking of Christ, Paul said in Ephesians 2:14-16 "For He Himself is our peace, who has made both one, and has broken down the middle wall of separation, having abolished in His flesh the enmity, that is the law of commandments contained in ordinances, so as to create one new man from the two, thus making peace, and that He might reconcile them both to God in one body through the cross." The Law of Moses God gave the Israelites was a temporary law that would be done away with when Christ died on the cross and that law was never intended to be observed by the Gentiles. The law Moses received was very lengthy and Moses was on the mountain for a long time. The law included every component of the Israelites life including the building of a tabernacle and various articles used for worship while they were in the wilderness. God's plan for redemption called for the people of Israel to remain faithful to the Old Law given by Moses until Jesus Christ died on the cross for the forgiveness of sin. After Jesus death the people who would have faith in Christ could without a priest obtain forgiveness of sin through faith in Jesus who is their high priest.

Moses was on the mountain for a long time and the people of Israel began to doubt if Moses would ever come down from the mountain, so they encouraged Aaron to take Moses' place. When they did that they rebelled against the Lord God and they asked Aaron to make some idols to be a god for them to worship. The Lord told Moses to go down the mountain to tend to the stiff-necked people. The Lord was angry enough to destroy them and start over with Moses and choose another nation of people, but Moses pleaded with the Lord to save the people of Israel. Moses reminded the Lord of His promise to Abraham and how He had told Abraham that he would bless and multiply his descendants. The Lord chose not to destroy the people of Israel and the Lord with compassion was willing to acknowledge them as His people after Moses pleaded for them. The promises God made to Abraham did not depend on the Law of Moses. The Law was added because the people were exceedingly sinful. God promised Israel that the time would come when he would make a new covenant with Israel, because redemption of sin could not come through the Law of Moses.

The new covenant in Christ would be a covenant of personal faith hope and love by everyone seeking God's forgiveness for sin. The Law of Moses regulated the external acts of morality without regards to the heart. The sacrifices for sin had to be offered continually. The attitudes of the hearts of the people did not change, and the people continued to sin. The Lord established the priesthood to administer the Law from the men of the tribe of Levi; so it was called the Levitical priesthood. Moses brother Aaron was chosen as the first high priest. Aaron's sons Nadab, Abihu, Ithamar and Eleazar were priests who assisted Aaron. The main duty of the priests included teaching the Law of Moses as well as offering the animal sacrifices and conducting the religious services at the tabernacle according to the Law.

God wanted His people to worship with their heart not with external rites and objects but He set up that type of worship on Mt Sinai to keep them united as a nation of people prepared for the coming of His Son. After the death of God's Son the Law of Moses would cease to be in effect and God's people would worship from the heart. The tabernacle service is defined in Hebrews 9:1-5 "Then indeed even the first covenant had ordinances of divine service and the earthly sanctuary. For the tabernacle was prepared: the first part in which was the lamp-stand, the table, and the showbread, which is called the sanctuary; and behind the second veil, the part of the tabernacle which is called the Holiest of All, which had the Golden censer and the ark of the covenant overlaid on all sides with gold, in which were the golden pot that had the manna Aaron's rod that budded, and the tablets of the covenant; and above it were the cherubim of glory overshadowing the mercy seat."

The people were instructed to make dishes and plates of gold and pitchers to pour out offerings. They were to make a table of acacia wood overlaid with gold, which was called the table of showbread. Twelve loaves of bread, one for each of the twelve tribes of Israel, were to be placed on the table. The bread was called the bread of presence indicating the presence of God. The altar for burning incense, the table for the bread of presence, and a lamp stand to give light were placed in the Holy Place.

God told them to build an ark (chest) made from acacia wood and cover it with pure gold inside and out. The Israelites moved from place to place for a long time before they were settled in the promise land, so the chest and the table had rings on each side and poles that could be inserted in the rings allowing men to carry them. Inside the ark were the stone tablets containing the Ten Commandments and Aaron's rod The chest was called the Ark of the Covenant and was the only thing placed in the Most Holy Place. On top of the Ark of the Covenant were two cherubim (angels) with their wings outspread covering the mercy seat where God's awesome presence was. The high priest was the only one who was authorized to enter the Most Holy Place. If anyone else entered the Most Holy Place they would die. The Most Holy place represented heaven as God's dwelling place and God's presence was there. The death of Jesus opened the way for anyone with faith in God and Christ to enter into the holy place of heaven.

Hebrews 9:6-10– When everything was prepared, the priests went into the first part of the tabernacle and performed the services. The high priest went alone once a year with blood, which he offered for himself and for the people's sins that were committed in ignorance. The Holy Spirit indicated this was the way into the Holiest of All but was not yet made manifest while the first tabernacle was still standing. It was symbolic for that time in which both gifts and sacrifices were offered but could not make him who performed the service perfect in regard to the conscience, because the sins were not forgiven. The service was concerned only with food and drinks, washings, and animal sacrifices. That type of worship would continue until the time of Christ who would sacrifice his own blood for the guilt of the sins of the people. The Law of Moses and the ordinances of the tabernacle and temple worship would end when Jesus died. Since the death of Jesus, His body and blood have become the sacrifice of atonement. In the courtyard of the tabernacle there was an altar for burnt offerings. The people would bring the animals to be sacrificed, and the priests would offer the animals on the altar for the people. There was also a copper basin called a laver, which was filled with water for the priests and high priest to wash their hands and feet before they entered the tabernacle.

The priesthood, the tabernacle and the animal sacrifices were only a foreshadowing of the salvation that would be provided by Jesus when He was sacrificed on the cross. A blood sacrifice was necessary for the remission of sins, but the blood of animals could never take away the guilt of sin; the sacrifices reminded the people year after year that they were sinners. After the death of the redeemer God's Son the Law of Moses would no longer be in effect.

The Israelites Struggle in the Wilderness

The Israelites often changed from faithful to becoming unfaithful to the Lord from the time of the wilderness wandering until God's Son was sacrificed. Israel would remain faithful to God for a time, then they would rebel against God's commandments. God would threaten them and inflict punishment to keep them faithful to the course he had planned for them. When the Israelites had been in the wilderness for about two years, they came to Kadesh Barnea close to the Negev in the Sinai Peninsula, a land inhabited by the Amalekites the descendants of Esau. God had promised Israel the land of Canaan but they were expected h to fight the people in the land and take the land from them. Moses was told to send twelve spies into the land to explore the land. Two of the spies, Joshua and Caleb, came back with a pleasing report and a sample of some of the fruit grown there, but ten of the spies said the people were powerful and so large that the Israelites looked like grasshoppers in their sight. When the people heard the report of the ten spies, they were afraid to go forward and they began to complain and grumble against Moses and Aaron.

They said, "If only we had stayed in Egypt." The Lord was displeased because of the people's complaining, and he said to Moses, "How long will these people treat me with contempt? How long will they refuse to believe in me in spite of all the miraculous signs I have performed among them?" God was very angry with the people of Israel but Moses intervened for them and God did not punish them but God decreed that not anyone of that generation would see the land of Canaan except for the two spies who had given them hope of entering Canaan with their good report. The Lord made the Israelites wander in the desert until all of that generation was dead.

It would be thirty-eight more years before they would get to enter the Promised Land of Canaan.

Deuteronomy – A Statement of the Law

After all the generation of those who came out of Egypt were dead, except for Moses, Joshua and Caleb, God told Moses to prepare the people to enter Canaan the land He promised them. Moses taught the people the Law that God gave them at Mt Sinai, and he warned them never to become idolaters but remain faithful to the Lord. He addressed the people with three important speeches and exhortations to encourage them. The Law would not make them righteous but it would reveal to them ho sinful they were and their need for redemption.

Deuteronomy 1:5-8 –On this side of the Jordan in the land of Moab, Moses began to explain this law saying, "The Lord our God spoke to us in Horeb (Sinai): saying you have dwelt long enough at this mountain. Turn and take your journey and go to the mountains of the Amorites, to all the neighboring places in the plain, in the mountains and in the lowland, in the South and on the seacoast, to the land of the Canaanites and to Lebanon, as far as the great river, the River Euphrates. See I have set the land before you; go in and possess the land which the Lord swore to your fathers- to Abraham, Isaac, and Jacob- to give them and their descendants after them."

The Israelites were told, what lands to go to in Canaan however idolatrous people had been living in those lands for many years and the Israelites were expected to drive them out. The Israelites would encounter opposition from the people that lived there but Moses encouraged the people to be courageous and cross over the Jordan River and take possession of the land of Canaan. The Jordan River was a dividing point between the wilderness and Canaan. The Israelites would have to fight for the land but God would help them if they remained faithful to Him. Moses was given great responsibility leading so many people, and he selected men from the twelve tribes of Israel who were wise and respected and Moses gave them jurisdiction over the people of Israel. The nation of Israel had grown to a large size in Egypt, and in the wilderness.

A census was taken according to the twelve tribes of Israel and they numbered approximately two million people. Every male twenty years or older that was able to fight in a war would be eligible and they were commanded to drive the idolatrous people out of the land and each tribe of Israel provided leaders for the army of Israel. The tribe of Levi was the tribe of the priests. They were not a part of the army and therefore would not fight. Ephraim and Manasseh, the two sons of Joseph, were leaders of tribes, and they would receive an allotment of land. Moses exhorted the people to carefully follow every command of the Law. Deuteronomy 7:9-11– The Lord your God, he is God, the faithful God who keeps His covenant and mercy for a thousand generations with those who love Him and keep His commandments; and He repays those who hate Him to their face, and destroy them. He will not be slack with Him who hates Him; He will repay Him. Therefore you shall obey the commandment the statutes and the judgments, which I command you.

Deuteronomy 8:1-2–You must be careful to observe every commandment which I command you that you may live and multiply, and go in and possess the land of which the Lord swore to your fathers. And you shall remember that the Lord your God led you all the way these forty years in the wilderness to humble you and test you, to know what was in your heart, whether you would keep His commandments or not. Moses warned the people to be careful not to worship the idols of the people in the land, which is an abomination to the Lord. Moses reviewed the Passover Feast and the other annual feasts the people were commanded to observe according the Law that God gave Moses at Sinai. When they conquered the people in the land they were to take possession of the land and live there and wait for the birth of Jesus the Messiah. The word Messiah means the 'Lord's Anointed One.' The New Testament reveals that the Messiah was the same Messiah that was promised when Jacob blessed his sons in Egypt (Genesis 49: 8-12). Jesus would be born in the land of Canaan in the first century A.D. Moses was now one hundred and twenty years old, and he had many things to do to prepare his people to go forward and take the land of Canaan. Moses encouraged the people of Israel to obey God's law, and he taught the law to the younger generation that had been born during the time they had wandered in the wilderness.

The Lord wanted Moses to urge the people to prepare for war and conquer the land of Canaan. The lord promised He would go with them as they drove out the people in the land. Moses told the Israelites that God's commandments were not too hard for the people to comply with, and they must choose life or death. If the Israelites loved God and obeyed His commandments, they would live and be blessed, but if they rebelled against God and His commandments, they would die. The Lord would not kill them, but He would not defend them against their enemies either unless they were faithful to obey Him. Moses told the people that if they obeyed the Lord, the Lord would fight for them like a destroying fire. Moses pleaded with God to let him live long enough to cross over the Jordan into the land of Canaan. God would not allow Moses to go into Canaan, because at one time Moses had taken credit for bringing forth water from a rock instead of giving God the glory.

(Numbers 20:12). In the book of Deuteronomy Moses taught about the importance of reiterating the covenant between God and the Israelites before they crossed the Jordan River and tribal leaders were to be appointed. Moses reminded the people of the events of the wilderness wandering. Deuteronomy 3:23-29 Paraphrase, Moses pleaded with the Lord to let him cross the Jordan and see the land between the Jordan and the mountains of Lebanon but the Lord was angry with Moses and would not listen to him. God refused to let Moses cross the Jordan and told him to go to the top of Mt Pisgah, and look in every direction so he could see the land. Joshua became the leader of the Israelites and Joshua would lead the children of Israel across the Jordan.

Joshua Becomes the Leader of the Israelites

The Lord told Moses to encourage Joshua to go forward and take the people across the Jordan into Canaan. Joshua was a young man from the tribe of Ephraim that had assisted Moses. Moses instructs the people not to add to or take away anything he had commanded them. The Lord commanded Moses at that time to speak to the people. Moses had warned the Israelites not to become idolaters like the people in the land where they would be going. Moses restated the ten commandments of the Law of Moses including the greatest commandment.

Deuteronomy 6:3-7 "Therefore hear, O Israel, and be careful to observe it, that it may be well with you, and that you may multiply greatly as the Lord God of your fathers has promised you– a land flowing with milk and honey.' Hear O Israel: The Lord our God, the Lord is one! You shall love the Lord your God with all your heart, with all your soul, and with all your strength. And these words, which I command you today, shall be in your heart. You shall teach them diligently to your children and shall talk of them when you sit in your house, when you walk by the way, when you lie down, and when you rise up." If the Israelites obeyed the Lord in every respect He would help them overcome the people in the land but the Israelites failed to obey the Lord in every respect and the children of Israel had fight their way in war to the land of Canaan.

Moses had a personal relationship with the Lord. He was a very humble man and the greatest of the prophets, because the Lord talked with him face to face (Num. 34:10), and no one has ever had access to the mighty miraculous power of the Lord like Moses did. The Lord performed awesome deeds for Israel. Moses taught Joshua everything he needed to know about taking command over Israel, and before he died, Moses climbed to the top of Mt Nebo, so he could see the Promised Land of Canaan. Moses died and was buried in a valley in Moab.

The children of Israel are now at the time for them to enter the Land of Canaan in force and battle the idolatrous people to take possession of the land and drive out the people there. Joshua in now the national leader. The book of Joshua and the book of Judges describes the conquest of Canaan to settle the land God promised them. God would help them but they were responsible to take the lead. As long as the Israelites obeyed the Lord He would fight for them but if they forsook the Lord He forsook them.. The Exodus from Egypt was approximately from 1240 B.C. to 1190 B.C. Joshua made three campaigns in the invasion of Canaan. The war with the people in Canaan began with the destruction of, Jericho on the other side of the river. Canaan was a land populated by city states with no central government, each city had its own king. The entire population worshiped idols and one popular idol is identified as Baal that was originally worshiped at Shechem but Baal worship spread throughout Canaan.

Joshua Leads Israel across the Jordan (1460 B.C.)

The book of Joshua is about the history of Israel's crusade to conquer the land of Canaan that God had promised them. The Law of Moses united the tribes of the nation of Israel and the land of Canaan would be divided among the tribes. A tribal leader governed each tribe. The Israelites were the direct descendants of Jacob's 12 sons. The combined twelve tribes are the united kingdom of Israel and Judah. They are the people referred to as Jews. Joshua 1:1-9–After the death of Moses the Lord spoke to Joshua and told him to go over the Jordan River with all the people to the land He was giving them. The Lord told Joshua that He would be with him like He was with Moses all the days of his life. The lord said I will not forsake, you or leave you, be strong and courageous and obey all of the Law of Moses and the Lord would be with him everywhere he went. Joshua had complete faith and hope in the Lord and he served his God.

God said to Joshua, "Every place that the sole of your foot will tread upon, I have given you, as I said to Moses." God gave the Israelites the land but they had to fight the people who were already living there and take the land from them. The people living in the land were idolaters. The promised territory extended from the wilderness area to Lebanon, and from The Mediterranean Sea (Great Sea) to the Euphrates River. God said from the land of the Hittites to the Great Sea shall be your territory. God also told them no one would be able to defeat them, because He would be with them and no man would be able to stand before them. God's promises depended on the faithfulness of the people who receive His promises. If they remained faithful to the Lord He would help them overcome the idolatrous people.

God said–"Be strong and of good courage, for to this people you shall divide as an inheritance the land, which I swore to their fathers to give them." Before Moses died he instructed them, "Do not turn from it to the right hand or to the left, that you may prosper wherever you go. This book of the Law shall not depart from your mouth, but you shall meditate in it day and night, that you may observe to do according to all that is written in it.

Then you will make your way prosperous, and you will have good success.' "Have I not commanded you? Be strong and of good courage; do not be afraid, nor be dismayed, for the Lord your God is with you wherever you go." The Israelites were told to make the Promised Land free of idolatry and free from the sins of the heathen people. The people of Israel were told to drive all the foreign people out of the land so that the people of Israel would not be tempted to engage in idolatry. God wanted to make Israel a holy nation to serve the Lord and His success would depend on the individual faith of the people of Israel to go to war and drive the idolaters out.

Joshua was chosen to lead Israel in military battles and take the land of Canaan by force. And the land would be divided among the twelve tribes. Joshua trusted God and the Spirit of God was with him, but the people of Israel often rebelled and failed to obey God's commandments. The conquest of Canaan was necessary for God's plan to bring His Son into the world. The nation of Israel, the descendants of Abraham, were chosen by the Lord for that purpose, and it was important for them to survive as a faithful nation of people until the right time for Jesus to be born. Under Joshua's leadership the Israelites defeated the kings of several cities and took their land.

There was not a single city that was too strong for the Israelites to conqueror, if they obeyed the Lord. Two kings of the Amorites were defeated and all of the cities of the plain. Reuben, Gad and Manasseh conquered territories east of the Jordan River. When they had settled their wives and children in the territories they conquered, the men of those tribes left their wives and children and went with the rest of the Israelites to help them conquer the territories west of the Jordan. The first city across the Jordan River was Jericho. Joshua sent spies across the River to the city of Jericho to gain information about the strength of the people because they would have to fight them for the land. When the spies entered Jericho, they went to the house of a harlot named Rahab for lodging.

While they were there, someone reported to the King that spies from Israel were in Rahab's house. By the providence of God, Rahab was informed that the Lord was going to take the city for the Israelites.

The spies promised Rahab that she and the lives of her household would be spared if she would hide them. Rahab knew the king would be looking for the two spies, so she took them up to the roof and covered them with flax so the king's men wouldn't find them. When the king sent his men to Rahab demanding her to bring the men out, she told them that the men had been there but had left the city. When the king's men went away, Rahab lowered the spies of Israel on a rope through a window in the wall to the outside of the city.

The two spies reported to Joshua all that had happened, and they were confident that the Lord would give them a victory over the city of Jericho. Then Joshua led the children of Israel to the Jordan River, but when the people neared the river, they were afraid and hesitant about crossing it. For three days the leaders of the tribes went to all of the people telling them to watch the Ark of the Covenant that would be carried across the Jordan River by the priests and the people were to follow the ark across the river. The ark was a rectangular box made of wood and covered with gold. The ark contained the two tablets of the Law of Moses, a golden pot of manna and Aaron's rod. Above it were, Cherubim's of glory overshadowing the mercy seat.

Exodus 25. The people watched the Ark, and as soon as the priests stepped into the water of the Jordan River carrying the Ark, the river stopped flowing, and there was a dry path all the way across the river to the other side for the Israelites to cross over. As long as the priests carrying the Ark stood in the water, the water ceased to flow, and all of the Israelites crossed over on dry ground, then the river began to flow again. The Israelites camped at a place called Gilgal east of Jericho from the place where they crossed. Gilgal became the Israelites first base of operations during their campaign to take the land. Joshua instructed one man from each tribe to pick up a stone from the riverbed as they crossed the river.

They took the twelve stones and built a memorial. Joshua told the people that in the future when their children asked what the stones meant, they were to tell them that God dried up the river and kept it dry until they had all crossed, just as he had done when they crossed the Red Sea with Moses. From Gilgal they advanced toward Jericho.

As the Israelites were nearing Jericho, Joshua saw an angel in the form of a man. Joshua asked him who he was, and the angel answered that he was the commander of the army of the Lord. Joshua asked the angel what he wanted him to do, and the angel said to Joshua, "Take off your shoes, because the place where you are standing is holy." The place was holy because the presence of God was there. God was watching over His people. The children of Israel were given specific instructions about how to destroy the city of Jericho.

The Lord told them to march around the city once every day for six days. Seven priests were to sound trumpets made from rams' horns while the other priests carried the Ark of the Covenant. On the seventh day they marched around the city seven times the priests blew the trumpets then they made a long blast on the trumpets, all the people shouted with a loud voice, and the walls of Jericho fell down. The Israelites rushed in and took the city. The only people in Jericho who were saved were Rahab and her household. The Israelites would be involved in many wars in the process of possessing all of the land of Canaan. Under the leadership of Joshua, with the help of the Lord, Israel gained many victories.

The Lord worked miracles to help the Israelites defeat the nations of the people in the land, however some of the tribes failed to drive out the Canaanites and their false gods from the land like the Lord had said and the Gentile nations lived among the tribes and tempted the Israelites to sin. Judges 2:1-4—The angel of the Lord came from Gilgal to Bochim, and said: I led you up from Egypt and brought you to the land of which I swore to your fathers; and I said, I will never break My covenant with you. And you were to never make a covenant with the inhabitants of this land; you were to tear down their altars. But you have not obeyed my voice. Why have you done this? I also said, I will not drive them out before you; but they shall be thorns in your side, and their god's shall be a snare to you. When the Angel of the Lord spoke these words to all the children of Israel the people wept. When Joshua dismissed the people each one went to their own inheritance to possess the land." Joshua died at the age of 110, and after his death Israel was without a national leader. The people's faith in God began to decline and the people engaged in the worship of foreign god's.

Most of Israel forgot the Lord, and there was no one to guide them and everyone did what he or she determined was right instead of following the Law of the Lord. Judges 2:20-23—The anger of the Lord was great against Israel; and He said, "Because this nation has transgressed My covenant which I commanded their fathers, and has not heeded My voice, I also will no longer drive out any of the nations which Joshua left when he died, so that through them I may test Israel, whether they will keep the ways of the Lord, to walk in them as their fathers kept them, or not." Therefore the Lord did not drive out their enemies immediately; and He did not deliver them into the hand of Joshua. God did not give up His people forever but they suffered great consequences and some defeats because they were not completely faithful to His word. The priesthood failed the people, and the tribes of Israel failed to govern themselves responsibly.

Without a national leader the people of Israel drifted away from following God. Israel needed someone with faith and integrity in the Lord to lead and govern them. The conquest of Canaan began with Joshua, but it was not complete before his death. After the death of Joshua, there was a time of disorganization and disunity among the twelve tribes of Israel. Israel's enemies took advantage of the Israelite tribes who had begun practicing idolatry. Israel broke their covenant with God and consequently God's protection was not with them any longer because the Israelites had not driven their enemies from the land of Canaan when they first occupied the land. The Lord allowed the enemies of Israel to defeat them. The Lord had said He would do that if they forsook Him. The Lord did not leave his people without national leadership for long.

God gave them leaders called Judges who judged the people according to the Law and delivered them from their enemies by the power of the Lord. The Judges were national leaders of Israel, until the people asked the Lord to give them a king. When a Judge died, the Israelites behaved even more corruptly than their fathers had. When enemies oppressed the nation of Israel the people would ask the Lord for help and He would appoint a Judge to help them defeat the enemy. God's Holy Spirit guided the Judges and helped them Judge the people.

God would protect His people as long as they obeyed the Law of Moses but when they forsook Him and worshiped false gods He did not prevent the godless nations from attacking them. God's plan of redemption depended on the birth, ministry and death of God's Son and god continued to rescue the Israelites from other nations. Judges Rule Israel 1374-1100. God gave the Judges power to do miraculous things to help Israel. The Hebrew word for Judges means 'one who administers justice.'

Othneil was the first of the Judges, and Samuel was the last. The book of Judges is a historical account of God's faithfulness to His people and Israel's failure to remain faithful to God. It was written to show the consequences of disobedience and the need for a national leader. The Judges took the place of Joshua as national leaders of Israel, until the time the people asked the Lord to give them a king and later the monarchy was established. The Judges became Israel's military leaders during battles with their enemies and the judges under God's supervision ruled Israelites. The book of Judges is a historical account of God's faithfulness to help and protect His people but Israel failed to remain faithful to God. The book of Judges is a record of the consequences of Israel's disobedience and the need for a strong national leader.

The Judges did not to rule continuously, God chose them to help Israel when they were being oppressed by other nations. God was continuing to help Israel prepare a nation of people for the birth of His Son. There were many times when there was not a Judge over the nation. When the people of Israel needed help to fend off their enemies they would ask the Lord for help and He would send them a Judge. The Judges became national heroes who governed the people according to the Law of Moses.

There were fifteen judges who ruled from the time of the first judge Othneil to Samuel, who was the last Judge. The Israelites continued to be involved in idolatry and worshiped false Gods called idols during that time. The king of Mesopotamia conquered the Israelites and ruled them. The Israelites asked the Lord for help and The Spirit of the Lord came upon Othneil and empowered him and they defeated the king of Mesopotamia.

Afterward the people of Israel had peace for forty more years then the children of Israel began to do evil again, and Eglon, the king of Moab, attacked and defeated the Israelites. Israel served Eglon for eighteen years, and then Ehud, the second Judge, killed Eglon. Judges 3– Ehud the Israelite came to Eglon when he was sitting upstairs in his cool private chamber. Ehud said "I have a message from God for you." So he arose from his seat. Then Ehud reached with his left hand, took the dagger from his right thigh, and thrust it into Eglon's belly. Even the hilt went in after the blade, and the fat closed over the blade. He did not draw the dagger out of his belly; and the entrails came out. Then Ehud went out through the porch and shut the doors of the upper room behind him and locked them.

Israel had peace for eighty years after Eglon's death but when Ehud died, the children of Israel began to do evil again, and Jabin, the King of Canaan, oppressed Israel for twenty years. Deborah was a prophetess as well as a Judge at that time. On one occasion Deborah sent for Barak, an Israelite from the tribe of Napthali, and told him that the Lord would deliver Jabin and his army of chariots into the hands of Barak and his troops. Barak wouldn't go to fight Jabin unless Deborah went with him. Deborah accompanied Barak along with ten thousand troops against nine hundred chariot troops of Sisera, the commander of Jabin's army. Jabin and his army were destroyed, and after that there was peace for forty years. Judges 6–The Midianites began to oppress Israel and the children of Israel complained to the Lord. The Lord sent a prophet to the children of Israel, and the prophet said the Lord God of Israel brought you from Egypt out of the house of bondage. Then He delivered you out of the hand of the Egyptians and out of the hand of all who oppressed you. He drove them out before you and gave you their land.

He also said "I Am the Lord your God; do not fear the gods of the Amorites, in whose land you dwell you did not obey Me. Each generation of the Israelites made the same mistakes their fathers made and worshiped the idolatrous gods of the Gentiles. The angel of the Lord came to a man named Gideon who was from the tribe of Manasseh and said to him, "The Lord is with you, you mighty man of valor!" The Spirit of God was with Gideon, and he became the next judge of Israel.

The Lord gave Gideon power through the Holy Spirit to defeat the Midianites and He convinced Gideon to do what the Lord told him. He was instructed to tear down the altar of Baal a false god and cut down the wooden image that was beside it. He was then told to build an altar to the Lord with the wood from the image he had cut down. Gideon waited until that night, and then he did everything he was told to do. So the Lord gave the Israelites victory over their enemies again. The Israelites had peace for forty years after Gideon. The Judges following Gideon were: Tola who judged for 23 years, Jair for 22 years, Jephthah for 6 years, Ibzan for 7 years, Elon for 10 years, Abdon for 8 years, and Samson for 20 years. The Bible tells us something interesting about Abdon. He judged Israel after Elon, and he had forty sons and thirty grandsons who rode on seventy young donkeys.

Samson was the last judge mentioned in the book of Judges, however the book of 1st Samuel mentions a priest named Eli who judged Israel for forty years after Samson. Eli was living in Shiloh situated north of Bethel. The tent of meeting (tabernacle, house of God) was set up there, and it was the principle sanctuary for the Israelites during the time of the Judges. The major enemy of Israel during the time of the judge Sampson was the Philistines. The Philistines came to the coastal plain around 1200 B.C. and attempted to settle in land belonging to Israel. Sampson waged war against the Philistines and by the providence of God he became a Judge. An angel announced Sampson's birth a man who would become a judge and the Lord gave Sampson superhuman strength to defeat the Philistines. The interesting story of Sampson is in Judges 13 through chapter 16. The Lord chose Samuel to be a judge even before he was born. There was a Jewish woman named Hannah who had no children, so she prayed to God and asked Him to give her a male child. She told God that if He would answer her prayer, she would give him to the Lord for all the days of his life. God answered her prayer, and she had a son and named him Samuel. The name Samuel means 'name of God.' When Samuel was weaned from his mother's breast, she took him to live in the Tabernacle with Eli, the priest. Hannah told Eli, "For this child I prayed, and the Lord has granted me my petition which I asked of Him. Therefore I also have lent him to the Lord; as long as he lives he shall be lent to the Lord." (1st Samuel 1:27)

Samuel ministered before the Lord, even as a child, wearing a linen ephod. Moreover his mother used to make him a little robe and bring it to him year by year when she came up with her husband to offer the yearly sacrifice." (1st Samuel 2:18-19) Eli was in the house of the Lord at Shiloh. Eli had judged Israel for forty years. Eli was very old and almost blind. One night after they had gone to bed, Samuel heard someone calling his name. He ran to Eli and asked him if he called him, but Eli told him he hadn't and told him to go back to bed. This happened three times. Samuel did not yet know the Lord, the word of the Lord had not been revealed to him. And the Lord called Samuel again the third time.

So he arose and went to Eli, and said, "Here I am, did you call me? Then Eli perceived that the Lord had called the boy. Therefore Eli said to Samuel, "Go, lie down; and it shall be, if He calls you, that you must say, "Speak, Lord, for Your servant hears."" So Samuel went and lay down in his place." (2nd Samuel 3:7-9)When the Lord called to Samuel the next time, Samuel did as Eli said, and the Lord talked to him about Eli's wicked sons and what He was going to do to them. As Samuel grew, the Lord was with him. God revealed himself to Samuel by the Holy Spirit, and Samuel acted as a priest, prophet and judge. Samuel spent his entire life serving the Lord and the people of Israel. The Lord blessed Samuel as he grew, and all the people from one end of Israel to the other recognized Samuel as a prophet. Samuel was the last judge who served God's people and the first in a line of the prophets. While Samuel was judge to the Israelites, the Philistines, the main enemies of Israel, captured the Ark of the Covenant, took it to Ashdod and set it up in the house of their god, Dagon. The Lord told the Israelites how to make the ark.

The Ark of the Covenant was made of wood and the first writing of the Ten Commandments of the Law that was given to the Israelites at Mt Sinai were kept in the Ark. The next morning, the idol Dagon had fallen on his face in front of the Ark. The Philistines set Dagon back up, but the following morning they found that Dagon had fallen again. This time his hands and his head were broken off and lay on the threshold of Dagon's temple. The Philistines never went into the temple again, because they were afraid. The Lord caused the people of Ashdod to come down with tumors.

The people became afraid of what the Israelite God would do to them next, so they moved the Ark to Gath. The Lord destroyed Gath, and the people there broke out with tumors. The ark was sent to the city of Ekron and the people there were stricken with tumors. The Philistines became afraid to keep the Ark of the Covenant any longer, so they returned the Ark to the Israelites and it was placed in Kirjath Jearim in the house of Abinadab. Samuel was the most important Israelite in the period between the judges and the monarchy. The Lord God communicated with Israel through the judges, but before Samuel died, God started communicating to the people by the word of men called prophets.

Samson was the last judge mentioned in the book of Judges. The book of 1st Samuel mentions a priest named Eli who judged Israel for forty years after Samson. Eli was living in Shiloh situated north of Bethel. The tent of meeting (tabernacle, house of God) was set up there, and it was the principle sanctuary for the Israelites during the time of the Judges. The Lord chose Samuel to be a judge even before he was born. There was a Jewish woman named Hannah who had no children, so she prayed to God and asked Him to give her a male child.

Hannah told God that if He would answer her prayer, she would give him to the Lord for all the days of his life. God answered her prayer, and she had a son and named him Samuel. The name Samuel means 'name of God.' When Samuel was weaned from his mother's breast, she took him to live in the Tabernacle with Eli, the priest. Hannah said to Eli– This child I prayed, and the Lord has granted me my petition which I asked of Him. Therefore I also have lent him to the Lord; as long as he lives he shall be lent to the Lord." Samuel ministered before the Lord, even as a child, wearing a linen ephod.

Samuel's mother used to make him a little robe and bring it to him year by year when she came up with her husband to offer the yearly sacrifice. Eli was very old and almost blind. One night after they had gone to bed, Samuel heard someone calling his name. He ran to Eli and asked him if he called him, but Eli told him he hadn't and told him to go back to bed. This happened three times. Samuel did not yet know the Lord, nor was the word of the Lord yet revealed to him.

And the Lord called Samuel again the third time. So he arose and went to Eli, and said, "Here I am, for you did call me." Eli realized that the Lord had called the Samuel. Eli said to Samuel, Go, lie down; and if He calls you say, Speak, Lord, for Your servant hears. Samuel went and lay down in his place. When the Lord called to Samuel the next time, Samuel did as Eli said, and the Lord talked to him about Eli's wicked sons and what He was going to do to them. As Samuel grew, the Lord was with him. God revealed himself to Samuel by the Holy Spirit, and Samuel acted as a priest, prophet and judge.

Samuel spent his entire life serving the Lord and the people of Israel. The Lord blessed Samuel as he grew, and all the people from one end of Israel to the other recognized Samuel as a prophet. Samuel was the last judge who served God's people and the first in a line of the prophets. For several years the Lord communicated with Israel through the Judges. Samuel was the most important Israelite in the period between the judges and the monarchy. The Lord God communicated with Israel through the judges, but before Samuel died, God had also started communicating to the people by the word of men called prophets. Samuel was the first in the line of prophets. The prophets weren't rulers like the kings; they served as spokesmen to deliver God's commands and messages to the kings and to the people.

Prophets

Prophets were men inspired by the Holy Spirit who spoke the word of God to the people the good word and the bad word of the Lord. The third chapter of 1st Samuel tells about God revealing his word to Samuel. The prophets were given a major role in the history of Israel after Israel became a monarchy. Samuel and the prophets who followed him worked directly with the Kings of Israel and Judah advising them, helping them, and warning them when they acted contrary to the Lord's will. A number of times during the ministry of Samuel, we read about a group of prophets who often prophesied together. The prophets preached, taught and instructed the people and their leaders. There are five major books of prophecy including Isaiah, Jeremiah, Lamentations, Ezekiel and Daniel. They are called Major Prophets because of the size of the contents of their book.

A number of times during the ministry of Samuel, we read about a group of prophets who often prophesied together. In the 19th chapter of 1st Samuel we read about Samuel being the leader of a group of prophets, and some believe that Samuel had a school for prophets. Elijah and Elisha were both associated with a company of prophets, and there were sometimes as many as fifty in the group. The company of prophets was known as 'sons of prophets.' Some suggest that the company of prophets lived together in a communal house or had a common place for them to gather and visit. Holy man was another title for the prophets. One day Elisha went to Shunem, and a woman there urged him to stay for a meal. When Elisha came by her place, he stopped there to eat (2nd Kings 4:8-9). The woman told her husband that Elisha was a holy man of God. The Lord often referred to the prophets as 'My servants.' Israel and Judah were warned by the prophets to repent of their evil ways and obey the entire law taught to them by the Lord's servants, the prophets (2ndKings 17:13). The prophets were inspired by God through the Holy Spirit to prophesy to the leaders of Israel. They were ordinary men prophesying for the Lord, and they faced many hazards, plus the wrath from the rulers of nations they prophesied against, however the prophets remained faithful to the Lord. The prophets were not paid to preach and didn't usually preach to large audiences; they often went alone to preach to individuals. The Lord's message delivered by the prophets varied according to the circumstances. Sometimes the prophet brought good news, but often the message involved doom and gloom, warnings, and a call for repentance. Sometimes the message was one of blessings and salvation. Sometimes they preached to people who hadn't invited them and who were hostile toward them.

The prophets had feelings for the people to whom they prophesied, mourning and praying for them. The prophets, beginning with Genesis through Revelation, weave God's plan of salvation into the scriptures all the way through the Bible. The prophets were God's watchmen who guarded against sin. The Bible contains seventeen books of prophecy written by the prophets. After several years the people complained because they wanted to be ruled by a king like the other nations. 1st Samuel 8:1-7–when Samuel was old that he made his sons judges over Israel in Beersheba. But his sons did not rule with honesty and took bribes perverting justice.

Samuel called the people of Israel together at Mizpah. The lord still gave directions to Israel through the words of the prophets when Israel needed guidance or punishment. The people of Israel were obligated to worship the Lord as Sovereign and God's commands even though a king ruled them. The blessings, advice, warnings and rebukes came upon the kings by the will and word of the Lord as the prophets spoke for the Lord. One of the duties of the prophets was to anoint God's selection of men to be king over Israel. Samuel, as judge and prophet, a

In the 19th chapter of 1st Samuel we read about Samuel being the leader of a group of prophets, and some believe that Samuel had a school for prophets. Elijah and Elisha were both associated with a company of prophets, and there were sometimes as many as fifty in the group. The company of prophets were known as 'sons of prophets.' Some suggest that the company of prophets lived together in a communal house or had a common place for them to gather and visit. The word prophet is an English word designating someone who is directed by the Lord to make known His will to people. The Greek word for prophet is prophetes and means 'one who speaks forth openly.' A good definition for a Bible prophet is 'one who speaks for the Lord' or a 'spokesman for the Lord.' The words of a true prophet always echoed the Lord's words. The common name for prophet in Hebrew is nabi. The word nabi means 'someone who utters, cries or speaks enthusiastically.'

Two Hebrew words associated with the prophets are hozeh and ro'eh. Hozeh and ro'eh are translated 'seer' in English, and both mean 'someone who sees with the mind and heart' and usually refers to seeing future events coming from the Lord. Hozeh or ro'eh describes a prophet who had the ability to foresee future events, but not all prophets were seers. Holy man was another title for the prophets.

One day Elisha went to Shunem, and a woman there urged him to stay for a meal. When Elisha came by her place, he stopped there to eat (2nd Kings 4:8-9). The woman told her husband that Elisha was a holy man of God. The Lord often referred to the prophets as 'My servants.' Israel and Judah were warned by the prophets to repent of their evil ways and obey the entire law taught to them by the Lord's servants, the prophets (2ndKings 17:13).

The prophets were inspired by God through the Holy Spirit to prophesy to the leaders of Israel. They were ordinary men prophesying for the Lord, and they faced many hazards, plus the wrath from the rulers of nations they prophesied against, however the prophets remained faithful to the Lord. The prophets weren't paid to preach and didn't usually preach to large audiences; they often went alone to preach to individuals. The Lord's message delivered by the prophets varied according to the circumstances.

Sometimes the prophet had good news, but often the message involved doom and gloom, warnings, and a call for repentance. Sometimes the message was one of blessings and salvation. Sometimes they preached to people who hadn't invited them and who were hostile toward them. The prophets had feelings for the people to whom they prophesied, mourning and praying for them. The prophets, beginning with Genesis through Revelation, weave God's plan of salvation into the scriptures all the way through the Bible. The prophets were God's watchmen who guarded against sin. The Bible contains seventeen books of prophecy. Prophecy always had its origin from the will of God. Paul told Timothy that all scripture is God breathed (2nd Tim 3:16). Peter stated that none of scripture was written according to the prophet's own interpretation.

The people respected the prophets, because they knew the prophet spoke for the Lord and received miraculous power from Him. God's prophets were truly courageous heroes who were faithful to deliver the Lord's message even when they were fearful. Prophets faced many dangers, even from their own people, who often put them to death, because they didn't like the message of God that was proclaimed. The prophets were sometimes stoned to death, sawed in two and put to death by the sword. They were often depressed, discouraged and fearful, yet their faith was usually steadfast. The prophets depended on the Lord for strength and safety, the Lord was there to lend comfort and encouragement to them and to rescue them from those who wished to harm them. Most of the prophets lived a solitary life. They went about in sheepskins and goatskins, destitute, persecuted and mistreated. They wandered in deserts and mountains and lived in caves and holes in the ground. All of God's prophets were commended for their faith, yet none of them lived to receive what had been promised. The world was never worthy of the prophets.

God continued to use prophets to proclaim His word in the first century when Christ was born and during the early years of the church. The foretelling of future events was not a necessary function of a prophet but most of the prophets did predict future events as the Lord revealed them. Some of the prophets served primarily to reveal the Lord's message for the present time or future events. The work of some prophets was similar to that of a teacher. The prophets preached, taught and instructed the people and their leaders. The prophets sometimes wandered in deserts and mountains and lived in caves and holes in the ground. All of God's prophets were commended for their faith, yet none of them lived to receive what had been promised. The prophets didn't usually preach to large audiences; they often went alone to preach to individuals. The Bible contains seventeen books of prophecy written by the prophets. Prophecy always had its origin from the will of God. Paul told Timothy that all scripture is God breathed (2nd Tim 3:16). Peter stated that none of scripture was written according to the prophet's own interpretation. People respected the prophets, because they knew the prophet spoke for the Lord and they received miraculous power from Him. There are five major books of prophecy including Isaiah, Jeremiah, Lamentations, Ezekiel and Daniel. They are called Major Prophets because of the size of the contents of their book. A number of times during the ministry of Samuel, we read about a group of prophets who often prophesied together.

In the 19th chapter of 1st Samuel we read about Samuel being the leader of a group of prophets, and some believe that Samuel had a school for prophets. Elijah and Elisha were both associated with a company of prophets, and there were sometimes as many as fifty in the group. The company of prophets was known as 'sons of prophets.' Some suggest that the company of prophets lived together in a communal house or had a common place for them to gather and visit. Holy man was another title for the prophets. One day Elisha went to Shunem, and a woman there urged him to stay for a meal. When Elisha came by her place, he stopped there to eat (2nd Kings 4:8-9). The woman told her husband that Elisha was a holy man of God. The Lord often referred to the prophets as 'My servants.' Israel and Judah were warned by the prophets to repent of their evil ways and obey the entire law taught to them by the Lord's servants, the prophets (2ndKings 17:13).

The prophets were inspired by God through the Holy Spirit to prophesy to the leaders of Israel. They were ordinary men prophesying for the Lord, and they faced many hazards, plus the wrath from the rulers of nations. The prophets remained faithful to the Lord and didn't usually preach to large audiences; they often went alone to preach to individuals. The Lord's message delivered by the prophets varied according to the circumstances. Sometimes the prophet brought good news, but often the message involved doom and gloom, warnings, and a call for repentance.

Sometimes the message was one of blessings and salvation. Sometimes they preached to people who hadn't invited them and who were hostile toward them. The prophets had feelings for the people to whom they prophesied, mourning and praying for them. The prophets, beginning with Genesis through Revelation, weave God's plan of salvation into the scriptures all the way through the Bible. The prophets were God's watchmen who guarded against sin. The Bible contains seventeen books of prophecy written by the prophets. After several years the people complained because they wanted to be ruled by a king like the other nations. 1st Samuel 8:1-7–when Samuel was old that he made his sons judges over Israel in Beersheba. But his sons did not rule with honesty and took bribes perverting justice. All the elders of Israel gathered together and came to Samuel at Ramah, and said to him, "Look you are old, and your sons do not walk in your ways. Now make us a king to judge us like all the nations." Samuel was not pleased with the attitude of the people of Israel, because Samuel thought they were rejecting his rule.

God spoke with Samuel telling him that the people were not rejecting him; they were rejecting the Lord. Under the leadership of Moses, Joshua the Judges and prophets, Israel was actually a theocracy. God appointed and directed the men who were in the leadership role by telling them what to do and what to say.. During the time of Samuel, God gave the nation of Israel a line of kings to rule over his people. The Lord told Samuel to let the people have a king, but to warn them what a king could do with the power given to only one man. The king would take whatever he wanted from the people, and the people would become like slaves in their own land. The king would have absolute authority.

Men who have that kind of power can't always be trusted. All the elders of Israel gathered together and came to Samuel at Ramah, and said to him, "Look you are old, and your sons do not walk in your ways. Now make us a king to judge us like all the nations." Samuel was not pleased with the attitude of the people of Israel, because Samuel thought they were rejecting his rule. God spoke with Samuel telling him that the people were not rejecting him; they were rejecting the Lord. Under the leadership of Moses, Joshua and the Judges, Israel was a theocracy. God appointed and directed the men who were in the leadership role by telling them what to do. During the time of Samuel, God gave the nation of Israel a line of kings to rule over his people. The Lord told Samuel to let the people have a king, but to warn them what a king could do with the power given to only one man. The king would take whatever he wanted from the people, and the people would become like slaves in their own land. The king would have absolute authority. Men who have that kind of power can't always be trusted. The first king chosen by the Lord was Saul the son of Kish from the tribe of Benjamin. Samuel took a flask of oil and poured it on Saul's head and kissed Saul saying the Lord has anointed you commander over His inheritance.

The first king chosen by the Lord was Saul the son of Kish from the tribe of Benjamin. Samuel took a flask of oil and poured it on Saul's head and kissed Saul saying the Lord has anointed you commander over His inheritance. Samuel called the people of Israel together at Mizpah. The lord still gave directions to Israel through the words of the prophets when Israel needed guidance or punishment. The people of Israel were obligated to worship the Lord as Sovereign and God's commands even though a king ruled them. The blessings, advice, warnings and rebukes came upon the kings by the will and word of the Lord as the prophets spoke for the Lord. One of the duties of the prophets was to anoint God's selection of men to be king over Israel. Samuel, as judge and prophet, anointed Saul as the first king of Israel.

United Monarchy Kings

Samuel warned the people what could happen if they had a king, but they wouldn't listen to him. At first, Saul was a good king and a mighty military leader, but God was not pleased with him, because Saul didn't obey God in everything He told him to do.

The heart of Saul was not completely converted to doing the Lord's will. In the earlier days of civilization when kings ruled nations, they also served as military leaders and warriors as well. Saul was a fierce warrior who could ably defend Israel, but he relied on his own judgment to rule wisely and failed to do what the Lord told him. The Lord was grieved for making Saul king because of his rebellious attitude, so the Lord rejected him and took the kingdom of Israel away from him.

The Lord told Samuel He had rejected Saul as the king and instructed him to anoint one of the sons of Jesse as king over Israel in the place of Saul. Samuel filled his horn with oil and went to Jesse's house in Bethlehem and anointed David to replace Saul as King over Israel. David was an ancestor of Judah, the son of Israel (Jacob), and David was chosen to be in the birth line of Christ. Of all the sons of Jesse, David was not the most likely choice for a king, because David was a shepherd boy and a musician. People look on the outward appearance of others and judge them, but the Lord looks at the heart. The Lord has the ability to see into the hearts of people and know things that people cannot know. The Lord knew that David was the best choice for king, because the Lord knew David's heart. Jesus was to be a descendant of David. The Lord said David was a man after His own heart because of David's attitude towards God.

David was endowed with many talents including musician, poet and singer. David became a great military leader and was engaged in several battles, especially with the Philistines. Even with all of his good qualities and his love for God, David became a sinful man who served God in his own generation. Nothing is known about Nathan's background except that he was from the tribe of Judah. Nathan appears without explanation in the 7th chapter of 2nd Samuel where he has a conversation with King David. Nathan was the prophet who spoke the word of the Lord to David, and it was he who spoke convicting words from the Lord when David sinned with Bathsheba.

Psalm, Chapter 31A psalm of David—O Lord, I put my trust in You. Let me never be ashamed; Deliver me in Your righteousness. Bow down Your ear to me. Deliver me speedily.

Be my rock of refuge, a fortress of defense to save me. You are my rock and my fortress; therefore, for Your name's sake, lead me and guide me. Pull me out of the net, which they have secretly laid for me, for You are my strength. Into your hand I commit my spirit; you have redeemed me, O Lord God of truth. I have hated those who regard useless idols; but I trust in the Lord. I will be glad and rejoice in Your mercy, for You have considered my trouble; You have known my soul in adversities, and have not put me into the hand of the enemy.

Have mercy on me, for I am in trouble; my eye wastes away with grief, yes, my soul and my body! For my life is spent with grief, and my years with sighing; my strength fails because of my iniquity, and my bones waste away. I am a reproach among all my enemies, but especially among my neighbors, and am repulsive to my acquaintances; those who see me outside flee from me.

I am forgotten like a dead man, out of mind; I am like a broken vessel. For I hear the slander of many; fear is on every side; while they take counsel together against me, they scheme to take away my life. But as for me, I trust in You, O Lord; I say, "You are my God." My times are in Your hand; deliver me from the hand of my enemies, and from those who persecute me. Make Your face shine upon Your servant; save me for Your mercies' sake.

Do not let me be ashamed, O Lord, for I have called upon You; let the wicked be ashamed; let them be silent in the grave. Let the lying lips be put to silence, which speak insolent things proudly and contemptuously against the righteous. Oh, how great is Your goodness, which You have laid up for those who fear You, which You have prepared for those who trust in You in the presence of the sons of men! You shall hide them in the secret place of Your presence from the plots of man; You shall keep them secretly in a pavilion from the strife of tongues. Blessed Be the Lord, for He has shown me His marvelous kindness in a strong city! For I said in my haste, "I am cut off from before Your eyes;" nevertheless You heard the voice of my supplications when I cried out to You. Oh, love the Lord, all you His saints for the Lord, preserves the faithful, and fully repays the proud person. Be of good courage, and He shall strengthen your heart, all you who hope in the Lord."

The Philistines were enemies of God's people, and one member of their army was a giant named Goliath. The Philistines and Goliath threatened the people of Israel and mocked the Lord. Everyone was afraid to go up against Goliath because of his great size. David believed the Lord would help him defeat Goliath, so David, with the Lord's help, killed Goliath, and he became a hero to the people. David was a person with a strong faith in God. God loved David because he was contrite and very humble in his attitude towards the Lord (1st Samuel 17). David wrote in the Psalms expressing the attitude of a heart that is humble. David's desire was to do the will of God, and he kept the law of God. Acts 13:16-23– The God Israel chose our fathers, and exalted the people when they dwelt as strangers in the land of Egypt, and with an uplifted arm He brought them out of it. Now for a time of about forty years He put up with your ways in the wilderness. And when He had destroyed seven Nations in the land of Canaan, He distributed their land to them by allotment. After that He gave them judges for about four hundred and fifty years, until Samuel the prophet. And afterward they asked for a king; and God gave them Saul the son of Kish a man of the tribe of Benjamin, for forty years.

And when He removed him, He raised up for them David as king to whom also He gave testimony and said, "I have found David, the son of Jesse, a man after My own heart, who will do all my will." From this man's seed, according to the promise, God raised up for Israel a Savior - Jesus." The kingdom of Israel under the leadership of David remained faithful to the Lord, and the Lord blessed Israel, and David's Kingdom was enlarged. David had several sons, including Solomon his son by Bathsheba. David selected Solomon to become his successor to the throne. Before David died, he called Solomon to his bedside and explained what his responsibilities would be when he ruled the kingdom after David's death. David told Solomon to walk in the ways, God showed him and to keep all of the commandments of the Law of Moses. David told Solomon that as long as he and his descendants were faithful to God with all of their heart and soul, God would be with them. Solomon was anointed King, the Lord appeared to him in a dream and told him he could ask for anything he wanted and his wish would be granted, Solomon asked for wisdom, and the lord was pleased.

The Lord gave Solomon wisdom as well as riches and honor. Solomon became known as the wisest man in the world, and under his rule the Kingdom of Israel became very wealthy. With all of Solomon's wisdom he accomplished many great things but in spite of his accomplishments Solomon was disobedient. God commanded Solomon not to worship false gods but he did not obey the Lord. When Solomon had reigned for four years he began building the temple in Jerusalem.

Solomon wrote the books of Proverbs, Ecclesiastes and Songs of Solomon. The book of Ecclesiastes is rich in wisdom. It describes some of the pitfalls of life and the misery that can occur in life. Solomon saw the tears of the oppressed and observed that death comes to everyone. He also discovered that everyone, the wise, the foolish, the rich, and the poor will all ultimately come face to face with death and their fate will be in God's hands. Solomon said that everything God has set in order is forever, and men cannot change it. He observed that there is nothing new in God's relationship with mankind and that there is nothing new under the sun. That which is now, has been before, and what is to be, has already been. Solomon summed up all of the activities in life and came to the conclusion that success in life is achieved only if we stand in awe of God and keep His commandments. He observed that this life is meaningless unless it leads to a greater life of faith in God.

With all of Solomon's wisdom he accomplished many great things, but in spite of all of his accomplishments Solomon disobeyed many of the commandments of the Lord and his heart turned away from strict obedience to the Lord. God commanded Solomon twice not to worship false gods, but he refused to obey what the Lord commanded. 1st Kings 5:1-6– Hiram king of Tyre sent his servants to Solomon when he heard that they had anointed him king in place of his father. Then Solomon sent to Hiram saying: You know how my father David could not build a house for the name of the Lord his God because of the wars which were fought against him on every side. Solomon said now the Lord my God has given me rest on every side there is neither adversary nor evil occurrence. And behold I propose to build a house for the name of the Lord my God, as the Lord spoke to my father David, saying, Your son, whom I will set on your throne in your place, he shall build the house for my name."

The tabernacle had served the Israelite nation for many years as the house of God, but it was a temporary structure. Four hundred and eighty years after the children of Israel left the land of Egypt and were settled in Canaan, and after Solomon had reigned for four years, he began building a temple in Jerusalem. When the temple was complete there was a dedication ceremony. The temple became the place for the presence of the Lord. The temple was still the focal point of the Jewish religion when Jesus was born in the first century. Solomon wrote the books of Proverbs, Ecclesiastes and Songs of Solomon. The book of Ecclesiastes is rich in wisdom. It describes some of the pitfalls of life and the misery that can occur in life. Solomon saw the tears of the oppressed and observed that death comes to everyone. He also discovered that everyone, the wise, the foolish, the rich, and the poor will all ultimately come face to face with death and their fate will be in God's hands. Solomon said that everything God has set in order is forever, and men cannot change it. He observed that there is nothing new in God's relationship with mankind and that there is nothing new under the sun. That which is now, has been before, and what is to be, has already been. Solomon summed up all of the activities in life and came to the conclusion that success in life is achieved only if we stand in awe of God and keep His commandments. He observed that this life is meaningless unless it leads to a greater life of faith in God. He concluded that the whole duty of man is to fear God and keep his commandments.

Ecclesiastes 12:9-14 "And moreover because the Preacher was wise, he still taught the people knowledge; yes, he pondered and sought out and set in order many proverbs. The Preacher sought to find acceptable words; and what was written, was upright-words of truth. The words of the wise are like goads, and the words of scholars are like well-driven nails, given by one Shepherd. In spite of Solomon's wisdom, he failed to take his own advice to fear God and keep His commandments. He observed that this life was meaningless unless you have faith in God. He observed that the whole duty of people is to fear God and keep His commandments.

1st Kings 11:9-13 "The Lord became angry with Solomon, because his heart had turned from the Lord God of Israel who had appeared to him twice, and had commanded him concerning this thing, that he should not go after other god's; but he did not keep what the Lord had commanded.

The Lord said to Solomon,' "Because you have done this, and have not kept My covenant and My statutes, which I have commanded you, I will surely tear the kingdom away from you and give it to your servant." "Nevertheless I will not do it in your days, for the sake of your father David; I will tear it out of the hand of your son. However I will not tear away the whole kingdom; I will give one tribe to your son for the sake of My servant David, and for the sake of Jerusalem which I have chosen." The nation of Israel is now a kingdom but it would still be many years before the kingdom of the Son of God would be established in the city of Jerusalem. The nation of Israel would go through many bad times before Jesus of Nazareth the Son of God would be born during the time of the Roman Empire. Kingdom of Israel Becomes Divided (931 B.C.) A few years after Solomon's son Rehoboam took his father's place on the throne. When Rehoboam became king he put a large tax on the people, and they rebelled.

God took ten tribes of Israel from Rehoboam and placed a king named Jeroboam over them and they were known as the ten northern tribes. The two southern tribes were, the Kingdom of Judah and Benjamin ruled by Rehoboam. The ten tribes of Israel chose the city of Samaria as their Capitol. The tribes of Judah and Benjamin, the Southern Kingdom, worshiped the Lord in the temple in Jerusalem. At times most of the Israelites turned away from following the Lord, but there was always a faithful remnant of the Israelites in Judah. The Lord blessed the remnant in Judah and continued to help them in order to complete the plan of redemption through His Son. Under Jeroboam's rule, the ten northern tribes worshiped idols and God became very angry with them, and He sent prophets to warn them. God's judgment would come against them if they didn't repent of their idolatry.

They made two golden calves and set them up as gods - one at each end of the kingdom - so the people of the northern kingdom could worship the golden calves instead of going to Jerusalem to worship God in the temple. There was constant conflict and war between the Northern Kingdom and the Southern Kingdom. Jeroboam led the ten northern tribes wholly into idolatry and the prophet Elijah, brought bad news from the Lord to Jeroboam and his household, denouncing Jeroboam.

1st Kings 14:7-10–Tell Jeroboam, the Lord God of Israel exalted you from among the people, made you ruler over My people Israel. I took the kingdom away from the house of David. David followed me with all his heart. And I gave the kingdom to you; and you have not kept My commandments and You did not do what was right in My eyes; and you have done more evil than all who were before you, for you have gone and made for yourself other gods and molded images to provoke Me to anger, and have cast Me behind your back, therefore I will bring disaster on the house of Jeroboam, and I will take away the remnant of the house of Jeroboam, as one takes away refuse until it is all gone.

Twenty kings reigned over the Israelites before Assyria defeated them. They went into captivity to the Assyrians in 722 B.C. The books of Kings and Chronicles give the history of the kings of both the Northern Kingdom of Israel, and the Southern Kingdom of Judah. The prophets also wrote about the sinful deeds and troublesome times of the two kingdoms. The Northern Kingdom was never restored to the fellowship of God. Ahab and Jezebel Ruled the Northern Kingdom of Israel. The sin of the Israelites did not prevent God from completing His plan of redemption. Ahab reigned from 874B.C. to 853B.C. and was on the throne during the time of the prophets Elijah and Elisha. Ahab was the son of Omri, and he reigned over the Israelites in Samaria for twenty-two years. Ahab fortified the cities of Israel and used his own Money. During his reign Israel had frequent wars with Syria.

A random arrow killed Ahab during a battle with Syria and he was buried in Samaria. Ahab did more evil to provoke the Lord than all of the kings of Israel before him. He built a temple for the false god Baal in Samaria, the capital city, and built a wooden image of Baal and worshiped it. Baal is the false God whose image was worshiped by the Gentiles. Jezebel, Ahab's wife, was not an Israelite. She was the daughter of Ethbaal, the king of Sidon. Jezebel worshipped the false god Baal, and she insisted that Baal have equal rights with the Lord God of Israel. Jezebel's insistence brought her into direct conflict with the prophet Elijah. Jezebel was so wicked that her name has always been associated with evil women.

Elijah, the prophet, warned King Ahab of Israel that as surely as the Lord God of Israel lived, and as he stood before God, there would not be any dew or rain for a few years. And It did not rain again until Elijah prayed to God for the rain to return. Ahab and Jezebel were very angry with Elijah and wanted to find him and kill him. The Lord Protected His prophet and told Elijah to travel eastward and hide from Ahab and Jezebel in the Kerith Ravine, east of the Jordan. There was a brook in the ravine where Elijah hid. He would have water. God sent ravens with food for him each day. Elijah had to depend on the providence of the Lord. After many days, the Lord told Elijah he would make it rain and Elijah was to go back to King Ahab. When Ahab saw Elijah, he said, "Is that you, O trouble maker of Israel?" Elijah said he was not the one who had made trouble for Israel but Ahab had. Ahab had forsaken the Lord and worshipped Baal. Elijah told Ahab to gather all the prophets of Baal and meet him on Mount Carmel.

When all the prophets of Baal were assembled on Mount Carmel, Elijah had a contest to see whose god was the real God. Each side built an altar to their God and placed a bull on the altar.

The prophets of Baal prayed long and hard for Baal to send fire down on the sacrifice, but no fire came. Elijah soaked his sacrifice with water and he prayed for God to send fire down on his sacrifice. God sent fire down and burned up the sacrifice of Elijah. When the people saw it they said, "The Lord, He is God!" After that, Elijah went off by himself and prayed to God to send rain. The sky turned dark, and it began to rain. Elijah had 450 prophets of Baal put to death in the Kishon valley. When Ahab told Jezebel what Elijah had done, Jezebel threatened to have Elijah killed. Elijah decided to hide in the wilderness, so he arose and ran for his life to Beersheba, which belonged to Judah. Elijah ran toward the wilderness, and sat down under a tree and prayed that he might die. He said, "It is enough! Now Lord, take my life, for I am no better than my fathers!" Fearing for his life, Elijah became very depressed and wanted to die there in the wilderness. An angel touched him and told him to get up and eat. Elijah saw a cake baked on coals, and a jar of water. He ate and drank and lay down again. And the angel of the Lord came back the second time, and touched him and said, "Get up and eat, because the journey is too long for you." Elijah had asked the Lord to take his life, but the Lord had other plans for him, and He treated Elijah with kindness.

The angel told Elijah to go to Mt Horeb, the mountain of God. When Elijah reached Mt Horeb, he spent the night in a cave. The next morning the Lord asked Elijah what he was doing there, and Elijah replied, "I have been very zealous for the Lord God Almighty. The Israelites have rejected your covenant, broken down your altars, and put your prophets to death with the sword. I am the only one left, and now they are trying to kill me too." Elijah was very distraught, he had served the Lord faithfully in all kinds of bad circumstances, and now the Lord was about to reward him for his faithfulness. The Lord told Elijah two important things to do: to go and anoint Hazael king over Israel, and then find Elisha and appoint Elisha to be a prophet of Israel. Elijah left the mountain, went to Hazael and anointed Hazael to be the king of Israel. Elijah found the prophet Elisha and made him his attendant.

God was going to take Elijah to heaven, and Elisha would take his place as the prophet of Israel, but before that took place, Elisha would witness a very unusual thing. Elijah would be taken up to heaven in a fiery chariot. The Lord would reward Elijah by taking him to heaven before he died. When the Lord was ready to take Elijah to heaven, he sent him to Bethel. Elijah and Elisha were coming back from Gilgal, and Elijah told Elisha to stay where he was and he would go on to Bethel alone. Elisha said, "As the Lord lives, and as your soul lives, I will not leave you!" (2nd Kings 2:2) And they both went to Bethel. There was a company of prophets there, and the prophets already knew the Lord was going to take Elijah. They told Elisha about it, and Elisha said he already knew and he asked them not to speak about it. It weighed heavily on Elisha knowing that Elijah would soon be gone, and he would be taking his place. Elijah told Elisha to stay at Bethel while he went to Jericho.

Elisha refused to stay at Bethel and he went with Elijah. When the two reached Jericho a group of prophets told Elisha that the Lord was going to take his master that day. Elisha said "Yes I know, but do not speak of it." Then Elijah told Elisha he was going to the Jordan River, and he told Elisha to stay there, but Elisha said, "As surely as the Lord lives and as you live, I will not leave you." When they got to the Jordan River, Elijah rolled up his cloak and struck the water with it.

The water parted and Elijah and Elisha walked across the river on dry ground. Elijah asked Elisha what he could do for him before the Lord took him. Elisha asked for a double portion of Elijah's spirit. The Holy Spirit of the Lord had been given to Elijah in a large measure. Elisha wanted to carry on Elijah's ministry with an even greater power than Elijah's. Elijah told Elisha he had asked for something that was hard to do, but it would be granted if Elisha were there when God took him. Elijah was testing Elisha to see if he would be faithful to replace him. Elijah and Elisha continued to walk away from the river. "Then it happened as they continued on and talked, suddenly a chariot of fire appeared with horses of fire, and separated the two of them; and Elijah went up in a whirlwind into heaven. Elisha saw it, and he cried out, "My father, my father, the chariot of Israel and its horsemen!" He saw him no more and he took hold of his own clothes and tore them into two pieces." Elijah ascended to heaven and Elisha picked up his cloak and walked back to the river, struck the waters with Elijah's cloak and called out to the Lord saying, "Where now is the Lord, the God of Elijah?" The waters parted again and Elisha walked across the river. Elisha wanted to know if the Lord had given him the power he promised.

A company of prophets witnessed what took place and the prophets said, "The spirit of Elijah is resting on Elisha." The Lord honored Elisha's request for a double measure of Elijah's spirit. Elijah was often described as a man of God. He was a Tishbite from the town of Tishbeh in Gilead, and his name means 'Yaweh is God.' He wore a garment of hair and a leather belt around his waist. His outer garment was probably made from sheepskin or goatskin and was loose fitting like a cloak. Ahaziah succeeded Ahab as the king of Israel but he died after two years, and Joram succeeded him. It was during the reign of Joram that Elijah went to heaven, and Elisha succeeded Elijah. The deeds of Elijah and Elisha are recorded from 1st Kings 17 through 2nd Kings 13. After Ahab, Israel was ruled by 12 kings in succession until 722 B.C. The last king on the throne of Israel is Hoshea, and the children of Israel continued to sin against the Lord. In the final difficult days of the Kingdom of Israel (from 760 to 722 B.C.), the prophet Hosea ministered to Israel.

This was during the days of the six kings who followed Jereboam the Second: Zechariah, Shallum, Menahem, Pekahiah, Pekah and Hoshea (2nd Kings 15-16, and 17).

Northern Kingdom of Israel Goes Into Exile

The nation of Israel was united under the first three kings Saul, David and Solomon. After the death of Solomon there was a civil war and the nation of Israel was split into two, the northern kingdom Israel and the kingdom of Judah. The capital city of Judah was Jerusalem where the temple was and the descendants of David through whom Christ would come ruled the southern kingdom of Judah. The northern kingdom Israel eventually became so wicked that it was destroyed by Assyria in 722 B.C. The books of First and Second Kings in the Bible reveal the history of the two kingdoms. The kings of Judah the southern kingdom ranged from good to bad and the Babylonians put the people of Judah in exile in Babylon in 586 B.C. Shalmaneser, the king of Assyria, invaded the land of Israel and laid siege to Samaria for three years.

During the reign of King Hoshea of Israel, the Assyrians completed the destruction of the northern kingdom, and in 722 B.C, Israel was exiled to Assyria. Shalmeneser settled them in Halah, in Gozan on the Harbors River, and in the towns of the Medes. (2nd Kings 17.) The prophet Amos threatened Israel with a judgment from the Lord several years before the exile, and the prophet Hosea had identified the enemy as Assyria. The purpose of Hosea's ministry was to point out Israel's sins and their unfaithfulness. Hosea put much of the blame for Israel's sin on their lifestyle, borrowed from their pagan neighbors in Canaan. The pagans worshiped the false god Baal, and the Israelites were influenced by their worship of Baal. Hosea wrote about the judgment of God and His salvation. God's judgment was altogether punitive. Out of love, God punished His people to bring them to repentance. The Lord reminded the Israelites that it was He who brought them out of Egypt, and that they should not acknowledge any God but Him (Hosea 13:4). According to Hosea 13:16, the people of Samaria would have to bear the burdens caused by their own guilt.

The Lord warned Israel about what other nations would do to Israel without His protection: they would be slaughtered with the sword, their little ones would be dashed to the ground, and their pregnant women would be ripped open. The prophet gave the Lord's warning in plenty of time for Israel to repent but Israel would not. The Lord would have turned away His anger if they repented. He sent the prophets to plead with the people to return to Him but the message of the prophets fell on deaf ears. The prophet Hosea prophesied about the Northern Kingdom of Israel in the eighth century B.C. Hosea issued the Lord's threats against Israel and rebuked them when they failed to heed His warnings.

Hosea prophesied that the Lord would destroy Israel but would save Judah. Judah would be saved because Jesus the Jewish Messiah would come from the descendants of Judah. Israel did not repent, and as Joel and Amos predicted, Israel was exiled to Assyria in 722B.C. In the first chapter of Hosea, the Lord compares Israel to a prostitute; she was married to the Lord, but she became unfaithful and served idols. The Lord is a jealous God and will not tolerate spiritual adultery. God's people symbolize his wife. The Lord commanded his prophet Hosea to marry Gomer; an adulterous wife with children of her unfaithfulness, to illustrate that Israel was guilty of spiritual adultery by leaving the Lord for other god's.

Beginning with chapter 1:10, there is a promise of restoration. Judah and Israel would be united under one leader, and they would be called sons of God. This is a prophecy of the coming of the kingdom of Christ that would be set up in the first century A.D. Paul quoted Hosea in Romans 9:25-26 saying that Hosea's prophecy predicted the restoration of Israel and Judah, which would include the Gentiles. God's plan for redemption would include all people on the earth that would accept Him and His Son by faith. The Kingdom of God's Son Jesus would be made up of the Jewish people of faith, the descendants of both kingdoms and the Gentiles that would obey the gospel of God's Son and become members of the kingdom of Christ. The Kingdom of Christ would soon be introduced after John the Baptizer and Jesus began their ministries in the first century A.D.

The gospel of Christ was preached to the Jews from every nation on the first Pentecost after Christ's death, burial, resurrection and ascension (Acts 2). The apostle Paul preached the gospel to the Gentiles later (Acts 10), and from then on the gospel was preached to people all over the world and still is today as Jesus the King of Kings reigns over His kingdom. Romans 9:22-25– Paul states that God chose to show his wrath during the events prior to the establishment of the kingdom. God showed His wrath against the stubborn unbelieving people that rejected His Son Jesus the Christ (Jewish Messiah). God had a difficult time with the Israelites (Jews) in His loving effort to establish redemption and salvation for all people.

The Lord became angry with Solomon because of his disobedience and told Solomon that He would take the kingdom away from his descendants but He promised to leave the kingdom in Solomon's hand as long as he lived. After Solomon's death, the kingdom was taken away from Solomon's son. 1st Kings 11:9-13– The Lord was angry with Solomon, because his heart had turned from the God of Israel who had appeared to him twice, and had commanded him concerning this thing, that he should not go after other god's; but he did not keep what the Lord had commanded.

The Lord said to Solomon,' "Because you have done this, and have not kept My covenant and My statutes, which I have commanded you, I will surely tear the kingdom away from you and give it to your servant." "Nevertheless I will not do it in your days, for the sake of your father David; I will tear it out of the hand of your son. However I will not tear away the whole kingdom; I will give one tribe to your son for the sake of My servant David, and for the sake of Jerusalem which I have chosen." You did not do what was right in My eyes; and you have done more evil than all who were before you, for you have gone and made for yourself other gods and molded images to provoke Me to anger, and have cast Me behind your back, therefore I will bring disaster on the house of Jeroboam, and I will take away the remnant of the house of Jeroboam, as one takes away refuse until it is all gone.

Twenty kings reigned over the Israelites before Assyria defeated them. They went into captivity to the Assyrians in 722 B.C. The books of Kings and Chronicles give the history of the kings of both the Northern Kingdom of Israel, and the Southern Kingdom of Judah. The prophets also wrote about the sinful deeds and troublesome times of the two kingdoms. The Northern Kingdom was never restored to the fellowship of God. Ahab and Jezebel Ruled the Northern Kingdom of Israel. The sin of the Israelites did not prevent God from completing His plan of redemption. The

Israelites would suffer through some very difficult times but some of the people would remain faithful to God until Jesus was born. Ahab reigned from 874B.C. to 853B.C. and was on the throne during the time of the prophets Elijah and Elisha.

Ahab was the son of Omri, and he reigned over the Israelites in Samaria for twenty-two years. Ahab fortified the cities of Israel and used his own Money. During his reign Israel had frequent wars with Syria. A random arrow killed Ahab during a battle with Syria and he was buried in Samaria. Ahab did more evil to provoke the Lord than all of the kings of Israel before him. He built a temple for the false god Baal in Samaria, the capital city, and built a wooden image of Baal and worshiped it. Baal was the false God whose image was worshiped by the Gentiles. Jezebel, Ahab's wife, was not an Israelite. She was the daughter of Ethbaal, the king of Sidon. Jezebel worshipped the false god Baal, and she insisted that Baal have equal rights with the Lord God of Israel. Jezebel's insistence brought her into direct conflict with the prophet Elijah. Jezebel was so wicked that her name has always been associated with evil women. Elijah, the prophet, warned King Ahab of Israel that as surely as the Lord God of Israel lived, and as he stood before God, there would not be any dew or rain for a few years. It did not rain again until Elijah prayed to God for the rain to return. Ahab and Jezebel were very angry with Elijah and wanted to find him and kill him. The Lord Protected His prophet and told Elijah to travel eastward and hide from Ahab and Jezebel in the Kerith Ravine, east of the Jordan. There was a brook in the ravine where Elijah hid. He would have water. God sent ravens with food for him each day. Elijah had to depend on the providence of the Lord. After many days, the Lord told Elijah he would make it rain and Elijah was to go back to King Ahab.

When Ahab saw Elijah, he said, "Is that you, O trouble maker of Israel?" Elijah said he was not the one who had made trouble for Israel but Ahab had. Ahab had forsaken the Lord and worshipped Baal. Elijah told Ahab to gather all the prophets of Baal and meet him on Mount Carmel. When all the prophets of Baal were assembled on Mount Carmel, Elijah had a contest to see whose god was the real God. Each side built an altar to their God and placed a bull on the altar. The prophets of Baal prayed long and hard for Baal to send fire down on the sacrifice, but no fire came. Elijah soaked his sacrifice with water and he prayed for God to send fire down on his sacrifice. God sent fire down and burned up the sacrifice of Elijah. When the people saw it they said, "The Lord, He is God!"

After that, Elijah went off by himself and prayed to God to send rain. The sky turned dark, and it began to rain. Elijah had 450 prophets of Baal put to death in the Kishon valley. When Ahab told Jezebel what Elijah had done, Jezebel threatened to have Elijah killed. Elijah decided to hide in the wilderness, so he arose and ran for his life to Beersheba, which belonged to Judah. Elijah ran toward the wilderness, and sat down under a tree and prayed that he might die. He said, "It is enough! Now Lord, take my life, for I am no better than my fathers! Fearing for his life, Elijah became very depressed and wanted to die there in the wilderness. An angel touched him and told him to get up and eat. Elijah saw a cake baked on coals, and a jar of water. He ate and drank and lay down again. And the angel of the Lord came back the second time, and touched him and said, "Get up and eat, because the journey is too long for you." Elijah had asked the Lord to take his life, but the Lord had other plans for him, and He treated Elijah with kindness.

The angel told Elijah to go to Mt Horeb, the mountain of God. When Elijah reached Mt Horeb, he spent the night in a cave. The next morning the Lord asked Elijah what he was doing there, and Elijah replied, "I have been very zealous for the Lord God Almighty. The Israelites have rejected your covenant, broken down your altars, and put your prophets to death with the sword. I am the only one left, and now they are trying to kill me too."

Elijah was very distraught, he had served the Lord faithfully in all kinds of bad circumstances, and now the Lord was about to reward him for his faithfulness. The Lord told Elijah two important things to do: to go and anoint Hazael king over Israel, and then find Elisha and appoint Elisha to be a prophet of Israel. Elijah left the mountain, went to Hazael and anointed Hazael to be the king of Israel. Elijah found the prophet Elisha and made him his attendant. God was going to take Elijah to heaven, and Elisha would take his place as the prophet of Israel, but before that took place, Elisha would witness a very unusual thing. Elijah would be taken to heaven in a fiery chariot. The Lord was going to reward Elijah by taking him to heaven before he died. When the Lord was ready to take Elijah to heaven, he sent him to Bethel.

Samuel warned the people what could happen if they had a king, but they wouldn't listen to him. At first, Saul was a good king and a mighty military leader, but God was not pleased with him, because Saul didn't obey God in everything He told him to do. The heart of Saul was not completely converted to doing the Lord's will. In the earlier days of civilization when kings ruled nations, they also served as military leaders and warriors as well. Saul was a fierce warrior who could ably defend Israel, but he relied on his own judgment to rule wisely and failed to do what the Lord told him. The Lord was grieved for making Saul king because of his rebellious attitude, so the Lord rejected him and took the kingdom of Israel away from him. The Lord told Samuel He had rejected Saul as the king and instructed him to anoint one of the sons of Jesse as king over Israel in the place of Saul. Samuel filled his horn with oil and went to Jesse's house in Bethlehem and anointed David to replace Saul as King over Israel. David was an ancestor of Judah, the son of Israel (Jacob), and David was chosen to be in the birth line of Christ.

Of all the sons of Jesse, David was not the most likely son to chosen for a king, David was a shepherd and a musician. People look on the outward appearance of others and judge them, but the Lord looks at the heart. The Lord has the ability to see into the hearts of people and know things that people cannot know.

The Lord knew that David was the best choice for king, because the Lord knew David's heart. Jesus was to be a descendant of David. The Lord said that David was a man after His own heart because of David's attitude towards God. David was endowed with many talents including musician, poet and singer. David became a great military leader and was engaged in several battles, especially with the Philistines. Even with all of his good qualities and his love for God, David became a sinful man who served God in his own generation. Nothing is known about Nathan's background except that he was from the tribe of Judah. Nathan appears without explanation in the 7th chapter of 2nd Samuel where he has a conversation with King David. Nathan was the prophet who spoke the word of the Lord to David, and it was he who spoke convicting words from the Lord when David sinned with Bathsheba. The Philistine people were enemies of God's people, and one member of their army was a giant named Goliath. The Philistines and Goliath threatened the people of Israel and mocked the Lord. Everyone was afraid to go up against Goliath because of his great size. David believed the Lord would help him defeat Goliath, so David, with the Lord's help, killed Goliath, and he became a hero to the people. David's desire was to do the will of God, and he kept the law of God in his heart, even though he was weak in the flesh and sinned.

Psalm, Chapter 31A psalm of David–O Lord, I put my trust in You. Let me never be ashamed; Deliver me in Your righteousness. Bow down Your ear to me. Deliver me speedily. Be my rock of refuge, a fortress of defense to save me. You are my rock and my fortress; therefore, for Your name's sake, lead me and guide me. Pull me out of the net, which they have secretly laid for me, for You are my strength. Into your hand I commit my spirit; you have redeemed me, O Lord God of truth. I have hated those who regard useless idols; but I trust in the Lord. I will be glad and rejoice in Your mercy, for You have considered my trouble; You have known my soul in adversities, and have not put me into the hand of the enemy. Have mercy on me, for I am in trouble; my eye wastes away with grief, yes, my soul and my body! For my life is spent with grief, and my years with sighing; my strength fails because of my iniquity, and my bones waste away.

I am a reproach among all my enemies, but especially among my neighbors, and am repulsive to my acquaintances; those who see me outside flee from me. I am forgotten like a dead man, out of mind; I am like a broken vessel. For I hear the slander of many; fear is on every side; while they take counsel together against me, they scheme to take away my life. But as for me, I trust in You, O Lord; I say, "You are my God." My times are in Your hand; deliver me from the hand of my enemies, and from those who persecute me. Make Your face shine upon Your servant; save me for Your mercies' sake. Do not let me be ashamed, O Lord, for I have called upon You; let the wicked be ashamed; let them be silent in the grave. Let the lying lips be put to silence, which speak insolent things proudly and contemptuously against the righteous. Oh, how great is Your goodness, which You have laid up for those who fear You, which You have prepared for those who trust in You in the presence of the sons of men!

You shall hide them in the secret place of Your presence from the plots of man; You shall keep them secretly in a pavilion from the strife of tongues. Blessed Be the Lord, for He has shown me His marvelous kindness in a strong city! For I said in my haste, "I am cut off from before Your eyes;" nevertheless You heard the voice of my supplications when I cried out to You. Oh, love the Lord, all you His saints for the Lord, preserves the faithful, and fully repays the proud person. Be of good courage, and He shall strengthen your heart, all you who hope in the Lord."

David King of Israel

The Philistines were enemies of God's people, and one member of their army was a giant named Goliath. The Philistines and Goliath threatened the people of Israel and mocked the Lord. Everyone was afraid to go up against Goliath because of his great size. David believed the Lord would help him defeat Goliath, so David, with the Lord's help, killed Goliath, and he became a hero to the people. David was a person with a strong faith in God. God loved David because he was contrite and very humble in his attitude towards the Lord (1st Samuel 17).

David wrote in the Psalms expressing the attitude of a heart that is humble. David's desire was to do the will of God, and he kept the law of God in his heart, even though he was sometimes weak in the flesh and sinned. Saul was jealous of David because the people loved him, and Saul tried to capture and kill him, but the Lord kept him safe. David had several opportunities to kill Saul, but he wouldn't kill the king of Israel. On one occasion, when Saul was in battle with the Philistines, he was wounded. To avoid being captured by the Philistines, Saul took his own life by falling on his sword. Saul had much potential, but he was a tragic failure, because his heart was not right with the Lord. The main difference between the successes of David over Saul was their attitudes toward the Lord. After Saul's death, David inquired of the Lord what he should do. The Lord guided him to the tribal town of Judah where he was anointed king over Israel. His royal residence was in Hebron.

David was only thirty years old when he began to reign over Israel, and during his reign, the nation of Israel experienced a golden age. David reigned for forty years; he reigned in Hebron for seven years and six months and later in Jerusalem for thirty-three years. Early in the life of David, he conquered the city of Jerusalem, which became the capital city of the Israelites. The Ark of God was placed on a new cart and brought to Jerusalem, and Jerusalem became known both as the city of God and the city of David. The word Zion is mentioned several times in the Bible in reference to the city of Jerusalem. Zion was the name of a hill in Jerusalem. Zion is the place where the royal palace of David was built and later where Solomon built the temple, the seat of Jewish worship and government. The name Zion was also used in reference to the home of the Israelites. Zion took on the meaning of the heavenly city or heavenly home, the city of God. 'The daughter of Zion' makes reference to Jerusalem and the people of God. Zion has a special significance to the Jewish people. David was favored by God because he did everything the Lord asked him to do. David was the greatest and best loved king in the history of the nation of Israel, and the Jews today still favor him as the greatest. In many ways he was a good person who had a good heart.

Like all men, David was not a perfect or sinless person. He committed some grievous sins, but he confessed his sins and repented. God accepted his humble repentance and promised that his descendants would be heirs to the same promise the Lord had made to Abraham by establishing a royal line from which the Messiah would come. David committed some grievous sins, but God accepted David's humble repentance and He promised that his descendants would be heirs to the same promise the Lord had made to Abraham by establishing the royal line of David, from which the Messiah, Jesus would come. After David, the royal line continued to follow the line of David until Jesus was born in the first century A.D. David was favored by God, because he did everything the Lord asked him to do. David was the greatest and best loved king in the history of the nation of Israel, and the Jews today still favor him as the greatest.

Acts 13:16-23– The God of this people Israel chose our fathers, and exalted the people when they dwelt as strangers in the land of Egypt, and with an uplifted arm He brought them out of it. Now for a time of about forty years He put up with your ways in the wilderness. And when He had destroyed seven nations in the land of Canaan, He distributed their land to them by allotment. After that He gave them judges for about four hundred and fifty years, until Samuel the prophet. And afterward they asked for a king; so God gave them Saul the son of Kish a man of the tribe of Benjamin, for forty years. And when He had removed him. He raised up for them David as king to whom also He gave testimony and said, "I have found David, the son of Jesse, a man after My own heart, who will do all my will." From this man's seed, according to the promise, God raised up for Israel a Savior - Jesus."

The kingdom of Israel under the leadership of David remained faithful to the Lord, and the Lord blessed Israel, and David's Kingdom was enlarged. David had several sons, including Solomon his son by Bathsheba. David selected Solomon to become his successor to the throne. Before David died, he called Solomon to his bedside and explained what his responsibilities would be when he ruled the kingdom after David's death. David told Solomon to walk in the ways, God showed him and to keep all of the commandments of the Law of Moses.

He told Solomon that as long as he and his descendants were faithful to God with all of their heart and soul, God would be with them. When David died, Solomon became the king of Israel. After Solomon was anointed king, the Lord appeared to him in a dream and told him he could ask for anything he wanted, and his wish would be granted. Solomon asked for wisdom, and the Lord was pleased and gave him great wisdom as well as riches and honor. Solomon became known as the wisest man in the world, and under his rule the kingdom of Israel became very wealthy. With all of Solomon's wisdom he accomplished many great things but in spite of all of his accomplishments Solomon disobeyed many of the commandments of the Lord and his heart turned away from strict obedience to God. God commanded Solomon twice not to worship false gods, but he refused to obey what the Lord commanded.

Solomon desired to carry out is father David's wishes and build a temple to the Lord as a place of worship. 1st Kings 5:1-6– Hiram king of Tyre sent his servants to Solomon he heard that they had anointed him king in place of his father. Then Solomon sent to Hiram saying: You know how my father David could not build a house for the name of the Lord his God because of the wars which were fought against him on every side, until the Lord put his foes under the soles of his feet. But now the Lord my God has given me rest on every side there is neither adversary nor evil occurrence. And behold I propose to build a house for the name of the Lord my God, as the Lord spoke to my father David, saying, Your son, whom I will set on your throne in your place, he shall build the house for my name." The tabernacle had served the Israelite nation for many years as the house of God, but it was a temporary structure. Four hundred and eighty years after the children of Israel left the land of Egypt and were settled in Canaan, and after Solomon had reigned for four years, he began building a temple in Jerusalem. When the temple was complete there was a dedication ceremony. The temple became the place for the presence of the Lord. The temple was the focal point of the Jewish religion when Jesus was born in the first century. Solomon wrote the books of Proverbs, Ecclesiastes and Songs of Solomon. The book of Ecclesiastes is rich in wisdom. It describes some of the pitfalls of life and the misery that can occur in life. Solomon saw the tears of the oppressed and observed that death comes to everyone.

He also discovered that everyone, the wise, the foolish, the rich, and the poor will all ultimately come face to face with death and their fate will be in God's hands. Solomon said that everything God has set in order is forever, and men cannot change it. He observed that there is nothing new in God's relationship with mankind and that there is nothing new under the sun. That which is now, has been before, and what is to be, has already been. Solomon summed up all of the activities in life and came to the conclusion that success in life is achieved only if we stand in awe of God and keep His commandments. He observed that this life is meaningless unless it leads to a greater life of faith in God. He concluded that the whole duty of man is to fear God and keep his commandments.

Ecclesiastes 12:9-14 "And moreover because the Preacher was wise, he still taught the people knowledge; yes, he pondered and sought out and set in order many proverbs. The Preacher sought to find acceptable words; and what was written, was upright-words of truth. The words of the wise are like goads, and the words of scholars are like well-driven nails, given by one Shepherd. In spite of Solomon's wisdom, he failed to take his own advice to fear God and keep His commandments. The Lord became angry with Solomon because of his disobedience and told Solomon that He would take the kingdom away from his descendants but He promised to leave the kingdom in Solomon's hand as long as he lived. After Solomon's death, the kingdom of Israel was taken away from Solomon's son.

1st Kings 11:9-13 "The Lord became angry with Solomon, because his heart had turned from the Lord God of Israel who had appeared to him twice, and had commanded him concerning this thing, that he should not go after other god's; but he did not keep what the Lord had commanded. The Lord said to Solomon,' "Because you have done this, and have not kept My covenant and My statutes, which I have commanded you, I will surely tear the kingdom away from you and give it to your servant." "Nevertheless I will not do it in your days, for the sake of your father David; I will tear it out of the hand of your son. However I will not tear away the whole kingdom; I will give one tribe to your son for the sake of My servant David, and for the sake of Jerusalem which I have chosen."

Kingdom of Israel Becomes Divided (931 B.C.)

The Lord's prophetic words were fulfilled a few years after Solomon's son Rehoboam took his father's place on the throne. When Rehoboam became king he put a large tax on the people, and they rebelled against him. At that time, the Lord split the kingdom. God took ten tribes of Israel from Rehoboam and placed a king named Jeroboam over them and they were known as the ten northern tribes. The two southern tribes were, the Kingdom of Judah and Benjamin ruled by Rehoboam. The ten tribes of Israel chose the city of Samaria as their Capitol. The tribes of Judah and Benjamin, the Southern Kingdom, worshiped the Lord in the temple in Jerusalem.

At times most of the Israelites turned away from following the Lord, but there was always a faithful remnant of the Israelites in Judah. The Lord blessed the remnant in Judah and continued to help them in order to complete the plan of redemption through His Son. Under Jeroboam's rule, the ten northern tribes worshiped idols and God became very angry with them, and He sent prophets to warn them. God's judgment would come against them if they didn't repent of their idolatry. They made two golden calves and set them up as gods - one at each end of the kingdom - so the people of the northern kingdom could worship the golden calves instead of going to Jerusalem to worship God in the temple. There was constant conflict and war between the Northern Kingdom and the Southern Kingdom.

When Jeroboam led the ten northern tribes wholly into idolatry the prophet Elijah, brought bad news from the Lord to Jeroboam and his household, denouncing Jeroboam. 1st Kings 14:7-10–Tell Jeroboam, the Lord God of Israel exalted you from among the people, made you ruler over My people Israel. I took the kingdom away from the house of David, and gave it to you; and you have not kept My commandments. David followed me with all his heart, You did not do what was right in My eyes; and you have done more evil than all who were before you, for you have gone and made for yourself other gods and molded images to provoke Me to anger, and have cast Me behind your back, therefore I will bring disaster on the house of Jeroboam, and I will take away the remnant of the house of Jeroboam, as one takes away refuse until it is all gone.

Twenty kings reigned over the Israelites before Assyria defeated them. They went into captivity to the Assyrians in 722 B.C. The books of Kings and Chronicles give the history of the kings of both the Northern Kingdom of Israel, and the Southern Kingdom of Judah. The prophets also wrote about the sinful deeds and troublesome times of the two kingdoms. The Northern Kingdom was never restored to the fellowship of God. Ahab and Jezebel Ruled the Northern Kingdom of Israel. The sin of the Israelites did not prevent God from completing His plan of redemption. Ahab reigned from 874B.C. to 853B.C. and was on the throne during the time of the prophets Elijah and Elisha. Ahab was the son of Omri, and he reigned over the Israelites in Samaria for twenty-two years. Ahab fortified the cities of Israel and used his own Money. During his reign Israel had frequent wars with Syria. A random arrow killed Ahab during a battle with Syria and he was buried in Samaria. Ahab did more evil to provoke the Lord than all of the kings of Israel before him. He built a temple for the false god Baal in Samaria, the capital city, and built a wooden image of Baal and worshiped it.

Baal was a false God whose image was worshiped by the Gentiles. Jezebel, Ahab's wife, was not an Israelite. She was the daughter of Ethbaal, the king of Sidon. Jezebel worshipped the false god Baal, and she insisted that Baal have equal rights with the Lord God of Israel. Jezebel's insistence brought her into direct conflict with the prophet Elijah. Jezebel was so wicked that her name has always been associated with evil women. Elijah, the prophet, warned King Ahab of Israel that as surely as the Lord God of Israel lived, and as he stood before God, there would not be any dew or rain for a few years. It did not rain again until Elijah prayed to God for the rain to return.

Ahab and Jezebel were very angry with Elijah and wanted to find him and kill him. The Lord Protected His prophet and told Elijah to travel eastward and hide from Ahab and Jezebel in the Kerith Ravine, east of the Jordan. There was a brook in the ravine where Elijah hid. He would have water. God sent ravens with food for him each day. Elijah had to depend on the providence of the Lord. After many days, the Lord told Elijah he would make it rain and Elijah was to go back to King Ahab. When Ahab saw Elijah, he said, "Is that you, O trouble maker of Israel?"

Elijah said he was not the one who had made trouble for Israel but Ahab had. Ahab had forsaken the Lord and worshipped Baal. Elijah told Ahab to gather all the prophets of Baal and meet him on Mount Carmel. When all the prophets of Baal were assembled on Mount Carmel, Elijah had a contest to see whose god was the real God. Each side built an altar to their God and placed a bull on the altar. The prophets of Baal prayed long and hard for Baal to send fire down on the sacrifice, but no fire came.

Elijah soaked his sacrifice with water and he prayed for God to send fire down on his sacrifice. God sent fire down and burned up the sacrifice of Elijah. When the people saw it they said, "The Lord, He is God!" After that, Elijah went off by himself and prayed to God to send rain. The sky turned dark, and it began to rain. Elijah had 450 prophets of Baal put to death in the Kishon valley. When Ahab told Jezebel what Elijah had done, Jezebel threatened to have Elijah killed. Elijah decided to hide in the wilderness, so he arose and ran for his life to Beersheba, which belonged to Judah. Elijah ran toward the wilderness, and sat down under a tree and prayed that he might die. He said, "It is enough! Now Lord, take my life, for I am no better than my fathers!" Fearing for his life, Elijah became very depressed and wanted to die there in the wilderness.

An angel touched him and told him to get up and eat. Elijah saw a cake baked on coals, and a jar of water. He ate and drank and lay down again. And the angel of the Lord came back the second time, and touched him and said, "Get up and eat, because the journey is too long for you." Elijah had asked the Lord to take his life, but the Lord had other plans for him, and He treated Elijah with kindness. The angel told Elijah to go to Mt Horeb, the mountain of God. When Elijah reached Mt Horeb, he spent the night in a cave. The next morning the Lord asked Elijah what he was doing there, and Elijah replied, "I have been very zealous for the Lord God Almighty. The Israelites have rejected your covenant, broken down your altars, and put your prophets to death with the sword. I am the only one left, and now they are trying to kill me too."

Elijah was very distraught, he had served the Lord faithfully in all kinds of bad circumstances, and now the Lord was about to reward him for his faithfulness.

The Lord told Elijah two important things to do: to go and anoint Hazael king over Israel, and then find Elisha and appoint Elisha to be a prophet of Israel. Elijah left the mountain, went to Hazael and anointed Hazael to be the king of Israel. Elijah found the prophet Elisha and made him his attendant. God was going to take Elijah to heaven, and Elisha would take his place as the prophet of Israel, but before that took place, Elisha would witness a very unusual thing. Elijah would be taken up to heaven in a fiery chariot.

The Lord would reward Elijah by taking him to heaven before he died. When the Lord was ready to take Elijah to heaven, he sent him to Bethel. Elijah and Elisha were coming back from Gilgal, and Elijah told Elisha to stay where he was and he would go on to Bethel alone. Elisha said, "As the Lord lives, and as your soul lives, I will not leave you!" (2nd Kings 2:2) And they both went to Bethel. There was a company of prophets there, and the prophets already knew the Lord was going to take Elijah. They told Elisha about it, and Elisha said he already knew and he asked them not to speak about it. It weighed heavily on Elisha knowing that Elijah would soon be gone, and he would be taking his place.

Elijah told Elisha to stay at Bethel while he went to Jericho. Elisha refused to stay at Bethel and he went with Elijah. When the two reached Jericho a group of prophets told Elisha that the Lord was going to take his master that day. Elisha said "Yes I know, but do not speak of it." Then Elijah told Elisha he was going to the Jordan River, and he told Elisha to stay there, but Elisha said, "As surely as the Lord lives and as you live, I will not leave you." When they got to the Jordan River, Elijah rolled up his cloak and struck the water with it. The water parted and Elijah and Elisha walked across the river on dry ground. Elijah asked Elisha what he could do for him before the Lord took him, and Elisha asked for a double portion of Elijah's spirit.

The Holy Spirit of the Lord had been given to Elijah in a large measure. Elisha wanted to carry on Elijah's ministry with an even greater power than Elijah's. Elijah told Elisha he had asked for something that was hard to do, but it would be granted if Elisha were there when God took him. Elijah was still testing Elisha to see if he would be faithful to replace him. Elijah and Elisha continued to walk away from the river.

"Then it happened as they continued on and talked, suddenly a chariot of fire appeared with horses of fire, and separated the two of them; and Elijah went up in a whirlwind into heaven. Elisha saw it, and he cried out, "My father, my father, the chariot of Israel and its horsemen!" He saw him no more and he took hold of his own clothes and tore them into two pieces." (2nd Kings 2:11-12) Elijah ascended to heaven and Elisha picked up his cloak and walked back to the river, struck the waters with Elijah's cloak and called out to the Lord saying, "Where now is the Lord, the God of Elijah?" The waters parted again and Elisha walked across the river. Elisha wanted to know if the Lord had given him the power he promised. A company of prophets witnessed what took place and the prophets said, "The spirit of Elijah is resting on Elisha." The Lord honored Elisha's request for a double measure of Elijah's spirit. Elijah was often described as a man of God. He was a Tishbite from the town of Tishbeh in Gilead, and his name means 'Yaweh is God.' He wore a garment of hair and a leather belt around his waist. His outer garment was probably made from sheepskin or goatskin and was loose fitting like a cloak.

Ahaziah succeeded Ahab as the king of Israel but he died after two years, and Joram succeeded him. It was during the reign of Joram that Elijah went to heaven, and Elisha succeeded Elijah. The deeds of Elijah and Elisha are recorded from 1st Kings 17 through 2nd Kings 13. After Ahab, Israel was ruled by 12 kings in succession until 722 B.C. The last king on the throne of Israel is

Hoshea, and the children of Israel continued to sin against the Lord. In the final difficult days of the Kingdom of Israel (from 760 to 722 B.C.), the prophet Hosea ministered to Israel. This was during the days of the six kings who followed Jereboam the Second: Zechariah, Shallum, Menahem, Pekahiah, Pekah and Hoshea (2nd Kings 15-16, and 17).

Northern Kingdom of Israel Goes Into Exile

The nation of Israel was united under the first three kings Saul, David and Solomon. After the death of Solomon there was a civil war and the united nation of Israel was split into two, the northern kingdom Israel and the kingdom of Judah. The capital city of Judah was Jerusalem where the temple was and the descendants of David through whom Christ would come ruled the southern kingdom of Judah.

The northern kingdom of Israel eventually became so wicked that it was destroyed by Assyria in 722 B.C. The books of First and Second Kings in the Bible reveal the history of the two kingdoms. The kings of Judah the southern kingdom ranged from good to bad and the Babylonians put the people of Judah in exile in Babylon in 586 B.C. Shalmaneser, the king of Assyria, invaded the land of Israel and laid siege to Samaria for three years.

During the reign of King Hoshea of Israel, the Assyrians completed the destruction of the northern kingdom, and in 722 B.C, Israel was exiled to Assyria. Shalmeneser settled them in Halah, in Gozan on the Habor River, and in the towns of the Medes. (2nd Kings 17.) The prophet Amos threatened Israel with a judgment from the Lord several years before the exile, and the prophet Hosea had identified the enemy as Assyria. The purpose of Hosea's ministry was to point out Israel's sins and their unfaithfulness. Hosea put much of the blame for Israel's sin on their lifestyle, borrowed from their pagan neighbors in Canaan.

The pagans worshiped the false god Baal, and the Israelites were influenced by their worship of Baal. Hosea wrote about the judgment of God and His salvation. God's judgment was altogether punitive. Out of love, God punished His people to bring them to repentance. The Lord reminded the Israelites that it was He who brought them out of Egypt, and that they should not acknowledge any God but Him (Hosea 13:4). According to Hosea 13:16, the people of Samaria would have to bear the burdens caused by their own guilt.

The Lord warned Israel about what other nations would do to Israel without His protection: they would be slaughtered with the sword, their little ones would be dashed to the ground, and their pregnant women would be ripped open. The prophet gave the Lord's warning in plenty of time for Israel to repent but Israel would not. The Lord would turn His anger away if they repented. He sent the prophets to plead with the people to return to Him but the message of the prophets fell on deaf ears. The prophet Hosea prophesied about the Northern Kingdom of Israel in the eighth century B.C. Hosea issued the Lord's threats against Israel and rebuked them when they failed to heed His warnings. Hosea prophesied that the Lord would destroy Israel but would save Judah.

Judah would be saved by the providence of God because Jesus the Jewish Messiah would come from the descendants of Judah. Israel did not repent, and as Joel and Amos predicted, Israel was exiled to Assyria in 722B.C. In the first chapter of Hosea, the Lord compares Israel to a prostitute; she was married to the Lord, but she became unfaithful and served idols. The Lord is a jealous God and will not tolerate spiritual adultery. God's people symbolize his wife. The Lord commanded his prophet Hosea to marry Gomer; an adulterous wife with children of her unfaithfulness, to illustrate that Israel was guilty of spiritual adultery by leaving the Lord for other god's.

Beginning with chapter 1:10, there is a promise of restoration. Judah and Israel would be united under one leader, and they would be called sons of God. This is a prophecy of the coming of the kingdom of Christ that would be set up in the first century A.D. Paul quoted Hosea in Romans 9:25-26 saying that Hosea's prophecy predicted the restoration of Israel and Judah, which would include the Gentiles. The Kingdom of Christ would be made up of Jewish people the descendants of both kingdoms in the beginning then the gentiles would receive the gospel and be members of the kingdom of Christ. The Kingdom of Christ would soon be introduced after John the Baptizer and Jesus began their ministries in the first century A.D. The gospel of Christ was preached to the Jews from every nation on the first Pentecost after Christ's death, burial, resurrection and ascension (Acts 2). The apostle Paul preached the gospel to the Gentiles later (Acts 10), and from then on the gospel was preached to people all over the world and still is today as Jesus the King of Kings reigns over His kingdom.

Romans 9:22-25– Paul states that God chose to show his wrath during the events prior to the establishment of the kingdom in order to make His power known. Throughout the history of the Old Testament, the people of Israel and Judah sinned the Lord demonstrated His wrath, then they would repent. Israel's sins were many, but God's compassion and love was enduring. The Gentiles had been sinners from the beginning, but God graciously sent his Son to die for all people. From the time of their exile till the coming of Christ in the first century Israel sowed the wind and reaped the whirlwind. (Hosea 8:7)

The nation of Israel sowed the wind of disregard for God's law and became idolatrous, and as a result, they reaped a whirlwind of judgment from the Lord. Israel sowed idolatry, and they reaped the mighty power of God and were taken captive by the Gentile nations.

Chapters 9 and 10–The prophet Hosea wrote about Israel's punishment for rejecting the Lord; they would become wanderers among the nations. The people of the nation of Israel went into exile in 722 B.C. and afterwards did become wanderers throughout the world. Chapter 11–Hosea wrote about God's love for Israel. God loved his people, the descendants of Abraham, but he punished them because of their many sins and stubborn refusal to repent. God's purpose in punishing his people was to make them return to Him. God's love for his people didn't change even when they sinned or failed to repent. The more God called on them to return to him, the further they drifted into sin and idolatry. Chapters 12-13, Hosea continued to expose the sins of Israel and Judah and exhorted the two nations to return to the Lord and maintain love and justice. Justice points to the sin of selfishness, greed, and pride. The merchants used dishonest scales; they loved to defraud the poor. Ephraim boasted about becoming wealthy. He thought his wealth would cover his sin. The Lord loves all those whose hearts are right regardless of their economic position. The kingdom of Israel continued in their sinful ways, and in the ninth year of King Hoshea, the king of Assyria besieged the city of Samaria. Israel was carried away from their own land to Assyria in 722 BC. The people of the Northern Kingdom mixed with people from other countries and their religion became mixed with paganism. The Samaritans were a mixture of the intermarriage of people from the Northern kingdom and people of other races and the other Jews hated them.

Southern Kingdom of Judah (626-586 B.C)

Before the exiles would return to Jerusalem, the combined nations of the Medes and Persians conquered the Babylonian empire, fulfilling the word of the Lord. Jeremiah 30, Jeremiah prophesied of a time when the Lord would restore Israel and Judah to the land. This was a promise of restoration to the fellowship of the Lord and, most likely, a prophecy with dual meaning.

The first was a prophecy of the return of the exiles in Babylon to Jerusalem after 70 years, and instead of serving Babylon, they would serve the Lord. The second was a prophecy of Messianic fulfillment; Christ the King would sit on David's throne when He came and His spiritual kingdom was established (The Church). The Lord had promised to discipline his people with justice, but he would not completely destroy them. The Lord would leave a remnant of the Jews through whom Jesus the Messiah would come. Christ was born in the first century A.D. and His parents Mary and Joseph were both descendants of David. The people during the time of the Old Testament lived by faith in God but they did not receive the things that were promised while they were living - they saw them by faith in the distant future. They longed for a better country - a heavenly city that God had prepared for them. Jeremiah 23:5-6, Jeremiah wrote about a righteous branch of David, referring to the birth of Christ.

Jeremiah 33:15, Jeremiah set the time of the beginning of the restoration when he wrote: "In those days, at that time, I will make a righteous branch sprout from David's line." This is the time in history when Christ would be born in the first century A.D. The remnant of Judah would provide an ancestor of King David through whom Christ would come. The Israelite people from Judah would spend seventy years in Babylon, and in the latter years of their time there, the Persians would conquer Babylon, and Cyrus, the king of Persia, would allow some of the exiles to return to Jerusalem and build another temple.

The Babylonian Exile -Book of Ezra -
Return of the Exiles to Judea

The Medes and Persians defeated Babylon during the time of the exile, and the Israelites who became known as Jews were under the rule of the Medes and Persians. During the reign of King Cyrus of Persia, Cyrus let the people of Judah return to Jerusalem. Cyrus became a part of God's divine plan for the Jews. The Lord influenced Cyrus in such a way that he was moved to fulfill Jeremiah's prophecy of the return of the Jews. The Lord commanded Cyrus to build Him a house in Jerusalem, so the family heads of the tribes of Judah and Benjamin, the priests and Levites, and all the people who were anxious to help would return to Jerusalem to build another temple of the Lord.

Cyrus gave the silver and gold articles taken from Solomon's temple to Sheshbazzar, the prince of Judah, to take back to Jerusalem with him. The Jews began their return in 537-538 B.C. As they returned, the people settled in their homes and rebuilt the altar for burnt sacrifices and sacrificed to the Lord. Worship to the Lord was restored in Jerusalem. Ezra 2:64-67 "The whole assembly together was forty two thousand three hundred and sixty, besides their male and female servants, of whom there were seven thousand three hundred and thirty seven; and they had two hundred men and women singers.' "Their horses were seven hundred and thirty six, their mules two hundred and forty five, their camels four hundred and thirty five, and their donkeys six thousand seven hundred and twenty."

The Jewish exiles who returned to Jerusalem were people who had lived well in Babylon and Persia and had amassed great wealth. The people were intelligent and talented and were able to rebuild their civilization and practice their religion freely. The people banded together in unity and were determined to restore the city of Jerusalem and the temple of the Lord. Among those who returned to Jerusalem was a Levitical priest named Zerubbabel. Zerubbabel and some of the other Jews were determined to re-establish the sacrifices of worship to the Lord in a new temple. The Jews were very liberal in their offerings for the work. First they built an altar for sacrifices on the site of the first temple and later laid out the foundations for a new temple.

When the people from Samaria who were Israelites from the former northern kingdom heard about the building of the temple, they offered to help, but Zerubbabel and the leading families of the Jews refused their help. They didn't want to have any association with the people of Samaria. The Samaritans were a mixture of the northern tribes of Israel and the Gentiles. The Samaritans There were still bad feelings between the people of the southern kingdom an opposed the re-building of the temple, so the work ceased until the second year of the reign of Darius over Persia in 520 B.C. Then the prophet Haggai delivered the word of the Lord to Zerubbabel. The message from the Lord encouraged the people to work harder to complete the rebuilding of the temple. Be strong, Zerubbabel,' says the Lord; and be strong, Joshua, son of Jehozadak, the high priest; and be strong, all you people of the land,' says the Lord, 'and work; for I am with you,' says the Lord of hosts.

According to the word that I covenanted with you when you came out of Egypt, so My Spirit remains among you; do not fear!' For thus says the Lord of hosts: 'Once more (it is a little while) I will shake heaven and earth, the sea and dry land; and I will shake all nations, and they shall come to the Desire of All Nations, and I will fill this temple with glory,' says the Lord of hosts. 'The silver is Mine, and the gold is Mine,' says the Lord of hosts. 'The glory of this latter temple shall be greater than the former,' says the Lord of hosts. 'And in this place I will give peace,' says the Lord of hosts."

Haggai's message stirred up the people to complete the rebuilding of the temple. He encouraged the people by assuring them that they would be successful, because the Lord was with them. Haggai preached during a period of four months in 520 B.C. The temple was completed in 516 B.C. when Darius the Mede was reigning over Persia. Ezra, the priest, was sent to Jerusalem in 458 B.C. He was well educated in the scriptures and taught the Law of Moses to the people who returned from Persia. The priests, singers and temple servants also returned to Jerusalem, and temple worship was restored in the seventh year of King Artaxerxes the king of Persia. Zechariah a priest and a prophet, prophesied to the people who were returning to Jerusalem at the end of the exile. Zechariah encouraged the people to return their hearts to the Lord. Zechariah made them realize that they deserved to be exiled, because they had turned away from the Lord God of Israel. Zechariah rekindled their belief in a Messiah Jesus Christ who would come and bring eternal peace to God's people.

Nehemiah

Ezra had led a group of the Jews back to Jerusalem around 458 B.C. to rebuild the temple and restore the worship of the Lord in the hope that the kingdom would be restored like it was in the time of David. Nehemiah led a group back to Jerusalem to rebuild the walls of the city of Jerusalem. The book of Nehemiah records the restoration of the walls. The great walls of a city were the city's best protection against their enemies. In the twentieth year of King Artaxerxes, there was a Jew named Nehemiah who was the cupbearer for the king. He had the responsibility of tasting the king's wine, a position of great trust. Nehemiah served King Artaxerxes during the period of 465-424 B.C. It was during this time that Nehemiah learned of the desolate state of Jerusalem.

Nehemiah asked King Artaxerxes for permission to go to Jerusalem to help rebuild the city and its walls, and the king agreed he could go. God's plan to preserve a remnant of the Jews for the birth of Christ was renewed in the Jews that returned from the exile. Nehemiah 2:1-6 "And it came to pass in the month of Nisan, in the twentieth year of King Artaxerxes, when wine was before him, that I took the wine and gave it to the king. Now I had never been sad in his presence before." The king said to me, "Why is your face sad, since you are not sick? This is nothing but sorrow of heart." So I became dreadfully afraid and said to the king, "May the king live forever! Why should my face not be sad, when the city the place of my father's tombs lie's waste, and its gates are burned with fire? Then the king said to me, "What do you request? So I prayed to the God of heaven. And I said to the king, "If it pleases the king, and if your servant has found favor in your sight, I ask that you send me to Judah, to the city of my father's tombs, that I may rebuild it." Then the king said to me (the queen also sitting beside him), "How long will your journey be?" "And when will you return?" So it pleased the king and I set him a time. The king gave Nehemiah permission to go back to Jerusalem. He also gave him lumber to rebuild the gates. When Nehemiah arrived in Jerusalem, he surveyed the damage to the walls. Then he went to the people and told them how God had blessed him in the king allowing him to go back to Jerusalem, and he told them what he had observed in surveying the walls. Then the people said, "Let us rise up and build." Then they set their hands to this good work. (Nehemiah 2:18)

Sanballat, an official in Samaria who had married into an Israelite family, wanted control of Judea and he was against the rebuilding of the walls of Jerusalem. When Sanballat heard that the Jews were rebuilding the walls, he tried to hinder the work. Nehemiah 4:1-3– When Sanballat heard about the Jews rebuilding the walls he was angry and he mocked the Jews. He spoke before his people and the army of Samaria, and said, "What are these feeble Jews doing? Will they fortify themselves?" will they offer sacrifices? Will they complete it in a day? Will they revive the stones from the heaps of rubbish- stones that are burned? Tobias the Ammonite was beside him, and he said, "Whatever they build, even if a fox goes up on it he will breakdown their stone wall.

Nehemiah made no reply to Sanballat, but he prayed to the Lord, "Hear, O our God, for we are despised turn their reproach on their own heads, and give them as plunder to a land of captivity! Do not cover their iniquity and do not let their sin be blotted out from before you; for they have provoked You to anger before the builders." So we built the wall, and the entire wall was joined together up to half its height, for the people had a mind to work." The Jews continued the work on the wall in spite of opposition from their enemies, and the wall was completed in 52 days. The people of the nations around Jerusalem were disheartened, because they realized that the Lord had helped Judah re-build the walls.

The Book of Daniel

Daniel and Ezekiel were among the young princes of Judah who were taken to Babylon in 605 B.C. before the exile of Judah. Both young men became prophets during the exile. Daniel prophesied about God's plan of redemption and wrote about his own life in Babylon around 530 B.C. Daniel recorded the events of the Babylonian captivity of God's people and about future events in history all the way to the end of time. Daniel was a talented young man and God gave Daniel the ability to prophesy and interpret dreams. Daniel prophesied about the future of God's people after they would leave Babylon because God revealed the future to him through dreams and the inspiration of the Holy Spirit.

The book of Daniel presents the history of the exiles from Judah during the seventy years they were in captivity until their return to Jerusalem. The people of Judah carried God's plan of redemption forward after their captivity. The theme of the book of Daniel is the sovereignty of God and His triumph over the kingdoms of men. The people of Judah became known as Jews while they were in Babylon. They were allowed to raise families as long as they didn't rebel against the Babylonian rulers. The Jews could not worship the way they did in the temple in Jerusalem, but they worshiped the Lord from their hearts, which is the way God always wanted His people to do. The Babylonians held Daniel in high esteem, because the Lord had given him special gifts of prophesying and the ability to interpret dreams.

The Lord spoke through Daniel about future events in history even events concerning the future spiritual kingdom of Christ in the first century. The Lord's plan was, that the Jews would return to Jerusalem, rebuild the walls of the city, build another temple, and serve Him in Jerusalem as they waited for the birth of the Messiah and His kingdom. The prophecies of Daniel and Jeremiah reinforced the faith and hope for God's people to return to Jerusalem. One night the king of Babylon King Nebuchadnezzar had a dream, and he was troubled by his dream and couldn't sleep because he did not understand the meaning of the dream. The king's astrologers, wise men, and magicians in the kingdom could not explain the king's dreams. Daniel was chief over the magicians, astrologers, Chaldeans and soothsayers, because God had blessed him with knowledge, understanding and wisdom plus the ability to interpret dreams, solve riddles and explain enigmas, so the king sent for Daniel and asked him if he could interpret his dreams.

Daniel told the king that he couldn't interpret his dreams, but his God could. That very night, the meaning of the king's dream was revealed to Daniel, and Daniel was able to interpret the king's dreams. Daniel praised God for revealing deep and mysterious things to him. Daniel understood that God controlled world events by deposing and establishing the kings he wanted on the throne, God gives wisdom to the wise. Daniel told the king what he dreamed, and then he explained the interpretation of the dream. In Nebuchadnezzar's dream he saw a huge statue of a man that frightened him. The head of the statue was made of gold, the chest and arms were silver, its belly and thighs were bronze, the legs were iron and the feet were a mixture of clay and iron. Daniel told the king that the head of gold represented the king of Babylon. Daniel told

Nebuchadnezzar that God is Sovereign over heaven and earth and that it was God who made the kings who rule over the earth.

Daniel said the kingdom of Babylon would be replaced by another kingdom. The chest and arms of silver in the dream represented that kingdom. Then a third kingdom, represented by a bronze belly and thighs, would replace the second kingdom. A fourth kingdom, represented by iron and miry clay, would replace the third kingdom, and it would crush all previous kingdoms and be strong like iron.

The kingdoms represented in the dream were kingdoms that would arise in this order after Babylon: the Medo-Persian Empire, the Greek Empire and the Roman Empire. The Roman Empire would be the last and most significant kingdom, because during the time of that empire Jesus the Son of God would be born in Bethlehem and become a sacrifice, providing redemption for sinners. From world history, we know that the king's dream proved that it was God that decided who would be King over the Babylonian, Persian, Greek and Roman Empires that existed in succession. The most important part of the interpretation of the dream was that during the time of the Roman Empire, Christ's kingdom, the church, would be established. In the days of the last kingdom in the dream, the God of heaven would set up a kingdom on earth, which shall never be destroyed. The kingdom of Christ the church is that kingdom and it will remain on earth until Jesus returns. The dream is certain, and its interpretation is sure. The Kingdom of the Son of God was established in the first century A.D. and has members all over the world at this time.

Belshazzar the King of Babylon

After the death of Nebuchadnezzar, his son Belshazzar became king over Babylon. Daniel 5:1-2 "Belshazzar the king made a great feast for a thousand of his lords, and drank wine in the presence of the thousand. While he tasted the wine, Belshazzar gave the command to bring the gold and silver vessels which, his father Nebuchadnezzar had taken from the temple which had been in Jerusalem that the king and his lords, his wives, and his concubines might drink from them." King Belshazzar insulted God when he and his guests drank wine from the gold and silver vessels that were taken from God's temple in Jerusalem.

God responded to Belshazzar's insult in this way. As the king and his guests were drinking from the gold and silver vessels in the great room where the feast was held, the fingers of a man's hand appeared on the wall and wrote a message to the king. "Then the king's countenance changed, and his thoughts troubled him, so that the joints of his hips were loosened and his knees knocked against each other." (Daniel 5:6) The king was afraid of God's power and he called for his wise men to explain the writing on the wall, but no one could explain what was meant by the message.

The queen told the king, "There is a man in your kingdom in whom is the Spirit of the Holy God." She said during the time that his father Nebuchadnezzar was king, Daniel interpreted, his dreams. So Daniel was brought before the king to explain the meaning of the writing on the wall. This is the inscription that was written: Mene, Mene, Tekel, Upharsin. This is the interpretation of each word. Mene: God has numbered your kingdom, and finished it; Tekel: You have been weighed in the balance and found wanting; Peres (singular for Up-Harsin): your kingdom has been divided, and given to the Medes and Persians." Then Belshazzar gave the command, to clothe Daniel with purple and put a chain of gold around his neck, and made a proclamation that he should be the third ruler in the kingdom.

The Jews in Babylon could raise families as long as they didn't rebel against the Babylonian rulers. The Jews could not worship the way they did in the temple in Jerusalem, but they worshiped the Lord in their hearts. Daniel and Ezekiel were among the young princes of Judah who were taken to Babylon in 605 B.C. before the exile of Judah. Both young men became prophets during the exile. Daniel prophesied about God's plan of redemption the time for the birth of Jesus the Son of God was drawing nearer and God through the Holy Spirit was using Daniel to prepare the descendants of Judah for the time of His birth and His Kingdom.

The Babylonians held Daniel in high esteem, because the Lord had given him special gifts of prophesying and interpreting dreams. The Lord spoke through Daniel about future events in history and events concerning the future spiritual kingdom of Christ. The Lord had determined that the Jews would return to Jerusalem, rebuild the walls of the city, build another temple, and serve Him in Jerusalem as they waited for the birth of the Messiah and His kingdom. The prophecies of Daniel and Jeremiah reinforced the faith and hope for God's people to return to Jerusalem. From history, we know that the king's dream proved that God was the one that decided who would be king over the Babylonian, Persian, Greek and Roman Empires that existed in succession.

The most important part of the interpretation of the dream, was that during the time of the Roman Empire, Jesus the Christ's kingdom, the church, would be established. God would set up a kingdom on earth, which would never be destroyed. The kingdom of Christ's the church would be established in the first Century A.D. and it was and it will remain on earth until the end of time. The men who saw Daniel praying reported him to the king and Daniel was thrown into the den of lions. Darius was the king at that time and he was concerned about Daniel so early the next morning he went to lion's den and called to Daniel and asked if his God had saved him. Daniel told the king God sent His angel to shut the mouth of the lions and he was not hurt because he was innocent. Daniel was released from the lion's den and Darius the King proclaimed that in every part of his kingdom people must accept Daniel's God.

Daniel fared well in the reign of King Darius and in the reign of Cyrus. In the 7th chapter of Daniel he had a vision from heaven of four beasts that represented four kingdoms that would reign on earth. God revealed the future history of great kingdoms that would exist before the kingdom of Christ. The fourth kingdom the Roman Empire, would control the people of the earth during the time Jesus was born. God gives Daniel an outline of world history leading up to the time for the kingdom of Jesus Christ.

Daniel 7:1-14– In Daniel's vision he saw four great beasts and he wrote down what he saw. The beasts represented kingdoms of men. After the four beasts, Daniel saw one like the Son of Man (Jesus) coming with the clouds of heaven! To Him was given dominion and glory and a kingdom where all peoples, nations, and languages should serve Him. His dominion would be an everlasting dominion, which shall not pass away, and His kingdom will be one, which shall not be destroyed. Daniel asked for an explanation of what he saw, and he was told the interpretation of the things he saw. The great beasts represented four kingdoms. He said: "The fourth beast shall be a fourth kingdom on earth, which shall be different from all other kingdoms, And shall devour the whole earth, Trample it and break it in pieces. The ten horns are ten kings who shall arise from this kingdom. And another shall arise after them; He shall be different from the first ones, and shall subdue three kings.

He shall speak pompous words against the Most High, Shall persecute the saints of the Most High, and shall intend to change times and law." Then the saints shall be given into his hand for a time times and half a time. The court shall be seated, and they shall take away his dominion, and the greatness of the kingdoms under the whole heaven shall be given to the people, the saints of the Most High. The church was dominated by the Roman Empire during the Empires rule. The kingdom of Christ is an everlasting kingdom, and all dominions shall serve and obey Him. Daniel's vision predicts that God's kingdom the Kingdom of Christ would be established during the time of the fourth kingdom the Roman Empire. (Revelation) The kingdom of Christ (church) would be a kingdom that would never be destroyed.

The four successive empires the beasts represented are: (1) the Babylonian Empire (lion) that exiled the kingdom of Judah, (2) the Persian Empire (bear) that allowed the people of Judah to return to Jerusalem and helped them in their efforts to restore their nation and their religion, (3) the Greek Empire (leopard) under the rule of Alexander the Great that conquered the world and spread Greek culture and the Greek language all over the world making communication among the peoples of the world possible, (4) the Roman Empire (the terrifying beast) allowed the Jews to live in the Roman Empire as long as they paid taxes to Rome. The reference to the four beasts are given to show how other nations would affect the lives of God's people throughout history and at the time Jesus was born. The three beasts (the Babylonian, Persian and Greek Empires) had already been stripped of their power when Daniel saw the slaying of the fourth beast, the Roman Empire. Daniel saw one like the son of man (Christ) and God gave Him authority, glory and Sovereign power over all peoples of the earth.

Christ is now in heaven at the right hand of God ruling over His kingdom the church, but He will return some day to glorify His people. At that time all of the kingdoms of this world will be destroyed, and God's people will inherit a new heaven and a new earth God prepared for them. Revelation 21 "Now I saw a new heaven and a new earth, for the first heaven and the first earth has passed away." The church on the earth, which is the kingdom of God, will at the end of time be given a new home somewhere in God's heavens.

The existing earth will be destroyed by fire at that time. The vision Daniel saw was prophetic, a prediction that the worldly empires would fall. The mighty empires are like pawns in the hands of God who can do as He wills with them. God's glorious kingdom will prevail over all kingdoms when Christ the King of Kings comes back to gather up His church and take it to the new heaven and earth, therefore the Kingdom of God shall never be destroyed. Today the church on earth represents the Kingdom of God. The battle for the hearts and souls of mankind is a spiritual battle that continues and will continue until Christ returns.

The account of God's redeeming plan in the Old Testament ends with the books of the two prophets Zechariah and Malachi. Zechariah wrote about the coming of Christ, His humanity, His rejection and His betrayal. He predicts Christ's crucifixion, His priesthood, and His kingship. The prophet Zechariah had a vision of a man on a red horse. Behind this man were red, brown and white horses. The horses were sent by the Lord on a mission throughout the earth to search out the condition of the people. The man on the red horse may have been the angel of the Lord, and the other horses may have represented angelic messengers who reported to the angel of the Lord. The messengers represented by the horses reported that the whole earth was at peace.

The angel asked the Lord how long he would withhold mercy from Jerusalem and Judah. The insinuation is that if the Lord was merciful and would soon return his people to Jerusalem. The people of Judah had been in exile for sixty-six years, but they would begin returning in four more years. The Lord said He would return to Jerusalem with mercy, and his house would be rebuilt. The people did return and rebuild the temple at the end of the seventy years of exile because of the influence the Lord had on King Cyrus of Persia. There were four different temples in the plan of redemption, Solomon's temple, Zerubbabel's temple built by the exiles, Herod's temple that was destroyed in 70 A.D. The fourth temple is the church, a spiritual temple still being, built by people obeying the gospel of Christ. The definition of the temple is a place on earth where the presence of God resides. Jesus said, "Destroy this temple, and I will raise it again in three days." Jesus was speaking of his body.

The Father lives in Jesus and Jesus lives in our hearts, and we are members of the kingdom of God which is the church on earth. The judgment of Israel's enemies was seen in the light of the coming of Christ, the Prince of Peace. Alexander spared the city of Jerusalem and the temple during his conquest. Zechariah 9:9-17 is about the Messiah King who would come with righteousness and salvation riding on a colt, the foal of a donkey. The fulfillment of this prophecy was announced when Christ triumphantly entered Jerusalem (Mt 21:1-5).

Christ's kingdom would be a universal kingdom of peace, a spiritual kingdom that is not of this world but will exist in the world. The kingdom of Jesus in within the hearts and minds of people of faith. Jesus told his disciples that they did not belong to the world even though he chose them out of the world (John 15:19). John 18: 36 "Jesus answered, "My kingdom is not of this world. If my kingdom were of this world, My servants would fight, so that I should not be delivered to the Jews; but now my kingdom is not from here." The kingdom of Christ is within believers, and Christ rules from heaven over their hearts. People of any nation can enter the kingdom of God and find peace with God there. The Kingdom of God, the Kingdom of Heaven, and the Kingdom of Christ are synonymous. The Law of Moses was replaced by the gospel of Christ, and God's people are those who have faith in Christ as the Savior and obey the gospel of Christ written in the New Testament. The church is a spiritual temple that replaced the temple built by men.

Book of Malachi (400 B.C.)

The Hebrew word Malachi means 'My messenger,' and it describes the function of the prophet rather than his name. The one who wrote the book was a messenger of the Lord, and it was written to a people who had become skeptical of the Lord's promise to send the Messiah to them. Malachi is the last of the written prophets until the time of John the Baptist in the first century A.D. The date of the writing of Malachi was around 420 to 400 B.C. After the Jews returned from the Babylonian captivity there was prophetic silence until John the Baptist began his ministry in the first century A.D. The people of Judah had the Old Testament scriptures but they were in a state of sin and apostasy.

The priests were ignoring the written word of God. The ministries of Zechariah and Malachi focused on bringing the people back to the Lord. In Malachi, chapter one, the Lord denounces the Jews, His beloved people, because the priests were corrupt and offering polluted sacrifices. The people were guilty of infidelity to God. The descendants of a faithful remnant of God's people still remained in the first century and they were the people through whom Christ would be born.

Malachi 3:1-4 states that the Lord promised to send his messenger to prepare the way for the Messiah of Israel and the redeemer of all people of faith. The Messiah would be a descendant of David and would inherit his throne. Throughout the years following King David's reign, the days of the Kingdom of Heaven had been advancing; they had been drawing nearer and nearer to being fulfilled. When the messenger came, the Messiah whom the Jews were seeking. He would come to cleanse and bring judgment on earth. John the Baptist was the messenger who came before Jesus to prepare the way for Jesus Christ the Messiah to begin His ministry. John was sent first to get the people ready to welcome the Messiah. He was preaching in the wilderness and baptizing people preparing them to receive Jesus by convicting them of sin. John warned people to repent and be baptized to cleanse them of their sins. When Jesus first came to John in the wilderness, Jesus told the crowd that John was the messenger sent by the Lord.

Luke 1:78-79 "Because of the tender mercy of our God, by which the rising sun will come to us from heaven to shine on those living in darkness and in the shadow of death, to guide our feet into the path of peace." The rising sun symbolizes the Messiah (Jesus Christ) who God was sending to bring peace to those who were separated from the fellowship of God because of sin. The sacrifice of Christ made it possible for people with faith to have peace with God and redemption for those who were guilty of sin.

Malachi 4:2 The Sun of Righteousness shall arise with healing in his wing. Christ is the 'Sun of Righteousness' who came to provide salvation for all people of faith. There was a period of approximately 400 years after Malachi's ministry before John the Baptist, the first New Testament prophet, was born.

Jesus was born soon after the birth of John. When both Jesus and John were grown, John began his ministry first in order to prepare the way for Jesus' ministry. Jesus began His ministry around 30 to 35 A.D. Judea the land where the Jews settled was Hellenistic and the people spoke the Greek language in their political, social and religious life. The Jews were allowed to live in Jerusalem and worship in the temple, but there were many who lived a distance from Jerusalem worshiped in the synagogue a Jewish house of worship and at least once a year, they went to the Jewish temple in Jerusalem to worship and observe the Jewish feasts. When Alexander died, his empire was divided between four generals of his army.

The Herod family had earlier been converted to Judaism. Herod the Great was born in 72 B.C. and He was the Herod on the throne that ruled in Judea at the time of Jesus' birth. Herod later ordered the slaughter of the male children in Bethlehem in order to procure the death of the infant Jesus. Herod was the name of a family from Idumaea that ruled in Palestine from 40 B.C. to about A.D. 100. The Romans appointed the Herod's kings of Judea. There were several Herod's that ruled in line and had authority over Judea where the Jews lived. Archelaus was the next Herod after the death of Herod the Great, but the Romans removed him from the throne after ten years.

Herod Antipas was on the throne in Galilee during the time of John the Baptist. Herod Antipas was the king that had John the Baptist beheaded and opposed Jesus. The territory of Judea included Galilee, Samaria and Judea and the cities and towns within them. Jerusalem and Bethlehem were in Judea. Judea ranged from the Sea of Galilee in the north to the Dead Sea all the way to Zoar. The Jordan River flowed from the Sea of Galilee to the Dead Sea. Judea prospered under the reign of Herod Antipas and he increased trade and built fortresses, aqueducts, and theaters. Herod began the rebuilding of the Temple and acted as protector and spokesman for various Jewish communities scattered about the world. In the age when the existence of the smaller states depended on the will of Rome, Herod kept Judea safe, secure, and prosperous. The four gospels of the Bible, Matthew, Mark, Luke and John, all give an account of the history of the birth of Jesus and His ministry, life, death, and resurrection.

The Jewish people were a small nation subject to the laws of the Roman Empire as well as Jewish law. God appointed the time to send His Son to earth and he sent John the Baptist first.

"I will send my prophet, and he will prepare the way before me." This was God's promise to send John the Baptist to prepare the way for Jesus. John the Baptist came in the first century A.D. and he lived in the wilderness area of the Jordan River. Christ was born in Bethlehem of Judea during Herod's reign in the first century A.D.

Jesus of Nazareth

This is the story of Jesus of Nazareth the Son of God, His life and ministry but not everything Jesus said or did. I have attempted to present the events of the story of Jesus' life in the order in which they occurred in the scriptures, and I do not claim my listing of events to be in exact chronological order due to the difficulty of following the writings of four different authors telling the story in their own order and style. Matthew, Mark, Luke and John each give an account of the life and ministry of Jesus. Jesus came through the birth line of David. He was the Messiah of the Jews that God had promised. He would become the Savior and redeemer of all people who would have faith in Him. Jesus is the Redeemer God promised to send soon after the creation. Jesus Christ is the Jewish Messiah, the Anointed of God.

Malachi was the last of the Old Testament prophets, and he prophesied about the coming of John the Baptist who would come ahead of Jesus to prepare the minds of the people to accept Jesus as the Messiah. Chapter 3–I send My messenger and he prepares the way. The Lord you are waiting for He will come suddenly. Malachi– But for you who revere my name, the sun of righteousness will rise with healing in His wings." (V 4-6) Remember the Law of Moses, My servant, which I commanded Him for all Israel, with the statutes and judgments, behold I will send you Elijah the prophet before the coming of the great and dreadful day of the Lord. And he will turn the hearts of the fathers to the children, and the hearts of the children to their fathers, lest I come and strike the earth with a curse."

Malachi 3:1-4 states that the Lord promised to send his messenger to prepare the way for Jesus Christ. The messenger was John the Baptist who would come with power like the prophet Elijah to prepare the way for Christ. John was called the Baptist because he was sent to baptize the people who were willing to repent of their sins and accept Jesus as the Messiah. Jesus was a descendant of King David, and He was born to be a King in the line of David, and the Sun of Righteousness. Jesus' kingdom is a spiritual kingdom. Throughout the years following King David's reign, the days of the Kingdom God promised had been drawing nearer and nearer each year to being fulfilled.

Jesus the Jewish Messiah, was coming to bring judgment against sinners and a way of redemption for the guilt of sin. The coming of Jesus fulfilled the promises of God from the time of Adam and Eve in the Garden of Eden to the end of time. In the first century A.D. the Jewish people, a small nation, was under the power of the Roman Empire and was subject to Roman law. The people were allowed to have their own king, but the king was appointed or approved by the Romans who had power over them. In 37 BC, Herod Antipater governed the Jews by the authority of the Roman Empire. The Jewish people were obligated in their religion to continue to keep the Law of Moses until the Messiah came. Most Jews lived in Palestine, Judea, Galilee and Samaria at the time Jesus was born.

Under the rule of the Romans, the Jews had religious identity and some freedom under the leadership of their priests. The high priest served as a magistrate. The Jews were allowed to keep their temple in Jerusalem for religious purposes, and they followed, to some extent, a corrupted view of the Law of Moses. There were two Jewish religious parties who had different views about obeying the Law of Moses. The religious parties were the Pharisees and the Sadducees. They were united in the decision to reject Jesus as the Messiah and conspired to put Him to death. The Pharisees were a major religious party from the second century BC to the second century AD. The Pharisees were middle class and in touch with the common people, and they accepted the written word to be inspired by God. They believed in the resurrection and an afterlife. They also believed in an appropriate punishment or reward based on the individual.

The Sadducees were an upper class group of Jews who were wealthy and influential and were more concerned with politics than religion. The Sadducees denied life after death, the resurrection and the existence of the spiritual world including angels and demons. The scribes were writers, copyists and the interpreters of the Law. The scribes served as priests and teachers of the Law and were usually associated with the Pharisees. Some scribes became members of the Sanhedrin, a legal administrative body in the Jewish population. The Scribes were professional students of the Law of Moses and its defenders.

Jesus the Son of God

God's Son Jesus the promised redeemer came to earth born to a virgin woman by the seed of God – making Him both God and human. He lived on earth as the Son of God in a human form and died as the Son of God in human form, thereby becoming a sacrifice for our sin. Jesus lived approximately 33 years on earth. The story of Jesus' birth, ministry, death, burial and resurrection is in Matthew, Mark, Luke and John. The Bible tells the story of Jesus of Nazareth and His life and ministry. During the time before and after the first century A.D, the Jewish people were allowed to maintain their temple in Jerusalem and practice their religion based on the Law of Moses.

The Jewish temple in Jerusalem was the focal point of Jewish religion, but there were also other meeting places of worship called synagogues scattered throughout the land in places that were a distance from Jerusalem. The people who lived a distance from Jerusalem could go to the Synagogue to worship God on the Sabbath day. Once a year they would all go to the temple in Jerusalem to worship. The temple in Jerusalem was a focal point for Jesus ministry. There was still a remnant of faithful God-fearing Jews on earth who had been patiently waiting for the Messiah but the religion of the Jews had become corrupted and divided.

Jesus was born in Bethlehem a few months after the birth of John. At the time of Jesus birth, Herod the Great was on the throne in Judea. Most of the story of Jesus in the New Testament took place in Galilee. Joseph and Mary lived in Nazareth of Galilee. Jesus was a descendant of King David, and He left heaven and was born on earth to become a spiritual King in the line of David over a spiritual kingdom.

Throughout the years following King David's reign, the time of the Kingdom of Christ had been drawing nearer and nearer to being fulfilled each year. When the messenger John the Baptist came in the first century the Messiah whom the Jews were seeking was born to bring judgment against sinners and provide a way for those who would have faith in Him to be redeemed from the guilt of sin. John the Baptist was the messenger that Malachi prophesied would come to prepare the way for Christ.

John preached about Jesus and he baptized the people who were willing to repent of their sins and accept Jesus as the Son of God and their redeemer. John was born approximately 400 years after the prophet Malachi's ministry. John the Baptist and Christ were both born during the reign of Herod in the first century A.D. John was born first and his ministry preceded Jesus, because he was to prepare the way for Jesus, the Messiah. John was called the Baptist, because he baptized people. Baptism is an immersion of a person in water sometimes called a burial because the sin of the baptized person is dead and was removed, by Jesus sacrifice for sin.

The parents of John the Baptist, Zacharias and Elizabeth, were chosen by the Lord. They were righteous people who obeyed all the commandments and ordinances of the Lord. John's birth was miraculous because Elizabeth was very old and beyond the age to conceive. Zacharias and Elizabeth lived in the hill country of Hebron. They were Levites, and Zacharias was a priest who served in the temple at Jerusalem. His duty was to burn incense in the Holy Place in the temple. Zacharias had been praying for a son for a long time. Around the first century A.D. it became

Zacharias' turn to offer the incense. He was an old man and had waited a long time to take a turn at burning the incense in the Holy Place, so Zacharias and Elizabeth went to Jerusalem for Zacharias to fulfill his priestly duty.

He was alone in the Holy Place when an angel of the Lord appeared to him standing on the right side of the altar of incense. The sight of the angel frightened Zacharias, but the angel told him not to be afraid. The angel told him his prayer had been heard. His wife was to have a son, and they were to call him John.

Luke 1:15-17 "For he will be great in the sight of the lord, and shall drink neither wine nor strong drink. He will also be filled with the Holy Spirit, even from his mother's womb. And he will turn many of the children of Israel to the Lord their God. He will go before Him in the spirit and power of Elijah, 'to turn the hearts of the fathers to the children,' and the disobedient to the wisdom of the just, to make ready a people prepared for the Lord."

The Lord answered Zacharias' prayer but Zacharias wanted to see a sign for proof since his wife was barren. Gabriel told Zacharias what the sign would be. He would not be able to speak again until the child was born. When Zacharias came out of the temple, the people waiting outside decided that Zacharias could not speak because he had seen a vision while he was in the temple. When Zacharias completed his days of service in the temple, he and Elizabeth left Jerusalem and went back to their home in the hill country. Sometime later Elizabeth became pregnant and she hid herself saying that God had taken away her reproach among women. It was a shameful thing among the people of Israel if a woman could not conceive.

Elizabeth gave birth to her son, and on the eighth day they circumcised him. Zacharias was still unable to talk. They wanted to call the child Zacharias after his father, but Zacharias asked for a writing tablet and he wrote, "His name is John." When he wrote the name for the baby, Zacharias was filled with the Holy Spirit and was able to speak, and he praised God. Zacharias praised God. Zacharias realized that God was fulfilling His promise to raise up a savior from the line of David to fulfill the promise made to Abraham to bless all people through God's Own seed. Zacharias, being filled with the Holy Spirit, prophesied about a horn of salvation from the house of David. The Holy Spirit was speaking of Mary's child Jesus, and prophesying that He is the one the prophets spoke of and the descendant that God promised to Abraham saying that He would bless all people through Him.

Mary's son Jesus would be the Messiah whom the Jews had been waiting for since the time of the prophets. Elizabeth and Zacharias' son, John, was a prophet of God who would prepare the way for Jesus. John was called the Baptist because he baptized people. John lived by himself in the wilderness area near the Jordan River, and he was strong in the Holy Spirit.

The Birth of Christ

Six months after Elizabeth became pregnant with John the Baptist, God sent the angel Gabriel to Nazareth in Galilee to a Virgin named Mary. The angel Gabriel announced that Mary was to have a son. Mary wasn't married, but she was betrothed to a young man named Joseph who was in the birth line of Jesus. Gabriel told Mary she was to call her baby boy Jesus. Gabriel said her son would be great and would be the Son of God, he would be given the throne of David and reign forever; there would be no end of His kingdom. Jesus was born to fulfill God's promise to send a savior to redeem people from the guilt of sin, adding them to the kingdom of Christ.

The kingdom would be recognized after the death, burial and resurrection of Jesus. Mary was confused, how could a virgin give birth. Gabriel told her that the Holy Spirit would come upon her and she would conceive. Mary believed the Holy Spirit and she said, "Behold the maidservant of the Lord! Let it be to me according to your word." Mary chose to become the mother of the Son of God by the Seed of God. Gabriel also informed Mary that her cousin, Elizabeth, was going to have a child in her old age, so Mary went to the hill country to see Elizabeth and tell her what the angel said.

Mary was betrothed to Joseph and at that time betrothed was the same as being legally married even though they had not yet come together as husband and wife. When Joseph learned that Mary was pregnant before they were married he wanted to dissolve the marriage contract secretly. Normally a man would publicly put away a woman under these circumstances, but Joseph was a good man and did not want to expose Mary publicly. While Joseph was thinking about what to do, an angel from heaven appeared to him and explained that Mary was pregnant with the Son of God. The angel said "Joseph, son of David, do not be afraid to take to you Mary your wife, for that which is conceived in her is of the Holy Spirit. And she will bring forth a Son, and you shall call His name Jesus, for He will save His people from their sins." "So all this was done that it might be fulfilled, which was spoken by the Lord through the prophet saying: "Behold, the virgin shall be with child, and bear a Son, and they shall call His name Immanuel." Which is translated, "God with us."(Matt. 1:19-23)

Joseph took Mary as his legal wife, but they did not consummate the marriage until after the birth of their Son Jesus. The name Jesus is a transliteration of the name Joshua and means 'Jehovah is salvation.' Jesus grew up in Nazareth, which was a very small village in Galilee. Joseph and Mary lived in Nazareth after their betrothal. Joseph was a carpenter in Nazareth. While Mary was pregnant, she went into the hill country to the house of Zacharias to see Elizabeth before Elizabeth's son was born. When Mary saw Elizabeth, she greeted her, and when Elizabeth heard the greeting of Mary, the baby leaped in her womb, and Elizabeth was filled with the Holy Spirit. Elizabeth spoke with a loud voice and said, "Blessed are you among women, and blessed is the fruit of your womb! But why is this granted to me, that the mother of my Lord should come to me?" For indeed as soon as the voice of your greeting sounded in my ears, the babe leaped in my womb for joy. Blessed is she who believed, for there will be a fulfillment of those things which were told her from the Lord."

Mary and Elizabeth talked about their sons, and Mary magnified the Lord by singing a song about the Lord and what He had done for her. Mary cited scripture from the prophecies of the Old Testament, including an understanding of the seed of Abraham. Mary's son was to be the Seed of God and Her Son would be a blessing to all people. Mary remained with Elizabeth about three months and then went home to Nazareth. Before Jesus was born, the Roman Emperor Caesar Augustus issued a decree for a census to be taken in the entire Roman world. Everyone was ordered to go to his own hometown to register, so Joseph, being a descendant of David, had to go to Bethlehem, the city of David.

Mary was pregnant, but she went with Joseph to Bethlehem in Judea to be registered in the census. While Mary and Joseph were in Bethlehem, the time came for her baby to be born. There were no unoccupied rooms in the local inn, so Joseph and Mary had to stay in a stall where they kept cattle. Mary gave birth to her baby boy, wrapped Him in swaddling cloths, and laid Him in a manger a crib used to feed cattle. In Bible times the crib was a ledge or projection at the end of the stall where hay or other food was placed.

Travelers with animals would use the stalls to feed their animals by placing food there. Bethlehem was situated in an area surrounded by fields where shepherds brought their flocks. The shepherds stayed in the fields at night and watched over their flocks. On the night Jesus was born, the shepherds were watching over their flocks when an angel of the Lord came and stood before them. The glory of the Lord shone around them and frightened them. The expression 'the shepherds were surrounded by the glory of the Lord' probably makes reference to a bright light shining around them as the angel spoke of the birth of God's Son.

The angel told the shepherds to not be afraid because he brought them good news that was joyful. The people of Israel, including the shepherds, had been waiting many years for the Messiah to come they knew what the scriptures revealed. The angel announced that the Savior (Messiah) had been born that very day in Bethlehem. Luke 2:12-14–And this will be the sign to you: you will find a Babe wrapped in swaddling clothes, lying in a manger." Suddenly there was with the angel a multitude of the heavenly host praising God and saying: "Glory to God in the highest, And on earth peace, Good will toward men!" Then the angels left and returned to heaven, and the shepherds went to Bethlehem to see the baby Jesus. When the shepherds came to Bethlehem they found Joseph and Mary and the baby Jesus and they went out and told others about the birth of the Messiah. The shepherds then returned to the fields glorifying and praising God. (The prophets had foretold the birth of the Son of God many years before Jesus' birth.)

Wise men from the east came to Jerusalem to visit with baby Jesus who was to be the king of the Jews. The Greek word for wise men is magi referring to astrologers. The wise men had been searching the stars for many years for the sign of the Messiah's birth and they knew He would be born in the vicinity of Jerusalem. At the time of His birth a certain star would be the sign of His birth, and the child was to become the King of the Jews. The people did not know Jesus would be a spiritual king over a spiritual kingdom and when the wise men said they were looking for the sign of the King of the Jews, Herod was troubled. He knew about the prophecies of the coming of the Jewish Messiah.

So he gathered some of the religious leaders of the Jews together and questioned them about where the Messiah was to be born. Herod was told that Jesus would be born in Bethlehem of Judea quoting the words of the prophet Micah in 5:2 "But you, Bethlehem Ephrathah, Though you are little among the thousands of Judah, yet out of you shall come forth to Me The One to be Ruler in Israel, whose going forth are from of old, From everlasting." Herod asked the wise men what time the star had appeared. Then he sent the men to Bethlehem to search for and find the Christ child, because he planned to kill Him.

The wise men from the east saw a bright star in the sky and followed it to the place where Jesus was. The men went into the house and saw the baby with Mary. They worshiped Him and gave Him gifts they had brought with them. Before they left, they were warned in a dream not to return to Herod, because he was looking for the Christ child so he could kill Him. The wise men left and went home a different way. When Herod learned the wise men had deceived him, he became very angry and ordered all the male children in Bethlehem who were two years of age and younger to be put to death. An angel of God came to Joseph in a dream and told him to take Mary and the baby Jesus and go to Egypt instead of going home to Nazareth. The angel said to stay in Egypt until he was told that it was safe to go home. Joseph and his family went to Egypt and remained there until Herod died. When Joseph heard that Herod had died, he Mary and baby Jesus left Egypt and went back to Nazareth, a town in the region of Galilee.

When the baby was eight days old, they circumcised him and named him Jesus. After Mary's days of purification according to the Jewish law was completed, they took Jesus to the temple in Jerusalem. There was an old man in Jerusalem named Simeon, a devout man who had been waiting for the consolation of Israel by the Messiah for many years. Simeon described the birth of Jesus as God's salvation that was for all people and as a Light to reveal acceptance and salvation of the Gentiles. Jesus Christ, came to provide salvation for all people. Mary, Joseph and Jesus were descendants of the Jewish people in the birth line of King David.

The Jewish people regularly observed several feasts in accordance with their religion. The feasts acknowledged God as the One who provided for His chosen people. The Feast of Unleavened bread, also called the Passover Feast, commemorated their deliverance from bondage in Egypt. The Feast of Weeks, called the Feast of Harvest and the day of first fruits was later called the feast of Pentecost. The Feast of Tabernacles or Feast of Booths was also called the Feast of Ingathering. The Sabbath was regarded as a feast and was called a Sabbath of rest. There is no record in the Bible of the early years of Jesus life with His parents in Nazareth. Joseph and Mary did everything that was required by Jewish law after Jesus was born. Then they returned to their home in Nazareth, and Jesus lived with his parents until He was twelve years old.

Near the beginning of His thirteenth year Jesus went with His parents to the temple in Jerusalem for the Passover Feast. They went with a large group of people from Nazareth. Joseph and Mary left Jerusalem after the Passover and were on their way back to Nazareth when they discovered that Jesus was not among the people returning with them. Joseph and Mary went back to Jerusalem to search for Jesus, and after three days they found Him sitting in the temple court listening to the teachers and asking them questions. Joseph and Mary didn't know what to think of Jesus being among the teachers of the Law. Mary scolded Him telling Him she had been worried. She asked Him why He treated them that way. Jesus must have known by that time that He was the Messiah, and He answered, "Didn't you know I had to be in My Fathers house?" Joseph and Mary knew Jesus was a special child given to them by God, but at that time they did not realize that He was the Messiah. According to Jewish law, a male becomes an adult at the end of his twelfth year. Jesus lived with His family and became strong in Spirit and increased in wisdom.

John the Baptist began his ministry and people went to the wilderness to hear John preach. John was baptizing many people that came to him. Jesus was also baptized and as He was praying, the Holy Spirit of God descended on Him in the form of a dove and the voice of God from heaven said to Him "You are My beloved Son; in whom I am well pleased. The time had come for Jesus to begin His ministry when He was about thirty years old. After his baptism Jesus returned to His home in Nazareth.

The people in the Synagogue in His hometown of Nazareth rejected Jesus claim to be the Messiah sent by God, so He went to Capernaum in Galilee. Jesus was aware that the Holy Spirit was with Him. Jesus ministry would last around three years, then He would be crucified, becoming the long awaited Messiah of Israel and the Savior of all people who would have faith in Him. The mission of Jesus was to come to as the Son of God, teach the good news (gospel), then die on the cross to redeem people of faith.

Jesus is now with His Father in heaven waiting to return at the end of time and claim those who belong to Him, and take them to heaven to a place prepared for them. John said Jesus did many other things that were not written in the gospels, but the things that are written were written to produce faith in Him. The Bible is available to most if not all of the people in the world and people can acquire faith in Jesus from what has been written about Jesus life on earth and His ministry that is recoded in the New Testament. One of Jesus disciples John wrote the gospel of John and by the inspiration of the Holy Spirit, he wrote about how to find eternal life in Jesus. John identifies Jesus as the Word that was with God in the beginning. All of the words in the Old Testament looked forward to the birth of Jesus.

John establishes the divinity of Christ and declares that Jesus was with God in the creation. John wrote that the evidence of Christ had been revealed, but many people still did not understand that Jesus was God's Son. God chose to send his Son into the world as the son of man so that He could experience life as a human being, and experience the same weakness and temptations that other people experience. The gospel writers Matthew, Mark, Luke and John all wrote a record of Jesus life and ministry including His death burial and resurrection.

The first chapter of John's gospel records a preamble of the story of the life and ministry of Christ so that people could believe, have faith in Christ and become children of God. John 1:1-14– "In the beginning was the Word, and the Word was with God and the word was God. He was in the beginning with God." All things were made through Him, and without Him nothing was made, that was made.

In Him was life, and the life was the light of men. And the light shines in the darkness, and the darkness did not comprehend it."–There was a man sent from God, whose name was John. This man came for a witness, to bear witness of the Light (Jesus) that all through Him might believe. John was not that Light, but was sent to bear witness of that Light. Verse 9-11–"That was the true Light that gives light to every man coming into the world. He was in the world, and the world was made through Him, and the world did not know Him. He came to His own, and His own did not receive Him."

Verse 12–"But as many as received Him, to them He gave the right to become children of God, to those who believe in His name." Verse 14–"And the word became flesh and dwelt among us, and we beheld His glory, the glory as of the only begotten of the Father, full of grace and truth." Before Jesus began His ministry John who was called the Baptist was sent to tell people Jesus was the Messiah and they needed to prepare their hearts to receive Him by confessing their faith in Jesus and being baptized. John called Jesus the light, because Jesus came to reveal the knowledge of the righteous plan of God to redeem those who are guilty of sin. Jesus is the true Light who gives light, the knowledge of salvation to the world. Jesus was rejected by many of His own people, and the Jewish nation rejected. However many individual people accepted Him, obeyed him and became children of God, born of God through faith in Christ. Jesus lived among the people of the earth for approximately 33 years and taught grace and truth. John called Jesus the Word because Jesus taught the good news of redemption from sin.

John the Baptist begins Teaching and Baptizing

According to the prophet Malachi, God promised to send a messenger to prepare the way for Jesus. John the Baptist was that messenger. With the birth of John the Baptist the first part of God's redeeming plan was taking place. John was filled with the Holy Spirit of God at an early age, and he knew he was the prophet, sent by the Lord to prepare the minds of the Jews to accept Jesus as the Messiah.

MT 3–John was about thirty years old when he began to preach in the desert area of Judea near the Jordan River and baptizing people. John preached a baptism of repentance for the remission of sin. He lived by himself and he wore clothing made from camel's hair and ate locusts and wild honey. John told people to repent, because the Kingdom of God was coming to the earth. The kingdom of God came first in the person of Jesus and was formally established on earth after the death of Jesus. The Kingdom would consist of all the people who would accept Christ as God's Son and obey the gospel message of Jesus Christ. Gospel means good news and it refers to the good news of redemption through faith in Christ. Repentance means a sincere confession to God from the mind and heart that you are a sinner, and a commitment to turn away from a life of sin and obey the gospel of Christ. Baptism means to immerse, and when a person was baptized by John, Jesus or His disciples they were immersed in water. Baptism and repentance are acts of faith that demonstrate a person's belief in Christ and a conviction to serve Him and God. The Jewish people who believed in God had been waiting a long time for Christ the Messiah but they had to be convinced that Jesus was the Messiah. Some of the people thought John was the Messiah, but John told them that he was not the Messiah but was sent to baptize people with water in preparation for the Messiah before He was ready to begin His ministry. He told those who came to him for baptism to bear fruit, which meant to obey the teachings Christ who was coming after him and live to remain faithful to Jesus for the rest of their life.

Jewish people came from Jerusalem and the whole area of the Jordan, and they confessed their sins and John baptized them. Those who believed in Jesus and were baptized by John would become members of the kingdom of Christ and they would be formally introduced after Jesus death. Many of the religious teachers, the scribes and Pharisees came to hear John. When he saw them coming, he called them a brood of vipers and asked them, "Who told you to turn away from the wrath of God that is coming?" John was angry with them because they were living in sin. John told the people that one mightier than he was coming. John spoke of Jesus, and he told them Jesus would baptize them with the Holy Spirit and with fire.

The word baptism also means to be overwhelmed. In the act of water baptism a person is overwhelmed by water, when they are plunged beneath the water. Baptized with the Holy Spirit would mean to be filled with the help of the Holy Spirit, the Holy Spirit would be given to them in a measure to help them in a spiritual way. Baptized with fire means to be overwhelmed with persecution and suffering, those who obeyed Jesus would be persecuted by unbelievers. All people receive, the Holy Spirit after water baptism. Some people in the first century received great power from the Holy Spirit to do miraculous things in the name of Christ. The Jews sent some officials of the people to ask John the Baptist who He was? John had stirred a lot of interest with his teaching and baptizing. They probably wanted to find out if he was the Messiah. John emphatically said he was not the Christ (Messiah). They asked if he was Elijah or one of the other prophets. John told them he was someone crying in the wilderness. John was in a wilderness area. John was lifting up his voice declaring the word of God.

Jesus Baptism

(MT 3) At the age of thirty Jesus, prepared for His ministry by going to the Jordan River where John was teaching people about the Kingdom of God and baptizing them. When John saw Jesus coming to be baptized, he recognized Jesus immediately as the Messiah, and he said, "Behold the Lamb of God who takes away the sin of the world." John baptized Jesus, and as Jesus was arising from the water the heavens divided and the Holy Spirit came down in the form of a dove and sat on Jesus. Then a voice came from heaven said, "You are My beloved Son in whom I am well pleased." Mark 3:9-11 John 1:32-34 "And John bore witness, saying, "I saw the Spirit descending from heaven like a dove, and He remained on Him. I did not know Him, but He who sent me to baptize with water said to me, 'Upon whom you see the Spirit descending and remaining on Him, this is He who baptizes with the Holy Spirit.' And I have seen and testified that this is the Son of God." Jesus was sinless but he submitted to baptism as an example to show that baptism was a part of God's righteous plan for people to be redeemed. Jesus was both human and divine and He submitted to baptism as a human to fulfill all righteousness.

While Jesus was on earth in the flesh, He looked, felt and acted like any person. Jesus could be tempted as a man, so He understood the weakness of the flesh allowing Him to practice compassion, love and mercy for those who were sinners. When Jesus first came from Galilee to be baptized, John did not want to baptize Him, because he knew Jesus was the Messiah and He was righteous. Jesus told John to baptize Him to fulfill all righteousness, so John Baptized Jesus in the Jordan River. Baptism is a righteous act of faith and a way to demonstrate a person's faith. John called Jesus a lamb metaphorically because He was an innocent person with no sin, who had a meek and gentle attitude. Jesus would offer no resistance later when He was taken before the authorities and crucified, like a lamb led to be slaughtered.

Jesus Tempted by Satan

Matt. 4–After His baptism, the Holy Spirit led Jesus into the wilderness of the Judean desert to be tempted by the Devil. Jesus fasted for forty days before He was tempted. The Devil tempted Jesus by telling Him to perform a miracle and turn the stones into bread to satisfy His hunger. Jesus had the power to turn stones into bread, but He told the devil that life is not sustained by bread alone but by living and obeying the word of God. Jesus said "It is written, 'Man shall not live by bread alone, but by every word of God." Jesus had faith that God would sustain Him. Satan attempted to make Jesus disobey God's commandments by offering Him power and riches, telling Jesus he would give Him all the kingdoms of the world if He would worship him, but Jesus said, "Get behind Me, Satan! For it is written, 'You shall worship the Lord your God and Him only you shall serve." Jesus taught that people should not deliberately tempt God. Everything Satan asked Jesus to do was against the will of God but Jesus would not disobey His Father.

Satan tried again to tempt Jesus to prove that God would protect Him. He said go up to the highest part of the temple and jump off. A fall from that height would kill or seriously maim anyone. Satan told Jesus the angels would save him from harm. Jesus didn't doubt that the angels would save Him, but He would not deliberately tempt God.

Jesus refused and said, "It has been said, 'You shall not tempt the Lord your God." Jesus' mission was to prove that He was the Messiah that that God promised to send in the beginning of time to save people from the guilt of sin. Jesus performed many miracles recorded in the gospels to prove who He was. Jesus willingly submitted to being sacrificed on a cross for the sins of the world. He voluntarily submitted to those who accused Him and crucified Him in order to, obey God and save people from their guilt of sin. He went with His accusers without fighting or offering resistance in order to please His Father in heaven and because of His love for people.

Jesus Begins His Ministry

MT 4–During the course of His ministry, Jesus went through the land of Galilee teaching in the synagogues, preaching the good news of the kingdom and healing people of all kinds of disease. His fame spread throughout Syria, and He healed sick people of various diseases, cast out demons, cured epilepsy and paralytics. A great many people followed Him from Galilee to Jerusalem, and Judea and beyond the Jordan River. Jesus selected 12 men who were, His disciples to travel with Him. These twelve men were later called apostles. The apostles would accompany Jesus during His ministry and then would continue to teach the gospel after Jesus death. The men chosen by Jesus would eventually, become leaders in the establishment of the church. They were all ordinary men. Peter, Andrew, James and John were fishermen who fished for a living. Matthew was a tax collector. The men had different personalities that varied from impulsive, passionate, thoughtful and pessimistic, and all but one would remain faithful to Jesus.

A disciple is a follower of a person or idea; one who follows their teacher. Jesus Apostle's would be sent to teach people about Jesus during His ministry and after Jesus death, the apostles would continue to teach about Jesus and the plan of redemption. The apostles would establish the kingdom of Christ and invite all people to become members. In the book of (John-1) Jesus chose Peter, Andrew and Philip. (MT-4) James and John. (MK-3) Bartholomew and Thomas Matthew, James the son of Alphaeus, Thaddeus, Simon the Canaanite and Judas Iscariot who betrayed Him.

When Jesus heard that John the Baptist had been put in prison, He left Galilee and went to Capernaum on the shore of the Sea of Galilee. Matthew's account says as Jesus walked by the Sea of Galilee, He saw Peter and Andrew casting a net into the Sea. Matthew 4:19 "Then He said to them, follow Me, and I will make you fishers of men." Peter and Andrew left their nets and followed Jesus. The next day Jesus met Philip and told Philip to follow Him. Jesus saw James and John, the sons of Zebedee, in their boat with their father. Jesus called to them, and they left their boat and followed Him.

Following Jesus means to accept Jesus as the Messiah sent by God. Philip began following Jesus and he found Nathanael and told him that Jesus was the one spoken of by Moses and the prophets and Nathanael joined them. Nathanael said he knew Jesus was the Son of God, the King of Israel. John 1:50-51 "Jesus answered and said to him, because I said to you, 'I saw you under the fig tree,' do you believe? You will see greater things than these." And He said to him, "Most assuredly, I say to you, hereafter you shall see heaven open, and the angels of God ascending and descending upon the Son of Man."

Jesus Family in Capernaum

(JN 4) Jesus family left Nazareth and went to live in Capernaum after leaving Nazereth. The apostle John gives testimony of Christ. (John 2) Jesus disciples followed Him and stayed with Him day and night everywhere He went. Three days after the disciples joined Jesus, they were with Him in Capernaum and went to a wedding in the city of Cana near Capernaum. Mary, the mother of Jesus, was at the wedding. During the wedding feast Jesus changed water into wine, His first miracle. The miracle in Cana demonstrated that Jesus was the Son of God.

John12-12–When Jesus did miraculous signs in Cana of Galilee, He manifested His glory; and His disciples believed in Him. Jesus went back to Capernaum called the city of comfort. It was located on the shore of the Sea of Galilee also known as Tiberias or the lake of Gennesaret. Capernaum was a large fishing village and trading center. Jesus often traveled from there to teach and perform miracles, and there is frequent mention of Capernaum in the gospels.

Peter, Andrew, James and John also lived in Capernaum near the shore of the Sea of Galilee. They were fishermen when Jesus called them. Jesus made many trips back and forth from and to Capernaum. He taught and healed many people around the area of the Sea of Galilee. Capernaum was a relatively large and prosperous city. Jesus' mother and brothers had a house in Capernaum, and they went to Capernaum after leaving Cana. Jesus and His disciples didn't stay long at any place, because Jesus was eager to take his ministry to other places. Jesus traveled throughout Galilee and taught in the cities, villages, on the mountains, in a boat on the Sea of Galilee and in the synagogues.

Passover feast in Jerusalem

(Book of John)–Jesus, being a Jew, went to Jerusalem in Judea for the Passover feast. On one occasion while He was in Jerusalem He entered the temple area and found people selling animals and doves for sacrifices. There were also changers of money there. Jesus made a whip from cords and drove them from the temple. To those who sold doves He said John 2:16 "Take these things away! Do not make My Fathers house a house of merchandise!" The temple was the Jews place of worship, and Jesus didn't think it was right to make it into a place of merchandise. The Jews at the temple asked Jesus for a sign to prove that He had authority to drive them out, so Jesus told them of a forthcoming sign. He said that if He were put to death, He would be alive again in three days. He was speaking of His resurrection. When that took place, they would know Jesus was the Messiah sent by God, however most of the Pharisees and Sadducees the religious sects of the Jews rejected Jesus and plotted to put him to death.

During the time Jesus was on earth, Satan lied and deceived people in an attempt to destroy the effect of the gospel Jesus was teaching. Some people gladly responded to the gospel, but not all who obeyed remained faithful. Some of the people who heard the word of the gospel wanted to believe, but the cares of the world kept them from becoming faithful believers. The term gospel means the good news of redemption through faith in Christ. While Jesus was in Jerusalem, He met a Pharisee named Nicodemus.

Nicodemus knew Jesus was the Messiah because of the miracles He was performing, and he called Jesus a teacher who came from God, but he didn't know of the Kingdom of God. Jesus seemed to be surprised that Nicodemus, a leader of the Jews, would not have already known about the Kingdom. The prophets of Israel clearly prophesied about the coming of the Kingdom. Jesus then taught Nicodemus about the Kingdom of God and how one can become a member. Jesus said to him "Most assuredly, I say to you, unless one is born again, he cannot see the kingdom of God." John 3:4 "Nicodemus said to Him, "How can a man be born when he is old? Can he enter a second time into his mother's womb and be born?" Born again simply means you begin a new life with faith in Jesus. You leave the old life of sin and live in a way to serve God.

Jesus was speaking of a spiritual birth. When a person acquires faith in Jesus, they are baptized in water and receive the Holy Spirit into their lives and are spiritually joined to Jesus. After being baptized, they are a new person because their sins are washed away, and they are joined with Christ in a spiritual relationship. They have been born again and they are a new person that is dedicated to obeying the will of God. All people who have been forgiven of their past sins are added to the kingdom of God. (John 3) John the Baptist baptized people in Aenon where there was a lot of water. Jesus and His disciples went to Judea and the disciples baptized people there. John continued to baptize people until he was arrested and put in prison. Jesus was converting people, and his disciples were baptizing more people than John. John said he baptized to help Jesus gain disciples. John the baptizer said he would be going away. John was murdered before Jesus completed His ministry. Luke 3–When John first began to baptize, people wondered, if John was the Messiah, but John told them, he was not. He told them Jesus was coming and He would baptize with the Spirit and with fire. Baptism of the Spirit came after water baptism. After the disciples were baptized in water they received the baptism of the Holy Spirit meant power from the Holy Spirit came into them enabling them to teach and preach about salvation in Jesus. Later Herod put John in prison and eventually executed him. Jesus came to Galilee and preached the gospel saying His time had come the kingdom of God was near. The people that Jesus and His disciples baptized were, forgiven of their sin.

Jesus and the Disciples go to Samaria

(John 4)–Jesus left Jerusalem in Judea to go back toward Galilee, but on His way He decided to go to Samaria because there were people there who needed to hear the gospel. The Samaritans were a race of people that was formed when the Jews from the northern kingdom married non-Jews. They weren't all Jewish. The Jews from the southern kingdom despised Samaritans and would not associate with them. Jesus and the disciples came to the city of Sychar in Samaria near a plot of land that Jacob had given to his son Joseph long ago. Jacob's well was there, and since it had been a long walk and Jesus was tired, He set down by a well to rest. A Samaritan woman came to the well to get water, and Jesus asked her for a drink. Jesus was alone because the disciples had gone to buy food. The woman was surprised that Jesus even spoke to her. Jews did not associate with Samaritans.

She said, "How is it that you, being a Jew, would ask me, a Samaritan woman, for a drink?" Jesus said, John 4:10 "If you knew the gift of God, and who it is who says to you 'Give Me a drink,' you would have asked Him, and He would have given you living water." Living water represents the gospel that leads to faith in Christ and in eternal life. God's plan of redemption is for all people of all nationalities that will accept Jesus as the Son of God by faith and obey His teaching. The woman didn't understand living water, so she told Jesus that the well was deep and He had nothing to draw water with. Then she asked him where He was going to get this living water. Jesus answered and said to her, "Who ever drinks of this water will thirst again, but who ever drinks of the water that I shall give him will never thirst. But the water I shall give him will become in him a fountain of water springing up to everlasting life." John 4:13-14 Jesus used water in a figurative sense. The water Jesus spoke about represents the Holy Spirit that would be given to Christians; "rivers of living water." According to John 7: 38-39 "He who believes in Me, as the scripture has said, out of his heart will flow rivers of living water." But this He spoke concerning the Spirit, whom those believing in Him would receive; for the Holy Spirit, was not yet given, because Jesus was not yet glorified."

The woman could tell that Jesus was a prophet but she did not know He was the Messiah. She told Jesus that her ancestors worshiped on this mountain they were on but the Jews say that Jerusalem is the place to worship. The woman's ancestors were Samaritan people. John 4:21-26 "Jesus said to her, "Woman, believe Me, the hour is coming when you will not worship on this mountain, or in Jerusalem. You do not know Him you worship we know what we worship, for salvation is of the Jews. But the hour is coming, and now is, when the true worshipers will worship the Father in spirit and truth. Jesus told the woman that He was the Messiah. Worship comes from the heart and is not directed at objects worship is a matter of the heart. The nation of Israel and the Samaritans, worshiped the God of Israel according to the Law of Moses but After Jesus was sacrificed for the guilt of the peoples sin the people would worship Him in the spirit and the truth.

The Jews worshiped God in the temple and offered animal sacrifices according to the Law of Moses, but a time was coming soon when people everywhere would worship God in spirit in their hearts. Christians can worship anywhere because their worship is spiritual. They can worship

God in song and prayer that issues from the heart instead of rituals and animal sacrifices. Their hearts represent God's temple. God accepts broken spirit, a broken and contrite heart. If there is iniquity in the heart God will not accept it. The Spirit of God lives in the humble, those who have a contrite heart God revives. True worship of God comes from a redeemed heart of a person who has been justified by faith and is trusting in the Lord Jesus.

Jesus let the woman know that now that He had come, all people, including Samaritans, could become God's spiritual people. Many of the Samaritan people believed that Jesus was the Messiah. The woman who had come to draw water left her water pot and went to the city to tell the people about the man that knew everything she had ever done. She wondered if He was Jesus the Messiah. The people from the city came to the well to see Jesus and He taught them. The disciples came back from the city and they were amazed that Jesus had talked to the Samaritan woman. Jesus remained in Samaria two more days, and many Samaritans became believers and pleaded with Jesus to stay there.

Jesus left there and returned to Galilee in the power of the Spirit. The people of Galilee welcomed Him, because they had been at the feast in Jerusalem and had seen all the things He did there.

Jesus goes to Nazareth

(Luke 4)–Jesus went to His hometown of Nazareth. On the Sabbath day He entered the Synagogue and read from the book of Isaiah, chapter 61. "The Spirit of the Lord is upon Me, Because He has anointed Me To preach the gospel to the poor; He has sent Me to heal the broken hearted, to proclaim liberty to the captives And recovery of sight to the blind, To set at liberty those who are oppressed; To proclaim the acceptable year of the Lord." Luke 4:18-19 Jesus closed the book and sat down. All the people in the synagogue stared at Him. Jesus said, "Today this Scripture is fulfilled in your hearing." Many of the people there were astonished. The people wondered where Jesus got His wisdom and knowledge of the things He taught. The people wondered about who Jesus was and some said, "Is this not Joseph's son." Some recognized Jesus as the carpenter, the son of Mary. Jesus' brothers and sister were also there. Jesus began to speak about the people's unfaithfulness, and they became filled with anger towards Him. The people failed to honor Jesus as the Messiah or a prophet. They ran Jesus out of the city and took Him to the edge of a cliff to throw Him off, but He miraculously escaped. Jesus said, "A prophet is not without honor except in his own country, among his own relatives, and in his own house." Jesus wasn't accepted in that town and He didn't perform many works there.

John 4–After two days, Jesus went to Galilee and was received well by the Galileans who had been in Jerusalem. Jesus then went to Cana in Galilee, the place where he turned water into wine, but he soon left there and went to Capernaum. While he was in Capernaum, a nobleman came to him and told Jesus his son was sick and at the point of death. He asked Jesus to heal Him. Jesus said, "Unless you people see signs and wonders, you will by no means believe." Jesus then told him, "Go your way; your son lives." The nobleman believed what Jesus said, so he left to go home. On the way home his servants met him and told him his son was well. This was Jesus second miracle.

MT 4–Jesus left Capernaum by the Sea, to go to the region of Zebulun and Naphtali and began to preach saying, "Repent and believe in the gospel for the kingdom of heaven is near." Jesus walked near the Sea of Galilee and He saw Peter and Andrew, two of His disciples casting a net in the sea. Mark 1:17 'Then Jesus said to them, "Follow Me, and I will make you become fishers of men." They left their nets and followed Jesus. Jesus went a little farther and He saw James and John in their boat mending nets. Jesus called them and they left Zebedee, their father, and followed Jesus. Jesus was in Capernaum on the Sabbath. He taught at the synagogue and the people were amazed, because He taught with authority. Jesus healed a man who had a demon in him. When the demon saw Jesus, he knew Jesus was the Son of God and he asked Jesus if He came to destroy him. Jesus told the demon to come out of the body of the man and the demon left.

Jesus and the disciples left the synagogue and went to Simon Peter's house in Capernaum. Peter's mother was sick, so when they told Jesus, He went in to her and healed her. He then took her by the hand and she got up. That evening people brought all who were sick with various diseases, and Jesus healed them. Jesus also cast out many demons. The next morning Jesus rose early and went to a private place to pray. Jesus often went off by himself to pray and be away from the crowd for a while. The disciples found Him and told Him that everyone was looking for Him. Jesus then decided to go to other towns close by so He could preach to the people there. Mark 1:38 "He said to them, "let us go into the next towns that I may preach there also, because for this purpose I have come forth."

LK 5–Jesus stood by the lake of Gennesaret (Sea of Galilee) and the people crowded in close to Him in order to hear Him teaching the Word of God. While He was there, He saw two boats standing empty by the lake and the fishermen washing their nets nearby. One of the fishermen was Simon Peter, one of His apostles, so Jesus got into Simon Peter's boat and asked him to push out a little way from shore. Jesus sat in the boat and taught the people on shore. After a while He stopped speaking and He asked Peter to go further out into deeper water and let down the nets to catch some fish.

Peter told Jesus they had fished there all night without catching any fish, but he did what Jesus said and let down the nets again. They caught so many fish in the net that Peter had to call for help to get them in the boat. Peter fell to his knees telling Jesus to leave him, because he was a sinful man. Peter was overwhelmed by the miracle Jesus performed and felt unworthy to be in His presence. Jesus told Peter to not be afraid. Jesus said from then on they would all be fishers of men. The twelve disciples became the twelve Apostles and Jesus commissioned them to go out and become fishers of men by preaching the gospel. When the disciples came on shore they left everything and followed Jesus.

Mk 2-Lk-5 A few days later Jesus went to Capernaum to the house where his mother and brothers lived. As soon as the people heard He was there, many came to see Him. The house soon became so full that no one else could enter. Jesus left Capernaum the next day and again went to a deserted place to rest, but the people found Him and pleaded with Him to stay with them. He told them, "I must preach the kingdom of God to the other cities also, because for this purpose I have been sent." (Luke4: 43) Jesus went throughout Galilee, and in each city on the Sabbath He would go to the synagogue and teach about the kingdom of God. Jesus healed all kinds of sickness and disease, and His fame spread throughout the Roman Empire. Jesus and the disciples traveled from place to place and in one city a man with leprosy came to Jesus, and kneeled down before Him. The man told Jesus, he believed Jesus could heal him if He was willing. Jesus was moved with compassion, and because the man had expressed faith in Jesus, He put out His hand and touched the man saying "I am willing; be cleansed." Jesus then told the man to tell no one that he was healed and to go to the priest and make an offering as a testimony. News of the healing spread everywhere, and great multitudes assembled to hear Jesus teach and to be healed. Jesus often became very tired and went into a wilderness area and rested and prayed. Mark 2, Luke 5–After a few days Jesus went to Capernaum to the house where his mother and brothers lived. As soon as the people heard He was there, many came to see Him. The house soon became so full that no one else could enter.

Jesus was teaching the Pharisees and a paralyzed man was brought to the house carried by four men. The house was full of people and they could not bring the man inside. The roof was un-covered and the paralyzed man's bed was let down into the room through the roof where Jesus was. Jesus said to the man 'Son your sins are forgiven you' There were some scribes and Pharisees there, and they reasoned in their hearts that Jesus was speaking blasphemies for saying your sins are forgiven. They believed that God was the only one who could forgive sins. They did not believe Jesus was the Son of God even though He demonstrated who He was with many miraculous acts including healing. Jesus knew what they were thinking in their hearts and He said, "Why do you reason about these things in your hearts? Which is easier, to say to the paralytic, 'Your sins are forgiven you,' or to say, 'Arise, take up your bed and walk'? But that you may know that the Son of Man has power on earth to forgive sins"—He said to the paralytic, I say to you, arise take up your bed, and go to your house." The paralytic arose, picked up his bed and carried it. The crowd saw it and was amazed, and they glorified God. Jesus took advantage of every opportunity He had to convince people that He was the Messiah that had come from God. Many people believed Him but those who did not believe planned to kill him later.

Jesus Chooses Matthew

Jesus, still in Capernaum, walked to the seashore of the Sea of Galilee. The crowd followed Him and He taught them. As they were walking along Jesus saw Levi Matthew, the son of Alphaeus, at the tax office, because he was a tax collector. Jesus told Matthew Levi to follow Him. He followed Him and became a disciple of Jesus. The Scribes and the Pharisees observed Jesus eating with tax collectors and sinners, and they asked Jesus' disciples why He would do that. No respectable Jew wanted to be seen with people they thought were sinners, especially tax collectors. Jesus heard their remarks and answered them saying, "Those who are well have no need of a physician, but those who are sick. I did not come to call the righteous, but sinners to repentance." LK 5–The Pharisees complained about Jesus and the disciples because they did not observe fasting.

Fasting is a voluntary abstinence from eating food. Fasting was a common practice among the Jews. The fast celebrates the Jewish Day of Atonement. The observation of fasting was commanded in the book of Leviticus. Jesus came to take away the observance of the old Law of Moses and establish the gospel. The Law of Moses could not take away the guilt of sin, because no one could keep the Law perfectly so they were condemned because of sin. Jesus often spoke in figurative language, and He taught a parable calling Himself a bridegroom who was celebrating with his friends. The kingdom of heaven would also called the church and the bride of Christ. Jesus celebrates with His disciples who would be the first members of the kingdom. Jesus told them the time is coming when He, the bridegroom, will be taken away - referring to His death. Jesus used figurative language and parables so His disciples would understand Him but His enemies would not understand. There are no parables recorded in the book of John, but parables taught by Jesus are recorded in the other three gospels. A parable is a brief story that is told to compare a familiar story drawn from nature or everyday events to a story with spiritual significance. Jesus spoke many parables to attract interest and provoke an inquiry, giving Him an opportunity to teach a spiritual lesson.

Jesus told a parable about making a garment out of new cloth before it is shrunk, and putting new wine in old wineskins. The parable taught that the kingdom of God was coming and it would be different than the Law of Moses, which would go away and all people would be welcomed into the kingdom of Christ.. The Jewish people fasted twice a week, but that was a tradition not prescribed by the Law. According to the Law fasting was to be observed on the Day of Atonement. The people questioning Jesus wanted to know why His disciples did not fast. They mistakenly believed the disciples were disobeying Moses Law. Jesus said you don't put a new patch on an old garment. Jesus using figurative language Jesus meant God's Law was changing and God's people would no longer under the gospel of Christ be subject to the old Law of Moses. Instead they would observe the gospel of Jesus a law of liberty that would not contain rituals like feasting and fasting. The Old Law is compared to old wineskins that would burst if you put new wine in them.

The new wine represents the gospel of Jesus. The kingdom of God that Jesus would establish would not be a reformed kingdom adhering to the Law of Moses. The law under the new covenant of faith in Christ is a law of liberty according to James 1. Christians are under a system of grace and liberty instead of a law of strict rules and regulations and are not subject to the Law of Moses. Christians do not earn their salvation it is given to them as a gift from Jesus who died to pay for the guilt of their sins. Christians are saved by grace through faith in Christ, it is a gift of God, Ephesians 2:8 so they could do good works. According to James 1, Christians must be doers of the law of liberty that set them free from the Law of Moses. The law of liberty that sets Christians free from the Law of Moses is the gospel of Christ taught in the Bible. The law of liberty teaches people that there are many works to be done when living by the law of liberty. 1st Corinthians 9:19 "For though I am free from all men, I have made myself a servant to all, that I might win the more; and to the Jews I became as a Jew, that I might win Jews; to those who are under the Law as under the Law, that I might win those under the Law. To those who are without law, (not being without law toward God, but under law toward Christ) that I might win those who are without law; to the weak I became as weak, that I might win the weak. I have become all things to all men that I might by all means save some. Now this I do for the gospels sake, that I might be partaker of it with you." Jesus said 'if you love Me keep My commandments'. Christians are obligated to keep the commandments of Christ. John 14"15.

The parables illustrated that you do not mix the rules of the Law of Moses with the teachings of the gospel. The, Law of Moses would no longer be in effect when Jesus died. The gospel of Christ would be preached, and people would come into the Kingdom of God. Jesus taught the new law of the gospel when He was on earth and He established the law of the gospel when He died on the cross. The Law of Moses was given for a good purpose, but the Jewish people would not obey the Law perfectly therefore they became unrighteous sinners with no way to regain their righteous status for there was no provision for forgiveness of sin by observance of the Law of Moses.

Christ became our sacrifice for sin when he was crucified, the sacrifice of Christ makes all followers of Christ righteous through their faith, repentance and prayer. Kingdom of God, Kingdom of heaven, and Kingdom of Christ are all names for the same kingdom, which was later called the church in the first century.

Jesus goes to Jerusalem for the Passover

(John 5) One day Jesus went to Jerusalem for the Jewish Passover Feast. While there, He went to the pool called Bethesda near the Sheep Gate. The place where the pool was located had five porches for those who were sick, blind, lame or paralyzed. The people came there to wait for the moving of the water in the pool. There was a belief that an angel would come at a certain time and stir up the water, and the first person in the pool would be healed. On the day Jesus came, there was a man with an infirmity that he had for thirty-eight years. The man had not been able before to be the first in the pool, because he had no one to put him in the pool when the water was first stirred. Jesus saw the man and asked him, "Do you want to be made well?" The man told Jesus he had no one to put him in the pool when the water stirred. "Jesus said to him "rise, take up your bed and walk." And immediately the man was made well and he took up his bed, and walked. The Jews saw the man walking and carrying his bed and they accused him of unlawfully working on the Sabbath, a ridiculous accusation. The Jews became aware that Jesus was the one who healed the man on the Sabbath and they persecuted Jesus and waited for an opportunity to kill Him. Jesus answered the undeserved outrage of the Jews saying, "My Father has been working until now, and I have been working."

Jesus claimed to be the Son of God and He explains that God has always worked for the good and the salvation of mankind and now Jesus was working for the same reason. The Jews wanted to kill Jesus because He healed on the Sabbath and He claimed that God was His Father. Jesus continued to teach and explain the unity between Himself and God. Jesus said that His Father would show greater works to do than the work He had already performed.

John 5:21 For as the Father raises the dead and gives life to them, even so the Son gives life to whom He will." Jesus lets them know that everything He did was because of His father. Jesus claims the same power as God, which identifies Him as the Son of God. John 5:26-29 "For as the father has life in Himself, so He has granted the Son to have life in Himself, and has given Him authority to execute judgment also, because He is the Son of Man. Do not marvel at this; for the hour is coming in which all who are in the graves will hear His voice and come forth, Those who have done good, to the resurrection of life, and those who have done evil, to the resurrection of condemnation." Jesus revealed that His reason for coming to earth was to die and provide redemption for the guilt of sin. Jesus performed many miracles and did great works among the people so people would believe He was the Messiah the Son of God.

Jesus wanted to establish faith in Him and the gospel so that people would voluntarily submit to God's plan of salvation. There is only one God given plan of redemption given by the Holy Spirit through the Word and people should obey it. The works of John the Baptist and the works of Jesus bear witness that Jesus Christ is the Son of God. The Scriptures from Genesis through Revelation bear witness of Christ. John 5:24-30 "Most assuredly, I say to you, he who hears My word and believes in Him who sent Me has everlasting life, and shall not come into judgment, but has passed from death into life. Most assuredly, I say to you the hour is coming, and now is, when the dead will hear the voice of the Son of God; and those who hear will live. For as the

Father has life in Himself, so He has granted the Son to have life in Himself, and has given Him authority to execute judgment also, because He is the Son of Man.

Do not marvel at this; for the hour is coming in which all who are in the graves will hear His voice and come forth—those who have done good, to the resurrection of life, and those who have done evil, to the resurrection of condemnation. I can of Myself do nothing. As I hear I judge; and My judgment is righteous, because I do not seek My own will but the will of the Father who sent Me. Jesus talked about the witness of John the Baptist who was a witness of the truth. Jesus told them, John was a burning and shining lamp, and people were willing to listen to John for a time.

Many of the Jews at first believed what John said about Jesus. Jesus said His works were greater than John's. John 5:36 "But I have a greater witness than John's; for the works John 5:36 "But I have a greater witness than John's; for the works which the father has given Me to finish—the very works that I do—bear witness of Me, that the Father has sent Me." When Jesus healed a man on the Sabbath, He was doing the work that God had sent Him to earth to do. Jesus faced the difficulty of establishing the law of liberty, freedom from the guilt of sin the gospel. The religious leaders were still teaching the Old Law. Under the Old Law it was unlawful to work on the Sabbath. As Jesus and the disciples walked through the grain fields one day, the disciples pulled and ate some of the grain, and the Pharisees accused them of unlawfully working on the Sabbath. The charge made by the Pharisees was ridiculous, and Jesus said to them the Son of Man is the Lord of the Sabbath. Jesus is the King of the kingdom of heaven, and His gospel is the rule for the life and behavior of His disciples.

Jesus continued to defend Himself by showing that the religious leaders missed the true meaning in the scriptures that people were supposed to live by. The Jews believed the scriptures taught them how to have eternal life but they failed to know that the scriptures taught that eternal life comes through faith in the Son of God. The, scriptures in fact do teach and they testify that eternal life comes through the Messiah. They didn't believe Jesus was the Messiah.

Jesus Heals in a Synagogue

On another Sabbath Jesus went into the synagogue and saw a man with a withered hand. The Scribes and Pharisees were watching Jesus to see what He would do hoping they could make a charge against Him. Jesus knew their thoughts, and He told the man with the withered hand to stand up. Jesus asked the Scribes and Pharisees if it was lawful to do, good on the Sabbath or to do evil, to save life or destroy life? Then Jesus told the man to stretch out his hand and Jesus restored his hand. The Scribes and Pharisees went into a rage. The Pharisees planned to kill Jesus but He knew their intentions, so Jesus and His disciples left and went to the Sea of Galilee. A great crowd from Galilee, Judea, Jerusalem, Idumea, Tyre and Sidon came to Him because they heard about the great things Jesus was doing.

Jesus healed many and the crowd closed around Him to touch Him. The demons he cast out fell down at His feet saying, "You are the Son of God." The demons knew who Jesus was, because they were fallen angels that served Satan. The demons left heaven and came to the earth to torment God's people. Jesus stood with His disciples and a great crowd of people from Judea, Jerusalem and the seacoast of Tyre and Sidon and He healed them. The people tried to touch Him because they saw the power to heal that had come out of Him. During his ministry Jesus had many disciples, or followers, besides the twelve who became apostles. A disciple is a follower of a certain person or movement. Jesus' disciples were simply those who followed Jesus because they had faith in Him. We who follow Christ's teaching today are disciples of Jesus Christ and we believe in the validity of the scriptures in the Bible. (LK 6) Jesus went to a mountain to pray, and He prayed all night. The next morning He called His disciples to Him, and he chose twelve men to be His apostles to continue His teaching after He ascended to heaven.

Jesus gave the Disciples special power from the Holy Spirit so they could continue His ministry after he was crucified. In order to be an apostle, they had to have been an eyewitness of the teaching and works of Jesus and especially to have been with Him after His resurrection. They had to have the ability to testify to everything Jesus did. Jesus officially chose the twelve who would serve as apostles. They would continue to follow Him and serve Him and the kingdom of God for the rest of their lives. The apostles were Peter, James, John, Andrew, Philip, Bartholomew, Matthew, Thomas, James the son of Alphabets – Thaddaeus, Simon the Cananite, and Judas Iscariot. These twelve disciples were called apostles. The word apostle means one sent on a mission. Jesus sent His apostles on a mission to preach and to teach about Him and His Kingdom after His death. They were there in the beginning of Jesus' Kingdom here on earth.

Jesus Preaches the Sermon on the Mount

Most of Jesus' time on earth was spent in Galilee proper and the area of the Sea of Galilee. The Sea of Galilee was near the middle of Galilee on the far eastern side. The Hebrew word for hill and mountain were sometimes used interchangeably.

There are many references to Jesus going up on a mountain to speak to the people so everyone could see him. Some of the larger mountains in Galilee were Mt Hermon, Meron, Gilboa, Lebanon, Tabor, and Carmel, and then there were many smaller mountains.

(Matt 5- 8, Luke 6) Jesus went up on the mountain and sat down, and He called His disciples to him and taught a Sermon on the Mount. At the beginning of His sermon Jesus taught about people being blessed if they have certain attitudes toward Him, His kingdom, and their fellow man. We call these blessings the beatitudes. NIV–Luke 6:17-23 "He went down with them and stood on a level place. A large crowd of His disciples were there and a great number of people from all over Judea, from Jerusalem and from the coast of Tyre and Sidon, who had come to hear Him and be healed of their diseases. Those troubled by evil spirits were cured and the people all tried to touch Him because power was coming from Him and healing them all. Looking at His disciples He said: "Blessed are you who are poor, for yours is the kingdom of God. Blessed are you who hunger now, for you will be satisfied. Blessed are you who weep now for you will, laugh. Blessed are you when men hate you, when they exclude you and insult you and reject your name as evil, because of the Son of Man. "Rejoice in that day and leap for joy, because great is your reward in heaven. For that is how their fathers treated to prophets." Jesus compares the way the people who have faith in Him then are treated, with the way those who have faith in Him now will be blessed when they enter eternal life in heaven.

Jesus continued to teach many other things concerning living a Christian life. Mt 8:28 "And so it was, when Jesus had ended these sayings, that the people were astonished at His teaching. For He taught them as one having authority, and not as the scribes." Jesus' teaching was recorded in the scriptures for all people in every generation. The work of the apostles ceased after their death, but they left an inspired record in the scriptures. Jesus taught about the proper attitude and behavior expected of a disciple.

Mt 5-6-7, Luke 6:20-49 Matthew and Luke give a similar, but not the exact, version of the Sermon on the Mount. Some believe the writers in Matthew and Luke were writing about two different times. Matthew 5:3-12–The poor in spirit are blessed because theirs is the kingdom of heaven. Blessed are those who mourn, they will be comforted. Blessed are the meek, they shall inherit the earth. Blessed are those who hunger and thirst after righteousness, they shall be filled. Blessed are the merciful, they shall obtain mercy. Blessed are the pure in heart, they shall see God. Blessed are the peacemakers they shall be called sons of God. Blessed are those who are persecuted for righteousness sake, theirs is the kingdom of heaven.

The word blessed means to be praised by God and you will receive God's gifts, especially the gift of eternal life in heaven. Jesus described those in His kingdom as being blessed. They will be accepted and blessed by God and will be happy. Jesus taught that God would bless those who were poor in spirit. The poor in spirit are meek and they are willing to trust God and Jesus. They have faith in Christ and follow His teaching. Jesus taught that those who mourn would be comforted. Mourning is an expression of deep grief, especially when someone you love is hurt, seriously ill or dies. Jesus' disciples would experience deep grief when Jesus was tortured and died on the cross. There are other times when people express sorrow and grief over the misfortune of someone else. Sorrow and grief for the misfortune of other people shows that a person has deep feelings for other people. They will be comforted by the Holy Spirit and by the word of God. God will bless them because they are the kind of people God takes delight in. Jesus said 'those who are meek shall inherit the earth.' A meek person is humble not haughty, does not boast, does not think too highly of themselves, and do not set themselves above others.

Inheriting the earth does not mean the earth we now live on. Inheriting the earth refers to entrance into the new heaven and new earth at the end of time. Isaiah 66:22 "For as the new heavens and the new earth, which I will make shall remain before Me," says the Lord, So shall your descendants and your name remain. And it shall come to pass That from one New Moon to another, And from one Sabbath to another, All flesh shall come to worship before Me," says the Lord."

Those who are hungry and thirsty for righteousness are those who have a desire to learn God's word and obey. They will be filled, because they will feed on God's word every day. Jesus said, "My Father gives you the true bread from heaven. For the bread of God is He who comes down from heaven and gives life to the world." (John 6:32b-33) "I am the bread of life." (John 6:48) Those who show mercy to other people will receive mercy from God. James 2:13: "For judgment is without mercy to the one who has shown no mercy. Mercy triumphs over judgment."

Christians are admonished to have a pure heart, because the pure in heart will see God after the resurrection. Pure means unadulterated faith, hope and love not mixed with sin. Matt. 12:34b "For out of the abundance of the heart the mouth speaks." Christians are to keep their hearts pure so that what they speak and do will be acceptable to God. The peacemakers will be called the sons of God. Romans 12:17-18 "Repay no one evil for evil. Have regard for good things in the sight of all men. If it is possible, as much as depends on you, live peaceably with all men. Beloved, do not avenge yourselves but rather give place to wrath; for it is written, 'Vengeance is Mine, I will repay,' says the Lord."

V.21 "Do not be overcome by evil, but overcome evil with good." Jesus said you are blessed if you are persecuted for righteousness sake. People may be persecuted because they are striving for righteousness. Matthew's account of the teaching of Jesus also compares Jesus' disciples to light. Jesus said a city that is on a hill, cannot be hid, everyone can see the lights from the city. Then He said that you wouldn't light a candle and then cover it up with a basket, but instead put it out where it can give light. The life of God's people should be like a light illuminating the gospel of Christ to those around us as they see their godly lives, and are drawn to their godliness in Christ.

Matthew compared Jesus' disciples to salt. Salt has many good characteristics such as seasoning, and preserving. God's people can by example change the attitudes of people towards faith, hope and love for God and Christ by being good examples of living by the teaching of Christ and by promoting the teaching of the Bible. The life of those who live in obedience to the gospel are preserving their life for eternity.

The religious leaders of the Jews in the first century were bad examples. They mistreated and discouraged people by their own bad example of unrighteousness. Jesus said to those who would be disciples that their righteousness must be greater than the righteousness of the scribes and Pharisees who were the teachers of the Law of Moses.

Mt 5– Jesus said He did not come to establish the Law of Moses He came to fulfill the Law meaning to bring it to an end. The Law of Moses could not take away the guilt of sin; in fact it caused sin to multiply, because people failed to obey the Law. Fulfilling the Law of Moses means it would cease to be in effect after the death, burial and resurrection of Jesus. The Law was given to teach morals through legalism. The gospel of Christ teaches morality by faith, hope and love not only for God and Jesus but for all people. Jesus life and ministry was a demonstration of His love for all people. Jesus continues His sermon teaching about murder, adultery, divorce, oaths, retaliation and love.

Matthew 5:43-48 "You have heard that it was said, 'You shall love your neighbor and hate your enemy.' But I say to you love your enemies, bless those who curse you, do good to those who hate you, and pray for those who spitefully use you and persecute you, that you may be sons of your Father in heaven; for He makes His sun rise on the evil and on the good, and sends rain on the just and on the unjust.' "For if you love those who love you, what reward have you? Do not even the tax collectors do the same? If you greet your brethren only, what do you do more that others? Do not even the tax collectors do so? Therefore you shall be perfect, just as your Father in heaven is perfect." People who have faith in Christ will be saved from the guilt of sin by faith.

MT 6–Jesus continued His teaching on the mountain with a lesson about charitable deeds. Disciples, by nature, would be inclined to be charitable which is good, and Jesus taught that people must have the right attitude when they give to people and do favors for people. Jesus said do not glorify your self before others for praise, because that is like a hypocrite. Jesus advised not to let wealth or the pursuit of wealth, hinder your responsibility to serve God. Jesus applied the same advice about praying. Do not pray to attract favorable attention to yourself. Jesus advised to pray in secret.

Jesus did not say you should not pray publicly, He said when you do pray do so with the proper attitude of humility towards God. Pray that God's will be done in all things, pray for your daily sustenance, pray for your inadequacies, and pray for the moral strength to do the right thing. Ask God for the things you need and He will give you what you need, God in heaven gives good things to those who ask. Mt 7:12 "Therefore, whatever you want men to do to you, do also to them, for this is the Law and the prophets." MT 7–Jesus said do not judge, Jesus was referring to making unjust and condemning judgments about other people.

God is the judge of all people and people who judge other people need to remember their own sins instead of being hypocritical. Be considerate and kind to other people and leave the judging to God. At this time the Jewish people were still obligated to keep the Law of Moses, so Jesus told them to continue to obey the Law of Moses. He then taught them about a new righteousness that would take the place of the Law of Moses. After His death, burial, resurrection and ascension. Jesus taught about two paths in life that people could follow, and He compares them to a path that leads to a narrow gate and a path that leads to a wide gate. The narrow gate represents obedience to the gospel of Christ and it gives entrance to those who have forsaken the evils of the world and narrowed their activities to following the word of God.

The wide gate suggests engaging in all kinds of evil desires and it leads to destruction. Jesus said only a few enter the narrow gate. Jesus warns that there will be false teachers that proclaim to be righteous but are actually like wolves that will destroy you by their false teaching. (MT 7) The person who hears Jesus teaching and does what He says is wise like a man who builds his life on a solid foundation. Those who hear God but fail to do what He says is foolish, and his house is built on a foundation that will crumble and he will not be able to withstand the storms of life. In the life of everyone there will be some difficult times and some good times, and those who have a solid foundation of faith, hope and love in Christ will be able to withstand the difficult times. Jesus teaching astonished the people because He taught them as one having authority.

When Jesus came down from the mountain, a great many people followed Him and Jesus healed a man with leprosy.

Jesus Goes to Capernaum

Luke 7–After Jesus came down the mountain He and the disciples went to Capernaum. There was a centurion, an official in the Roman army, in Capernaum who had a servant who was very sick and about to die. When the centurion heard that Jesus was in Capernaum, he sent some elders of the Jews to ask Jesus to come and heal his servant. Jesus agreed to go with them. When Jesus and the men came to the house, the centurion came out and asked Jesus not to come into his house, because the centurion felt he was worthy to even ask Jesus. But he told Jesus that if he would just say the word, his servant would be healed. The centurion had faith and a hope that Jesus would heal his servant. When he said this, Jesus said to the crowd following him, "I say to you, I have not found such great faith not even in Israel!"(Luke 7:9) When the men who were with Jesus went into the house, the servant was healed.

Luke 7:11– The next day Jesus went to a city called Nain in the plain of Jezreel and many of His disciples went with Him, and a large crowd. Nain means pleasant or green pastures because it overlooks the Plain of Esdraelon and the valley of Jezreel. Jesus came near the gate of the city and saw a dead man being carried out. The dead man was the only son of a widow. Jesus had compassion for her and told her not to cry. Jesus touched the open coffin and told the young man to arise and he set up. The people were afraid, and they glorified God when they recognized that Jesus as a prophet of God. The report of Jesus raising a person from the dead was spread throughout Judea and the surrounding area.

LK 7–The disciples of John the Baptist told John about the things Jesus was doing, so John sent two of his disciples to Jesus to ask Him if He was the Messiah. The men came to Jesus and asked, "Are You the Messiah, or should we keep looking?" While John's disciples were there, Jesus healed many people of infirmities, evil spirits and other afflictions.

Jesus told John's disciples to go tell John that the blind see, the lame walk, the lepers are cleansed, the deaf hear and the dead are raised and the poor have the gospel preached to them. John would then know Jesus was the promised Messiah. Jesus did many marvelous things in approximately three years before He ascended to heaven. Jesus did many works in numerous cities but he was not pleased with the result of His teaching and healing in some of the cities. Many people would not believe in Jesus and follow Him. Matthew 11:20-24 "Then He began to rebuke the cities in which most of His mighty works had been done, because they did not repent; "Woe to you, Chorazin! Woe to you Bethsaida! For if the mighty works, which were done in you had been done in Tyre and Sidon, they would have repented long ago in sackcloth and ashes. But I say to you, it will be more tolerable for Tyre and Sidon than for you in the day, of judgment. And you Capernaum, who are exalted to heaven, will be brought down to Hades; for if the mighty works which were done in you had been done in Sodom, it would have remained until this day. But I say to you that it shall be more tolerable for the land of Sodom in the judgment than for you."

Jesus was talking about sinners who will not repent of their sin - warning them about going to a place called Hades. Hades is a place in the heavens where the spirits of the dead go to wait for the second coming of Christ. There is a place in Hades for the spirits of the righteous and a separate place for the spirits of the unrighteous. Hades is also referred to as hell. Hell was used by Jesus as the hell of fire indicating a place of torture or death. In the Old Testament the word Sheol was translated as grave or pit - a place of both the saved and unsaved spirits. When the New Testament was translated into Greek, Sheol was translated as Hades Thayer's Greek- English Lexicon. Luke 16:19-31 "There was a certain rich man clothed in purple and fine linen and he fared sumptuously every day. There was a certain beggar named Lazarus, full of sores, who was laid at his gate, desiring to be fed with the crumbs which fell from the rich man's' table. Moreover the dogs came and licked his sores. So it was that the beggar died and was carried by the angels to Abraham's bosom. The rich man also died and was buried. And being in torment in Hades, he lifted up his eyes and saw Abraham afar off, and Lazarus in his bosom.

He cried and said, 'Father Abraham, have mercy on me and send Lazarus that he may dip the tip of his finger in water and cool my tongue; for I am tormented in this flame.' "But Abraham said, 'Son, remember that in your lifetime you received your good things, and likewise Lazarus evil things; but now he is comforted. And besides all this, between us and you there is a great gulf fixed, so that those who want to pass from here to you cannot, nor can those from there, pass to us." According to this parable, when people die their spirits go to Hades. There are two places in Hades. One is for the spirit of those who are saved by their faith, hope and love and they are in a place of paradise. People without faith are assigned a place of torment. When people die, their fate is already determined, and their spirit has no choice or chance to change their destination in hell or paradise. The spirits wait there until the day of God's judgment at the end of time.

Jesus Eats at the House of a Pharisee

LK 7– A Pharisees named Simon invited Jesus to eat with him, so Jesus went to his house and sat down to eat. A woman who was a sinner came to the house when she learned that Jesus was there. She brought with her some expensive fragrant oil and stood at Jesus' feet crying. She then began to wash His feet with her tears and wipe them with her hair. She kissed Jesus' feet and rubbed fragrant oil on them. The Pharisee saw her and reasoned to himself that Jesus must not be a prophet, because He did not know the woman was a sinner. Otherwise He would not have let her touch Him. But Jesus knew everything about the woman. Jesus told Simon that He had something to tell him. He then told him a parable about two men who each owed a debt to a creditor. One man owed a large sum of money and the other one owed quite a bit less.

Neither of the debtors had the money to repay the creditor, so the creditor forgave the debt of each man. Jesus asked Simon, "Which one do you think loved the creditor more?" Simon said he supposed the one with the largest debt. Jesus told Simon he had correctly judged. He reminded Simon about how loving and gracious the woman had treated Him, The debt of sin of the woman was great, but her faith in Jesus saved her.

Luke 7:50–Then He said to the woman, "Your faith has saved you. Go in peace." The redeeming power of Jesus is great enough to nullify the penalty of all kinds of sin. LK 8–Jesus and His twelve disciples continued to travel. They went through every city and village and Jesus taught about the kingdom of God. Some of the women who had been healed provided them with food. Mary Magdalene, Joanna, the wife of Herod's steward and Susanna.

Jesus left Capernaum the next day and went to a deserted place to rest, but the people found Him and pleaded with Him to stay with them. Jesus said, Luke 5: 43 "I must preach the kingdom of God to the other cities also, because for this purpose I have been sent." Jesus wanted to teach the gospel there while He had an opportunity, and each Sabbath He went to the synagogues to teach. He went to Galilee and the surrounding regions teaching about the kingdom of God and healing all kinds of sickness and disease. His fame spread throughout the Roman Empire.

MT 12– A blind and mute man who had a demon in him was brought to Jesus, and Jesus healed him. The people were amazed and wondered if Jesus could be the descendant of King David. They knew the Messiah was to come from the birth line of David. Jesus was the Messiah they had been expecting for many years. Jesus healed the man and the Pharisees accused Jesus of casting out demons by the power of Beelzebub. Beelzebub was a false god that was worshiped by the Philistines in the city of Ekron. He was associated with Satan, the ruler of the demons. Jesus could read the thoughts of people so He asked them, if Satan would cast out his own demons? Demons are Satan's angels. Jesus said a house divided against its self could not stand, implying that he could not be casting out Satan by the power of Satan. Jesus was casting out demons by the power of God. Jesus told them every sin could be forgiven, even blasphemy against men, but blasphemy against the Holy Spirit would not be forgiven. Mark 3-28-29 "Assuredly, I say to you, all sins will be forgiven the sons of men, and whatever blasphemies they may utter; but he who blaspheme against the Holy Spirit never has forgiveness, but is subject to eternal condemnation."

Blasphemy means speaking evil against the Holy Spirit. The work of the Holy Spirit includes spiritual guidance and comforting God's people.

The Pharisees demanded to see Jesus perform a miracle to prove that He was the Messiah. Jesus called them an adulterous generation. Faith hope and love once established, does not require a sign, and Jesus said only a wicked and adulterous generation would ask for a sign. Jesus said there would be no sign except the sign of Jonah. Even the Gentiles believed in the story of Jonah. God had before sent Israel's prophet Jonah to preach to the people in Nineveh, but Jonah didn't want to obey God, so God punished him. Jonah went aboard a ship trying to run away from God, but God caused a great wind to come up. The waves were high, and Jonah told the frightened crew of the ship to throw him in the sea, and the winds would cease. So Jonah was thrown into the sea and a great whale swallowed him. When Jonah was in the whale's belly, Jonah prayed to God for forgiveness. After three days and nights in the whale's belly, the whale spit Jonah out on dry land. After that Jonah preached to the people in Nineveh. God saved Jonah's life in a strange way to prove that He is God Almighty Who can do anything. Jesus was comparing what happened to Jonah to His upcoming death, burial and resurrection. Jesus would be three days and nights in the grave, and then He would come out of the grave and resume His mission on earth.

MT 12, LK8–On one occasion while Jesus was talking to the people, His mother and brothers came to speak with Him. Someone told Jesus they wanted to speak with Him and Jesus said, "Who is My mother and who are My brothers?" Then he pointed to His disciples and said, "Here are My mother and My brothers! For whoever does the will, of My Father in heaven, are my brother and sister and mother."

Parables

The term parable literally means placing beside. A parable puts thoughts side by side similar to an allegory. A parable tells a short story with interesting illustrations of moral and religious truth, a story that is familiar in nature or in every day life. Many of Jesus' parables related to the characteristics of the kingdom of God. They enlightened the knowledge about the kingdom of God for some people but hardened the hearts of those who did not believe the gospel truth. Jesus spoke in parables to attract interest and provoke an inquiry, giving Him an opportunity to teach a spiritual lesson.

Matthew 13:10-17 "And the disciples came and said to Him, "Why do you speak to them in parables?" He answered and said to them, "Because it has been given to you to know the mysteries of the kingdom of heaven, but to them it has not been given. For whoever has, to him more will be given, and he will have abundance; but whoever does not have, even what he has will be taken away from him." Therefore I speak to them in parables, because seeing they do not see, and hearing they do not hear, nor do they understand. And in them the prophecy of Isaiah is fulfilled, which says: Hearing you will hear and shall not understand, and seeing you will see and not perceive; for the hearts of this people have grown dull. Their ears are hard of hearing, and their eyes they have closed, lest they should see with their eyes and hear with their ears, lest they should understand with their hearts and turn, so that I should heal them."

Wise people without prejudice and with an honest heart would be able to understand Jesus' parables, but those who were prejudice against Jesus would harden their heart. There were some things about the kingdom that Jesus wanted to teach his disciples without revealing the meaning to His enemies, so He taught in parables and explained the meaning of the parables. There are many parables in the book of Luke that reveals Christ's understanding of the attitudes of all kinds of people, as He examines their responses and attitudes toward God and Christ. Some of Jesus' parables are illustrations about the attitudes and actions of the rich and the poor. The middle class was not wide spread in the first century. There were only a small degree of those who might be classified as the middle class. The majority of the people were poor. Jesus accomplished two purposes with the parables: to point out the improper attitudes of those who were rich, and to express God's attitude towards people. Jesus taught about the attitudes of the various Jewish sects. In order to understand the meaning of a parable a person must be interested enough to listen and thoughtfully consider what they hear. Parables reveal the truth to those with understanding hearts. Potential believers accept the truth taught in the parable and learn from the parable. Unbelievers would not understand the true meaning of Jesus parables and they would leave Jesus alone. Jesus taught in parables to reveal the truth to the righteous and conceal it from the wicked.

(MT 13) (Luke 8). A great many people came from every city to see and hear Jesus teach. In Matthew 13, Luke 13, 14 and Mark 4 Jesus taught 38 parables. MT 13-MK 4-LK 8– List some of Jesus parables. The parable of the Soils, Wheat, and the Mustard seed, Leaven, Tithes, Tares, Hidden Treasure, The Pearl of Great Price, Parable of the Dragnet, parable of the Householder.

The disciples asked Jesus why He taught people in parables Jesus explained that they knew about the secrets of the kingdom of heaven because it was given to them but it was not given to other people. When the Apostles taught the Holy Spirit inspired them with knowledge and truth. The parable of the soils is about a farmer that sowed seed in four different types of soil, and he received a different yield from each soil. The seed represents the gospel of Christ that is preached to all people but yields different results from the people hearing the parable. Mark 4–The, parable of the soils makes a comparison between the people who hear the gospel message and respond to it. The soil represents the heart of those who hear. In the parable of the soils, the types of ground represent four types of people with different attitudes toward the gospel message. People who believe the gospel and respond in a positive way are the people with an obedient heart; they represent the good soil. The people represented by the other types of soil will reject the gospel of Christ.

The parable of the wheat is about a farmer. The farmer planted good seed in his field, and an enemy planted bad seed among the farmer's good seed. All of the seeds produced plants. The good seed represents people who hear the gospel and respond to it in a positive way by obeying the gospel and remaining faithful. The plants that grow from the bad seed represent people who hear the gospel message and respond to the message in a negative way refusing to obey the gospel. Jesus said both kinds of people will remain on earth together, but when He comes, He will separate the good people from the bad people and destroy the bad people represented by the weeds.

The parable of the mustard seed compares the kingdom of God to a mustard seed. The mustard seed is a very tiny seed when planted, but it yields a very large plant. The kingdom of God started with Jesus and a few disciples and began to grow and eventually grew into a large kingdom. Jesus predicts that the Kingdom of God (church) will grow and spread out on earth.

The parable of the leaven is about leaven that is added to dough to make the lump of dough grow larger, one example is yeast. Without the leaven, the dough would not grow larger. The gospel of Christ that is actively taught is like leaven and will make the kingdom of God grow larger.

Parable of the hidden treasure Matthew 13:44 "Again the kingdom of heaven is like treasure hidden in a field, which a man found and hid; and for joy over it he goes and sells all that he has and buys that field." The hidden treasure is membership in the kingdom of God, which is so great that a person of faith will do whatever is necessary to gain entrance into the kingdom of God. Jesus taught a parable about a lamp that gives light. A lamp that is lit should not be hidden so that its light can shine all around. The light from the lamp represents the Word of God including the gospel of Christ. God's word should be taught all over the world. Parable of the pearl of great price is like a merchant looking for beautiful pearls. He found one very expensive pearl and he sold everything he had and bought the pearl. The pearl represents faith in Christ. Parable of the dragnet is about casting a net into the sea and catching all kinds of fish. It is about the separation of the saved from the unsaved at the end of time. Some people will be good enough for God to keep and some will be thrown into the fire to be burned.

The angels at the end of time will separate the people that are saved from those who are lost. The Parable of the householder is about the generation that was living during the time Jesus was on earth. The scribe is like the religious members of Judaism. The householder is God who made a covenant with people during Moses time but made a new and better covenant in Christ. The scribes, Pharisees and other religious leaders held on to the old Law of Moses and rejected the gospel of Christ.

Jesus and His Disciples Cross the Sea of Galilee

MT 8– To avoid the great multitude coming toward Him, Jesus told His disciples to cross the sea in their boat to the other side. Before Jesus could go with them, a scribe came to Him and told Jesus he would follow Him anywhere He went. Jesus said, "Foxes have holes and birds of the air have nests, but the Son of Man has nowhere to lay His head."

Jesus did not have a permanent place to stay, because He constantly moved from one place to another place. One person wanted to follow Jesus, but he told Jesus that he must first go and bury his father. Jesus said, "Follow Me, and let the dead bury the dead." Jesus' meaning was to let those who will not follow Him bury the dead. Spiritual matters are more important than other matters and should be given priority. There is nothing more important than obeying the gospel of Christ.

At another time Jesus and the disciples were in their boat in the middle of the sea. A great storm came up and the waves of the sea were high. Jesus was asleep in the boat, and His disciples became scared and woke Him saying, "Lord, save us." But Jesus said to them, "Why are you fearful, O you of little faith?" Jesus was disappointed, because His disciples were still afraid after all of the things they had witnessed Him do. Jesus got up and said to the wind and waves, "Peace, be still." And He calmed the waters. The disciples were amazed that Jesus had the power to make even the sea and the wind obey Him. The disciples didn't yet realize that Jesus had such great power even over the forces of nature, and they wondered who He was that even the wind and sea obeyed Him. On the other side of the sea they came to the country of the Gergesenes (also called the Gaderenes) who lived in the large region east of Galilee.

The people were residents of Gadara, one of the cities of the Decapolis. Gadara was located east of the Jordan River. Jesus came ashore and a man from the city who had been possessed by demons for a long time came to Him. The man was naked. He didn't live in a house. He lived in the tombs where people were buried. The man fell down in front of Jesus, and in a loud voice said, "What have I to do with you, Jesus Son of the Most High God?" The demons in the man knew who Jesus was, because demons are the Devil's fallen angels who lived in heaven at one time. Jesus told the demons to come out of the man. The man was shackled and chained because of the demons, but he broke free from them, and the demons drove him into the wilderness. Jesus asked the demon his names and he said legion, because many demons had entered the man.

God created the angels before the creation of the universe, they are heavenly creatures, they have the ability to go between heaven and earth and they serve God day and night. Some angels rebelled against God and served Satan the Devil. The angels who serve Satan are antagonistic towards God's people. Demons have much greater power than humans, but they are subject to God. Demons are enemies of Christ and the Jews who were God's people. During the days of Jesus' ministry, the demons persecuted the Jews and some demons even lived inside people. Matthew records an incident of two men who were possessed by demons. These demons saw Jesus and called Him the Son of God. They asked Jesus if He had come to torment them. The demons feared He would cast them out of the two men, and they asked Him to let them go into a herd of pigs that was nearby. Jesus told them to go, and they entered the pigs and the whole herd ran down a slope into the sea. MK 5–Jesus and His disciples crossed over the sea again and went back to Capernaum. One of the rulers of the synagogue in Capernaum by the name of Jairus came and fell at Jesus' feet begging Him to come lay His hands on his little daughter who was at the point of death and heal her. Jesus told him to not be afraid but believe in Him and she would be well.

Jesus then went with Jairus. He entered the house but only allowed Peter, James and John and the father and mother of the girl to go in the house with Him. They all wept because they thought the girl was dead, Jesus told them not to weep because she was only sleeping. But they still believed she was dead. Jesus made all of them go outside, and then He took her hand and told her to arise. Her spirit returned to her and she immediately arose. Her parents were astonished at what Jesus had done.

MK 5–There was a woman there among the people who had been bleeding for twelve years. The doctors weren't able to help her, and she was getting worse. When she saw Jesus, the woman made her way through the crowd and touched His clothes. When she touched His clothes her bleeding stopped. Jesus realized that power had gone out of Him so He asked, who touched His clothing? The woman came and fell down before Jesus and told Him she had touched Him. Jesus told her that her faith made her well.

MT 9–When Jesus left Jairus house two blind men followed Him and called out to Him saying, "Son of David, have mercy." Jesus went into the house and they came to Him, and Jesus asked them if they thought He could heal them. They said, "Yes Lord" and He touched their eyes and He said, "According to your faith let it be to you." Jesus told them not to tell anyone but to spread the news about Him. A man was brought to Jesus who was possessed by a demon and couldn't speak. Jesus cast the demon out of him and the man was able to speak.

MT13–Jesus and His disciples went to Nazareth where He grew up, and on the Sabbath He entered the synagogue and taught the people. Everyone was puzzled by His wisdom and teaching and of the mighty works He was doing. The people of Nazareth recognized Jesus as the son of Joseph and Mary, and they knew His brothers James, Joses, Judas, Simon and His sisters. They thought Jesus was an impostor who only claimed to be the Messiah. Jesus was rejected in His own hometown, and He said, "A prophet is not without honor except in His own country, among His own relatives, and in His own house."(Mark 6:4) He didn't perform many miracles in Nazareth, because the people there didn't believe in Him.

The Twelve Apostles Are Sent to Preach

LK 9–Jesus gave the twelve apostles power and authority over demons and the power to heal diseases. He told them to go and preach about the kingdom of God and to heal the sick. He also told them not take anything with them when they went, not a staff, baggage, bread or money. When they entered a house, they were to stay there while they were teaching. If anyone would not invite them in, they were to go on their way. Jesus was preparing them for the work of an apostle. The apostles would finish their work after Jesus' death. The apostles obeyed Jesus, and then they returned and reported what they had done and taught, and Jesus allowed them to go to a deserted place by boat so they could rest.

MK 6–King Herod began to hear about Jesus, because his name was becoming well known, but He thought Jesus was John the Baptist who had come back from the dead. Herod had previously ordered the execution of John the Baptist by having him beheaded.

Jesus and His disciples got in a boat and crossed over the Sea of Galilee to get away from the crowd, but the people saw them leave and ran from the cities and arrived where Jesus and the apostles were going before they got there. When Jesus got there and saw the multitude and He had compassion for them.

JN 6– Jesus went up a mountain and sat down and started teaching them. It was beginning to be late in the day, and Jesus saw a great multitude of people who had come to hear him. He turned to Philip and asked where they could buy bread to feed the people that followed them because they were in a deserted place. Jesus was testing Philip, Jesus already knew that He would miraculously supply enough food to feed the five thousand people. Later As the day became longer the disciples asked Jesus to send the people away so they could go to town and get food. But He said, "You give them something to eat." Andrew said that there was a boy there with five loaves of bread and two fish, but that was not enough food for five thousand people. Jesus had the people sit down on the grass, and then He miraculously supplied enough food for everyone. Jesus had the people assemble in groups of fifty. He blessed the small amount of food the disciples had and broke it into pieces and told the disciples give it to the crowd. Everyone had enough to eat and there were twelve baskets full left over. Jesus told the disciples to pick up the food left over so that nothing would be wasted. The people witnessing the miraculous feeding said Jesus was truly a prophet.

MK 6, MT 14–After feeding the five thousand, Jesus was afraid the people would attempt to make Him their king by force. He told His disciple to go alone by boat to the other side of the sea then Jesus went up the mountain by himself to pray. When evening came Jesus was alone, and the disciples were in their boat. That evening when it became dark the disciples were in the middle of the sea, and a strong wind was blowing. Jesus began walking to the disciples on the water. When Jesus was a distance from the boat, the disciples saw Him and they were afraid because they thought He was a ghost, and they cried out. Jesus called to them and told them to be of good cheer because it was He, and He told them not to be afraid. Peter asked Jesus to command for him to come to Him on the water, and Jesus told him to come.

Peter got out of the boat and began to walk on the water to Jesus, but the waves were washing around him, and he became frightened. He began to sink, and he cried out for Jesus to save him. Jesus put out His hand and helped Peter into the boat and the wind died down. His apostles worshiped Jesus saying, "Truly, You are the Son of God."

MK 6–They crossed the sea and came to Gennesaret and the disciples left the boat and the people on shore recognized them. They went through that territory and began to bring sick people on beds for Jesus to heal. Jesus entered the cities, villages and market places and the people begged Him to let them touch the hem of His garment. Those who touched him were healed.

JN 6– The next day the people Jesus had fed on the mountain went to the place where they saw Jesus disciples in their boats. Jesus wasn't there, so they left in boats to find Him. Jesus had already gone into Capernaum by then, so they went to Capernaum and found Him there. Jesus took an opportunity at that time to teach a lesson about the benevolence of God. He told them that the only reason they were looking for Him was to get more food. He told them to not be more concerned with finding food to eat than being concerned with finding spiritual food that could give them everlasting life. Jesus said he could give them that kind of food, because God had chosen Him for that work. The people wanted to know' what they could do to work the works of God? John 6:29–"Jesus answered and said to them. "This is the work of God that you believe in Him whom He sent."

When Jesus said for them to believe, He was saying to have faith in Him. The people then asked Jesus to perform a miracle so they could believe in Him, and they reminded Him of the fathers of old who miraculously received bread in the wilderness wandering in the Sinai desert. Jesus said, John 6 – I say to you, Moses did not give you the bread from heaven, but My Father gives you the true bread from heaven. For the bread of God is he who comes down from heaven and gives life to the world." Jesus identifies Himself as the true bread from heaven sent by God who could give them eternal life.

Jesus Goes to Capernaum then leaves for Tyre

Jesus and the disciples left Capernaum and went to the area of Tyre and Sidon. Tyre was a seaport on the Phoenician coast and Sidon was not far. Jesus secretly entered a house so he could be hidden from the crowd of people for a while. (Sometimes Jesus sought privacy so He could rest. Jesus had not been in the house long before a woman who had a daughter possessed by a demon found Him. The woman came and fell at Jesus' feet. She was a Greek, a Syro-Phoenician. The woman asked Jesus to cast out the demon, but Jesus said, Mark 7:27 "Let the children be filled first, for it is not good to take the children's bread and throw it to the little dogs."

The woman was not satisfied with Jesus' answer and she said, "Lord, even the little dogs eat the crumbs under the table that fall from the children." Jesus came to His own people the Jews first because they had been God's people for many years and it was through them that Jesus would be born. The Jews were the children of God throughout the old covenant, and the woman and her daughter were Gentiles. The Jews considered gentile people to be no better than dogs. Mark 7:29-30 "Then He said to her, 'For this saying go your way; the demon has gone out of your daughter.' And when she had come to her house, she found the demon gone out, and her daughter lying on the bed."

MK 7–Jesus and His disciples left Tyre and Sidon and went through the region of Decapolis to the Sea of Galilee. Decapolis was a Gentile area during that time, but a small Jewish population also lived there. Decapolis bordered Galilee and Perea. The people brought a deaf mute with a speech impediment to Jesus and begged Him to heal the man. Jesus took him out away from the crowd. Jesus put his fingers in the man's ears. Then He spat and touched his tongue. Jesus looked toward heaven and said "Ephatha," meaning 'be opened.' The man was immediately able to hear and he could talk plainly. The people were astonished at what Jesus had done. Jesus told the people not to tell anyone what He had done, however the more He commanded them not to tell anyone, the more they spread the news all over that area.

Jesus Miraculously Feeds Four Thousand

MT 15–Jesus left the area of Decapolis and went along the edge of the Sea of Galilee. Then He went up on a mountain there and sat down. A great many people came to where He was and brought the lame, blind, mute, and maimed to him for Him to heal. They placed people needing healing at the feet of Jesus, and He healed them and the people were amazed. Jesus called His disciples to come to Him, and He told them He felt sorry for the people because they had been with Him a few days and had nothing to eat. The disciples were concerned because they were in the wilderness and there was no place to get food. Jesus asked them what food they had and they said seven loaves of bread and a few fish. Jesus told the people to sit down and He gave thanks and broke them. Then He gave the bread and fish to the disciples and they fed the people, and the food did not run out. Jesus miraculously fed the four thousand people and they had seven baskets of food left.

Jesus and His Disciples Go to Dalmanutha

MK 8–Jesus sent the people away and He and the disciples left in a boat and sailed to Dalmanutha on the west shore of the Sea of Galilee south of Capernaum. Mary Magdalene was from Magdala in that same area. The Pharisees came to where Jesus was, they still did not believe He was the Messiah, and they were anxious to see if He could perform a miracle. Jesus was disgusted with them because of their unbelief. "He sighed deeply in His spirit and said, "Why does this generation seek a sign? Assuredly, I say to you no sign shall be given to this generation."

(Mark 8) Jesus was very disappointed because of their unbelief that He got into the boat and left Dalmanutha and went to the other side of the Sea of Galilee. Jesus disciples forgot to bring bread, and they only had one loaf in the boat. Jesus told them, "Take heed, beware of the leaven of the Pharisees and the leaven of Herod." (Mark 8) The disciples didn't understand what Jesus meant. They thought He was talking about having no bread. Jesus was aware of their thoughts and He said, "Why do you reason because you have no bread? Do you not yet perceive nor understand? Is your heart still hardened? Having eyes, do you not see? And having ears, do you not hear?

And do you not remember? When I broke the five loaves for the five thousand, how many baskets full of fragments did you take up? Mark 8 Jesus was very disappointed in the disciple's attitude, after all the miracles they had witnessed Him do, they still had little faith and understanding of His power and who He was.

MK 8–Jesus and the disciples came to Bethsaida on the north shore of the Sea of Galilee. A blind man was brought to Jesus, and the people begged Him to heal the man. Jesus led the blind man out of town and He spit on his eyes, put His hands on him, and asked him if he could see. The man said he could see men like trees walking. Jesus put His hands back on the man's eyes and his eyesight was restored. Jesus then sent him away but told him not to tell anyone that Jesus had healed him. The scriptures don't tell us why Jesus at times did not want the people He healed to tell anyone about it. He may have been so physically tired at times that He needed to rest.

MT 16-MK8-LK 9–Jesus and His disciples leave Bethsaida and travel to the towns in Caesarea Philippi located at the foot of Mt Hermon the main water source for the Jordan River. Jesus asked His disciples who the people thought He was. Some thought He was John the Baptist, Elijah, Jeremiah or one of the prophets. Jesus asked them who they thought He was. Peter said to Jesus, "You are the Christ." Jesus blessed Peter and told him that it was God who had revealed to Peter who He was. Matthew 16:18-20 "And I say to you that you are Peter, and on this rock I will build My church, and the gates of Hades shall not prevail against it. And I will give you the keys of the kingdom of heaven, and whatever you bind on earth will be bound in heaven, and whatever you loose on earth will be loosed in heaven." Jesus was saying, the church (Jesus Kingdom) would be built on Peter's confession that Jesus is the Messiah. Jesus then told Peter and the disciples that whatever they taught would be solid like a rock meaning it would be true and confirmed forever, because they taught by the inspiration of the Holy Spirit of God.

MK 9–Jesus and the disciples left Caesarea Philippi and went through Galilee, Jesus did not want anyone to know where He was, because He wanted a private time with the disciples so He could tell them about His death.

Mark 9:31 "The Son of Man is being betrayed into the hands of men, and they will kill Him. And after He is killed, He will rise the third day." This must have been a shock to the disciples that Jesus would face death after seeing the great power Jesus had already exhibited. They probably wondered what would become of them if Jesus died. Jesus had already hinted of His death, but the disciples were puzzled when Jesus said He would rise on the third day. The faith of the apostle grew as they traveled with Jesus and witnessed His miracles, but the things He told them puzzled them at times. The disciples asked Jesus who in the kingdom would be the greatest? Jesus told them that a member of the kingdom would be like a little child. Little children look to their parents with humility and accept what their parents tell them. Those who are in the kingdom must look to God and Christ with the humble attitude of faith, hope and love and accept what the scriptures teach them. The Kingdom of God was to be ruled by God through His word in the scriptures.

When Jesus spoke about the greatest in the kingdom, the disciples, no doubt, thought of authority, possibly pomp and splendor, but Jesus had a surprising answer that did not include any of those things. Jesus said one must change and become as a little child. One enters the kingdom with faith, hope, love and humility when they give their lives to God and Christ. Entering the kingdom of God involves a change of heart from worldly priorities, accepting Christ and the authority of His word with all of the heart. We must love the Lord our God with all our heart, soul, and mind. The love that the Father has lavished on us, Is very great because we are His children.

Disciples of Christ are united in one body, which is the Kingdom of Christ as brothers and sisters of Christ. Jesus asked the question "Who is my mother, and my brothers?" Then He said that whoever does the will of His Father in heaven is His brother, His sister and His mother." "If anyone says, "I love God," and yet he hates his brother, he is a liar. He who does not love his brother whom he has seen cannot love God whom he has not seen. Believers are many in number, yet we are one body in Christ, and individual members, one of another. Jesus said that if God's people love one another, God lives in us and His love is perfected in us.

1st Corinthians 13:1-7 "Though I speak with the tongues of men and of angels, but have not love, I have become a sounding brass or a clanging cymbal. And though I have the gift of prophecy, and understand all mysteries and all knowledge, and though I have all faith, so that I could remove mountains, but have not love, I am nothing. And though I bestow all my goods to feed the poor, and though I give my body to be burned, but have not love, it profits me nothing. Love suffers long and is kind; love does not envy; love does not parade itself, is not puffed up; does not behave rudely, does not seek its own, is not provoked, thinks no evil; does not rejoice in iniquity, but rejoices in the truth; bears all things, believes all things, hopes all things, endures all things."

Jesus Reveals His Suffering and Death

From that time, Jesus began to reveal to His disciples that He would have to go to Jerusalem and suffer at the hands of the elders, chief priests and scribes and be killed but He would be resurrected on the third day. The Pharisees, elders, scribes and the chief priest leading members of the Jewish religion did not believe Jesus was the Messiah they thought He was an impostor. They wanted to see Jesus perform a miracle to prove He was the Messiah. Jesus had already proved Himself many times by a great number of miracles and He was disturbed by their unbelief. He refused show them another miracle. Jesus told them they would see a miracle like Jonah, who was in the belly of the whale for three days and three nights then was spit out alive. Jesus referred to His death burial and resurrection comparing it to the familiar story of Jonah in the belly of a whale for three days. Jesus would be in the grave for three days and nights and Jesus would be resurrected and seen again after His resurrection.

When Jesus died, He was buried and He was resurrected on the 3rd day. Peter did not Believe Jesus when He said he would be killed and Jesus privately rebuked Peter and told him he did not understand the things of God. Jesus tells the disciples about the cost of following Him and said they must deny their own self and take up the cross and follow Him. The cross represents the persecution and suffering associated with being a disciple of Christ especially among the Jews in the first century.

The disciples suffered persecution from the Romans before and after the death of Christ and during their mission to establish the church on earth but they looked forward to the time when Jesus will return to reward the followers of Christ with eternal life in a place prepared for them in heaven. MT 16:27-28–For the Son of man will come in the glory of His Father with His angels, and then He will reward each according to his works. Assuredly, I say to you, some are standing here who shall not taste of death till they see the Son of Man coming in His kingdom. Jesus spoke those words to His disciples who would witness the transfiguration of Jesus coming in His kingdom six days after the prophecy of the second coming. Matthew 16. The transfiguration would strengthen the faith of Jesus apostles. Matthew 17:1-9–Six days later Jesus took Peter, James and John to a mountain and He was transfigured, His face shone like the sun and His clothes became white as a bright light. Moses and Elijah appeared and talked to them and the Disciples were so frightened they fell on the ground.

Peter told Jesus it was good for them to be there and Peter suggested making three tabernacles, one for Jesus, Moses and Elijah the great prophets of the Old Testament. Peter suggested making three shrines to honor these most notable people. Peter did not yet realize that that the things of the Old Law given to Moses would cease and all people could be redeemed by faith and obedience to the gospel of Jesus. God explains –A bright cloud came over them and the voice of God said, "This is My beloved Son, in whom I am well pleased. Hear Him!" God announced that now was the time for Moses and Elijah to be in the background, their work was completed. Now was the time to have faith in God's Son and obey Him.

MK 8– Jesus began to teach His disciples about what was ahead for Him in the future. Jesus tells them He will suffer many things and be rejected by the religious leaders. Be killed and resurrected after three days. This was hard for the disciples to believe and Peter rebuked Jesus. Jesus turned around looked at the disciples and began rebuking Peter. Mark 8:33 "Get behind Me, Satan! For you are not mindful of the things of God, but the things of men." Eight days after the vision Jesus took Peter, James and John up on a high mountain to pray probably Mt Hermon or Mt Tabor.

God identified Jesus as his Son and gave His approval of Jesus ministry. The disciples were frightened and they fell face down on the ground but Jesus touched them and told them not to be afraid. When they looked again Jesus was the only one they saw, Moses and Elijah had disappeared. The disappearance of Moses and Elijah meant their work had been completed and now people must follow Jesus. Jesus told the disciples not to tell anyone about what they had seen until after Jesus was resurrected. The disciples still did not understand the complete truth about everything that would take place in Jesus life as the Messiah and the Redeemer. Jesus told the disciples not tell anyone about the things they saw until He rose from the dead. The disciples wondered what rising from the dead meant. They asked Jesus about Elijah and wanted to know why the scribes taught that Elijah must come before the Messiah.

Mark 9:12– Jesus told them, Elijah was to come first and restore all things. Jesus replies that Elijah has already come making a reference to John the Baptist who came in the spirit and power of Elijah. Jesus called Himself the Son of Man, and told them that He would suffer many things and be treated with contempt. But I say to you that Elijah has come, and they did to Him whatever they wished, as it is written of him. Jesus told them that John the Baptist fulfilled the prophecy of the coming of Elijah. John ministered in the same spirit and power of Elijah.

MT 17– Jesus and the disciples caught up with the multitude and Jesus cast a demon out of a boy. The demon caused the boy to have epileptic fits and he often fell into the fire or the water. The disciples had tried to cast out the demon but they were not able. Jesus cast the demon from him. Jesus referred to that generation of people as faithless. The disciples privately asked Jesus why they could not cast out the demon and he told them they did not have enough faith. So Jesus said to them, "Because of your unbelief; I say to you, if you have faith as a mustard seed, you will say to this mountain, 'Move from here to there.' And it will move; and nothing will be impossible for you. However, this kind does not go out except by prayer and fasting." Jesus told the disciples about His death that was coming soon. Jesus said He was going to be betrayed and given to men who would kill Him.

Jesus said after His death He would be resurrected on the third day. The disciples were very sorrowful after hearing that Jesus would die.

Jesus and the Disciples go back to Capernaum

(MT 17) Jesus and the disciples go back to their home base in Capernaum. The men who received the taxes for the temple asked Peter if Jesus had paid the temple tax and Peter told him yes. Jesus knew what Peter was thinking and he asked him, do the kings of the earth take taxes from their sons or from strangers? Peter answered from strangers. Jesus replied then the sons are free. Jesus implies that the sons are not obligated to pay taxes but to keep from offending anyone for the sake of His ministry, Jesus told Peter to go to the sea, put in a fish hook and open the mouth of the first fish he caught and he would find a piece of money. Jesus told him to pay the taxes for Him and for your self.

Jesus paid the tax to avoid trouble with the religious leaders. Jesus knew the disciples had been arguing and He knew what they argued about but Jesus asked the disciples what they argued about when they were on the road. The disciples had argued about who would be the greatest in the kingdom and they did not answer Jesus. Jesus said those who desire to be first will be last of all and he will be the servant of all. There is to be equality in the Kingdom of God (church). The disciples did not understand that all disciples would be equal in authority but some would have better understanding and be more capable to teach and take a public lead not personal power in the church.

MT 18) Jesus set a child by them and told them that they would not enter heaven unless they become like a child. Jesus was talking about the humility of a little child. Jesus meant everyone in the church should have an attitude of humility like a little child. Little children are not concerned with being the greatest they are happy to be accepted and to accept God, Christ and those who are caring for them. Those who strive to be the greatest and have authority over others cause many problems within the church. The attitudes of Jesus disciples should be like the humble attitude of little children. Matthew 18:2-5 "Then Jesus called a little child to Him, set him in the midst of them, and said, "Assuredly, I say to you, unless you are converted and become as little children, you will by no means enter the kingdom of heaven.

Therefore whoever humbles himself as this little child is the greatest in the kingdom of heaven. Whoever receives one little child like this in My name receives Me."

Jesus called all the people to come Him hear Him and told them that the food they ate would not defile them. He told them it is the things that come out of the mouth that defiles blasphemy, lies and evil thoughts. Jesus is talking about being defiled morally in the eyes of God. Mark 7:20-23 "And He said. "What comes out of a man defiles a man. For from within the heart of men, proceed evil thoughts, adulteries, fornications, murders, thefts, covetousness, wickedness, deceit, lewdness, an evil eye, blasphemy, pride and foolishness. All these evil things come from within and defile a man." Jesus quoted the scriptures they knew and claimed to believe, in order to shame them because they did not honor the very scriptures they quoted.

Parable about Lost Sheep

LK 18 When Jesus talked to tax collectors and sinners the Pharisees and scribes complained saying He talked to sinners. The religious leaders and notable people thought they were too good to even speak to people who collected taxes and they criticized and shunned tax collectors and other people they thought were beneath them. Jesus came to bring salvation to all people because all people are sinners. Everyone needs to obey God and Christ so they can have personal forgiveness because all people sin. Jesus taught everyone obey His message of redemption. Jesus taught a parable about lost sheep and compared them to people who are lost because of sin. Sheep are docile and need someone to lead them in the right direction and protect them from their enemies.

Sinners are like lost sheep they have the same need and Jesus is the Good Shepherd that guides sinful people to a life of righteousness through faith in Him so they can be saved from the penalty of sin. Luke 15:7 "I say to you that likewise there will be more joy in heaven over one sinner who repents that over ninety-nine just persons who need no repentance." Faith in Jesus, repentance, baptism, hope and love are the essential ingredients for a successful life on earth that leads to a home in heaven.

Everyone was a sinner when Jesus came and like a good Shepherd Jesus provided a way of salvation for everyone who would come to Him in faith.

The Feast of Dedication is the same as the Feast of Lights and it took place at the same time as the feast of tabernacles. It was celebrated for eight days. Jesus went to Solomon's porch in the temple at the time of the feast and the Jews there surrounded Him. They asked Jesus how long He was going to keep them in suspense about who He was. They wanted Jesus to declare whether He was the Messiah. Jesus had plainly shown them that He was the Messiah by His works miraculous works but they did not believe Him. Jesus said the works He did in His Fathers name were witness that He was the Messiah. Jesus told them they did not believe because they were not of His sheep. Jesus sheep symbolizes the people who believe in Jesus and follow Him.

LK 9– Jesus knew everything that was going to happen to Him. When it was near the time for Jesus to be arrested He went to Jerusalem. Jesus was in Galilee and He went through Samaria on His way. Jesus sent messengers ahead of Him and they went into a Samaritan village to prepare the way for Him but the Samaritans refused to receive Jesus because they knew He was on His way to Jerusalem. James and John asked Jesus if they could, like Elijah call fire down on them. Jesus rebuked them telling them they did not understand what manner of spirit they were of. The disciples of Jesus were not taught to have a mean spirit when someone offended them. Jesus rebuked them and He told them He did not come to destroy people's lives, He came to save them and they went to another village.

Jesus teaches the disciples about the cost of discipleship. On the road to Jerusalem one of the disciples said to Jesus, "Lord I will follow you wherever you go." Jesus said, "Foxes have holes and birds of the air have nests, but the Son of Man has nowhere to lay His head." Jesus told another disciple to follow Him and He said he had to bury his father first. Jesus said, "Let the dead bury their own dead, but you go and preach the kingdom of God." Jesus emphasizes the importance of the mission of the twelve men He chose to be apostles. The main concern of the apostles would be the preaching of the gospel for the rest of their life.

The Jews came to Jerusalem every year to observe their annual feasts. There were seven annual feasts the, Passover of seven days including the weekly Sabbath and unleavened bread, first fruits, Pentecost, the day of Atonement, the first day of booths, and the eight day of booths. On the way to Jerusalem Jesus entered a village and was met by ten lepers and they stood at a distance. People were afraid of leprosy because it was a painful disease and there was no known cure. The lepers shouted out to Jesus and asked Him to have mercy on them. Luke 17:14–When Jesus saw them, He said to them "Go show yourselves to the priests." And as they went, they were cleansed." One of them that had been healed returned to Jesus and Glorified God with a loud voice. He was a Samaritan and he fell down at Jesus feet and thanked Him. Jesus asked him "Were there not ten cleansed? Jesus said where are the other nine? A foreigner was the only one that that gave God the glory for healing him. Jesus used the scriptures they knew and claimed to follow in order to shame them because they did not honor the very scriptures they quoted.

Jesus in the Temple

JN 7–Jesus brothers left for Jerusalem during the time for the feast and Jesus went in secret to Jerusalem. Jesus went to the temple and taught and the people were amazed because of His wisdom and knowledge they knew he had never studied in the Synagogues. Jesus told them the things he taught, came directly from God who sent Him. Jesus asked them why they wanted to kill Him and the people said he had a demon. They thought a demon gave Jesus His power to perform miraculous signs. Jesus asked them if they were angry because He healed a man on the Sabbath. Jesus said, do not judge by appearance but use righteous judgment. The people were discussing among themselves who Jesus was and where He came from. Jesus told them that they knew Him and knew where He was from, He told them God sent Him. The people were divided in their opinion of Jesus. Some accepted Him as a great prophet others said He is the Messiah but some wondered if the messiah would come from Galilee instead of Judea. The scriptures said He would come from Bethlehem.

Jesus remarks stirred up those who were talking about Him and they wanted to seize Him but no one touched Him. Some of the people were convinced that Jesus was the Messiah but they thought the Messiah would have done more signs than Jesus did. The Pharisees heard the people discussing the things Jesus said and they sent officers to arrest Him. Jesus had predicted His death. John 7:33-34 "Then Jesus said to them, "I shall be with you a little longer, and then I go to Him who sent Me. You will seek Me and not find Me, and where I am you cannot come." Jesus would soon be arrested, tried and crucified then He would go to God who sent Him. They would look for Him and would not be able to find Him because they could not go where He was going. He would ascend to heaven.

The Jewish Sanhedrin council and the people were confused about who Jesus was. During the last day of the feast Jesus stood up and said, "If anyone thirsts, let Him come to Me and drink. He who believes in Me, as the scripture has said out of his heart will flow, rivers of living water." JN 7–Jesus spoke about the Holy Spirit that would be given to those who believed in Jesus. Flowing waters is an endless stream of water figuratively representing the spiritual life of a disciple in whom the Holy Spirit lives. The evidence of the living waters is found in Acts chapter two on the day of Pentecost when the Holy Spirit was given to the Apostles.

JN 8–Everyone left the temple to go home and Jesus went to the Mt of Olives. Jesus came to the temple again early the next morning and the scribes and Pharisees brought a woman to Him that had committed adultery. Jesus said, John 8:7 "He who is without sin among you, let him throw a stone at her first." The people asking Jesus what to do were convicted by there own conscience because they knew they were sinners and they left. Jesus told the woman He did not condemn her. This does not mean Jesus approved of her sin. His time for judgment had not come. Judgment and condemnation belongs to God. Jesus left the temple and hid because He had aroused the anger of the people in the temple by His answers to their questions and they picked up stones to throw at Him. They asked Jesus what He thought they should do.

Jesus did not answer them directly instead He wrote on the ground "He who is without sin among you, let him throw a stone at her first." Jesus told the woman He did not condemn her and told her to go and sin no more. Jesus spoke to the people again and told them He was the light of the world and whoever follows Him will not walk in darkness but have the light of life. Light is used figuratively meaning Jesus has the real truth and knowledge that can enlighten their minds and teach them the way of righteousness. Jesus continued to talk to those who are in the temple. Jesus tells them His judgment is true because God is with Him in His judgment and He bears witness of Him. God bore witness of Jesus from the beginning and through the scriptures. Jesus told them they did not know God for if they did they would know Him also. The scriptures from the beginning taught about the coming of the Messiah but the Jews failed to believe. Jesus said he was going to God and they could not come. The people who refuse to accept Jesus will never see God. Jesus warned them that if they die and are still guilty of sin they would die in their sins. Jesus hinted that after they kill Him they would then realize who He was. Some of the people in Jerusalem did not know Jesus and they wondered if Jesus was the one the scribes and the Pharisees wanted to kill.

They reasoned that Jesus was not the Messiah because they knew where Jesus was from. Jesus cried out from within the temple "You both know Me, and you know where I am from; and I have not come of Myself, but He who sent Me is true, whom you do not know. "But I know Him, for I am from Him, and He sent me." The officers of the temple had apparently taken Jesus but they had not delivered Him to the officials. The officers were beginning to believe that Jesus was the Messiah and they said no man had ever spoken like Jesus.

The members of the Sanhedrin, the highest tribunal of the Jews were upset and they asked if any of the rulers or Pharisees had believed in Him? Then they cursed the crowd. Nicodemus a cautious Pharisee who believed Jesus would receive unlawful treatment reminded them that Jesus must receive a fair hearing under the Law. He asked if the law would judge a person before they heard them. They asked Nicodemus if he was also from Galilee and they, said no prophet had ever come from Galilee. Everyone left the temple and went home.

Jesus was not arrested and He went to the Mt of Olives that overlooks Jerusalem to spend the night, but early the next morning He returned to the temple and the people came to Him and He sat down and began to teach. The scribes and Pharisees brought a woman to Him that was caught in the act of adultery. They told Jesus what she had done then quoted from the Law of Moses that prescribed stoning an adulterer. They asked Jesus if He thought she should be stoned. Jesus did not speak but He wrote a note on the ground.

John 8:7— When they continued to ask Jesus questions He said to them, "He who is without sin among you, let him throw a stone at her first." Jesus did not condone sin or a lack of punishment for sin, He was teaching that they did not have the right to condemn and punish her because they were also guilty of sin. God is the only one with the right to punish the guilty. The accusers of the woman left and Jesus said He did not condemn her and He told her to go and do not sin anymore. John 8:12 "Then Jesus spoke to them again saying. "I am the light of the world. He who follows Me shall not walk in darkness, but have the light of life." Jesus uses light to mean, being able to understand God's word with the mind. The word of God enlightens the mind, allowing a person to know and understand God's will for them as taught in the Bible.

1st Corinthians 2:13 "These things we also speak not in words which man's wisdom teaches but which the Holy Spirit teaches, comparing spiritual things with spiritual." Jesus declares that He is the One that the scriptures reveal and anyone desiring to be righteous will find righteousness in Him. Jesus used the words living water when He sat at a well and ask a Samaritan woman for a drink.

Jesus told the woman He would give her living water. The living water promised by Jesus is the Holy Spirit that dwells in those who believe and accept Christ. Ephesians 1:13-14– "In Him you also trusted, after you heard the word of truth, the gospel of your salvation; in whom also, having believed, you were sealed with the Holy Spirit of promise, who is the guarantee of our inheritance until the redemption of the purchased possession, to the praise of His glory." The Holy Spirit was not given to all believers at that time, later after Jesus Death, burial and resurrection the Spirit would indwell all believers, and a greater measure of the Spirit was to be given, to those people directly chosen by Christ like the Apostles.

They would receive gifts from the Holy Spirit in a generous amount in order to enable them to accomplish their mission of preaching the gospel. In the early days of the church, certain members of the kingdom were given temporary gifts of the Holy Spirit so they could lead and teach the members of the church before the scriptures were complete. The special gifts eventually ceased to be given because the Bible scriptures were completed and the redemption plan of God was completely documented. It is up to each individual person now to examine the scriptures and learn about God's plan of redemption and obey the word in the scriptures and have faith in God and Christ.

Jesus spoke plainly to his accusers telling them that they did not know Him because they didn't know God. They knew there was a God that created everything but they failed to love and trust Him in a personal way and they failed know Jesus the Son of God and have faith in Him. Jesus told them he was going away meaning He was going back to heaven. Jesus told them they could not go there because they are of this world. Jesus enemies had no spiritual insight or yearning for heaven. Jesus knew they would still be guilty when they died because they would not accept Him as God's Son. And He told them if they did not believe in Him they would die in their sins. John 8:31 "If you abide in My word, you are My disciples indeed. And you shall know the truth, and the truth shall make you free." 8:34-36– Jesus answered them, I say to you, whoever commits sin is a slave of sin and a slave does not abide in the house forever, but a son abides forever. Therefore if the Son makes you free, you shall be free indeed."

The Jews insisted that they were God's children but Jesus told them if they were God's children they would not be trying to kill Him. Jesus accused the Jews of being the children of the devil because the devil had always been a murderer. The Jews who killed Jesus were murders and did not belong to God. John 8:47 "He who is of God hears God's words; therefore you do not hear, because you are not of God." The Jews were God's chosen people but they lost their place as His people because they failed to obey Him and they would not accept Jesus. The Jews accused Jesus of having a demon because of the things Jesus said and Jesus said he did not have a demon and He honors His Father, but they dishonor Him.

Jesus said again, those who obey His word will never see death. Jesus is referring to spiritual death. The spirit of people that are saved by faith in Jesus does not die, the spirit lives forever in a place of paradise. The Jews continue to ridicule Jesus and they call attention to His age and with sarcasm saying have you seen Abraham? Jesus tells them that He existed before the time of Abraham. The Jews picked up stones to kill Him but Jesus went out of the temple and disappeared.

Jesus Heals a Blind Man

JN 9–Jesus saw a blind man who had been blind since birth. The disciples thought blindness and other defects were caused by sin but Jesus knew that sin is not the cause of birth defects. Jesus told them the works of God are made known by Him and He must do those works while He is still here. The miracles Jesus performed were works that proved that He was the Son of God. People cannot perform real miracles unless they get their power from God. Jesus spit on the ground and mixed the spittle with the clay and anointed the blind man's eyes. He told him to go wash in the pool of Siloam, a public pool of rain, water used by the people of Jerusalem. The man washed in the pool and he was able to see. The water did not heal him his faith in God and Jesus caused God to heal him. The Pharisees found out about the miracle and they said Jesus was not from God because He broke the law of the Sabbath when He healed on the Sabbath. The Pharisees could not be convinced to believe that Jesus was from God and they told the man who was healed of blindness that he was born with sin and they threw him out of the synagogue.

No one is born with the guilt of sin because sin is a deliberate act of disobedience to God's commands. People sin when they are old enough to be accountable to God and not before. Jesus heard what the Jews did to the man and He looked for him and found him. Jesus asked him if he believed in the Son of God. The man did not know who the Son of God was and Jesus said, John 9:37 "You have both seen Him and it is He who is talking with you." Then the man told Jesus he believed Him and he worshiped Him. Jesus taught the disciples a parable about Himself, the Parable of the Good Shepherd.

There is a doorway that leads into the Good Shepherd's flock and the call goes out for sheep to enter His flock through the door. The door represents obedience to the Shepherd's message in the gospel and it is the only way into the Shepherds flock. The sheep represent the people who have faith in Jesus and Jesus Himself is the Good Shepherd. No one can enter heaven unless they believe in the Son of God and follow Him. Jesus only accepts those sheep that love Him and obey his voice. The shepherd guides His sheep by His voice and from then on and they follow no one else. If the sheep stray from the flock The Shepherd hunts for them until He finds them and brings them back into the fold. Jesus the Shepherd loved His sheep enough to sacrifice himself for them. The teaching of Jesus caused a division among the Jews, some accused Him of having a demon and being out of His mind but others realized that Jesus words were not the words of a demon and a few people and the disciples followed Him.

Jesus Selects Seventy Disciples to Teach

LK 10-13) Jesus appointed seventy disciples besides the twelve and sent them out two by two to all of the places where He would be going. He told them the harvest was very great and there was few workers. The seventy would be teaching about Jesus and the gospel. Jesus warned the seventy or as some say seventy-two that they will be like sheep among wolves. Being like sheep means they will be defenseless against the Jews who oppose Jesus. The disciples would be on the move constantly teaching about Jesus and there would not be time for them to do anything else.

The time was becoming short, the time for Jesus to be arrested. Jesus gave His disciples, power from the Holy Spirit so they would be able to teach the gospel message and to confirm the authority of their message. The apostles were, inspired by the Holy Spirit meaning the Spirit would give them the very words to speak as they taught. They were to tell those they taught that the kingdom of God was coming soon and they would be able to recognize the kingdom. The Jewish people were familiar with the story about Sodom and Gomorrah about how God destroyed the people of that city.

Jesus warned the people that in the Day He returns from heaven it will be a worse time for the unrighteous than it was on the day Sodom and Gomorrah was destroyed. Jesus pronounced a woe on the cities of Chorazin and Bethsaida, cities in Galilee a few miles from Capernaum. Jesus left Nazareth at the beginning of His ministry and His Home base was in the city of Capernaum where his mother and brothers and some of the disciples lived. The people in that area knew about many of the great things Jesus did but many still did not believe in Him. Jesus then pronounced a woe on Capernaum the town that had seen and felt, the mighty power of Jesus, but still would not accept Jesus as the Messiah.

Jesus said Capernaum would be brought down to Hades meaning the unbelieving people there will be condemned on the great judgment day of God at the end of time. Jesus told the seventy that the people who reject their message about Him are rejecting God. Luke 10:17-20 "And He said to them, I saw Satan fall like lightning from heaven. Every time a person accepts Jesus and obeys the gospel it is a victory for them and for Jesus. Behold I give you the authority to trample on serpents and scorpions, and over all the power of the enemy, and nothing shall by any means hurt you, but rather rejoice because your names are written in heaven." The statement Jesus made about Satan was directly connected with the Disciples report of success when they preached the gospel in the areas where Jesus sent them. The gospel message had a clear and successful impact on the hearts and minds of many of the people they taught and they obeyed the gospel (good news of redemption). Jesus often spoke in figurative language to teach the truth to some, and hide the meaning from others.

The influence of Satan corrupted the minds of people causing them to ignore the commands of God. The time of disobedience began with Adam and Eve in the Garden of Eden. Since the death of Christ people are still in a spiritual battle with Satan. In Ephesians 6 Paul states that God's people are engaged in a spiritual battle against the forces of darkness and wickedness. The only defense against the evil spiritual forces is the armor of God, which is the Word of God and faith in Christ that leads to righteousness.

Colossians 3:1-17 "And whatever you do in word or deed, do all in the name of the Lord Jesus, giving thanks to God the Father Through Him.

Luke 23-24 "Blessed are the eyes which see the things you see; for I tell you that many prophets and Kings have desired to see what you see, and have not seen it and to hear what you hear, and have not heard it." A lawyer tested Jesus by asking Him what he could do to have eternal life and Jesus asked him a question about the Law of Moses. The lawyer quoted from Deuteronomy where it says to love the Lord with all your heart, soul, strength and mind and to love your neighbor like you love yourself. Jesus told him that was the right answer and if he did that he would have eternal life.

Jesus and the Disciples Continue to Travel

Jesus and His disciples continued to travel and they entered another village and a woman named Martha welcomed Jesus to her house. Martha had a sister named Mary and Mary sat at Jesus feet and listened to Him teach about the kingdom. Martha was busy serving and Mary was not helping her, she was sitting at Jesus feet listening to Him. Martha asked Jesus if he cared that Mary had left her to do all the serving. Martha wanted Jesus to tell Mary to help her. Luke 10:41-42 "And Jesus answered and said to her, "Martha, Martha, you are worried and troubled about many things. But one thing is needed, and Mary has chosen that good part, which will not be taken away from her." Mary was doing what was right at the time because she was dedicated to listening to Jesus. Jesus did not say that either one of the women were not doing the proper thing, He suggested that Mary was doing a good thing by devoting her attention to hearing Him teach.

(LK 11) One of the disciples asked Jesus to teach them how to pray. "So He said to them, "When you pray, say: Our Father in Heaven Hallowed be your name. Your kingdom come, Your will be done on earth as it is in heaven. Give us this day our daily bread. And forgive us our sins, for we also forgive everyone who is indebted to us. And do not lead us into temptation, but deliver us from the evil one." Jesus told the disciples not to fear the Pharisees, but fear God who is able to cast you into hell. Jesus assures them that God will protect and provide for them if they will obey Him.

Jesus, warns the disciple of a time coming when He will be killed. He warns them about the persecution they will suffer. Jesus said there will be much division among the people when He goes away speaking of His death, burial, resurrection, then ascension into heaven. Someday, Jesus will return to earth to take all of the people who have faith in Him to a new home, eternal in heaven.

Jesus Warns People to be ready for His Return

Jesus advises the disciples and all people to prepare for the time of His return. Jesus said, for no one knows the day or hour when He will return. He exhorts them to have faith in Him do the things He has taught them. (LK 13) Jesus teaches about repentance a term that implies a change of ones purpose, mind and heart. Repentance in the Bible makes reference to sorrowfully regretting the guilt of sin against God and Christ and asking for God's forgiveness. Repentance involves changing one's mind or purpose to obey God instead of sin. Jesus said, unless you repent you will all perish. When Jesus sent the twelve disciples to preach they told people to repent. Mark 6: 12 "So they went out and preached that people should repent. And they cast out many demons, and anointed with oil many who were sick, and healed them." Jesus told a parable about a fig tree that had not been producing fruit for three years. The owner of the tree asked if he should cut it down. Jesus told them to fertilize it then if it does not produce fruit cut it down. Jesus compares the fig tree to people that do not repent and obey the Gospel. When a tree fails to produce fruit it is good for nothing and should be cut down. Jesus message was to teach and encourage everyone to have faith in Him and obey the gospel and if they refuse to accept Jesus as the God's Son and the Savior, leave them alone. No one can be forced into the kingdom (church). Jesus referred indirectly to the people of Israel but the message applies to all people. People must obey the gospel of Christ from a sincere heart of faith. God gave His people the Jews many opportunities to repent and accept Christ as the Messiah but most of them refused to accept Christ.

JN 10-During the time for the Feast of Dedication Jesus went to Solomon's porch at the temple and the Jews gathered around Him. The Feast of Dedication is now known as Hanukkah and is a memorial to the dedication of the temple by Judas Maccabeus several years earlier.

The Jews were very anxious to know if Jesus was truly the Messiah. They asked Him how long He would keep them in suspense. Jesus had fully demonstrated in their presence who He was but many failed to believe Him. They said if you are the Christ tell us in a way that we can understand. Jesus spoke to them in parables and they did not always understand Him. The Jews accused Jesus of blasphemy because they said you are a man but you claim to be God. Jesus gave the people of His time, proof that He was God's Son by the Miracles He performed and they still refused to believe Him.

Jesus argued from Psalm 82 where God talks to a group and He calls them gods and sons of the Most High. That was an example of mortals or angels being referred to as gods. Jesus asked why was He was accused of blasphemy if He referred to Himself as a Son of God. All of those that obey the gospel are children of God. John10: 37-38. "If I do not do the works of My Father, do not believe in Me; but if I do, though you do not believe Me, believe the works, that you may know and believe that the Father is in Me, and I in Him." The people wanted to arrest Jesus for blasphemy because they still refused to believe Him but He escaped from them and went to the area of the Jordan where John the Baptist had previously done his baptizing.

The people then believed in Jesus and they agreed that everything John said about Him was true. Jesus went through other towns and villages towards Jerusalem and He taught as he traveled.

Jesus told the people they must do something now while they are living before they can go to heaven, if they wait it will be too late. That same day the Pharisees came to Jesus and warned Him to leave because Herod wanted to kill Him. Jesus was not afraid of Herod, and He had not completed His work among the people but Jesus decided to leave. Jesus was resigned to the fact that He was going to suffer and die but He did not want to die outside of the city of Jerusalem. Jesus was going to be killed even though He had the power to prevent His death. Jesus died willingly to save those who would have faith in Him. He came to earth for the purpose of dying for the sins of the people, but it was not yet the right time.

Luke 13:34-35 "O Jerusalem, Jerusalem, the one who kills the prophets and stones those who are sent to her! How often I wanted to gather your children together, as a hen gathers her brood under her wings, but you were not willing! See!' "Your house is left to you desolate; and assuredly, I say to you, you shall not see Me until the time comes when you say, 'Blessed is He who comes in the name of the Lord!'" Jesus did everything He could to convince His own people that He was the Messiah but many Jews especially the religious leaders rejected Him and eventually were responsible for His death not knowing that they were dooming themselves to eternal destruction. Jesus went to the house of a Pharisee and there were other guests at the house besides Jesus. Jesus taught the people by asking questions with obvious answers in order to teach about relationships among the members of the Kingdom of God.

Jesus teaches Pharisees and Lawyers

Luke 16:14-17—The Pharisees who were lovers of money, heard what Jesus said and they made fun of Him. And Jesus said to them, "You are those who justify yourselves before men, but God knows your hearts. For what is highly esteemed among men is an abomination in the sight of God. The Law and the prophets were until John.' Since that time the kingdom of God has been preached, and everyone was coming into it." Jesus said—It was easier for heaven and earth to pass away than for one bit of the law to fail. The Law of Moses did not fail the Law was not meant to save people or make them righteous. Besides the people did not obey the Law. Jesus told them that a new law from God was coming that is not like the Law of Moses. The new law is the gospel of Christ that redeems people from the guilt of sin. If a person under the Law of Moses sinned there was no provision in the Law to forgive sin but the moment a person accepts Jesus by faith and repents of their sin and is baptized they are they are a child of God dedicated to serving Jesus God and others.

Jesus told a parable about a certain man that was rich and had everything he wanted every day. Jesus made a comparison between a rich man and a beggar named Lazarus to show that being accepted by God does not depend on wealth and fame but in a person's faith, hope and love. Lazarus was full of sores, and was laid at the rich man's gate hoping he would be fed with the crumbs from the rich man's table.

The dogs were the only ones that cared about Lazarus and they came and licked his sores. When the Lazarus died the angels took him to Abraham's bosom. The rich man also died and was buried and he was in torment in Hades. He could see Abraham far off and see Lazarus who was in his bosom. The rich man cried out and said, 'Father Abraham have mercy on me and send Lazarus that he may dip the tip of his finger in water and cool my tongue; for I am tormented in this flame.' But Abraham said to the rich man remember that in your lifetime you received good things, and Lazarus evil things; but now he is comforted. And besides all this, between us and you there is a great gulf fixed, so that those who want to go from here to you cannot, nor can those there come to us." The rich man did not suffer after death because he was rich. He suffered because he did not have in God's Son. The, Lord judge's people by what is in their heart not by their personal wealth. People must have faith, hope and love in and for God and Christ regardless of whether they are rich or poor. When people die their spirit goes to Hades a place reserved for the spirits of the dead. There are two places in Hades one for those who are saved because of their faith, and it is a place of paradise. There is also a place of torment for those who have little or no faith. When a person dies, their fate has already been determined.

Jesus Goes to Bethany to Raise Lazarus

JN 11–Lazarus lived in Bethany near Jerusalem the town where Mary and Martha lived. Martha sent a message to Jesus that Lazarus was dead. She was hoping Jesus would restore his life. Jesus was a close friend of the family and knew they believed in Him. Jesus told the disciples they were going to Judea again. The disciples did not believe they should go back to Judea but Jesus told them His friend Lazarus was dead and He was going to raise him from the dead. Jesus had told Martha He had the power to raise Lazarus from the dead. Jesus said those who believe in Him would not die. Jesus referred to the spirit of people. Lazarus spirit continued to live after his body died. His Spirit was in Hades the realm of the spirits of the dead. Martha had faith in Christ to raise Lazarus and she went to call her sister Mary.

Martha called to her sister Mary and told her the teacher had come and he was asking for her. The Jews in the house with Mary were comforting her as she grieved for her brother. They followed Mary when she let the house to go to the tomb where Lazarus was buried. When Mary came to Jesus she wept and fell down at His feet and told Him if He had been there Lazarus would not have died. Mary and the Jews that came with her were crying and Jesus was deeply moved. Jesus loved Mary, Martha and Lazarus. Jesus was disturbed in his spirit and He asked where Lazarus was buried. Jesus told them that Lazarus will rise again and said, "let us go to Him." When Jesus arrived at the tomb He could tell that Lazarus had been dead for four days. Since Jerusalem was close to Bethany many women from there had joined Martha and Mary to console them. And she confessed her faith in Christ by saying, "Lord if You had been here, my brother would not have died. But even now I know that whatever You ask of God, God will give You."

Martha thought Jesus meant Lazarus would live after the resurrection at the end of time. John 11:25-26 "Jesus said to her, "I Am the resurrection and the life. He who believes in Me, though he may die, he shall live. And whoever lives and believes in Me shall never die. Do you believe this?" The tomb was a cave and there was a stone covering the entrance. Jesus told them to move the stone and Martha said Lord by now there is a bad smell for he has been dead for four days. Jesus reminded them that He told them before that they would see the glory of God after their death. At the gravesite Jesus prayed to His Father God and called for Lazarus to come out of his grave. Lazarus emerged from the grave wearing his grave clothes and he was still bound up. Jesus told the people there to unbind him and let him go. Some of the Jews that had come with Mary to Lazarus tomb saw Jesus raise Lazarus from the dead and they believed in Him but some told the Pharisees.

The Pharisees and priests discussed what they should do about Jesus. They wanted to do something against Him because everyone might believe in Him then the Romans would take away their freedom as a nation. Caiaphas was the high priest that year and he suggested that Jesus should die for the nation.

Caiaphas did not have the authority to kill Jesus but he prophesied that Jesus would die for the nation and He would unite the people as one. From then on the Jews plotted to kill Jesus so

He no longer walked publicly among the Jews. Jesus went to a city called Ephraim and stayed there with His disciples. Jesus knew He was going to be killed but that was not the right time and He avoided being arrested.

The time for the Jewish Passover was near and many of the Jews went to Jerusalem to celebrate the Passover. The people looked for Jesus in the temple wondering if He would come to the Passover. The authorities were also looking for Jesus so they could arrest Him. LK 17– Jesus went toward Jerusalem and he passed through Samaria and Galilee. He entered a village and was met by ten lepers. The lepers were a distance from Jesus but when they saw Him they knew Him and shouted at Him saying "Jesus, Master, have mercy on us!" Jesus told them to go and show themselves to the priests. The lepers were healed and one of them a Samaritan with a loud voice glorified God. Jesus rebuffed the others who were Jewish.

Luke 17:17-19 So Jesus answered and said, "Were there not ten cleansed? But where are the nine? Were there any found who returned to give glory to God except this foreigner?" And He said to Him, "arise go your way. Your faith has made you well." The Pharisees asked Jesus when the kingdom of God would come they were referring to the kingdom of God on earth. They thought the kingdom would have all of the visible characteristics of an earthly kingdom. Jesus told them the kingdom (church) would not be visible because it is within the spirit (hearts) of people and cannot be seen. You cannot tell if a person is a member of the kingdom by a visual observation. The Pharisees were probably puzzled by Jesus answer and Jesus tells them a second time. The Kingdom of God is within the hearts of the members.

Jesus goes to Judea

(MT 19) Jesus and the disciples leave Galilee and go beyond the Jordan River in Judea and a great crowd of people followed Him and He healed them. The Pharisees came to test Him by asking Him questions about the law.

First they asked about marriage and divorce. Jesus answered that the reason God made people both male and female was so they could live together as a family. Jesus said people should not separate the union of a man and wife that God joins together. The Pharisees asked Jesus why Moses commanded a certificate of divorce. Jesus told them Moses permitted divorce because of the hardness of their heart. Hardness of the heart means stubbornness, a weakness that keeps people from doing what is right and sometimes keeps a person from obeying God.

Matthew 19:8-9–Jesus told them it was because of the hardness of their hearts that Moses permitted you to divorce, but from the beginning it was not so. And I say whoever divorces his wife, except for sexual immorality, and marries another, commits adultery; and whoever marries her who is divorced commits adultery. The disciples reasoned among themselves that it would be better not to marry at all but Jesus told them that not everyone would be able to remain single and everyone should use their own judgment about getting married. God honors marriage and has from the beginning of time. Little children were brought to Jesus so he could put His hands on them and pray for them.

The disciples did not agree with bringing children to Jesus but Jesus said let them come to Me. MK 10 13-16–They brought little children to Jesus so He could touch them; but the disciples rebuked those who brought them. When Jesus saw it, He was displeased and He said "Let the little children come to Me and do not forbid them; for of such is the kingdom of God. Assuredly, I say to you, whoever does not receive the kingdom of God as a little child, will by no means enter it." And Jesus took them in His arms, laid His hands on them and blessed them. Little children are innocent and without sin because they do not know or understand their moral obligations until they are taught as they mature. God does not punish those who are not morally accountable for their actions due to their age or the ability to think and reason clearly.

The Rich Young Ruler

A young man that was rich came to question Jesus about what to do to have eternal life? Jesus told the young one no one but God was good and to have eternal life, he must keep God's commandments.

Jesus uses the word good to mean righteous (without the guilt of sin). The young man asked which of the commandments? Matthew 19:18-19– Jesus said, "'You shall not murder, 'You shall not commit adultery', 'You shall not bear false witness, 'Honor your father and your mother,' and, 'You shall love your neighbor as yourself.'" The young man said he had always done those things and what else must he do? Jesus told him in order to be perfect, to sell the things you have and give to the poor. Follow Me then you will have treasure in heaven. Being perfect in order to save themselves is what one would have to be to be saved, but no one can save themselves, only God can save and God saves people not on their own merit but on the fact that they have faith in God's Son Jesus Christ. Faith in Jesus is known by a person's personal obedience to the gospel of Christ. The young man went away unhappy because he had many possessions. Jesus told His disciples it was hard for a rich man to come into the Kingdom of God. It would be harder for a rich person to obey the gospel, because they were too dependent on their riches to obtain what they wanted but it was possible. The disciples left everything to follow Jesus. Matthew 19:28-30–Jesus said to them, when the Son of Man sits on the throne of His glory, you who have followed Me will also sit on twelve thrones, judging the twelve tribes of Israel.' "And everyone who has left houses or brothers or sisters or father or mother or wife or children or lands, for My name's sake, shall receive a hundredfold, and inherit eternal life. But many who are first will be last, and the last first."

Regeneration is the rebirth of the spirit and it is accomplished by faith, hope and love. When people are reborn spiritually their priority in life is to serve God. John 1:12-13 "But as many as received Him, to them He gave the right to become children of God, to those who believe in His name: who were born, not of blood, nor of the will of the flesh, nor of the will of man, but of God." Those who are reborn will reign with Christ in eternal life. In the book of James, Peter said God gives us new birth through the resurrection of Jesus Christ. The parable of the laborers taught by Jesus in Matthew 20 is about the grace of God that is freely given to people from every culture if they are willing by faith to come into the kingdom of God (The Church). In the kingdom there is equality among the members.

Jesus and the Disciples go to Jerusalem

(LK 18) Jesus and the disciples begin a journey to Jerusalem. The events that the prophets in the Old Testament predicted concerning Jesus would soon begin to take place. Jesus spoke privately to the twelve disciples (Apostles). Jesus tells the twelve that he will be arrested and given to the Gentiles. They will spit on Him mock Him and insult Him. Then they will beat him and kill Him but on the third day He will be resurrected. Jesus could have avoided going to Jerusalem but Jesus was dedicated to accomplishing God's will.

The mother of James and John came to Jesus with her sons and Jesus asked her what she wanted. She told Jesus she wanted her sons to sit on each side of Jesus in the Kingdom. Jesus told her she did not understand what she was asking and it was not within His authority to grant what she asked. The other disciples were not pleased with the request of James and John and Jesus taught them about the proper relationship among the disciples. The Members of the kingdom (church) will not be given authority over one another. Those who will be great in the kingdom are those who serve the other members. Jesus is an example of serving the members of the church.

(LK 18) Jesus and the disciples continued on their way to Jerusalem and they came near Jericho and saw a blind man sitting by the road begging. A blind man heard the multitude following Jesus and he asked what was happening. He was told that Jesus of Nazareth was going by and he cried out saying Jesus the Son of David have mercy on me. The people in front of the multitude told him to be quiet but he cried out louder. Jesus stopped walking and commanded that the blind man be brought to Him. Jesus asked him what he wanted and the man asked that his sight be restored. Luke 18:42-43 "Then Jesus said to him, "Receive your sight; your faith has made you well."

Jesus came into Jericho and He saw a rich tax collector named Zacchaeus. Zacchaeus wanted to see Jesus but he was short and could not see over the crowd.

Zacchaeus climbed into a sycamore tree so he could see and Jesus looked up and saw him and told him to hurry and come down from the tree. Jesus told Zacchaeus He wanted to stay at his house. Zacchaeus hurried down the tree. The Jews complained because they said Jesus was going to the house of a sinner. The Jewish people did not like tax collectors they hated them because they often took a large portion of the money they collected for themselves. Zacchaeus was a Jew so Jesus called him a son of Abraham. Jesus said that He came to seek and save those who were lost, meaning sinners. Luke 19:9-10–Jesus said to him, "Today salvation has come to this house, because he also is a son of Abraham; for the Son of Man has come to seek and to save that which was lost." Jesus came to save all people but He went to the Jews first, the descendants of Abraham.

Jesus and Zacchaeus left Jericho and a large crowd followed them. They came to two blind men sitting near the road. The men heard Jesus and shouted have mercy on us, O lord, Son of David! Jesus called to them and asked what they wanted Him to do for them. They said they wanted their eyesight restored. Jesus had compassion for them and He touched their eyes and immediately their eyesight was restored.

154

(JN 14) Six days before the Passover Jesus was on His way to Jerusalem and He came to Bethany and ate with Martha, Mary and Lazarus. Mary anointed Jesus feet with some expensive oil. Judas Iscariot complained saying the ointment could have been sold and the money used to help the poor. Judas did not care about the poor he wanted the ointment to be sold and the money put in the common box because He carried the box and sometimes used the money for himself. John 12:7-8–Jesus said to them let her alone; she has kept this for the day of My burial. For the poor you have with you always, but Me you do not have always."

The Triumphal entry into Jerusalem

Jesus and the disciples came to Bethpage near Jerusalem and the Mt of Olives. Jesus sent two disciples to a village where they would find a donkey and a colt tied. He told them to bring them to Him and if anyone said anything tell him the Lord has a need, and then he will let you have the donkey and the colt.

This was done in fulfillment of an Old Testament prophecy. Zechariah 9:9 "Rejoice greatly, O daughter of Zion! Shout O daughter of Jerusalem! Behold your king is coming to you; He is just and having salvation, Lowly and riding on a donkey, A colt, the foal of a donkey." After Jesus and the disciples reached Jerusalem Jesus taught in the temple during the day and at night. He went to the Mt of Olives early in the morning then would return to the temple. During the Passover feast a Great crowd of people came to Jerusalem for the feast. They heard that Jesus would be coming there and they took palm branches and went to meet Him crying "Hosanna! 'Blessed is He who comes in the name of the Lord!' The King of Israel!'

Jesus found a young donkey and sat on it, as it is written: "Fear not, daughter of Zion; Behold, your King is coming, sitting on a donkey's colt." The disciples did as Jesus requested and they laid their clothes on the donkey and colt for Jesus to sit. A large crowd of people spread their clothes on the road and some cut branches from the trees and spread them on the road. Matthew 21:9 "Then the multitudes who went before and those who followed cried out, saying: "Hosanna to the Son of David! Blessed is He who comes in the name of the Lord!' Hosanna in the highest!" The King of Israel!

The disciples set Jesus on the donkey and colt. A large crowd of people spread their clothes on the road and some cut branches from the trees and spread them out on the road. Matthew 21– Then the multitudes who went before and those who followed cried out saying: Hosanna to the Son of David! Blessed is He who comes in the name of the Lord! Hosanna in the highest! When they entered Jerusalem the people were shaken and they asked, who is this? The multitudes said this is Jesus, the prophet from Nazareth of Galilee. The Pharisees said among them selves, you are accomplishing nothing. Look the world has gone after Him. Jesus was very popular with the people. Jesus came near the city of Jerusalem and He wept. Jesus knew ahead of time what was going to happen in Jerusalem. Luke 19 Jesus speaks of Jerusalem and the temple and He told them if you had known in this your day, the things that make for your peace! But now they are hidden from your eyes. Jesus was speaking of the great judgment that was coming against Jerusalem after His death.

Jesus said the days are coming when your enemies will build an embankment around you and close you in on every side, and level you, and your children within you, to the ground; and they will not leave in you one stone upon another. Jesus knew what was going to happen to Him soon, His death and burial and he wept over the city of Jerusalem. Jesus was aware of the cruel things they would do to Him but He had compassion for the people causing Him to weep. Jesus entered Jerusalem and went into the temple and looked around but the time was late so He went to Bethany with the disciples. Bethany was a small village on the other side of the Mt of Olives and the village where Mary, Martha and Lazarus lived it was not far from Jerusalem.

Jesus and the disciples go back to Jerusalem, Jesus went to the temple and drove out those who were buying and selling things in the temple. He turned over the tables of the changers of money and the seats of those who sold doves. Jesus did not believe it was right to bring merchandise into the temple. Mark 11:17 "Then He taught saying, "Is it not written, 'My house shall be called a house of prayer for all nations?' But you have made it a den of thieves'" The people were astonished at Jesus teaching and the Scribes and chief priests were afraid of Jesus because of the people and they discussed how they might kill Him. Then the blind and the lame came to Him in the temple and he healed them. The chief priests and scribes watched the wonderful things Jesus did and heard those who followed Jesus crying out "Hosanna to the Son of David!" The priests and scribes were angry and said do you hear what they are saying? Jesus said, "Yes, Have you never read, 'Out of the mouth of babes and nursing infants You have perfected praise?'"

When evening came Jesus went into the city of Bethany to spend the night. The next day when Jesus came out of Bethany he was hungry. He saw a fig tree with leaves still on it and thought there might be some figs but there were no figs. Jesus knew what was waiting for Him in Jerusalem and He took His frustration out on the tree and He said, "Let no one eat fruit from you ever again." Jesus went into the city of Jerusalem and went into the temple. The chief priests and elders of the people made a bold stand against Him while He taught, they asked him where he received authority to do the things He was doing?

Jesus answered them by asking a question. Where did John get authority to baptize? Was it from Heaven or from men? They were afraid to answer Jesus because if they said from heaven then Jesus would say, why didn't you believe him? If they said from men the people would attack Him because the people believed John was a prophet. The chief priest said we do not know.

MT 21 Jesus taught a parable about two sons that worked in their father's vineyard. The parable was meant to show the hypocrisy of the religious leaders and the attitudes of those who will obey the gospel. The Father in the parable represents God and the vineyard represents the people that respond to the message of the gospel of Christ. The owner of the vineyard said to the oldest son go work in the vineyard. The first son had said he would not go to work but later he repented and went to work in the vineyard. The second son said he would go but he changed his mind. Jesus asks which son obeyed his father and the people said the first. In this parable Jesus was rebuking the Jewish leaders for pretending to be righteous leaders of God's people but they did not keep the commandments of God and they rejected Jesus the Son of God. The leaders and ruling class of the Jews did not accept Jesus as the Messiah. The working class of the Jewish people accepted Jesus as the Messiah and became disciples and Jesus accepted them in His kingdom.

MT 21–Jesus teaches a parable about a landowner who planted a Vineyard put a hedge around the vineyard to keep out those who are undesirable, built a watchtower and leased it to tenants then he went away. The tenants are the leaders of Israel. God the owner of the vineyard cared for the people of Israel and sent leaders and prophets to advise and help Israel (the tenants) but the people killed, beat and stoned those sent to help them. Jesus was sent from God to redeem people but He would be crucified. God sent His Son Jesus and they were already conspiring to kill Him. The Jews who did not accept Christ as the messiah, tried many times to trap Jesus into saying or doing something against the government so they could have Him arrested. The enemies of Christ sent a Jewish group that was in the favor of Herod the King to trap Jesus.

They told Jesus they believed He was teaching the way of God truthfully and that He was not prejudiced. Then they ask Him a question to trap Him. They ask Jesus if it was lawful to pay taxes to Caesar the Roman emperor or to refuse to pay. Jesus knew they were trying to trick Him to say something that they could have Him arrested for. Matthew 22:18-22– But Jesus knew of their wickedness, and said, "Why do you test Me, you Hypocrites? Show me the tax money" So they brought Him a coin. And He said to them, "Whose image and inscription is this?" "They said to Him, Caesar's." And He said to them, "Render to Caesar the things that are Caesar's, and to God the things that are God's." When they heard these words, they marveled and went their way." God's people live in the world among people who are not believers. Some unbelievers are in positions of authority in the civil government and they make civil laws that all citizens must obey. Jesus taught that God's people must obey the commandments of God and also obey the laws of the civil authorities.

Jesus was leaving the temple and one of the disciples asked Him, what kind of stones were in the structure of the temple? Jesus surprised them with His answer. He told them the temple was going to be destroyed. The Jewish temple was a large magnificent building with beautiful stones. Jesus was sitting on the Mount of Olives with a view of the temple when He made those comments. Jesus told them that the days would come when the temple would be destroyed and He told them there would be signs before the temple was destroyed. James, John and Andrew asked Him in private what kind of sign there would be before the temple would be destroyed. Jesus answered.

Luke 21:20-24– "But when you see Jerusalem surrounded by armies, then know that its desolation is near. Then let those who are in Judea flee to the mountains, let those who are in the midst of her depart, and let not those who are in the country enter her. For those are the days of vengeance, that all things that are written may be fulfilled." Luke writes about Jesus prediction of the destruction of Jerusalem in A.D. 70 when the temple would be destroyed by the Roman army. Luke said there will be great distress and many people would be killed with the sword of the Romans.

Jesus told them to pay careful attention that no one deceives them. Jesus said many things would happen before the destruction of Jerusalem, but do not be troubled. He said they would hear rumors about war but do not be troubled by them. He said there would be earthquakes, famines, and other troubles before the destruction of the temple. Jesus said those things were bound to happen but they were just the beginning of trouble. A Jewish historian named Flavius Josephus recorded the events of the destruction in Jewish history. The kingdom of Christ (church) had already been established before then and Jesus was warning those who would be in the church what to expect when the time came and what to do to be safe.

The Jews began a revolt against the Romans in 66 A.D. Nero was the Emperor of Rome during the revolt and Nero the leader of the Roman army was sent to Jerusalem. He gave his son Titus the position of leader of the Roman army and in A.D. 70 The Roman General Titus completely destroyed Jerusalem and the temple fulfilling Jesus predictions. Jesus told the disciples there would be much trouble He was referring to the persecution of the Jews including His followers. They would be brought before councils and beaten in the synagogues. They would be arrested and brought before rulers and Kings because they were Jesus disciples. Jesus said the gospel must be preached first before the trouble from the Romans appears. The Apostles would begin their preaching after the death of Christ and preaching the gospel would be their first priority. Jesus told them the Holy Spirit would be with them and the Spirit would tell them where to go and what to say. Jesus said there would be a time of trouble for all people. He told them they would be hated because they believed in Him but if they endured to the end they would be saved.

MK 13–The second coming of Jesus will take place at the end of time and Jesus describes what will take place when He returns. The sun will become dark and the moon will not shine. The stars will fall and the powers of heaven will be shaken. Matthew writes that Jesus coming will be a spectacular sight and the carnage on earth will be great. Then the sign of Christ will be appear in heaven. People will be able to see Christ coming from the heavens with His angels on clouds with power and glory.

Christ will send His angels ahead with the loud sound of a trumpet. He will gather up all of those who are saved for eternal life and they will ascend to heaven. MT 24–Jesus said God is the only One that knows the day when he will return to earth for His Kingdom (Church) not even the angels. People will be busy with daily activities not knowing it is the time for the lord to return. Some will be taken for heaven when He comes and some will be left for destruction. Jesus advised everyone to be spiritually prepared for the day when He returns. LK 21–Before the time of the second coming there will be great tribulation on earth. Nations will be at war and there will be great earthquakes, famines and pestilences, fearful sights and great signs from heaven. John describes in more detail in the book of Revelation. Jesus told a parable about a fig tree, you can tell by looking at the tree and know by the beginning of the budding of the tree that it is almost summer time but no one knows when Jesus will return.

Jesus said when you see the things beginning to happen that I just told you about then you will know by those things that His return is beginning to take place. The time for the second coming of Jesus will not be known until people see Him coming in the clouds with His angels. However the people living in Jerusalem in A.D. 70 would be able to see the signs of Jerusalem's destruction by the Romans. Jesus taught a parable about the kingdom of heaven comparing it to ten virgins. The virgins prepared themselves to meet the bridegroom. Five of the virgins were wise and the other five were foolish. They were all waiting for the wedding procession. The parable foretells the return of Jesus at the end of time. Christ will return at an unknown time and His people the church will be ready for His return. The church represents the wise virgins, who prepared themselves for heaven by living according to Jesus teaching. They have faithfully waited for His return. Christians will be ready for Jesus return because they were born again through faith in Jesus. As born again followers of Jesus they are ready for Him to return. The five foolish virgins either did not prepare themselves by obedience to Christ or they failed to remain faithful.

The Old Testament portrayed the Messiah as a husband of the people and Jesus and John the Baptist both said the Messiah was the bridegroom. The five foolish virgins represented the people who will not be prepared for the return of Jesus at the end of time. Jesus will say to those who did not accept Him by faith that He does not know them. They will not be admitted into the new heaven and new earth with the bridegroom.

Jesus said to watch, meaning to be ready spiritually at all times because no one knows the day or the hour when Jesus will return. Jesus teaches a parable about the talents of those who are in the kingdom of God. Members of the kingdom must remain faithful and use their talents to serve the church during the time they are waiting for Christ to return. The Lord expects each one to be ready for His coming each one will be judged according to their faith in Christ. MT 26–Jesus talked to His disciples about the time for the Passover feast in Jerusalem. Sometime after the feast He would be arrested, tried and crucified. During the day Jesus taught in the temple and at night He went to the Mt of Olives. In the mornings Jesus returned to teach in the temple. The life of the Jewish people was centered on the temple for many years and their activities had been established for many years. There were several feasts during each year. The seven main feasts were Passover, Un-leavened Bread, Day of First fruits and The Feast of Pentecost, the Feast of Trumpets, The Day of Atonement and the Feast of Tabernacles.

Some Greeks came to Jerusalem and they approached Philip from Bethsaida about seeing Jesus. Philip told Andrew then, they told Jesus. Jesus taught the Greek people and He told them that the time had come for Him to be glorified. Glorified meant His time to be crucified. Jesus compared His death to a grain of wheat that does not produce other wheat unless it is put in the ground and dies. When it is planted it produces new life. Jesus sacrifice on the cross would provide new spiritual life leading to eternal life for those who would have faith in Jesus. Jesus said, "He who loves His life, will lose it." Jesus speaks figuratively. If a person loves their life on earth more than serving God they will lose eternal life in heaven because they will not be faithful to serve Jesus while they are waiting for His return. "He who hates his life in this world will keep it for eternal life, meaning that a person must love serving Jesus more than anything else in this life while we are waiting for His return.

MK 14–Two days later it was time for the Passover and the feast of Un-leavened bread and the Chief priests and the scribes were still discussing how they could kill Jesus. They were afraid to kill Him during the feast time because they were afraid of what the people would do to them.

They were looking for a way to turn the people against Jesus. Before the feast of Passover Jesus already knew the time had come for His arrest His trial and death. Satan entered Judas Iscariot the disciple that would betray Jesus. Judas went to the chief priests and captains and asked them what they would pay him if he identified Jesus and they gave him 30 pieces of silver and from that time Judas looked for an opportunity to betray Jesus. God had determined that Jesus would die and ascend to heaven. Jesus knew what He must do and He rose up after the meal and laid His clothes aside and girded Himself with a towel, poured water in a basin and washed the disciple's feet to teach them to love one another and maintain equal and humble among themselves and the other members of the kingdom.

When Jesus came to Simon Peter, Peter asked Him if He was going to wash his feet. Peter could not accept the idea of the washing of his feet by Jesus. Jesus told Peter that he Peter did not at that time understand why He was washing His feet but later he would know. Jesus taught His disciples to love one another and accept each other equally with humility. Peter told Jesus

He would never wash his feet but Jesus said, "If I do not wash you, you have no part with Me Jesus washed the disciples feet and sat down again and said to them, "Do you know what I have done to you? You call Me teacher and Lord, and you say well, for so I am. If I your Lord and Teacher have washed your feet, you also ought to wash one another's feet. For I have given you an example that you should do as I have done to you. Most assuredly I say to you, a servant is not greater than his master; nor is he who is sent greater than he who sent him." God looks with equality on all faithful Christians.

The Lord's Supper

(LK 22, MT26, MK 14)–When the day of unleavened bread came it was time to kill the animal for the Passover meal and Jesus sent Peter and John, to prepare the Passover. They asked where they should go to eat the Passover, Jesus told them to enter Jerusalem and they would see a man carrying a pitcher of water. Jesus said to follow the man into the house and tell the master of the house that the Teacher asks, where is the room? So they could eat the Passover meal.

He will show you a large upper room already furnished. The disciples did as Jesus said and prepared the Passover meal. When the proper time came Jesus and His disciples sat down to eat. Jesus said to His apostles that He desired to eat the pass over meal with them before it was time for Him to suffer. Jesus knew that after the pass over meal He would be arrested, tried and eventually crucified. Before that took place He wanted some time with His apostles. Satan had already tempted Judas to betray Him. Luke 22:19-23–Jesus took some bread and gave thanks for it, broke it and gave it to the apostles saying "This is My body which is given for you; do this in remembrance of Me." And in the same way he took the cup after they had eaten, saying, "This cup which is poured out for you is the new covenant in My blood.

1st Corinthians 11:23-25–For I received from the Lord that which I also delivered to you: that the Lord Jesus on the same night in which He was betrayed took bread; and when He had given thanks, He broke it and said, eat; this is my body which is broken for you; do this in remembrance of Me. He also took the cup after supper, saying, this cup is the new covenant (agreement) in My blood as often as you drink it in remembrance of Me. The new agreement between God and the people on earth was redemption for sin paid for by the blood (death) of Christ. The disciples of Jesus ate the bread and drank of the cup every first day of the week after Jesus death, burial and resurrection. The disciples disputed about which one was going to betray Jesus and which one of them would be the greatest. Jesus told them the one who is the greatest among them must become like the youngest and the one who leads like a servant.

Jesus told them they must serve one another. Jesus reminds them that He is the one who serves. Jesus and the disciples went to the garden of Gethsemane to the Mount of Olives. Jesus knew what was ahead of Him and He knelt down to pray. He asked His father if He would remove the suffering from Him but to let Your will be done. And angel from heaven appeared to Him and gave Him strength. Jesus was in agony, He knew what was ahead and His sweat became like drops of blood falling to the ground. The disciples were filled with sorrow and each one began to ask Him if they were the one. Jesus answered saying it is the one who dips his hand with Me in the dish.

Jesus said woe to the man that betrays Me it would be better if he had not been born. Judas asked if he was the one and Jesus replied, "You have said it." Jesus dipped a piece of bread and gave it to Judas Iscariot and Satan entered Judas. Jesus told Judas to do it quickly. None of the other disciples realized why Jesus said what He did to Judas. Judas knew what Jesus meant and he left and went out into the night waiting for an opportunity to betray Jesus.

Gospel of John—Jesus had revealed to His disciples that Judas one of them would betray Him. Jesus comforts His disciples and teaches them about the role of the Holy Spirit and their relation to each other and the need for Him to go away. He predicts His death and resurrection and their future glory. Jesus prays to His Father in heaven and prays for the future glory of the Apostles. Judas left to betray Jesus, Jesus and the other disciples went out into the night. Jesus told the disciples, now is the time that He would be glorified and God would be glorified in Him. The glory of God and Jesus would be magnified by Jesus death. John 12—Jesus answered them "The hour has come that the Son of Man should be glorified. Most assuredly, I say to you, unless a grain of wheat falls into the ground and dies, it remains alone; but if it dies, it produces much grain. Jesus said God had given Him authority over all people and He would give eternal life to as many as God gave Him. Jesus called the disciples little children at that time because like children they did not understand what was about to take place.

The disciples did not know beforehand of the real grief and sorrow that was in store for Jesus and for them. After Jesus had spoken to the disciples about His imminent death He and the disciples went over the ravine of Kidron to a garden. Judas knew the place because Jesus and the disciples went there often. Roman soldiers and officers came there with lanterns, torches and weapons. Jesus knew why they came and He asked who they came for. They answered Him, 'Jesus the Nazarene' and Jesus identified Himself. Judas was there with them. Peter drew his sword and cut off the ear of the high priest's slave but Jesus told him to put it up saying His Father had given Him that cup to drink meaning, it was God's will for Jesus to die and become the sacrifice for the sins of the world. The crowd and the religious leaders came for Jesus with swords and clubs like He was a robber.

The disciples all left Jesus and walked away frightened. Jesus was arrested and tied up without any real proof of a crime against Him. Jesus offered no resistance to those who arrested Him. Jesus asked the chief priest and captains of the temple why they came out against him like He was a thief. Jesus told them this was their hour and the power of darkness (ignorance). It was their hour to do what they wanted to at that time. Jesus said— The time was coming later when He would be resurrected. Jesus was taken to Annas a former high priest. LK 22—Peter went with the crowd following at a distance and he went into the courtyard and sat down by the fire. Annas sent Jesus to the reigning high priest Caiphas and Caiphas told them that it was a good thing for one man to die for the people, inferring they should put Jesus to death.

Simon Peter was outside warming himself by the fire. A servant girl saw Peter and she accused him of being with Jesus. Peter denied being with Jesus and said I do not know Him. Later someone else saw Peter and said he was with Jesus. Peter denied he was with those who were with Jesus. About an hour later someone else accused Peter of being with Jesus because he was a Galilean. For the third time Peter denied knowing Jesus and while he was speaking a rooster crowed. Jesus had told Peter before, that he would deny Him three times before the rooster crows. Peter remembered what Jesus said and He cried. Peter was ashamed of his weakness in denying that he knew Jesus. The disciples were afraid for Jesus but they could do nothing to help Him because of the Jewish and the Roman authorities.

The high priest questioned Jesus about His teaching and about the disciples. Jesus told Him He had done nothing secretly and had taught in the synagogues and the temple. Jesus told him to ask who had heard Him about the things He said. An officer slapped Jesus with the palm of his hand and said do you answer the high priest like that? Jesus replied that if He had spoken evil bear witness of the evil; but if well, why do you strike Me? Jesus was led to the Praetorian where they had assembled the whole garrison. They dressed Jesus in purple; made a crown of thorns and put it on His head and saluted Him saying Hail the King of the Jews. Jesus was beaten, spit on, hit on the head with a reed and they bowed down in mockery, pretending to worship Him.

When they were through mocking Jesus they put a scarlet robe on Him and led Him away to be crucified. For a full description of the events read all four gospel accounts in Matthew 27, Mark 15 Luke 22 and John 18 and19. Jesus was sent to Pilate the Roman Governor and accused of crimes against Rome. Pilate asked Jesus if he was the King of the Jews. Jesus answered him and said, 'it is as you say.' Pilate said he found no crime against Jesus but the multitude became furious and accused Jesus of stirring up the people. Pilate found out that Jesus was from Galilee and he sent Jesus to Herod. Pilate could release one person that was arrested but the chief priests of the Jews urged Pilate to release a criminal named Barrabbas instead of Jesus. Pilate wanted to please the crowd so he released Barabbas instead of Jesus. Pilate asked them what he should do with Jesus and they said crucify Him.

Jesus was dressed in purple; a crown of thorns was put on His head and the people saluted Him saying Hail the King of the Jews. Jesus was beaten, spit on, hit on the head with a reed and they bowed down in mockery, pretending to worship Him. When they were through mocking Jesus they put a scarlet robe on Him and led Him away to be crucified. For a full description of the events read all four gospel accounts in Matthew 27, Mark 15, Luke 22 and John 18and19. Pilate found out that Jesus was from Galilee and he sent Jesus to Herod.

The Sanhedrin tries Jesus

The Sanhedrin was the highest tribunal of the Jews in Jerusalem. They had authority to order arrests and the power to judge any case except one that required capital punishment. The Romans were the only authority over capital punishment. (JN 18) The Jewish troops that arrested Jesus tied Him up and took Him to Annas the father in law of Caiphas who was the high priest. Annas had been a high priest a few years earlier and had been deposed but the Jews considered the priesthood to be a lifetime office and still valued the opinion of Annas. Caiphas had previously said it was a good thing for one man to die for the people. He also said that it was good to let one person go free.

Peter and one of the other disciples followed Jesus into the courtyard of the high priest. Peter stayed outside waiting by the door. The high priest knew the disciples and he told the girl that guarded the gate to have Peter come inside. The men holding Jesus made fun of Him and beat him. Jesus was blindfolded and they hit Him in the face and said, prophesy! They said tell us who hit you in the face? They accused Jesus of being evil and said if you are the Christ tell us. Jesus said to them Luke 22:67-69 "If I tell you, you will by no means believe. And if I also ask you, you will by no means answer Me or let Me go. Hereafter the Son of Man will sit on the right hand of the power of God." Then they asked Him if He was the Son of God and He affirmed that He was. The officials believed that Jesus was an impostor. The chief priests, the elders and the council wanted someone to testify against Jesus and two false witnesses came forward and accused Jesus of saying, that He was able to destroy the temple and build it again in three days.

Jesus was referring to His body when He said that. He was predicting His death, burial and resurrection. Jesus remained silent and the high priest said to Jesus do You have nothing to say? Jesus still remained silent and the high priest put Him under oath and told Him to tell them if He was the Christ, the Son of God. Matthew 27: 64 "Jesus said to them, "it is as you said. Nevertheless, I say to you, hereafter you will see the Son of Man sitting at the right hand of the power, and coming on the clouds of heaven." Jesus had said before that He would return to heaven after He was resurrected and now He tells them He will come back. Jesus would be resurrected soon after His death. The high priest was so angry he was beside himself he tore his clothes and accused Jesus of blasphemy. Jesus had not blasphemed He always spoke the truth. Those trying Jesus all agreed that He deserved to die and they spit in His face and slapped Him. Jesus was then ordered to the residence of the provincial governor.

MT 27– The next morning all the chief priests and the elders agreed to kill Jesus and they bound Him and led Him to Pontius Pilate. Judas Iscariot was very remorseful after Jesus was condemned and he brought the thirty pieces of silver to the chief priests and the elders and confessed that Jesus was innocent but they said they did not care. When Jesus stood before Pilate he was asked if He was the king of the Jews.

Jesus told him yes but He said nothing when the chief priest and elders questioned Him. Pilate heard Jesus was from Galilee and he sent him to Herod who had jurisdiction over Galilee. Herod was glad to see Jesus because he had wanted to meet him for a long time. Herod had heard much about Jesus and was hoping that he would see Jesus perform a miracle. He questioned Jesus but Jesus remained silent even though the chief priests and scribes were accusing Him. Herod and his soldiers treated Jesus with contempt and made fun of Him. They dressed Jesus in a beautiful robe and sent him back to Pontius Pilate. MK 15–The next morning Jesus was taken to Pilate and Pilate asked him if He was the King of the Jews? Jesus answered yes and the chief priest accused Him of being guilty of many things but Jesus said nothing. Pilate asked Him why He did not answer but Jesus still remained silent. There was a custom then to release one prisoner every year. Pilate found no crime against Jesus. He thought the chief priest's were jealous of Him and that is why they arrested Him. Pilate was willing to let Jesus go free. There was a custom that every year one prisoner could be set free. Pilate let the people choose the person that would be set free to honor their custom. They could have chosen Jesus but the chief priest encouraged the crowd to choose a prisoner named Barabbas instead of Jesus and Barabbas was set free. Pilate asked what he should do with Jesus the one called the king of the Jews.

The people shouted out crucify him. Pilate still did not want to do any thing to Jesus but they shouted out louder crucify Him! (JN 18, 19) Pilate asked Jesus what crimes had He committed? John 18:36-37 Jesus answered, "My kingdom is not of this world. If My kingdom were of this world, My servants would fight, so that I should not be delivered to the Jews; but now My kingdom is not from here. Pilate therefore said to Him, are you a king then? Jesus answered You say rightly that I am a king. For this cause I was born, and for this cause I have come into the world, that I should bear witness to the truth. Everyone who is of the truth hears My voice."

When Jesus said His kingdom was not of this world He did not mean His kingdom would not be in the world. Not of the world means it is not a worldly kingdom. The kingdom of God is a spiritual kingdom.

Pilate told Jesus he had the power to do anything he wanted to with Him even the power to crucify Him. The kingdom would soon be established in the world in the hearts of those who would have faith in Jesus. Jesus told Pilate he would have no power unless God gave it to him. The Jews knew Pilate wanted to release Jesus but they insisted that He be charged with a crime. They said if you let Him go you are no friend of Caesar. Caesar was the supreme ruler of the Roman Empire. Pilate brought Jesus and set Him in the judgment seat in a place called the pavement but in Hebrew it is Gabbatha and was probably a part of the public square where the mob of people gathered. They led Jesus towards the place where the cross was. The cross was heavy and Jesus was weak because of the things He had suffered. They gave the cross to a man named Simon who was a Cyrenian. Simon carried the cross for Jesus.

A great many people followed them on their way to where the cross would be put in the ground and some of the women were mourning and Jesus spoke to them. Luke 23:28-31–But Jesus turned to them and said, "Daughters of Jerusalem, do not weep for Me, but weep for yourselves and for your children. For indeed the days are coming in which they will say, 'Blessed are the barren wombs that never bore, and breasts which never nursed! Then they will begin to say to the mountains, "Fall on us! And to the hills, "Cover us! For if they do these things in the green wood, what will be done in the dry?" Jesus warned of an event coming in the future that would be much worse than what was happening to Him. There were two future events coming that would be much worse, the destruction of Jerusalem that would come in A.D. 70 and the tribulation that would come at the end of time.

John 19–They came to a place called Golgotha or Place of the Skull and they gave Jesus some sour wine mingled with gall (Myrrh). Jesus tasted it but would not drink it. The soldiers placed Him on the cross and divided His garments among them. Psalms 22. They cast lots to determine what each one would take. The chief priests, scribes and elders mocked Him and said. "He saved others; Himself He cannot save. If He is the King of Israel let Him now come down from the cross, and we will believe Him. He trusted in God; let Him deliver now if He will have Him; for He said, 'I am the Son of God."

It was the third hour (9A.M.) and written above Jesus head was an inscription that read, Jesus of Nazareth, The King of The Jews. Two criminals were also crucified at that time one on Jesus left and one on the right. One of the criminals blasphemed Jesus mocking Him saying if you are the Christ save yourself and save us. The other criminal rebuked him for mocking Jesus and he said do you not fear God? Then he asked Jesus to remember him when He came into His kingdom. Jesus told him that today he would be in Paradise with him. The chief priest, Scribes and elders mocked Him saying He saved others but He cannot save Himself. 'If He is the king of Israel, let Him now come down from the cross, and we will believe Him. He trusted God; let Him deliver Him now if He will have Him; for He said, I am the Son of God.' The robbers who were crucified with Him reviled Him.

The people who passed by the cross blasphemed Jesus and mocked him. When it was the sixth hour (noon) it was dark all over the earth until the ninth hour (3 p.m.) Mark 15: 34 "And at the ninth hour Jesus cried out with a loud voice, saying, Eloi, Eloi, Lama Sabachthani?" Which is translated, "My God, My God, why have You forsaken Me?" Some who were standing there heard Jesus and they said look He is calling for Elijah. Someone ran and filled a sponge full of sour wine, and put it on a reed and told Jesus to drink. Jesus cried out in a loud voice, then took His last breath. The Centurion said truly this Man was the Son of God! There were women looking on from away off who had followed Jesus and had ministered to Him in Galilee. Jesus bore the sins of the world in His own body and at that moment God abandoned Him. Then the sun was darkened and the veil of the temple was torn in two.

The veil of the temple is the curtain that separates the Holy place from the Most Holy signifying that access to God would now be available to all people not Jews only. Jesus cried out with a loud voice and said "Father, into your hands I commit My Spirit." The earth quaked, the rocks split, and graves were opened. Bodies of the saints who were dead were resurrected and came out of the graves. After His resurrection, the disciples went into Jerusalem and were seen there by many. Some of those who were watching Jesus as He suffered on the cross said He was crying for Elijah.

One of the men standing there offered Jesus a drink of vinegar the other men said to let Him alone, they wanted to see if Elijah would come to save Him. Jesus cried with a loud voice and died. JN 19–Because it was the day of preparation they did not want the bodies left on the cross on the Sabbath so they asked Pilate if they could break their legs and carry them away. They came and began breaking the legs but when they came to Jesus He was already dead and they did not break

His legs. They broke the legs of the two criminals so they would die sooner. One of the soldiers stuck his spear in Jesus side and blood and water poured out. Zechariah 12:10 "And I will pour on the house of David and on the inhabitants of Jerusalem the Spirit of grace and supplication; then they will look on M e whom they pierced. Yes, they will mourn for Him as one mourns for his only son, and grieve for Him as one grieves for a firstborn."

The Burial of Jesus and the Empty Tomb

A man named Joseph, who was from Arimathea a good man that was waiting for the kingdom of God, did not agree with the decision to kill Jesus. Joseph was a good friend of Jesus. Joseph was wealthy and a member of the Sanhedrin. Joseph asked Pilate for the body of Jesus and he took it down from the cross. Nicodemus brought a large mixture of myrrh and aloes to prepare the body. They wrapped the body with strips of linen cloth with spices and put it in the burial tomb that was cut out of the rock. The tomb was new no one had been buried in it. It was the day of preparation and the Sabbath was about to begin. There was a garden at the place they selected with a new tomb and they laid the body there. The women from Galilee followed Joseph and saw the tomb and the body. They went home and prepared spices and perfume for Jesus body. Then they rested to obey the Sabbath. Tombs of that kind hewn from rock were very large. After the body was prepared, Joseph and Nicodemus placed Jesus body on a stone ledge in the tomb and rolled a stone in front of the tomb that would serve as a door. Mk 15– The Centurion and those with him that guarded the grave were afraid when they saw the earthquake and the other things that happened. They said this was truly the Son of God. The women watched from a distance. Among them were Mary Magdalene, Mary the mother of James the less, and of Joses and Salome and many other women who followed Jesus.

Jesus Resurrection

MT-MK–Early in the morning of the first day of the week Mary Magdalene and another Mary came to the tomb and there was a great earthquake and an angel came from heaven and rolled back the large stone that sealed the tomb. An angel sat on the stone. His face shone like lightning and his clothes were as white as snow. The men guarding the tomb were so frightened they shook. An angel told the women not to be afraid and they said Jesus is not here. An angel at the grave showed the women the place where Jesus had been laid and said go quickly and tell His disciples He is in Galilee. The women ran to tell the disciples.

LK 24–Luke said there were two angels and they asked the women why they were looking for the living among the dead and they told them Jesus had been resurrected. The angels reminded them that Jesus had told them that he would be crucified and then be resurrected on the third day. The women left the tomb and told the eleven disciples about Jesus resurrection. Judas had hanged himself previously after he had betrayed Jesus. The disciples did not know whether they should believe the women, they thought it might be gossip but Peter ran to the tomb to see for himself. JN20–When Mary Magdalene saw that Jesus was not in the tomb she ran and found Peter and John the disciple Jesus loved. Mary told them someone had removed Jesus from the tomb and she did not know where they put Him. Peter and John ran towards the tomb but John got there first and looked in. Peter came from behind him and went into the tomb.

Peter saw the burial clothes and the handkerchief that had been on Hid head was not with the other clothes John arrived and entered the tomb and saw that Jesus was not there and He remembered the scriptures that said He would rise again from the dead and he believed Jesus was alive. Mary was outside the tomb crying and she told the two angels someone had taken away the Lord and she did not know where he was. Right after saying that she turned and saw Jesus but she did not recognize Him and thought he was the gardener. Jesus asked her why she was crying. Mary thought the man she was talking to had taken Jesus body away.

When Jesus called her Mary she recognized Him. John 20:17 ' Jesus said to her, "Do not cling to Me, for I have not yet ascended to My Father; but go to My brethren and say to them, I am ascending to My father and your Father, and to My God and your God." Mary Magdalene told the disciples that Jesus had talked to her and she told them that He said do not be afraid and go tell His brethren (disciples) to go to Galilee and they will see me there. Jesus was going to come to the disciples in Galilee. They left quickly and ran from the tomb and did not tell anyone because they feared. Two travelers were walking on the road that goes to Emmaus, which was about seven miles from Jerusalem. They were talking about the amazing things that happened in the last few days. Jesus came near them and walked along with them. Miraculously their eyes were restrained and they could not recognize Him and they did not know who He was. LK 24 Jesus could see that they were sad and He asked them what they were talking about. They told Him they were talking about Jesus of Nazareth the mighty prophet. They told about Jesus arrest, being condemned to die and His crucifixion. They were disappointed because they thought Jesus was going to redeem Israel. This was the third day since His death and the women told them Jesus was not in the tomb, and they saw a vision of angels who said He was alive.

Luke 24:25-27 "Then He said to them, "O foolish ones, and slow of heart to believe in all that the prophets have spoken! Ought not the Christ to have suffered these things and to enter into His glory?" Jesus explained to the travelers that God had designed the things that happened to Him, and the prophets prophesied about them many years before. Jesus began with Moses and explained from all of the prophets and scriptures the things that were taught about Him. They came near a village, Jesus was planning to go further, but the travelers invited Jesus to go home with them and He went with them. Jesus sat at the table with them to eat and he broke bread and blessed it and gave them some. They had not been able to recognize Jesus before, but now their eyes were opened and they recognized Him, then He vanished. The travelers were disappointed their hearts had been excited when He was with them, and talked to them explaining the scriptures.

The two men left and returned to Jerusalem, they found Jesus disciples and told them Jesus had risen from the dead. The men told the disciples about the things that happened on the road and said the Lord has indeed risen. As they were talking Jesus appeared among them and said "Peace to you." They thought they were seeing a spirit. Luke 24:38 "And he said to them, "Why are you troubled? And why do doubts arise in your hearts? Behold My hands and My feet, that it is I Myself. Handle Me and see, for a spirit does not have flesh and bones as you see I have." Jesus showed them His hands and His feet where the nails had pierced the. Jesus asked them for some food and they gave Him broiled fish and honeycomb and He ate.

Luke wrote that Jesus later appeared to the eleven disciples and sat at the table with them and rebuked them for not believing. Mark 16:15-18 "And He said to them, "Go into all the world and preach the gospel to every creature. He who believes and is baptized will be saved; but he who does not believe will be condemned. And these signs will follow those who believe: In My name they will cast out demons; they will speak with new tongues; they will take up serpents; and if they drink anything deadly, it will by no means hurt them; they will lay hands on the sick, and they will recover." In the last words recorded by Mark's gospel Jesus was received into heaven, where He sat down at God's right hand. The apostles preached the gospel everywhere and the Lord helped them by confirming their word with miraculous signs. LK 24—Jesus promised to send them the power of the Holy Spirit and He told them to wait in Jerusalem until they were given that power from heaven. Jesus was giving them the power from the Holy Spirit because He would soon ascend to heaven and they would need the Holy Spirit to guide into all truth as they continued to teach the gospel of Christ and establish the Kingdom of Christ (church).

Jesus reminded the disciples of some of the things He previously told them about, things that must be fulfilled according to the Law of Moses the prophets and Psalms. Jesus gave the disciples the ability to understand the scriptures about Him and emphasized that His death was necessary for the remission of sins and that the gospel should be preached in His name all over the world beginning in Jerusalem. The disciples were witnesses of all those things that took place in the first century.

They were openly exposed nothing was done in secret. The last words of Jesus in Luke, "behold, I send the Promise of My Father upon you; but tarry in the city of Jerusalem until you are endued with power from on high." The power from heaven the Holy Spirit would come to the apostles to give them power and understanding. Jesus led the disciples to Bethany, lifted up His hands and blessed them. While He was blessing them He was carried up into heaven. Mary Magdalene told the disciples she had seen Jesus and He talked with her. That same day, the first day of the week the disciples were inside with the doors shut because they feared the Jews and Jesus came and stood with them and said "Peace be with you." Jesus breathed on the apostles and said, "Receive the Holy Spirit. If you forgive the sins of any, they are forgiven them; if you retain the sins of any, they are retained." The apostles would teach and preach under the direct influence of the Holy Spirit who would inspire them to speak the truth of the Word of God. God is the only one who has authority to condemn and to forgive sins.

JN 20 A few days later the disciples were inside again and Thomas was with them. Jesus came in and the door was shut and Jesus stood and said "Peace to you!" Thomas had before doubted Jesus resurrection and for that reason Jesus told him to look at His hands and put his hand in His side. Thomas saw the results of Jesus crucifixion and called Jesus Lord and God. Jesus said Thomas believed because He saw the evidence of Jesus crucifixion and he said those who believe without seeing Him are blessed. Today we believe Jesus is the Son of God that died to redeem us from the guilt of our sins. Christians believe in Jesus because of the overwhelming evidence that is in the Bible. Jesus performed many miracles that were witnessed by the disciples that are not in the scriptures but those that are written were written so that people would have faith in Christ. Jesus appeared to the disciples one more time at the town of Tiberius on the western shore of the Sea of Galilee, before He ascended to heaven. The disciples that saw Him were Simon Peter, Thomas the twin, Nathaniel from Cana in Galilee, the sons of Zebedee and two other disciples. Peter said he was going fishing and they all said we are going with you. They caught no fish that night. Jesus was standing on the shore but the disciples did not recognize Him because they were in the boat.

Jesus asked them if they had food and they said no. Jesus told them to cast the net on the right side of the boat and when they did the net was very heavy because of the catch and they could not draw it in. The disciples then recognized Jesus and John told Peter and he put his outer garment on and jumped into the sea. The other disciples came to Jesus in a boat, they were not far from the shore and they dragged the net full of fish on shore. They saw a fire and fish on the coals and some bread ready to be eaten. Jesus told them to bring some of the fish they caught. Peter dragged the net full of one hundred and fifty three fish and the net did not break. Jesus told them to come eat breakfast. The disciples were afraid to ask Him who He was but they knew He was the Lord and they came ashore and ate. This was the third time the disciples had seen Jesus after His resurrection. After they ate breakfast, Jesus questioned Peter. John 21:15-18– "So when they had eaten breakfast, Jesus said to Simon Peter, "Simon, son of Jonah, do you love Me more than these?" He said to Him, "yes, Lord; you know that I love you." He said to him, "Feed My lambs." He said to him a second time, "Simon, son of Jonah, do you love Me?" And he said to Him, "Lord You know all things; You know that I love you." He said to him, "Tend My sheep." Jesus said for the third time Simon, son of Jonah, do you love Me?"

Peter was grieved because Jesus said for the third time, "Do you love Me?" And he said to Him, "Lord, You know all things; You know that I love You." Jesus said to him, "Feed My sheep. Most assuredly, I say to you, when you were younger, you girded yourself and walked where you wished; but when you are old, you will stretch out your hands and another will gird you and carry you where you do not wish." Jesus said those things to signify by what death Peter would glorify God. Peter had a strong faith and strong will and Jesus asked him to look after the other disciples. Jesus would soon ascend to heaven. Peter did not receive a position of authority over the other apostles but he led them by example with his own strength and passion for the Lord. The Bible does not have a record of Peters suffering and death but according to tradition Peter's death occurred near the end of Nero's reign over Rome and at Peter's request he was crucified upside down.

Jesus did many things that were not written and if they were, even the world could not contain all the books that could be written. Matthew 28:18-20–And Jesus came and spoke to them, saying, "All authority has been given to Me in heaven and on earth. Go therefore and make disciples of all the nations, baptizing them in the name of the father and of the Son and of the Holy Spirit. Teaching them to observe all things that I have commanded you; and lo, I am with you always, even to the end of the age." The end of the age would be the same as the end of the earth at the end of time. Jesus would soon ascend to heaven and He asked Peter to look after the other disciples. Jesus knew that as the disciples grew older they would need someone with strength to lead them. Peter assured Jesus that he loved Him. Peter saw John the disciple whom Jesus loved, behind them. (John was the one who had asked Jesus at the last supper who would betray Him.) Peter said to Jesus, Lord what about this man? Peter was asking about John. Jesus told Peter, if He willed that John would remain till He returned. Jesus told Peter to follow Him. A rumor spread that Jesus had said the disciples would not die. Jesus had said if it was His will.

The Apostles establish the Kingdom of Christ

Jesus had told the apostles to wait in Jerusalem until they received supernatural power from the Holy Spirit. After Jesus had spoken to His disciples, they watched Him ascend to heaven and a cloud obscured Him from their sight. The Apostles were left alone but the Holy Spirit would inspire them and they would preach the gospel Kingdom of Christ would be publicly established in Jerusalem. Then two men in white clothing said, "Men of Galilee, why do you stand gazing up into heaven? This same Jesus, who was taken up from you into heaven, will so come in like manner as you saw Him go into heaven. The kingdom of God (church) was introduced first by John the Baptist who was preaching and baptizing people before Christ began His ministry. John the Baptist was sent by God to baptize people in preparation for the kingdom. The New Testament clearly states that the Kingdom of Christ (church) was in view while Christ and the apostles were on earth. The kingdom became a visible reality in the first century on the day of Pentecost after the resurrection of Christ according to the second chapter of the book of Acts.

Before His ascension Jesus had emphasized that His death was necessary for the remission of sins and that the gospel should be preached in His name all over the world beginning in Jerusalem. The disciples received instructions to make Disciples of Christ among all people in every nation. The teaching about Jesus Christ was God's redeeming message to sinful people everywhere. Before Jesus ascended to heaven He told the His apostles to establish His kingdom on earth. Mark 16:15-16 "Go into all the world and preach the gospel to every creature. He who believes and is baptized will be saved: but he who does not believe will be condemned." "But you shall receive power when the Holy Spirit has come upon you; and you shall be witnesses to Me in Jerusalem, and in all Judea and Samaria, and to the end of the earth."

The Jewish apostleship ceased after the establishment of the church and the death of the Apostles. It was necessary at that time on the day of Pentecost for the apostles to demonstrate the power of the Holy Spirit with divine inspiration because the New Testament scriptures were not yet available. Peter preached on the first day of Pentecost after Jesus death. He was inspired by the Holy Spirit enabling him to know what to say. Peter and the other Apostles who were also inspired stood before the crowd of people declared that the things that were happening were a fulfillment of Joel's Prophecy.

Acts 2:1-12 "When the day of Pentecost had fully come, they were all with one accord in one place. The Apostles and some other of Jesus disciple were together waiting for the Holy Spirit. 2. And suddenly there came a sound from heaven, as of a rushing mighty wind, and it filled the whole house where they were sitting." The Holy Spirit could have come silently but he came in a way to attract a lot of attention to the presence of God's Spirit so that all would know that this was an event from God. There were people (Jews) from every nation and language that were in Jerusalem to attend the feast that day.

The apostles were all inspired and with full agreement in one place. And suddenly there came a sound from heaven, as of a rushing mighty wind, and it filled the whole house where they were sitting. Then there appeared to them divided tongues, as of fire, and one sat upon each of them.

And they were all filled with the Holy Spirit and began to speak in other languages that the Holy Spirit gave them.

The tongues were a sign to the people that they were speaking with the authority of God. Jesus told the Apostles beforehand that they would be witnesses for Him in Jerusalem, Judea, Samaria, and all over the world. Jesus told them what happened in Jerusalem on the day of Pentecost was the beginning of witnessing to people from every nation. From then until the end of the world people would be witnesses for Jesus and the gospel message. Some of the crowd attributed the miraculous speaking to God but some said these men are drunk on new wine. The promise of the kingdom of Christ would form right before their eyes but they would not recognize what was happening.

The kingdom of Christ would consist of people on earth who would willingly become Christ's disciples through faith in Christ and obey the requirements taught by Christ. Peter was selected to speak as he stood with the other apostles. Peter reminded the Jews that they were guilty of crucifying Jesus. The message cut them to the heart and they asked what they could do, to receive God's forgiveness for the guilt of their sin. Peter told them to repent of their sin and be baptized for the remission of their sins. The people that heard Peter realized they were guilty of sin and asked Peter what they could do in order to be forgiven by Jesus and God. Peter told the people to repent and be baptized in the name of Jesus for the remission of sins. Peter said the promise of remission of sins was to be given to everyone who obeyed.

There was a common bond among those who obeyed the things Peter taught and they continued to fellowship each other. The Lord continued to add to the number of people that repented and were baptized. On that day about three thousand people obeyed the words of Peter and were added to the kingdom of Christ (church). Peter had told them all to repent and be baptized so their sins could be forgiven. Those who heard the gospel message of Peter and the apostles were baptized and soon after their baptism they were called Christians. The things they heard and saw was a fulfillment of God's promise to pour out the Holy Spirit on all people. The message of faith, repentance and water baptism became the formula for obtaining the remission of sins from that first Pentecost day Peter preached the message to the end of time.

The kingdom of Christ still continues to expand every day. Jesus preached the same message before His death. Peter said the promise of forgiveness of sin would be given to all who would obey the message the Apostles preached. The Apostles were not left alone to teach what they wanted to, the Holy Spirit inspired them to preach the gospel of the Kingdom of Christ. The kingdom would be publicly established in Jerusalem. Then two men in white clothing said, "Men of Galilee, why do you stand gazing up into heaven? This same Jesus, who was taken up from you into heaven, will so come in like manner as you saw Him go into heaven. Two angels confirmed the gospel message of the Holy Spirit.

The apostles continued to teach and preach for several years after the church in Jerusalem was established and other disciples were gifted by the Holy Spirit to preach the gospel. Speaking in tongues was a temporary gift of the Holy Spirit that ceased when the tongues and other miraculous gifts were no longer necessary because the Bible was being written and the scriptures were available. The demonstration by the Holy Spirit was only temporary as a sign for the beginning of the church. Miraculous gifts of the Holy Spirit would cease later and the church would depend on the written Word of God in the Bible.

Jesus is the king of the kingdom the church, which is a group of people that are joined together in unity and love for one another. The king has absolute power over the kingdom. When we see the word kingdom associated with God or Christ we should not think of one geographical area. The people in the room where the Apostles were, heard the sound and saw something that looked like tongues of fire that sat on each of the Apostles. The Bible describes the event of speaking in tongues in reference to the existence of the many languages of the people that were present. The dramatic appearance of divided tongues of fire proved they spoke from God, and when they spoke everyone heard in their own language. The term other tongues, simply means other languages. People from every nation were present and they heard in their native language signifying that redemption was offered to all people everywhere. Peter continued to preach encouraging people with the gospel of Christ and many believed him and about three thousand people were baptized and became members of the church.

The church met in the temple daily praising God and the people were pleased and many were added to the church. Peter and John were arrested but many had believed and of the men there were about five thousand. Peter and John were threatened for preaching but they were let go. The apostles were still being threatened but a Jewish man named Gamaliel a man who taught the Law asked the Jews to leave the apostles alone then the Apostles were beaten and told they should not speak in the name of Jesus anymore then they were freed. However they continued to preach the gospel daily in the temple and from house to house. Gospel means the good news of Jesus Christ the Redeemer.

The last words of Jesus that are recorded in Matthew's gospel are in, Matthew 28:18-20 Jesus came and spoke to them, saying, "All authority has been given to Me in heaven and on earth. Go therefore and make disciples of all the nations, baptizing them in the name of the father and of the Son and of the Holy Spirit. Teaching them to observe all things that I have commanded you; and lo, I am with you always, even to the end of the age." Jesus commanded the apostles to preach the gospel all over the world by His authority. The gospel of Christ is, for all people for all time throughout the earth Jesus spiritually rules over the many individual church groups everywhere. Then two angels said, "Men of Galilee, why do you stand gazing up into heaven? This same Jesus, who was taken up from you into heaven, will so come in like manner as you saw Him go into heaven. An indwelling of the Holy Spirit was given to Christians to help them walk in fellowship with Christ before the scriptures were complete and made available to everyone. The miraculous signs on the day of Pentecost were signs that ushered in the new age of God's act of redemption.

Miraculous signs and supernatural gifts of the knowledge of God's Word proved that the apostles and other inspired people were speaking by the power of the Holy Spirit, proof that what they said was from the Word of God. After miraculous gifts of the Holy Spirit ceased Christians continued to teach about the kingdom of Christ with an understanding they gleaned from the scriptures in New Testament and miraculous gifts were no longer needed. God and Jesus wants people to accept them and the gospel message with their heart by faith not by miraculous signs.

Jesus said –Luke 17: 20-21 When He was asked by the Pharisees when the kingdom of God would come, He answered them, "The kingdom of God does not come with observation; nor will they say, 'See here!' or 'See there!' For indeed, the kingdom of God is within you." Everyone in the kingdom of Christ comes into the kingdom by faith in Jesus Christ when they voluntarily submit themselves to the rule of Jesus by obedience to the gospel message. Jesus is a king over a spiritual kingdom of people (church) that have been redeemed from the guilt of sin. The kingdom of Christ, the church is a spiritual kingdom within the hearts of those who have obeyed Jesus. The members of the church, the kingdom of God on earth have love for one another and other people and they desire for all people to have faith, hope and love and follow the teachings of Jesus. Acts 2:42-45 "And they continued steadfastly in the apostles doctrine and fellowship, in the breaking of bread and in prayers. The spiritual gifts of the Holy Spirit did not cease until the Word of God in the written scriptures was available.

Before that time fear came upon every soul, and many wonders and signs were done through the apostles who were still inspired by the Holy Spirit. Now all who believed were together and had all things common and sold their possessions and goods, and divided them among all, as anyone had need." The Disciples of Christ grew to a large number of people in Jerusalem. Many of them living in other towns came to Jerusalem for the feast and heard Peter preach about the kingdom. The members of the church in Jerusalem sold their possessions so that everyone could have what they needed to live. The sharing in common among the church members was a freewill offering from their heart.

Christ never assumed carnal or political authority on earth, in the New Testament He is called Lord of Lord's and The King of Kings. Jesus is the King of Kings and Lord of all Christians in His spiritual kingdom and Christians are directly under His authority. Jesus Christ the Son of God has become the most popular and influential person that has ever existed. He is known by more than ninety names, titles, and references listed in the Bible. Jesus told the apostles they would have the keys to the Kingdom of Christ (Church). Matthew 16–Jesus promised to give the keys to heaven to the apostles. Keys represent the terms of membership in the kingdom as stated in the Bible. The keys to the kingdom are in the New Testament.

The Book of Acts is a record of the Apostles work of preaching the gospel after Jesus' death and ascension. The Bible has a complete record of everything people need to know about Christianity and the book of Acts furnishes us with the gospel message taught by the apostles to introduce the kingdom of Christ (church) to the Jews and the Gentiles including all people even the eve of the end of time. The apostles continued to teach and preach about the kingdom until their death.

After the death of the apostles the keys to the kingdom of Christ still existed in the inspired word of God in the Bible then and today. The kingdom continues to grow today because faithful members of the kingdom continue to preach the good news of the kingdom converting people to Christ. The scriptures of the Old Testament revealed the coming of Christ and His mission of redemption. The scriptures did not come from the mind and imagination of the prophets. God revealed the scriptures to the prophets and the writers of the Bible by direct inspiration of the Holy Spirit.

The scriptures reflect the light of God's word and will, like a light shining in a dark place, give understanding to those in sin and cause Christ the Morning Star, to rise in their hearts by faith giving them hope and teaching them to love. The gospel and church membership is free to all willing to learn the gospel and obey Jesus. 1st John 2:1-2 "My little children, I am writing these things to you so that you may not sin. And if anyone sins, we have an Advocate with the father, Jesus Christ the righteous and He Himself is the propitiation for our sins; and not for ours only, but also for those of the whole world. Now by this we know that we know Him, if we keep his commandments. He who says, I know Him," and does not keep His commandments, is a liar, and the truth is not in Him." Jesus will reign over the churches until the end of time then He will return to earth to transport the members of the churches to their home in heaven.

Ephesians 1:22-23 "And He put all things in subjection under His feet, and gave Him as head over all things to the church, which is His body, the fullness of Him who fills all in all." The apostles preached the gospel everywhere, and the Holy Spirit helped them by confirming their word with miraculous signs.

Some people including myself believe the kingdom of Christ was established in the first century A.D. as a spiritual kingdom and includes everyone who will have faith in Christ and will submit to the terms of the gospel of Christ recorded in the Bible.

NLT Bible–Philippians 2:12-13 "Dear friends you always followed my instructions when I was with you. And now that I am away, it is even more important to work hard to show the results of your salvation, obeying God with deep reverence and fear. For God is working in you, giving you the desire and the power to do what pleases Him." Salvation and church membership is a personal thing that is freely open to anyone that will obey the gospel of Christ. Salvation depends on personal obedience not on human authority.. The word church refers to people who have been saved by obedience to the gospel of Christ. The kingdom of God is universal and the church can be a local group or any number of groups in other areas. The redemption of sin is free for any individual that has faith and repents of their sin and is baptized in water like Jesus as a sign of their faith in Jesus.

Jesus is the Head of the church also called the kingdom of God, Kingdom of Christ. A kingdom suggests the idea of invisibility and power. You cannot know if a person is a member of the Kingdom of God by looking at them because they do not look any different from anyone else but you can recognize them by their demonstration of faith, hope and love. The Jews in the first century were expecting a king that would deliver them from the bondage of the Roman Empire. Jesus did not come to rule over a worldly kingdom or to remove the people of his kingdom from a worldly empire. Jesus is a king over a spiritual kingdom of people that have been redeemed from the guilt of sin no matter where they live or whatever Government they are subject to. Christ never assumed carnal or political authority on earth yet in the New Testament He is called Lord of Lord's and The King of Kings because He accepts all people who have faith in Him. Faith in Jesus always means obedience to the gospel. Jesus is the King of Kings and Lord of all Christians. Jesus will reign over the churches until the end of time then He will return to earth and transport the members of the churches to their home in heaven.

Ephesians 1:22-23 "And He put all things in subjection under His feet, and gave Him as head over all things to the church, which is His body, the fullness of Him who fills all in all." The apostles preached the gospel everywhere, and the Holy Spirit helped them by confirming their word with miraculous signs. In the NIV—and other versions of the Bible it says to work out you own salvation with fear and trembling. No one on earth can save a soul and people cannot save themselves but they can obtain salvation by obeying the gospel of Christ taught by the New Testament writers. Salvation is a personal achievement that anyone willing to obey the gospel message can obtain.

A young disciple of Christ named Stephen was chosen by the apostles to preach the gospel, they laid their hands on him afterwards to impart a gift of the Holy Spirit during the days before miraculous gifts ceased. Stephen had great faith and was gifted by the Holy Spirit. Stephen taught about Jesus in the Synagogue using very strong language against those who crucified Christ. Some people argued with Stephen but they were not able to resist the wisdom and the spirit by which he spoke. Stephen was falsely accused of blasphemy and false witnesses testified against him. Stephen began to preach to them about how God had made a promise to Abraham to bless all nations through him and how it was fulfilled in Jesus Christ.

Stephen taught about Jesus in the Synagogue using very strong language against those who crucified Christ. Some people argued with Stephen but they were not able to resist the wisdom and the spirit by which he spoke. Stephen was falsely accused of blasphemy and false witnesses testified against him. The Jewish members became very angry threatening Stephen but he, being filled with the Holy Spirit looked to heaven and he saw the glory of God and Jesus was standing at the right hand of God. As Stephen stood before them, his face began to glow like the face of an angel. When Stephen was asked if the accusations were true, Stephen began to preach to them about how God had made a promise to Abraham to bless all nations through him and how it was fulfilled in Jesus Christ. Stephen accused the Jews of being stubborn and refusing to accept the will of God before and now they were murderers. The Jewish leaders became irate with Stephen.

Stephen full of the Holy Spirit, looked up into heaven. He saw Jesus standing at the right hand of God, and he told the people what he saw. The crowd ran at Stephen, dragged him out of the city, and began to stone him. Just before Stephen died from the stoning, he prayed, "Lord, receive my spirit" and he knelt down and cried out in a loud voice "Lord, do not charge them with this sin." Then Stephen died.

Saul was born in Tarsus and was a Roman citizen. There is no evidence that Saul was involved in any way with Jesus before his conversion to Christianity. In the 9th chapter of Acts we find that Saul who was later called Paul the Latin name for Saul persecuted Christians, and he threatened to put them to death. Saul was a Jewish man who was zealous for the Law and persecuted Christians but He was converted to Christ and became zealous for preaching the gospel of Christ.

When the Jews stoned Stephen, they laid their coats at the feet of a young man named Saul who had been persecuting the followers of Christ. Saul and those he led entered the houses of Christians and took them to prison. The Lord chose certain people during the early history of the church to give gifts of the Holy Spirit to, so the gospel would be preached and spread all over the world. Saul was chosen by God to preach the gospel of Christ. After Stephen's death a light from heaven shone all around Saul, He was afraid and he fell to the ground. Then he heard a voice say, "Saul, Saul, why are you persecuting Me? Saul said, "Who are you, Lord?" The voice replied, "I am Jesus, whom you are persecuting. It is hard for you to kick against the goads." Goads are sharp pointed sticks used to drive cattle. It was hard for the cattle to stray from the herder because the pricks from the sharp goads hurt them. The message for Saul was that he was going against the will of God and of Christ when he persecuted Christians. Saul was zealous for God before he was chosen but he did not realize that He was going against God's will when he was persecuting Christians and resisting the teaching of Jesus God's Son. Saul persecuted Christians threatening them with death. Saul thought he was doing what God wanted him to do.

The Lord told Saul to go to the city of Damascus and someone would tell him what to do. God had plans for Saul whose name was changed to Paul. Saul was a zealous man that was capable of wielding a great influence in the kingdom of Christ and converting the Gentiles to Christ. The voice of the Lord from heaven quickly convinced Saul that he was wrong to resist the gospel of Christ. Saul was frightened, believing that he had been wrong and he asked what he could do. Jesus told Saul to go into Damascus and he would be told what to do. Saul was unable to see because he had been deliberately blinded but he was led into the city and went to the house of a man named Judas.

There was a disciple in the city name Ananias and in a vision the Lord told Ananias to go to Judas house and ask for Saul of Tarsus. Saul was praying and he saw a vision of a man named Ananias coming and putting his hand on him to restore his sight. Ananias was reluctant to go to Judas house but the Lord told him, to go because he Saul was chosen by God to bear God's name before Gentiles, kings, and the children of Israel. "For I will show him how many things he must suffer for My name's sake." Saul spent three days and nights without sight, and during that time he didn't eat or drink anything. Ananias went to the house where Saul was and restored his sight and baptized him. Even though Saul had been a non-believer that persecuted Christians God chose to save him in the same way everyone was saved. Saul whose name became Paul converted many people Christ and was a strong person with the ability to lead the church. Paul emphasized that God has only one kingdom and all people of faith are in the one kingdom even that Kingdom would be spread all over the world.

Philip one of the men chosen to be a deacon in the church at Jerusalem preached the gospel in Samaria and many people believed in the Lord Jesus and both men and women were baptized. An angel of the Lord told Philip to go to Samaria and on his way he met a man in a chariot on the road home and the spirit sent Philip to preach the gospel to him. Philip preached about Jesus and further down the road they found a pool of water and the man asked Philip to baptize him. After the man confessed his faith in Christ, Philip baptized him in the pool of water. The Holy Spirit sent Philip somewhere else and the man who was baptized continued on his way rejoicing.

God intended for the gospel to be preached to all people and He opened the door for Gentiles in the first century. Gentiles were accepted into the Kingdom of Christ as brothers and sisters. The conversion and the acceptance of the gentiles into the church began in Caesarea with a Roman soldier named Cornelius who was a centurion in the Roman army. Cornelius was a Gentile but he and his family believed in God and they were interested in the Jews religion. One day about the ninth hour Cornelius saw a vision, an angel of God came to him in the vision and called him by name. Cornelius fearing the angel said "What is it Lord." The angel told Cornelius that God had heard his prayer and Cornelius was told to send for Peter who was in Joppa and Peter would tell him what he must do to become a Christian. The next day Peter went to the top of his house to pray and he fell into a trance and saw a vision sent by God. Peter was thinking about what the vision meant and the Holy Spirit told him three men were coming to him and he should go with them.

The purpose of the presence of the power of the Holy Spirit was to convince the Jews that God also accepted the Gentiles that had faith in Christ. Peter accepted the fact that God accepted the Gentiles and he knew they should be taught the gospel and become members of the church. Peter told the Gentiles to be baptized in the name of the Lord. The gentiles were baptized in the name of Jesus and were added to the church. From that time forward the gospel was preached to all people regardless of their nationality. Cornelius was baptized in accordance to what the Holy Spirit taught the apostles about baptism.

The news about the Gentiles became known in Jerusalem by the apostles and the church there agreed that God had granted repentance and eternal life to the Gentiles, which included all people. Members of the church taught the gospel of Christ to the people in Antioch and they were added to the church. The church in Jerusalem heard about their conversion and sent Barnabas to Antioch. Barnabas witnessed the grace of God there and he encouraged the Christians there. Barnabas left Antioch to look for Paul and he brought Paul to Antioch and they worshiped with the church there for a year and the Disciples of Christ were called Christians first in Antioch.

There were certain Christians in Antioch in the early days of the church before the scriptures were available that were given gifts from the Holy Spirit to minister, prophesy and teach God's Word and the Lord told Barnabas and Saul (Paul) to go to other areas and preach the Word of God. During the early days of the church some members were given supernatural gifts of the Holy Spirit because the complete written Word of God was not yet available in the Bible. In the first Century members of the church were enabled to teach the gospel in an effective way with the help of the Holy Spirit and people were being added to the church. People have natural wisdom and an ability to reason and the people Paul preached to, already had a concept of God. Paul taught, there is only one real God and He created everything. Paul said God made people in a way that He expected them to look for Him and find Him, which is an easy thing because the evidence of God is everywhere and people are God's offspring (children). Paul preached to the people of Athens telling them that God made the world but since He is the Lord of heaven and the earth He does not live in earthly dwellings and He is not worshiped with people's hands as if He needed anything because He gives life, breath and all things to the people He created. Before Jesus was born people attempted to worship God with or by things they made with their own hands and that way of worship was not acceptable to God.

People have the ability to reason that there is a real God and they should look for God and find Him because God is not far from anyone since He is the creator of all things. The Book of Acts is a record of the Apostles work of preaching the gospel to establish churches after Jesus' death. Jesus said, "I will build My church and the gates of Hades shall not prevail against it." Satan worked against the establishment of the church but he was not able to prevent its establishment. The church that Jesus built can only be identified by the faith, hope and love of the members of that church. Church came into existence in various places all over the world eventually because the gospel was preached and people obeyed the gospel message of faith, hope and love. The church–the Kingdom of Christ will continue on earth until the end of time then it will be taken into heaven. Today all Christian religions believe the Bible is the word of God and they base their doctrine on a study of the Bible but they do not all agree on what the Bible teaches or on church doctrine.

In the NIV—and other versions of the Bible it says to work out your own salvation with fear and trembling. This message came from the Apostle Paul who had originally delivered the message of salvation to the members of the church. Paul urged the members of the church to remain faithful to the word of God they received. Paul was inspired by the Holy Spirit therefore his message came from God through the Holy Spirit. People should listen to the word preached and study the Bible and work out their own salvation from what they read and are taught by carefully examining the scriptures.

The kingdom of Christ on earth would consist of church groups located all over the world. The Lord wants each member of the church to learn the scriptures in the Bible and by their own faith and initiative, teach other people from the scriptures. In chapter 13 of 1st Corinthians Paul told each member to examine them selves to see if they are living according to the faith they learned about in the Bible. There should only be one kind of Christian and all Christians are to be of the same mind by following the teaching about the church in the New Testament so they can live and worship God in peace. Since humans are very diverse the churches may and do vary in some ways like choosing various names to identify their group and conducting their worship in various ways but each group should stay within the Bible example of a church.

The word of God in the Bible is the only God given authority for the church. Paul urged the members of the church to remain faithful to the word of God they received. Paul was inspired by the Holy Spirit therefore his message came from God through the Holy Spirit. Church groups depend on their own understanding of the gospel message and of faith, hope and love as taught in the Bible. Christians were told to continue to meet together on the first day of the week. By meeting together church members support each other's faith. The first century members met in the temple and in homes, praising God and they were in favor with other people. The miraculous spiritual gifts ceased after a time when the scriptures were complete. We do not need miraculous signs today because we can read the complete will of God in the Bible.

Peter an apostle with a strong influence in the church told the Jews that God had given the Gentiles the same gift He gave them and they agreed saying, "Then God has also granted to the Gentiles repentance to life." God opened the door of redemption to the Gentiles. After the days of Holy Spirit inspiration Christians depended on the Bible. Christians today are convinced that the Bible contains the complete plan of redemption and God's complete will for people. The Bible guides Christians in the truth and is the ultimate source of the truth of God's will. The Holy Spirit that inspired the writers of the Bible still works on people's hearts through the written and spoken word of God. The Spirit lives in some degree within Christians and He is our comforter and guide. Jesus told the disciples that the Spirit would guide them into all truth. People are encouraged to read the bible and gain an understanding of the scriptures according to their ability. A church is a group of Christians that meet together to worship God and Christ. All of the churches together represent the kingdom of Christ, also noted as the kingdom of God or kingdom of heaven. A kingdom suggests the idea of invisibility and power.

You cannot know if a person is a member of the Kingdom of God by looking at them because they do not look any different from anyone else. Jesus spiritual kingdom is invisible because it exists in the hearts of individuals. The other books of the Bible record the early history of the churches and the many problems within the church groups. The book to the churches in Thessalonica and the book of Revelation prepares Christians for a time in the future when the church will be faced with great persecution prior to the end of time when Christ will return.

Revelation 20:11-15 Then I saw a great white throne and Him who sat on it, from whose face the earth and the heaven fled away. And there was found no place for them. And I saw the dead, small and great, standing before God, and books were opened. And another book was opened, which is the Book of Life. And the dead were judged according to their works, by the things, which were written in the books. The sea gave up the dead who were in it, and Death and Hades delivered up the dead who were in them. And they were judged, each one according to his works.

Then death and Hades were cast into the lake of fire. This is the second death. And anyone not found written in the Book of Life was cast into the lake of fire." The end of the world will not come until Jesus returns to earth. His coming will be unexpected and sudden like lightning. This indicates that those who are alive when Jesus comes back will see and hear Him as He descends from heaven with the angels. Matthew 24:29-31 "But immediately after the tribulation of those days the sun will be darkened, and the moon will not give its light, and the stars will fall from the sky, and the powers of heaven will be shaken. And then the sign of the son of Man will appear in the sky, and then all the tribes of the earth will mourn, and they will see the Son of Man coming on the clouds of the sky with power and great glory. 'And He will send forth His angels with great power.

1st Peter 2—Peter wrote about those who accepted Jesus and obeyed the gospel, saying: "You are like living stones being built up as a spiritual house for a holy priesthood, to offer up spiritual sacrifices acceptable to God through Jesus Christ. You are a chosen race, a royal priesthood, A Holy Nation, A people for God's own possession so that you may, proclaim the excellencies of Him who has called you out of darkness into His marvelous light; for you once were not a people, but now you are the people of God; you had not received mercy, but now you have received mercy."

The Lord Jesus Himself will come from heaven and the dead in Christ will be resurrected. Then all Christians will be caught up in the clouds to meet the Lord in the air, and will remain with the lord forever. In the second letter to the church in Thessalonica Paul speaks to all Christians and especially those who have suffered persecution saying you are worthy of the kingdom of God and God is just to repay with affliction those who afflicted the church. Paul said "The Lord Jesus will be revealed from heaven with His mighty angels in flaming fire, dealing out retribution to those who do not know God and to those who do not obey the gospel of our Lord Jesus. God's plan of redemption was revealed many years ago and millions of people have become Christians and before the end of time many more people will obey the gospel of Christ.

The Bible teaches that some day the earth will be destroyed after God's people have been removed from the earth. The Bible also informs us that prior to the end of time there will a great falling away from the faith during a period known as the end time a time period prior to the second coming of Christ. In the second chapter of 2nd Thessalonians Paul writes about a man of lawlessness referring to a personality on earth that will exalt himself above the God of heaven or any other so called god because He will declare that he is God. The man of lawlessness is also called the man of destruction. The man of lawlessness will be an ally of Satan and Satan will give him the power to perform signs and wonders to fool the people on earth, attempting to persuade them to follow him instead of God.

Paul wrote to Timothy and warned him that the last days before the end of time will be difficult times because "men will be lovers of self, lovers of money, boastful, arrogant, revilers disobedient to parents, ungrateful, unholy, unloving, irreconcilable, malicious gossips, without self control, brutal, haters of good, treacherous, reckless, conceited, lovers of pleasure rather than lovers of God." Paul wrote to the church in Ephesus admonishing them to be strong in the Lord and put on the armor of God so they could stand against the Devil, the one that will empower the lawless one.

Paul said Christians will struggle against the world forces of darkness the spiritual forces of wickedness in the heavenly places. The devils demons will wage a spiritual warfare against Christians during the end times before Jesus returns. Paul said a Christian's defense would be to stand firm in the truth and righteousness. Take the helmet of salvation, and the sword of the Spirit, which is the word of God. Peter said there would be false prophets who will secretly introduce false heresies that are destructive and many will follow them. 1st Peter chapter 3– The heavens and the earth are reserved for fire on the day of God's judgment when Jesus returns. Peter said "By His word the present heavens and earth are being reserved for fire kept for the day- of judgment and destruction of ungodly men."

(NASB). 2nd Peter 3:10-12–The day of the Lord will come like a thief, in which the heavens will pass away with a roar and the elements will be destroyed with intense heat, and the earth and its works will be burned up.

"Since all these things are to be destroyed in this way, what sort of people ought you to be in holy conduct and godliness, looking for and hastening the coming day of God, because of which the heavens will be destroyed by burning, and the elements will melt with intense heat! But according to His promises we are looking for new heavens and a new earth, in which righteousness dwells." There will be a new place for all of God's people in a place that has been prepared for all who have been saved by Christ. Christians are waiting for the return of Jesus but before Jesus comes back a time of great tribulation and persecution will have begun. 2nd Thessalonians when the man of lawlessness is allied with Satan he will have great power and he will use miracles and lying wonders, with all unrighteousness and deception. Jesus will return at the time described by Matthew 24:27-31. The angels will gather up those who are saved.

Luke 21:25-28, people on earth will see Jesus coming in a cloud with power and great glory. Mark 13: 24-27 "But in those days, after that tribulation, the sun will be darkened, and the moon will not give its light; the stars of heaven will fall, and the powers in the heavens will be shaken. Then they will see the Son of Man coming in the clouds with great power and glory. And then He will send His angels, and gather together His elect from the four winds, from the farthest part of earth to the farthest part of heaven." During the end of time, Jesus returns and all the dead will be resurrected in the proper order 1st Corinthians 15:20-26 Paul affirms that Christ was resurrected from the dead and those who belong to Christ will be resurrected to life.

Paul said the resurrection would take place at the time of Christ's second coming. And at that time the kingdom of God the church will be delivered to God in heaven and Christ Himself will also be subject to God that God may be all in all. Paul also says those who are resurrected will have a glorious body. The dead body is corrupted but when it is resurrected in glory it will be a spiritual body and bear the image of the heavenly. There are several references in the New Testament warning the church about suffering great persecution before Christ returns. The scriptures reflect the light of God's word and will, like a light shining in a dark place, give understanding to those in sin and cause Christ the Morning Star, to rise in their hearts by faith giving them hope.

1st John 2:1-2 "My little children, I am writing these things to you so that you may not sin. And if anyone sins, we have an Advocate with the father, Jesus Christ the righteous and He Himself is the propitiation for our sins; and not for ours only, but also for those of the whole world. Now by this we know that we know Him, if we keep his commandments. He who says, I know Him," and does not keep His commandments, is a liar, and the truth is not in Him.

Revelation

The book of Revelation completes the story of the redeeming plan that began in the book of Genesis. There are several references to the end time in other books of the Bible, but Revelation specifically focuses on the future events of the end times. God made sure the church would be prepared for the end time. He inspired the Apostle Paul to write two letters to the church in Thessalonica. These two letters prepare us to understand the events of the end of time. In 1st Thessalonians Paul emphasized the second coming of Christ at an unknown time and warned the church to be ready at all times.

Matthew 24:4-14–And Jesus said "See to it that no one misleads you. For many will come in My name, saying, 'I am the Christ,' and will mislead many. You will be hearing of wars and rumors of wars. See that you are not frightened, for those things must take place, but that is not yet the end. For nation will rise against nation, and kingdom against kingdom, and in various places there will be famines and earthquakes.' "But all these things are merely the beginning of birth pangs. Then they will deliver you to tribulation, and will kill you, and you will be hated by al nations because of My name. At that time many will fall away and will betray one another and hate one another. Many false prophets will arise and will mislead people.

Christians will experience persecution and tribulation from the Antichrist at the end of time when the Anti-Christ appears. No one knows when the Anti-Christ will appear with great power to persecute God's people but Jesus will return while the Anti-Christ is on earth. When Jesus appears the church will be involved in a period of great persecution instigated by Satan and carried out by a world empire governed by a person referred to as the lawless one in the second letter of Thessalonians. Paul said God would be just and would repay those who were responsible for the tribulation.

The coming of Christ will take place while the Anti-Christ is on earth. His coming will be sudden like lightning. This indicates that those who are alive when Jesus comes back will see and hear Jesus as He descends from heaven with the angels. Matthew 24:29-31– After the tribulation the sun will be darkened, and the moon will not give its light, and the stars will fall from the sky, and the powers of heaven will be shaken. And then the sign of the son of Man will appear in the sky, and all the tribes of the earth will mourn, and they will see the Son of Man coming on the clouds of the sky with power and great glory.

Jesus returns to earth at the end of time. The sea will give up the dead who are in it, and Death and Hades will be delivered and the dead who are in them. And all who have ever lived will be judged, each one according to his works. Then all who belong to the unsaved on earth and in Hades, be will cast into the lake of fire. This is the second death. And anyone not found written in the Book of Life was cast into the lake of fire." The book of life represents the life of every person while they were alive on earth and God will make His judgment according everyone's life of faith, hope and love. The end of the world will come at a time when people are not expecting it. The time of the second coming of Christ is not known and cannot be known until the very day Christ returns. Christians who are dead and alive are still waiting for Jesus to return.

Revelation 20:11-15 Then I saw a great white throne and Him who sat on it, from whose face the earth and the heaven fled away. And there was found no place for them. And I saw the dead, small and great, standing before God, and books were opened. And another book was opened, which is the Book of Life. And the dead were judged according to their works, by the things, which were written in the books. The books are figurative and they represent a record of the life of people including their works. All people at the end of time will be resurrected so they can receive God's final judgment. Some may wonder what kind of body they will have. The Christians in Corinth asked Paul about the resurrection of the dead. 1st Corinthians 15 Paul writes about various types of bodies then he describes the bodies of the people who are resurrected. 1st Corinthians– 15 Paul exhorts Christians to wake up and do not sin. Some Christians doubted the resurrection of the dead body. Paul told those who doubted that God gives dead people a body "as He pleases." The natural body is corruptible and will decay after death. In the resurrection, the dead who were Christians will be given a spiritual body not made of dirt.

1St Corinthians 15–God will give Christians a body that is incorruptible, and immortal. The resurrected body is the image of a heavenly body.

Tribulation of the last Days on Earth

The last days on earth refer to a period of time called the end time before Jesus returns when there will be greater tribulation than has existed before. Christians expect Jesus to return someday near the end of time. The sign of the imminence of the coming of Christ and the resurrection of the dead will be known when the terrible events of the last days of earth are being experienced. The Apostle Paul warned the church about the coming of a great apostasy that would occur before He returns. There will be enemies of Christianity until the end of time but during the end time tribulation will be greater than ever before. In the first chapter of 1st John–John wrote about an antichrist that will arise and deny the divinity of Christ and persecute Christians. He attempts to control all people on earth. 1st John 4 John warned the church that there would be false spirits and false teachers in the world that will not confess that Jesus is from God.

John said Christians know that they are of God but the whole world will lie in the power of the evil one before Jesus comes back. Satan the Devil will empower the evil one and with his great power he will attempt to destroy the faith of God's people using lies and deceit. In 2nd John Christians are encouraged to live according to the Lord's commandments. John said that God has given us eternal life in His Son regardless of the Devil's evil that will be present on the earth at the end of time. In 1st Peter 2 Paraphrase: Peter wrote about those who accepted Jesus and obeyed the gospel, saying: "You are like living stones being built up as a spiritual house for a holy priesthood, to offer up spiritual sacrifices acceptable to God through Jesus Christ. You are a chosen race, a royal priesthood, A Holy Nation, A people for God's own possession so that you may, proclaim the excellencies of Him who has called you out of darkness into His marvelous light; for you once were not a people, but now you are the people of God; you had not received mercy, but now you have received mercy."

1st Thessalonians chapter four Paul wrote to encourage Christians not to be uninformed and worry about all of those who die before Christ returns. Paul said if we believe Jesus died and rose from the dead to live again, so we will be resurrected at the end of time. The Lord Jesus Himself will come from heaven and the dead in Christ will be resurrected. Then all Christians will be caught up in the clouds to meet the Lord in the air, and will remain with the lord forever.

In the second letter to the church in Thessalonica Paul speaks to all Christians and especially those who have suffered persecution saying you are worthy of the kingdom of God and God is just to repay with affliction those who afflicted the church. Paul said "The Lord Jesus will be revealed from heaven with His mighty angels in flaming fire, dealing out retribution to those who do not know God and to those who do not obey the gospel of our Lord Jesus. These will pay the penalty of eternal destruction, away from the presence of the Lord and the glory of His power." In the second chapter of 2nd Thessalonians Paul writes about a man of lawlessness referring to a person on earth that will exalt himself above the God of heaven. He will declare that he is God. The man of lawlessness is also called the man of destruction. The man of lawlessness will be an ally of Satan and Satan will give him the power to perform signs and wonders to fool the people on earth, an attempt to prove he is God. Paul wrote to Timothy and warned him that the last days before the end of time will be difficult times because "men will be lovers self, lovers of money, boastful, arrogant, revilers disobedient to parents, ungrateful, unholy, unloving, irreconcilable, malicious gossips, without self control, brutal, haters of good, treacherous, reckless, conceited, lovers of pleasure rather than lovers of God." Paul wrote to the church in Ephesus admonishing them to be strong in the Lord and put on the armor of God so they could stand against the Devil, the one that will empower the lawless one. Paul said Christians would struggle against the world forces of darkness the spiritual forces of wickedness in the heavenly places.

The Devils Demons will wage a spiritual warfare against Christians during the end times before Jesus returns. Paul said a Christian's defense would be to stand firm in the truth and righteousness.

Take the helmet of salvation, and the sword of the Spirit, which is the word of God. Peter said there would be false prophets who will secretly introduce false heresies that are destructive and many will follow them. 1st Peter chapter 3- "The present heavens and the earth are reserved for fire at the day of judgment when Jesus returns. Peter said "By His word the present heavens and earth are being reserved for fire kept for the day- of judgment and destruction of ungodly men." (NASB). 2nd Peter 3:10-12 "But the day of the Lord will come like a thief, in which the heavens will pass away with a roar and the elements will be destroyed with intense heat, and the earth and its works will be burned up. "Since all these things are to be destroyed in this way, what sort of people ought you to be in holy conduct and godliness, looking for and hastening the coming day of God, because of which the heavens will be destroyed by burning, and the elements will melt with intense heat! But according to His promises we are looking for new heavens and a new earth, in which righteousness dwells."

Hebrews 12:28-29 "Therefore, since we receive a kingdom that cannot be shaken, let us show gratitude, by which we may offer to God an acceptable service with reverence and awe; for our God is a consuming fire." Christians are waiting for the return of Jesus but before Jesus comes back a time of great tribulation and persecution will have begun. Described by Paul in 2nd Thessalonians when the man of lawlessness will be allied with Satan. Satan will have great power and he will use miracles and lying wonders, with all unrighteousness and deception. C.S Lewis said, "God whispers to us in our pleasures, speaks in our conscience, but shouts in our pains. It is His megaphone to rouse a deaf world." Bad things are allowed to happen to remind us that God made us and we are responsible to Him, and he sees us when we are good or bad. Jesus will return at the time as described by Matthew 24:27-31. The angels will gather up those who are saved. Luke 21:25-28, people on earth will see Jesus coming in a cloud with power and great glory. Mark 13: 24-27 "But in those days, after that tribulation, the sun will be darkened, and the moon will not give its light; the stars of heaven will fall, and the powers in the heavens will be shaken. Then they will see the Son of Man coming in the clouds with great power and glory. And then He will send His angels, and gather together His elect from the four winds, from the farthest part of earth to the farthest part of heaven."

During the end times all the dead will be resurrected in the proper order 1st Corinthians 15:20-26 Paul affirms that Christ was resurrected from the dead and those who belong to Christ will be resurrected to life. Paul said the resurrection would take place at the time of

Christ's second coming. And at that time the kingdom of God the church will be delivered to God in heaven and Christ Himself will also be subject to God that God may be all in all. Paul also says those resurrected will have a glorious body. The dead body is corrupted but when it is resurrected in glory it will be a spiritual body and bear the image of the heavenly. There are several references in the New Testament warning the church about suffering great persecution before Christ returns.

Book of Revelation

The word revelation means to reveal things that are hidden, such as an unveiling of future events. The literature of Revelation is describes the last and final events of God's plan of redemption, a time of great tribulation during the final judgment. The book of Revelation reveals future events that will begin at an unknown times prior to the end of the world. The events were revealed to the Apostle John by dreams and by direct revelation from heaven. The enemy is The church of the first century was familiar with figurative and apocalyptic literature. Many of the books in the Bible include that type of literature, especially the books of prophecy. The of God's people in Revelation The enemy is called the Antichrist and he is empowered by Satan. Revelation has seven sections and each section is independent from the other sections even though each section describes events that take place from the first coming of Christ to the second coming of Christ. "Then I saw an angel coming down from heaven, having the key to the bottomless pit and a great chain in his hand. He laid hold of the dragon, that serpent of old, who is the Devil and Satan, and bound him for a thousand years; and cast him into the bottomless pit, and shut him up, and set a seal on him, so that he should deceive the nations no more till the thousand years were finished. Satan is bound at this time but after these things he must be released for a little while." The abyss where Satan is imprisoned is referred to in Luke 8:30-31– "Jesus asked him, saying, "What is your name? And he said legion, because many demons had entered him. And they begged him that he would not command them to go out into the abyss." A bottomless pit somewhere in the heavens where the spirits of the dead who are unsaved will be sent, also the abode of the demons.

Revelation 9:1-2 Then the fifth angel sounded: And I saw a star fallen from heaven to the earth. To him was given the key to the bottomless pit (abyss). And he opened the bottomless pit, and smoke arose out of the pit like the smoke of a great furnace. Revelation 11:7 "When they finish their testimony, the beast (Satan) that ascends out of the bottomless pit (abyss) will make war against them, overcome them, and kill them." Revelation 17:8 The beast that you saw was, and is not, and will ascend out of the bottomless pit (abyss) and go to perdition" (hell). Satan had come to earth to persecute Jesus and God put him in the Abyss. Jude 6–5-7 I want to remind you, though you once knew this, that the Lord, having saved the people out of the land of Egypt, afterward destroyed those who did not believe. And the angels who did not keep their proper domain, but left their own abode, He has reserved in everlasting chains under darkness for the judgment of the great day; as the cities of Sodom and Gomorrah. In a similar manner these having given themselves over to sexual immorality and having gone after strange flesh, are set forth as an example, suffering the vengeance of eternal fire. Michael disputed about the body of Moses, dared not bring against him said "The Lord rebuke you!" Michael is an Archangel who is the protector of God's people and he protects them from Satan and the demons. The angels (demons) who left heaven and came to earth to torment God's people were put in the bottomless pit until the judgment time when they will be released from the Abyss for a little time before they are destroyed
Revelation has seven different sections and each section describes events that take place from the first coming of Christ to the second coming of Christ. Revelation 20:1-6 "Then I saw an angel

191

coming down from heaven, having the key to the bottomless pit and a great chain in his hand. He laid hold of the dragon, that serpent of old, who is the Devil and Satan, and bound him for a thousand years; and cast him into the bottomless pit, and shut him up, and set a seal on him, so that he should deceive the nations no more till the thousand years were finished. But after these things he must be released for a little while."

Satan's demons had access to the earth in the first century and they lied to, deceive and persecute God's people.

After the death of Christ they were limited in their power and influence because they were put in the Abyss. The abyss (bottomless pit) where Satan is imprisoned is referred to in Luke 8:30-31– "Jesus asked him, saying, "What is your name? And he said legion, because many demons had entered him. And the demons begged Jesus not to command them to go out into the abyss." Revelation 9:1-2 Then the fifth angel sounded: And I saw a star fallen from heaven to the earth. To him was given the key to the bottomless pit (abyss). And he opened the bottomless pit, and smoke arose out of the pit like the smoke of a great furnace." The abyss is a bottomless pit somewhere in the heavens and it is a holding place for the spirits of the dead who are not saved, evil angels, demons and Satan.

The Abyss is like a prison holding its occupants for future punishment. Satan and the demons were put in the abyss sometime after the death of Jesus. Sometime after the death of Jesus Satan was put in the abyss limiting his power against the people on earth. Near the end of time during a great persecution of God's people on earth Satan is released from the abyss and he attacks the church. Jesus will come and destroy Satan and all evil. God's people will be transported to heaven by Jesus and the angels. The thousand years that Satan is bound is a figurative time period that began in the first century. and will not end until Jesus returns at the end of time to take the church to heaven and to destroy the earth.

Revelation chapter 11– Describes the fate of the martyrs that died in the first century because they would not deny Jesus. Revelation 11:7 "When they finish their testimony, the beast (Satan) that ascends out of the bottomless pit (abyss) will make war against them, overcome them, and kill them." Revelation 17:8 The beast that you saw was, and is not, and will ascend out of the bottomless pit (abyss) and go to perdition" (hell). Satan had come to earth to persecute Jesus and God put him in the Abyss. He was on earth then he was not. Jude 6-9 "And the angels who did not keep their proper domain, but left their own abode, He has reserved in everlasting chains under darkness for the judgment of the great day; as Sodom and Gomorrah, and the cities around them in a similar manner to these, have given themselves over to sexual immorality and gone after strange flesh, reject authority, and speak evil of dignitaries.

Yet Michael the archangel, in contending with the devil, when he disputed about the body of Moses, dared not bring against him a reviling accusation, but said, "The Lord rebuke you!"

The angels (demons) who left heaven and came to earth to torment God's people. They were put in the bottomless pit. (Chains, darkness) the abyss until the judgment time when they will be released from the Abyss for a little time before they are destroyed. During that little time the Christians who are on earth will suffer from severe persecution. Jesus and the angels will return. "And I saw thrones and they sat on them, and judgment was committed to them." The judgment of all people who had been killed because of their faith in Jesus will be determined. Then I saw the souls of those who had been beheaded for their witness to Jesus, the martyrs who were killed for the word of God, who had not worshiped the beast or his image, and had not received his mark on their foreheads or on their hands. And they lived and reigned with Christ for a thousand years. The thousand years is a figurative time that describes the period of Christianity from its beginning until the time when Jesus returns to earth with His angels to destroy Satan and the lawless one that has been persecuting But the rest of the dead did not live again until the thousand years were finished. This is the first such the second death has no power, but they shall be priests of God and Christ, and shall reign with Him a thousand years."

No one knows what time in the future the persecution and tribulation will begin. Blessed and holy is he who has part in the first resurrection. Over Christians need to know about these future events and be ready, for the terrible events will test their faith. Satan is bound (in the Abyss) for a period of time symbolized by 1000 years. The abyss is a bottomless pit and it describes a place of immeasurable depth also called the underworld. A short time before the second coming of Christ the millennium 1,000 years ends. The word millennium figuratively makes reference to one thousand years and it is the term used for the time period that Satan is bound during the Christian dispensation. The Christian dispensation began with the first coming of Christ and the kingdom of Christ (church) will remain on earth until Christ returns and Satan is being restrained.

Satan will be set free before the end of time to return to the earth and cause great tribulation as explained in Revelation. Christ will return to earth and destroy Satan. The angel in heaven that bound Satan with the great chain, has the keys to the bottomless pit and God will order him let Satan out of the Abyss. Satan will be released from the abyss and go to earth and deceive the nations and the church. The great persecution of the church will challenge the faith of all Christians. The spirit of mankind does not die — life extends beyond the grave, and at the end of time God will deal justly with all people of every time period. According to Matthew's gospel, people will be divided into two groups, the righteous and the unrighteous.

Jesus and the angels will come to the earth to take vengeance on Satan, the Antichrist and the unrighteous people. Those who are still living will be able to see Christ and the angels descend on the clouds of the sky in glory with great power. Christ's coming will be a time of grief and sorrow for the unbelievers and the unrighteous, but it will be a time of joy and comfort for God's people. The righteous will be caught up in the clouds to meet the Lord in the air, and they shall ever be with the Lord. Then the earth and everything in it will be destroyed with a consuming fire. Since Revelation reveals events of the future that are still pending it is easier to understand the future events if we divide them into sections. 1st John chapter 4 John explains that the antichrist denies the divinity of Christ.

1st John 5 People who win the victory over sin and evil in the world are those who have faith–believe that Jesus Christ is the Son of God. Three things bear witness in heaven: The Father, the Word of God and the Holy Spirit. Three that bear witness on earth: the Spirit, the water, and the blood and the three agree as one. Holy Spirit, water baptism, and the blood shed on the cross. 1st John 5:18-19 "We know that whoever is born of God does not sin; but he who has been born of God keeps himself and the wicked one does not touch him." We know that we are of God, and the whole world lies under the sway of the wicked one." In 2nd Thessalonians the

2nd chapter, Paul writes about the antichrist and identifies him as the man of sin, also known as the Lawless One, who will appear at the end time. The end time is a short period of time near the end of time represented figuratively by Daniel as three and one half years, 42 months, 1260 days, or a time, times and half a time.

The end time and the end of time are in the future but the end time could begin to take place at any time. 1st John 2:18 "Little children, it is the last hour; and as you have heard that the antichrist is coming, even now many antichrists have come, by which we know that it is the last hour. The last hour figuratively refers to the last days prior to the destruction of the earth. We are presently living in the last hour figuratively speaking and the Anti-Christ could appear at any time. There were many people in the first century that denied the divinity of Christ and there are many now but John in revelation is referring to the antichrist that will come near the end of time before Christ returns.

2nd Thessalonians 2:1–4: Now brethren concerning the coming of our Lord Jesus Christ and our gathering together to him, we ask you, not to be soon shaken in mind or troubled either by spirit or by word or by letter, as if from us, as though the day of Christ has come. Let no one deceive you by any means; for that Day will not come unless the falling away comes first, and the man of sin is revealed, the son of perdition, who opposes and exalts himself above all that is called God or that is worshiped." In the first chapter of 2nd Thessalonians, Paul said he knew the end time was coming, but he did not know when it would begin. Paul wrote about the great apostasy during the end time that will take place before Christ comes back.

He said during that time many people will fall away from their faith in God and will follow a world leader called the Lawless One who is the Antichrist, the man of sin who is corrupted by the power of Satan. Satan will be on earth during the end time and will give power to helper the Lawless One who will help establish his evil empire and persecute the church. 2nd Timothy 3:1–7 "But know this, that in the last days perilous times will come: For men will be lovers of themselves, lovers of money, boasters, proud, blasphemers, disobedient to parents, unthankful, unholy, unloving, unforgiving, slanderers, without self-control, brutal, despisers of good, traitors, headstrong, haughty, lovers of pleasure rather than lovers of God, having a form of godliness but denying its power. And from such people turn away! For of this sort are those who creep into households and make captives of gullible women loaded down with sins, led away by various lusts, always learning and never able to come to the Knowledge of the truth."

Daniel wrote that the, time of trouble during the end time would be followed by the second coming of Christ. Daniel 12:1–3 "At that time Michael shall stand up, The great prince who stands watch over the sons of your people; and there shall be a time of trouble, such as never was since there was a nation, Even to that time. And at that time your people shall be delivered everyone who is found written in the book. And many of those who sleep in the dust of the earth shall awake, some to everlasting life some to shame and everlasting contempt. Those who are wise shall shine like the brightness of the firmament, and those who turn many to righteousness like the stars forever and ever." The idea has been presented that Christ will return to earth, establish His kingdom, the church on earth for a thousand years before the end of time. That theory is not correct because Christ has already established the kingdom, which is the church. When Christ returns the church (kingdom) will ascend to heaven for an eternity. Christ has continually reigned over the church since the beginning, In the first century, the kingdom of Christ was established on the first Pentecost day in Jerusalem and has been growing in number ever since. Christ's reign on earth ends at the end of time when the church will leave this earth bound for a new heaven and new earth.

Philippians 3:20-21"For our citizenship is in heaven, from which we also eagerly wait for the Savior, the Lord Jesus Christ, who will transform our lowly body that it may be conformed to His glorious body, according to the working by which He is able even to subdue all things to Himself. To reign with Christ means to be in fellowship with Christ. Christians belong to the kingdom of Christ as soon as they obey the gospel of Christ. Christ reigns from heaven in the hearts of every person who believes He is God's Son. The church is viewed as being here now and in heaven in the future, and all Christians already reign with Christ in His kingdom. Christ will come with the angels without any prior warning, but there will be no doubt about what is taking place when He returns. Everyone will see and hear Him as He descends in the clouds. There will be signs on the earth, signs in the sun, in the moon in the stars; and on the earth distress of nations, with perplexity, the sea and the waves roaring; men's hearts failing them from fear

Christians will realize what is happening during the end times and know that their redemption is near, and they will anticipate being caught up in the air to meet the Lord. Luke 21:25–28 –There will be signs in the sun, in the moon, and in the stars; and on the earth distress of nations, with perplexity, the sea and the waves roaring; men's hearts failing them from fear and and the expectation of those things which are coming on the earth, for the powers of the heavens will be shaken. Then they will see the Son of Man coming in a cloud with power and great glory. Now when these things begin to happen, look up and lift up your heads, because your redemption draws near. John saw thrones and they sat on them, and judgment was committed to them. Then I saw the souls of those who had been beheaded (martyrs) for their witness to Jesus and for the word of God, who had not worshiped the beast and they reigned with Christ during the thousand years (the time period from the beginning of the kingdom of Christ, the church until the time when Jesus returns), that is the first resurrection. The spirits of the martyrs went directly to heaven when they were killed and they reigned with Christ during the thousand years (Christian dispensation). Holy is he who has part in the first resurrection. Over such the second death has no power, but they shall be priests of God and Christ, and shall reign with Him a thousand years." The 7th and last section of Revelation is chapters 20-21-22. Section 7 begins with the beginning of the Christian age in the first century after the crucifixion, resurrection and ascension of Christ, and ends with the events of the second coming of Christ at the end of time. No one knows what time in the future the persecution and tribulation will begin, but Christians need to know about these future events and be ready, for they will test your faith when they appear. Satan was bound (in the Abyss) for a period of time symbolized by 1000 years.

The Abyss is located somewhere in the great expanse of space we call the heavens. After Satan was bound he could not use his power against the church (The Kingdom of Christ). The word millennium makes reference to one thousand years and is the term used for the time period that Satan is bound during the Christian dispensation.

The Christian dispensation began with the first coming of Christ and the kingdom of Christ (church) will remain on earth until Jesus removes it. Jesus and the angels will come to the earth to take vengeance on Satan, the Antichrist and the unrighteous people. Those who are still living will be able to see Christ and the angels descend on the clouds of the sky in glory with great power. Christ's coming will be a time of grief and sorrow for the unbelievers and the unrighteous, but it will be a time of joy and comfort for God's people. The righteous will be caught up in the clouds to meet the Lord in the air, and they shall ever be with the Lord. Then the earth and everything in it will be destroyed with a consuming fire.

Since Revelation reveals events of the future that are still pending it is easier to understand the future events if we divide them into sections. 1st John chapter 4 John explains that the antichrist denies the divinity of Christ. 1st John 5 People who win the victory over sin and evil in the world are those who have faith–believe that Jesus Christ is the Son of God. Three things bear witness in heaven: The Father, the Word of God and the Holy Spirit. Three that bear witness on earth: the Spirit, the water, and the blood and the three agree as one. Holy Spirit, water baptism, and the blood shed on the cross.

1st John 5:18-19 "We know that whoever is born of God does not sin; but he who has been born of God keeps himself and the wicked one does not touch him." We know that we are of God, and the whole world lies under the sway of the wicked one." In 2nd Thessalonians the 2nd chapter, Paul writes about the antichrist and identifies him as the man of sin, also known as the Lawless One, who will appear at the end time. The end time is a short period of time near the end of time represented figuratively by Daniel as three and one half years, 42 months, 1260 days, or a time, times and half a time.

The end time and the end of time are in the future but the end time could begin to take place at any time. 1st John 2:18 "Little children, it is the last hour; and as you have heard that the antichrist is coming, even now many antichrists have come, by which we know that it is the last hour. The last hour figuratively refers to the last days prior to the destruction of the earth. We are presently living in the last hour figuratively speaking and the Anti-Christ could appear at any time.

Many people in the first century denied the divinity of Christ and there are many now but John in revelation is referring to the antichrist that will come near the end of time before Christ returns. Thessalonians 2:1–4: Now brethren concerning the coming of our Lord Jesus Christ and our gathering together to him, we ask you, not to be soon shaken in mind or troubled either by spirit or by word or by letter, as if from us, as though the day of Christ has come. Let no one deceive you by any means; for that Day will not come unless the falling away comes first, and the man of sin is revealed, the son of perdition, who opposes and exalts himself above all that is called God or that is worshiped." In 2nd Thessalonians, Paul said he knew the end time was coming but he did not know when it would begin. Paul wrote about a great apostasy during the end time before Jesus returns.

Revelation Chapter 4 — Throne Room in Heaven

John received information about the seven churches in Asia then He saw an open door in heaven. The open door was an invitation for John to look into God's throne room where Christ, the angels, the elders, and the four living creatures receive their assignments. The open door and the expression of being in the Spirit means John had been given the ability from the Holy Spirit to see visions. John would be seeing visions of things that would take place during the end time Paul wrote about in 1st and 2nd Thessalonians.

Chapter 4:1–3 "After these things I looked, and behold, a door standing open in heaven. And the first voice, which I heard was like a trumpet speaking with me saying "Come up here, and I will show you things which must take place after this. Immediately I was in the Spirit; and behold, a throne set in heaven, and One sat on the throne. And He who sat there was like a jasper and sardius stone in appearance; and there was a rainbow around the throne, in appearance like an emerald." John heard a loud voice from heaven saying, "Come up here." John didn't physically go to heaven – In his mind he was able to see and hear things in heaven in a vision. John saw things that are never seen on earth, and the only way to describe those things was to figuratively compare them to earthly objects. The open door and the expression of being in the Spirit means John had been given the ability from the Holy Spirit to see visions.

John would be seeing visions of things that would take place during the end time Paul wrote about in 1st and 2nd Thessalonians. John saw the Majesty of God in resplendent glory in the throne room in heaven, God the Almighty Creator, who makes decisions and assigns duties to the other occupants of Heaven. John, being under the influence of the Holy Spirit, was able to see these things and write what he saw. The voice John heard was loud and clear like the sound of a trumpet.

The decisions made in the throne room will affect the troubling events of the end times coming in the future. Verses 4–5 "Around the throne were twenty-four thrones, and on the thrones I saw twenty-four elders sitting, clothed in white robes; and they had crowns of gold on their heads. And from the throne preceded lightning, thunder, and voices. Seven lamps of fire were burning before the throne, which are the seven Spirits of God." John saw a representation of God and His throne. Thrones represent authority, and those who are on thrones receive authority from God to carry out His commands. John saw twenty-four thrones surrounding God's throne. Twenty-four elders were sitting on the thrones. The elders are angelic creatures in heaven who serve God. The term elder means someone who is old in age and has acquired wisdom. The vision of elders on thrones represents God's ability to know the events of the future. God who makes and controls the lightning and thunder, He can determine and control future events. John also saw the Holy Spirit and described him as the seven spirits of God.

Seven lamps of fire symbolize the Holy Spirit. Lamps are symbols of knowledge, and the Holy Spirit is assigned to distribute the knowledge of God's word. The seven burning lamps symbolize the power of the Holy Spirit to enlighten the minds and hearts of people with the word of God. The number seven is a symbol of a complete number or perfection. Seven means complete perfect. The Holy Spirit is complete in every way to serve God and to take the word of God to people. The Holy Spirit of God with supernatural power is instrumental in accomplishing all things determined by God.

Verses 6–11 "Before the throne there was a sea of glass, like crystal. And around the throne were four living creatures full of eyes in front and in back. The first living creature was like a lion, the second living creature had a face like a man, and the fourth living creature was like a flying eagle.

The four living creatures, each having six wings, were full of eyes around and within. And they did not rest day or night, saying: "Holy, holy, holy, Lord God Almighty, Who was and is and is to come!" Whenever the living creatures give glory and honor and thanks to Him who sits on the throne, who lives forever and ever, the twenty-four elders fall down before Him who sits on the throne and worship Him who lives forever and ever, and cast their crowns before the throne, saying: "You are worthy, O Lord, to receive gory and honor and power; for You created all things, and by Your will they exist and were created."

The expanse that looked like glass in front of the throne of God was transparent like crystal. Being transparent signifies that things can be seen on either side front or back when looking through the crystal. God's intentions and actions are clearly seen in heaven and are broadcast to the people of the earth. The actions and the intentions of God from the beginning of time to the end of time can be understood by investigating the word of God in the Bible. John was going to see visions and hear about what was to be in the future plans of God. In the center of the throne and surrounding the throne were four symbolic winged creatures called living creatures. Creature refers to something that is created and is under the influence and control of the creator. The Cherubim on earth were symbolic representations of winged creatures that live in heaven.

They were represented on earth as statue like figures. Cherubim guarded the tree of life in the Garden of Eden. Cherubim were placed at either end of the mercy seat of the Ark of the Covenant. Cherubim decorated Solomon's temple, and they were carved around the walls of the temple. Read more about Cherubim in Ezekiel chapters 1 and 10. In the first chapter of Ezekiel, Ezekiel saw visions of God and he saw the four living creatures in heaven, and he gave a description of their appearance. Most likely, the creatures John saw in heaven are Cherubim. The Cherubim magnify the power and holiness of God. Cherubim visibly remind one of God's glory, majesty and power. God deserves great honor, respect, and the worship that is due Him from all creatures in heaven and on earth.

The living creatures continually praise, honor and give thanks to God. They are an example for all of God's creation to continually glorify praise, honor, obey and give thanks to the Lord God Almighty. John saw and received information about events that would take place soon. The word soon in the Greek could be translated immediately. John was immediately able to see the terrifying future events of the end times. These were not events that were about to happen right away but would come in the future during the end time. In a vision John was allowed to see Christ receive a scroll that contained events of the future of the church during the end time. Christ and the Apostles spoke of the time when the church and the people on earth will experience a great tribulation caused by Satan and a world leader called the Lawless One who is Antichrist.

Paul described the Lawless One as the man who will claim to be God and the man of sin who opposes God and exalts himself above God. This will take place on earth during the end time, and many will fall from the faith because of Satan and the Lawless One. 2nd Thessalonians 2:1–4 "Now brethren concerning the coming of our Lord Jesus Christ and our gathering together to

Him, we ask you, not to be soon troubled, either by spirit or by word or by letter, as if from us as though the day of Christ had come.'

"Let no one deceive you by any means; for that day will not come unless the falling away comes first, and the man of sin is revealed, the son of perdition, who opposes and exalts himself above all that is called God or is worshiped, so that he sits in the temple of God, showing himself that he is God." God's providential protection of the church will keep it from disappearing from the earth during the end time. In the Bible the church is symbolized by the following terms — golden lamp stands, Jerusalem, the Holy City, the New Jerusalem, 144,000 (those with the name of Christ and God written on their forehead), a woman, the bride of Christ, the kingdom of God, the kingdom of Christ, and the temple of God, which is the redeemed.

Chapter 5 — Lamb Receives a Scroll

John saw God sitting on His throne holding a scroll containing future events that would take place at the end time including the redemption of the saints.

The scroll was sealed — meaning no one could open the scroll and read the contents without being authorized by God. The seals on the scroll symbolize God's control over the events of the end times. When the first seal is opened, God has granted His permission to read from the scroll.

Verses 4–5 "The scroll contained information about the events that were to take place at the end times but the scroll was sealed so that no one could reveal its contents. The saints in heaven and on the earth were anxious to know the contents because it contained the coming judgments of God and the redemption of the saints on earth.' "So I wept much, because no one was found worthy to open and read the scroll or to look at it. But one of the elders said to me, "Do not weep. Behold, the Lion of the tribe of Judah, the Root of David, has prevailed to open the scroll and loose its seven seals.' The saints in heaven are the spirits of the redeemed. They are martyrs who are anxious to know what was written in the scroll, because it reveals the judgments of God for the future of the redeemed on earth. The elders around God's throne knew that Jesus was the only one worthy to open and read the scroll, because He died on the cross as a worthy sacrifice to provide redemption. They sang a new song about the worthiness of Christ.

Verses 6–10 "And I looked, and behold, in the midst of the throne and of the four living creatures, and in the midst of the elders, stood a Lamb as though it had been slain, having seven horns and seven eyes, which are the seven Spirits of God sent out into all the earth. "Then He came and took the scroll out of the right hand of Him who sat on the throne.' "Now when he had taken the scroll, the four living creatures and the twenty-four elders fell down before the Lamb, each having a harp, and golden bowls full of incense, which are the prayers of the saints. And they sang a new song, saying' "You are worthy to take the scroll, and to open its seals; for you were slain and have redeemed us to God by Your blood out of every tribe and tongue and people and nation, and have made us kings and priests to our God; and we shall reign on the earth." All Christians present them selves, both body and spirit, to God as living sacrifices. Christians share in the reign of Christ on earth now. The word reign makes reference to Christians prevailing over the power of sin and death on earth now.

Members of the kingdom are kings and priests in the eyes of God. Grace reigns, or exists, through the righteousness of those who have faith in Christ. God's grace gives eternal life through the death of Jesus Christ. The word exist or existed can be substituted for the word reign. Romans 5:17–21– "For if by the one man's offense death reigned through the one, much more those who receive abundance of grace and of the gift of righteousness will reign in life through the one Jesus Christ. Therefore, as through one man's offense judgment came to all men, resulting in condemnation, even so through one man's righteous act the free gift came to all men resulting in justification of life. For as by one man's disobedience many were made sinners, so also by one Man's obedience many will be made righteous. Moreover the law entered that the offense might abound.' "But when sin abounded, grace abounded much more, so that grace might reign through righteousness to eternal life through Jesus Christ our Lord." Death had power through Adam's sin and all people sin therefore they are subject to death. Eternal life exists, because the grace of God reigns through righteousness to those who are made righteous by faith in Christ.

Christians belong to the family of God as brothers and sisters of Christ, and as a family we share in the reign of Christ including the dead in Christ. Verses 11–14 "Then I looked, and I heard the voice of many angels around the throne, the living creatures, and the elders; and the number of them was ten thousand times ten thousand, and thousands of thousands, saying with a loud voice: "Worthy is the Lamb who was slain to receive power and riches and wisdom, and strength and honor and glory and blessing!' "And every creature which is in heaven and on the earth and under the earth and such as are in the sea, and all that are in them, I heard saying: Blessing and honor and glory and power be to Him who sits on the throne and to the Lamb forever and ever!" Then the four living creatures said, "Amen!" and the twenty-four elders fell down and worshiped Him who lives forever and ever." The song was a new song, because it had never been sung before the death of Christ. The angels praised Christ for being worthy to reign in heaven and on earth.

Chapter 6–Opening the Seals of the Scroll

Chapter 6:1–2 "Now I saw when the Lamb opened one of the seals; and I heard one of the four living creatures saying with a voice, like thunder, "Come and see."

And I looked, and behold, a white horse. He who sat on it had a bow; and a crown was given to him, and he went out conquering and to conquer:" When each seal was opened, the contents of the seal revealed judgments from God that would come upon the earth in succession during the time of Jesus' first coming until His second coming." The first seal was opened John saw a white horse. The rider had a bow and He was given a crown, and He went out to conquer sin and death. The crown signifies that the rider had the right, as a king, to exercise His authority. Christ is the rider on the white horse who came in the first century to fight a spiritual battle against sin and establish His kingdom called the church. The battle is symbolized by a bow, an instrument of peace. Christ taught the gospel of peace between God and mankind to His Apostles. The opening of the other five seals of the scroll will reveal events of the Christian dispensation including the future events at the end time and during the great tribulation.

Christ continued to open the seals of the scroll, and each time a seal is opened, a colored horse was seen. The colored horse reveals an event of tribulation. Verses 3–4 "When He opened the second seal, I heard the second living creature saying, "Come and see." Another horse, fiery red, went out. And it was granted to the one who sat on it to take peace from the earth, and that people should kill one another; and there was given to him a great sword." The large sword was a type of sword that is used for killing. The red horse symbolizes carnal warfare during the end time. Satan will be set free from the bottomless pit at the beginning of the end time and give power to the Lawless One (Antichrist), and he will rule over a world empire. He will cause warfare and distress among the nations. There will be much bloodshed — symbolized by the red horse and the sword.

Satan will give the Lawless One power over the people on earth, and the church will suffer great persecution. Paul's letters to the church in Thessalonica explain what will happen during the end time when Satan and the Lawless One takes control of the people on earth. Satan will be out of the Abyss and will be free to influence the people on earth. There will be a rebellion caused by Satan against God, Christ, and the church.

2nd Thessalonians 2:1–5–Concerning the coming of our Lord Jesus Christ and our gathering together to him, we ask you, not to be soon shaken in mind or troubled, either by spirit or by word or by letter, as if from us, as though the day of Christ had come. Let no one deceive you by any means; for that Day will not come until the falling away comes first. The man of sin will be revealed. He is the son of perdition, who opposes and exalts himself above all that is called God or that is worshiped, so that he sits as God in the temple of God, showing himself that he is God. God will let Satan out of the Abyss on purpose to give power to the man of sin called the Lawless One (Antichrist). He will claim to be God and will cause great tribulation for the people on earth. The tribulation of the end time will punish the enemies of God and will cause some people to repent and obey the gospel. God's judgments are righteous but His justice demands punishment.

Paul continued to write to the church about the second coming of Christ at the end of time and he warned, the church would suffer persecution before Christ returns. 2nd Thessalonians 1:3–10– "We are bound to thank God always for you brethren, as it is fitting, because your faith grows exceedingly, and the love of every one of you all abounds toward each other, so that we ourselves boast of you among the churches of God for your patience and faith in all your persecutions and tribulations that you endure, which is manifest evidence of the righteous judgment of God that you may be counted worthy of the kingdom of God for which you also suffer; since it is a righteous thing with God to repay with tribulation those who trouble you, and to give you who are troubled rest with us when the Lord Jesus is revealed from heaven with His mighty angels, in flaming fire taking vengeance on those who do not know God, and on those who do not obey the gospel of our Lord Jesus Christ.' "These shall be punished with everlasting destruction from the presence of the Lord and from the glory of His power, when He comes in that Day, to be glorified in His saints and to be admired among all those who believe, because our testimony among you was believed." Verses 5–6 "When He opened the third seal, I heard the third living creature say, "Come and see." So I looked, and behold, a black horse, and he who sat on it had a pair of scales in his hand.

And I heard a voice in the midst of the four living creatures saying, "A quart of wheat for a denarius, and three quarts of barley for a denarius; and do not harm the oil and the wine." The black horse with a rider symbolizes famine and economic depression. The depression and famine will negatively affect the life of the people on earth. The Lawless One (Antichrist) will receive power from Satan, and He will control the life of the people on earth.

Verses 7–8 "When He opened the fourth seal, I heard the voice of the fourth living creature saying, "Come and see." So I looked, and behold, a pale horse. And the name of him who sat on it was Death, and Hades followed with him. And power was given to them over a fourth of the earth to kill with sword, with hunger, with death, and by the beasts of the earth."

The rider on the pale horse is named death many people will die during the end time. More than a fourth of the people on earth will die because of the famine, bloodshed, disease and beasts.

The Fifth Seal is Opened — The Martyrs

Verses 9–11 "When He opened the fifth seal, I saw under the altar the souls of those who had been slain for the word of God and for the testimony, which they held. And they cried with a loud voice, saying, "How long, O Lord, holy and true, until You judge and avenge our blood on those who dwell on the earth?" Then a white robe was given to each of them; and it was said to them that they should rest a little while longer, until both the number of their fellow servants and their brethren, who would be killed as they were, was completed."

Some of the martyrs in heaven were those who were killed during the end time. The martyrs in heaven were anxious for God to send Christ to destroy the evil forces on earth and bring the church to heaven. During the end times Christians will be persecuted and some will be put to death. The martyrs were killed, because they would not deny Christ. Each of the martyrs received white robes, which are symbols of righteousness. The martyrs were anxious for God to bring forth His final judgment against Satan and the unrighteous people of the earth who murdered them.

But they must wait until the end of time when Christ returns. John saw their spirits under God's altar calling out for Him to avenge their death.

The Sixth Seal is Opened — Great Earthquake

Verses 12–14 "I looked when He opened the sixth seal, and behold, there was a great earthquake; and the sun became black as sackcloth of hair, and the moon became like blood. And the stars of heaven fell to the earth, as a fig tree drops its late figs when it is shaken by a mighty wind. Then the sky receded as a scroll when it is rolled up, and every mountain and island was moved out of its place." The sixth seal reveals visions of God's final judgment on earth at the end of time. In verse 12, the sixth seal was opened, and John saw visions of a great earthquake and the upheaval of the sun, moon and stars.

Upheaval of the earth and the universe are common figurative expressions in the Bible having to do with the end of time. Earthquakes are mentioned in Chapters 6, 8, 11, and 16 of Revelation as events of the end times. The events in chapter 6 of Revelation are very similar to Matthew 24 depicting the second coming of Christ. Jeremiah, Joel, and Zechariah all used the terms that are used in chapter 6 to describe the events of the end of time.

Earthquakes happen naturally, but during the end of time the greatest earthquake ever will come from an act of God at the final judgment. Darkness will fill the earth and Islands will disappear. The Earthquake will cause unbelievers and the ungodly to fear God, because they will realize that the wrath of God has come.

At the end of time the unrighteous will be filled with fear and call to the mountains and rocks to fall on them and deliver them from God's wrath. Most likely some will repent but not all of the unrighteous. The whole earth will be in chaos and turmoil, and everyone who is left on earth will realize that the final judgment of God has come. There will be great anguish for the unrighteous, but the righteous will shout with joy. These things take place at the end of time, but God's redeemed will be safe.

Chapter 7

Before the events at the end of time begin to take place God's people identified by the seal of God. In chapter 14 the 144,000 are standing on Mt Zion with God's name written on their foreheads, and John identifies them as the redeemed from the earth. The reason John identified the redeemed at the end of time with the twelve tribes of Israel is because the church was predominantly Jewish when he wrote. The redeemed will be from many cultures from all over the earth.

After the end of time, John saw the redeemed in heaven. Each section ends with events of the end of time. God holds back His destroying angels until the end of time after the redeemed are safe in heaven. After John saw the great earthquake at the end of time, John looked into heaven and saw the redeemed from every nation, tribe, and language including those who came out of the great tribulation during the end time. "John looked, and behold, a great multitude which no one could number, of all nations, tribes, peoples, and tongues, standing before the throne and before the Lamb, clothed with white robes, with palm branches in their hands, and crying out with a loud voice, saying, "Salvation belongs to our God who sits on the throne, and to the Lamb!

All the angels stood around the throne and the elders and the four living creatures, and fell on their faces before the throne and worshiped God, saying: "Amen! Blessing and glory and wisdom, Thanksgiving and honor and power and might, Be to our God forever and ever. Amen." 7:13-17"Then one of the elders answered, saying to me, "Who are these arrayed in white robes, and where did they come from?" And I said to him, "Sir, you know." So he said to me. "These are the ones who came out of the great tribulation, and washed their robes and made them white in the blood of the Lamb. Therefore they are before the throne of God and serve Him day and night in His temple. And He who sits on the throne will dwell among them. They shall neither hunger anymore nor thirst anymore; the sun shall not strike them, nor any heat; for the Lamb who is in the midst of the throne will shepherd them and lead them to living fountains of water. And God will wipe away every tear from their eyes."

Section 3– Chapter 8–11

7th Seal: Prelude to the Seven Trumpets

Beginning in chapter 8, when the seventh seal of the scroll is opened more events of the end time, were revealed. There is a period of silence in heaven for a short time indicative of a break in the time before the other events come upon the earth. Seven angels, each with trumpets, signal the beginning of an event during the end time. The first trumpet sounds, and hail and fire mingled with blood will be thrown to the earth, a symbol of destruction and death. The Second trumpet sounds, and something like a great mountain on fire is thrown into the sea killing a third of the creatures in the sea and destroying a third of the ships. The third trumpet sounds, and a great star falls on a third of the rivers and springs of water – a symbol of poisoned water. The fourth trumpet sounds, and a third of the sun, moon, and stars are darkened affecting the normal amount of light on earth.

Chapter 9 – The fifth trumpet sounds, and a star falls from heaven. A mighty angel comes to the earth and lets Satan out of confinement in the Abyss (bottomless pit). Demons terrorize the people of the earth. The sixth trumpet sounds and four angels kill a third of the people on earth.

Chapter 10 – A mighty angel with a little book declares that the mystery of God would be finished when the seventh angel sounds his trumpet for the end of time. John eats the little book, a symbol of learning the contents of the book.

Chapter 11 – God gives power to two witnesses to prophesy for 1,260 days during the end time. The two witnesses may be two prophets who can communicate with God. The two witnesses are symbolized by two olive trees and two lamp stands. The two witnesses have power to stop the rain, turn the waters to blood and strike the earth with plagues. The power of the two witnesses comes from God, and they will have the ability to invoke the power Of God to perform miracles to protect the church. Satan will be on earth, and he will make war against the two witnesses and kill them. Killing the two witnesses means to silence them for a while.

The two witnesses will be resurrected, and they will ascend to heaven. Then a great earthquake will kill seven thousand people. The ability of the witnesses to call on God will be restored after they are resurrected. The seventh trumpet sounds at the end of time, and the inhabitants of heaven, including the redeemed from the earth, worship God and thank Him, because has He used His great power against Satan and the forces of evil. The time had come for judging the dead and rewarding the redeemed. Section 3 ends with chapter 11.

Chapter 8:1-7 The 7th Seal– "When He opened the seventh seal, there was silence in heaven for about half an hour. And I saw the seven angels who stand before God, and to them were given seven trumpets. Then another angel, having a golden censer, came and stood at the altar.' "He was given much incense that he should offer it with the prayers of all the saints upon the golden altar, which was before the throne and the smoke of the incense, with the prayers of the saints, ascended before God from the angel's hand. Then the angel took the censer, filled it with fire from the altar, and threw it to the earth. "And there were noises, thunderings, lightnings, and an earthquake. So the seven angels who had the seven trumpets prepared themselves to sound.

"The first angel sounded: and hail and fire followed, mingled with blood, and they were thrown to the earth. And a third of the trees were burned up, and all green grass was burned up." The time of opening the seventh seal is near the end of time, and events become increasingly worse with time. The events will cause pain and sorrow on the earth. In chapter 8, the incense and prayers of the saints ascended before God, then the angel filled the censer with the incense and prayers mixed with fire and threw it to the earth causing noises, thundering, lightning, and an earthquake — sign's that God was answering the prayers of the saints with judgments against Satan and the unrighteous people of the earth.

Each time an angel sounds a trumpet an event of God's wrath takes place. The angels will hold back the four winds of the earth — winds from the east, west, north and south — waiting for the sound of the trumpet. The winds are symbols of God's destroying power. The four angels are given the power to harm the land and the sea. Thunder is associated with the voice of God, and lightning is regarded as an instrument of the judgment of God. God gave His approval to send a judgment against the unrighteous on earth to warn them to repent.

The first angel sounds his trumpet, followed by hail and fire mingled with blood burning up a third of the trees and all of the green grass on earth. Hail, fire, and blood symbolize death and great damage to one third of the earth.

2nd Trumpet Verses 8–9 "Then the second angel sounded: And something like a great mountain burning with fire was thrown into the sea, and a third of the sea became blood. And a third of the living creatures in the sea died, and a third of the ships were destroyed." John saw and heard the second angel blow his trumpet, and he saw the results of the judgment. Something similar to an enormous mountain that is on fire — possibly a huge meteorite — will fall into the sea. There will be blood in a third of the sea, and one third of the living things in the sea will die, and many ships will be destroyed.

Only one third of the area of the seas will be affected. The purpose of the object thrown into the sea will be to inflict great damage upon the earth to punish the unrighteous and to cause as many as will to repent. God makes known that He is real and He demonstrates His Almighty power during the end times. 3rd Trumpet Verses 10–11 "Then the third angel sounded: And a great star fell from heaven, burning like a torch, and it fell on a third of the rivers and on the springs of water. The name of the star is Wormwood. A third of the waters became wormwood, and many men died from the water, because it was made bitter." The large star was on fire like a torch when it fell from the sky, and it fell on a third of the rivers and springs of fresh water. The star was called wormwood.

Wormwood is a perennial bitter herb that is toxic and is used in a figurative sense to describe something bitter or extremely unpleasant suggesting sorrow and bitterness resulting from the death and destruction of the falling star. Falling stars and meteorites are common occurrences even now, but the one John writes about will be much greater in power. It will be huge, and it will cause the fresh water to be bitter and poisoned from contamination. The water will cause many people to die.

4th Trumpet Verse 12 "Then the fourth angel sounded: And a third of the sun was struck, a third of the moon, and a third of the stars, so that a third of them were darkened. A third of the day did not shine, and likewise the night."

The sounding of the fourth angel's trumpet signals a plague that will obscure a third of the light that normally illuminates the earth — the light that comes from the sun, moon, and stars. This plague means there will be a time of darkness upon the earth during the day as well as the night. The darkness will, most likely, cause great fear and cause a cease of most activities on earth. The darkness is a sign of the great woe that will be caused by the blowing of the other three trumpets.

Verse 13 "And I looked, and I heard an angel flying through the midst of heaven, saying with a loud voice, "Woe, woe, woe to the inhabitants of the earth, because of the remaining blasts of the trumpet of the three angels who are about to sound!"

John continued to look and listen, and he heard an angel flying through heaven. The angel was crying out with a loud voice saying, "Woe! Woe! Woe!" to the people on earth. The definition of a woe is something that causes great grief, trouble, or distress. There are three remaining trumpet judgments, and there is grief, trouble, and distress associated with each one.

The events of the three woe judgments that are coming will be much worse than the other judgments. The angel will call out to the inhabitants of the earth to warn them to repent because of the severity of the plagues that will follow the last three trumpet blasts. God has forever warned mankind of the consequences of disobedience, but most people ignore Him and continue to disobey Him. Some versions of the Bible use the word eagle instead of angel. Eagle and vulture are translated from the same Greek word. The vultures will have a feast on the dead bodies caused by the judgments.

When the next three angels blow their trumpets, Satan and his demons will be allowed to come out of the bottomless pit and cause a great tribulation of the people on earth during the end time. According to the woes in John's visions, the end times will last much longer than an instant of time, because several things will take place in succession. In between the events, the unbelievers and ungodly people will have an opportunity to turn to God and Christ and repent before the final destruction.

There will be three more trumpets of judgment, the 5th, 6th and 7th, signaling the three woes that will let the people of the earth know that the events of the end of time are taking place. The sounding of the 7th trumpet announces the last days of God's judgment at the end of time.

5th Trumpet Chap 9

The 5th angel is the first of the angels representing the three woes mentioned in chapter 8:13. The first woe represents an event much worse than any previous event. The angel sounds his trumpet, and Satan is released from the Abyss.

Chapter 9:1–2 "Then the fifth angel sounded: And I saw a star fallen from heaven to the earth. To him was given the key to the bottomless pit. And he opened the bottomless pit, and smoke arose out of the pit like the smoke of a great furnace. So the sun and the air were darkened because of the smoke of the pit." The release of Satan from the Abyss is the first of the three woes. When the fifth angel blew his trumpet, John saw a star fall out of heaven. The word star in the Bible is often used to designate an angel. The star in verse 1 is Michael, the Arch Angel, the protector of God's people. Michael is given the key to the Abyss to let Satan and his demons out of the

Abyss. The Abyss is a place of conscious existence, somewhere in the heavens. It's a place God has prepared for spirits who are waiting for the final judgment of God. The verb tartaro is not Sheol, Hades, nor hell, but it is the place where those angels who sin are confined to be reserved until the judgment. The region is described as pits of darkness. (Vines Expository Dictionary)

Luke 8:30–31–Jesus asked him, saying, "What is your name?" And he said "Legion", because many demons had entered him. And they begged Him that He would not command them to go into the abyss." Heaven is so vast that it consists of many areas called the heavens. There is the highest heaven where God and Christ are, and the Abyss is somewhere in the heavens below the highest heaven. Romans 10:6-7–The righteousness of faith speaks in this way, do not say in your heart, who will ascend into heaven to bring Christ down from above or, who will descend into the abyss, to bring Christ up from the dead. The Bible reveals that there are several heavens. The Bible speaks of at least three heavens and there may be more than three.

The word hell is used fourteen times in the New Testament, and it is described as a place of torment. There are four words that are all translated hell: the Hebrew word Sheol, the Greek words Hades, Gehenna, and Tartarus. Sheol signifies the grave or the state of death and the world of the dead. Sheol is parallel to the Hebrew words for pit or hell. Sheol is a place of consciousness for the spirits of the dead. Gehenna is the final destiny of those who reject God and is described as a place of unquenchable fire. Mark 9:45 "And if your foot causes you to sin, cut it off. It is better for you to enter life lame, rather than having two feet, to be cast into hell, into the fire that shall never be quenched." There is a clear description of Hades in Luke 16:19–31. Hades is described as a place in the heavens where departed spirits of the dead go. Hades consists of two separate places.

There is one place for the spirits of the righteous and a separate place for the spirits of the unrighteous. Spirits cannot go from one place to the other. The spirits of the righteous are in a place of paradise, and the spirits of the unrighteous are in a place of torment.

Revelation 20:1-2 "Then I saw an angel coming down from heaven, having the key to the bottomless pit and a great chain in his hand. He laid hold on the dragon, that serpent of old, who is the devil and Satan, and bound him for a thousand years; and he cast him into the bottomless pit, and shut him up, and set a seal on him, so that he should deceive the nations no more till the thousand years were finished. But after these things he must be released for a little while." Being in the Abyss meant Satan and the demons had lost the use of their evil power against people. They were prisoners confined to one area and could not go back and forth to the earth.

With instructions from the throne, Michael will let Satan and his demons out of the Abyss, and Satan will use his power to torment people on earth and empower the Lawless One (Antichrist) in a way that he rules on earth. God will allow this event to take place, because the time for the second coming of Christ will be near, and many of the people on earth will not have repented of their unrighteous ways and obeyed the gospel of Christ. The purpose of the torment is not to punish but to cause repentance.

Verses 3–4 "Then out of the smoke locusts came upon the earth. And to them was given power, as the scorpions of the earth have power. They were commanded not to harm the grass of the earth, or any green thing, or any tree, but only those men who do not have the seal of God on their foreheads." Where there is fire there is smoke, and when the Abyss is opened, smoke comes out. This act of God's judgment allows Satan and the demons to torment the people on earth during the end time to cause them to repent, and some will probably repent. The creatures from the Abyss will be Satan's demons, not literal locusts, and they will come in great numbers like locusts and will have power to harm mankind. The demons are symbolized by locusts because of their great number and their destructive power like a swarm or plague of locusts. These demons will harm people on earth causing pain compared to the sting of a scorpion.

Verses 5–6 "And they were not given authority to kill them, but to torment them for five months. Their torment was like the torment of a scorpion when it strikes a man. In those days men will seek death and will not find it; they will desire to die, and death will flee from them." The normal life of a locust is five months, and the demon's time to torture people will be limited to five months since their purpose is not to kill people but to cause the unrighteous to repent. The reason God will not allow the demons to kill the people is because He wants them to turn to Christ and obey the gospel of Christ. God is giving them a chance to repent before the end of time.

Verses 7–12 "The shape of the locusts was like horses prepared for battle. On their heads were crowns of something like gold, and their faces were like the faces of men. They had hair like women's hair and their teeth were like lions teeth. And they had breastplates like breastplates of iron, and the sound of their wings was like the sound of chariots with many horses running into battle.' "They had tails like scorpions, and there were stings in their tails. Their power was to hurt men five months. And they had as king over them the angel of the bottomless pit, whose name in Hebrew is Abaddon, but in Greek he has the name Apollyon. One woe is past. Behold, still two more are coming after these things." The locusts may symbolize Satan's demons that are let out of the Abyss." The king of the demons is Satan, the angel of the bottomless pit.

Satan's name in Hebrew is Abaddon. In Greek he has the name Apollyon. Abaddon and Apollyon mean destroyer. A figurative description is given to illustrate the appearance of the demons. The appearance of the demons will look like an army with armor, and they will make a loud noise. The demons will be animal-like creatures resembling horses and humans with large teeth. Their appearance will be terrifying and unlike anything ever seen on earth before. The sight of them will probably be almost as bad as their sting. They will appear like horses prepared for battle. On their heads will be crowns like gold, and their faces will be like the faces of men. They will have hair like women's hair, probably long, and their teeth will be like lions' teeth large and fierce looking. Their breastplates will look like breastplates of iron, and the sound of their wings will be like the sound of chariots with many horses running into battle. They will have tails like scorpions, and they will hurt people for five months. The torture caused by the demons will be so severe that people will long to die. The demons are commanded not to harm the grass of the earth, or any green thing, or any tree but only those men who do not have the seal of God on their foreheads. The seal of God on the forehead symbolizes some kind of identification showing they are Christians and must not be harmed in any way.

The Sixth Trumpet Sounds

Verses 13–15 "Then the sixth angel sounded: And I heard a voice from the four horns of the golden altar which is before God, saying to the sixth angel who had the trumpet, "Release the four angels who are bound at the great river Euphrates." So the four angels who had been prepared for the hour and day and month and year, were released to kill a third of mankind."

The first woe was a plague of demons symbolized by locusts. After the first woe, the sixth of the seven angels will blow his trumpet. The 6th trumpet sounds and the second woe proceeds. A voice from the horns of God's altar will be heard, and the sixth angel will be instructed to turn loose the four angels that are waiting at the Euphrates River for their instructions to kill a third of the earth's population. Those who are killed will not be Christians. They will be from among the unrighteous and may be from the army of the empire of the lawless one.

The order came from the golden altar in heaven, possibly from the voice of Christ. Four angels had been prepared and waiting for the time they would be sent to kill a third of the unrighteous people on earth. Christ gives the okay for the Angels to act. The Angels were already at the Euphrates River waiting for the time of the sixth angel to sound his trumpet. Angels from heaven symbolized by an army of horsemen will carry out the plague that follows the sound of the sixth trumpet.

Verses 16–19 "Now the number of the army of the horsemen was two hundred million; I heard the number of them. And thus I saw the horses in the vision: those who sat on them had breastplates of fiery red, hyacinth blue, and sulfur yellow; and the heads of the horses were like the heads of lions; and out of their mouths came fire, smoke, and brimstone." By these three plagues a third of mankind was killed—by the fire and the smoke and the brimstone, which came out of their mouths. For their power is in their mouth and in their tails; for their tails are like serpents, having heads; and with them they do harm." An army of two hundred million on horseback does not make reference to an army of humans and must refer to a supernatural army. "Then I heard a loud voice from the temple saying to the seven angels, "Go and pour out the bowls of the wrath of God on the earth.

The Seventh Trumpet

Verses 15–19 "Then the seventh angel sounded: And there were loud voices in heaven saying, "The kingdoms of this world have become the kingdoms of our Lord and of His Christ, and He shall reign forever and ever! And the twenty-four elders who sat before God on their thrones fell on their faces and worshiped God saying: "We give you thanks, O Lord God Almighty, the One who is and who was and who is to come, because you have taken your great power and reigned. The nations were angry, and your wrath has come, and the time of the dead that they should be judged, and that You should reward your servants the prophets and the saints and those who fear your name, small and great, and should destroy those who destroy the earth."

Then the temple of God was opened in heaven, and the ark of His covenant was seen in His temple, and there were lightning, noises, thunder an earthquake, and great hail."

The seventh and last angel blowing his trumpet is a sign that it is time for the mystery of God to be completed at the end of time. The third woe will take place and the full wrath of God will come upon all of those who refuse to accept Christ. Verse 15 is looking forward to and anticipating the second coming of Christ when the entire number of the redeemed will ascend to heaven and all of the kingdoms of men will be destroyed. Christ God and the church will reign forever in heaven. The population of heaven gives thanks to God in anticipation of God using His great power to complete the end of time when all the faithful people of God are rewarded.

The temple of God is opened in heaven, and the ark of His covenant is seen in His temple (the redeemed church) a sign that God and Christ have used their great power to save the redeemed. And will destroy the unrighteous at the end of time. The martyrs and the Ark of the Covenant are witnesses of the faithfulness of God and His word and His judgments. In the book of Daniel, an angel told Daniel that the events at the end will be for a time, times, and half a time: 3 and ½ years, 1260 days or 42 months the length of the end time. Christ will rescue his church from the wrath that will come upon the earth. When the angel blew his trumpet, John heard loud voices and saw a vision in heaven.

He saw the Ark of the Covenant, the meeting place where the Lord reveals His will to His servants. John saw the coming judgment of God symbolized by lightning, thunder, an earthquake and a hailstorm. This is an indication that the coming wrath of God will be very severe. The power of God and Christ will have taken control of the nations on earth that were under the dominion of Satan and the Lawless one. The nations that are allied with Satan will be angry because of God's judgments. God will send a great earthquake to reveal himself to the people in an effort to make them repent before the final and total destruction of the earth. The survivors of the earthquake will be terrified, and some will turn to God, glorify Him, and repent because of the resurrection of the two witnesses and the earthquake.

The mystery of God will be accomplished, and those who are on earth at that time will understand the true meaning of John's message. There will be great distress upon the earth at the end time and end of time, because Satan, the Antichrist, and the Lawless One (Antichrist) will be on earth. God doesn't want anyone to perish; He wants everyone to have faith in Christ and repent of sin. God does everything he can to reach the hearts of people, even if He must use drastic and punishing measures to convince them. For more information about the Antichrist-Lawless One, read the second chapter of Paul's second letter to the church in Thessalonica and the twelfth chapter of Daniel. Daniel said during the end times many people would be made pure. They will be made spotless and be refined because of the judgments of God that caused them to repent and obey the gospel. Daniel prophesied that the dead will be resurrected, and everyone whose name is written in the book of life will be saved. After the resurrection of the dead God will judge the people on earth and reward His servants, the prophets, and all the faithful will ascend to heaven with Jesus and the angels. After the faithful have been removed from the earth there will be great anguish for those who are left. The unbelievers and ungodly will have one last opportunity to repent during that time. The events in section 3 ends with events of the end time and the end of time.

Section 4 reveals more end time events–Chapters 12 through 14 Section 4 begins with the birth of the church and ends with the second coming of Christ to reap the grapes of wrath at the end of time. The central theme of section 4 is the ultimate victory of Christ and the church over Satan and his evil forces. Chapters 12 through 14 portray a spiritual war between Christ and Satan featuring the beast out of the sea, the beast out of the earth, the false prophet, and the Lawless One (Antichrist). The focus is on the events of the end time and the end of time. Chapter 12 is a Synopsis of the beginning of Christianity in the first century. Satan is cast out of heaven to earth.

A Jewish woman named Mary from the nation of Israel gives birth to the Messiah named Jesus. Jesus came to provide redemption for mankind from the guilt of sin. Satan called the dragon attempted to prevent Jesus from accomplishing God's plan of redemption.

The horsemen are literal angels that had been bound at the Euphrates River for that purpose. The word 'bound' indicates the angels were prevented to act by the power of God and could not act until God allowed them to. With the approval of God, they were to kill a third of the number of the unrighteous people on earth. Christians should not fear because God's angels will not harm them. The release of the angels will be the answer to the prayers of the saints Christians who are suffering persecution from Satan and an evil generation. The large number of unrighteous people killed will be a warning sign from God.

There are references in the Old Testament when God's angels were sent to kill. The army will be sent against the unbelieving and ungodly people of the earth with the purpose to make them repent, but many still will not repent. The Euphrates River may be a symbolic reference that would be understood by the Jewish Christians in the first century. In the Old Testament, the enemies of Israel traditionally gathered at the Euphrates River in advance of assaulting God's people. The river was a natural boundary between Israel and her enemies.

The fact that the Euphrates River is mentioned doesn't necessarily mean this event will occur at the Euphrates River. The place where the battle begins is not important, because God is the only one who will have complete control of the events of the end time and the end of time. Revelation gives readers a mental picture of the great amount of evil and idolatry that will exist during the end time.

The army of horsemen will not harm Christians at the end time. Some of the unrighteous at the end time that did not repent were not killed and they continued to engage in sexual immorality and idolatry. The unwillingness of some to repent after witnessing the torture by the horsemen is a testimony to the depth of their wicked character.

Verses 20–21 "But the rest of mankind, who were not killed by these plagues, did not repent of the works of their hands, that they should not worship demons, and idols of gold, silver, brass, stone and wood, which can neither see nor hear nor walk. And they did not repent of their murders or their sorceries or their sexual immorality or their thefts."

The Mighty Angel and the Little Scroll

Chapter 10:1–7 "I saw still another mighty angel coming down from heaven, clothed with a cloud. And a rainbow was on his head his face was like the sun, and his feet like pillars of fire. He had a little book open in his hand. And he set his right foot on the sea and his left foot on the land, and cried with a loud voice, as when a lion roars. When he cried out, seven thunders uttered their voices. Now when the seven thunders uttered their voices, I was about to write; but I heard a voice from heaven saying to me, "Seal up the things which the seven thunders uttered, and do not write them." "The angel whom I saw standing on the sea and on the land raised up his hand to heaven and swore by Him who lives forever and ever, who created heaven and the things that are in it, the earth and the things that are in it, and the sea and the things that are in it, that there

211

should be delay no longer, but in the days of the sounding of the seventh angel, when he is about to sound, the mystery of God would be finished, as He declared to His servants the prophets."

John saw a mighty angel like the angel in chapter nine. Mighty may refer to an Arch Angel, possibly Michael or Gabriel. Michael is an Arch Angel that is spoken of as being like God. He is the guardian of God's people, and was an intercessor for Israel. The name Gabriel means the strength of God or man of God. Gabriel is one of the Arch Angels that stands before the throne of God. The angel was holding an open book in his hand and is seen in a vision, not a literal sighting.

The term seven is sometimes used symbolically for fullness and is often associated with the voice of God. The little book revealed the mystery of the events God planned for the end of time. The angel John saw was standing on the land and the sea, because the coming events would be great and affect both the land and the sea. John was told to eat the little book that was open in the hands of the angel. He was to fully digest or memorize what was revealed and not to write anything down. The events of the end of time would be revealed and written down later. When the seventh angel sounds his trumpet, the events of the end of time will take place and the mystery of God's plan for the end of time and the second coming of Christ will be completed.

After several partial judgments there will be one final judgment, and everything on earth, including the atmosphere above the earth, will be destroyed with fire. There will be no more time for repentance after the seventh angel sounds his trumpet. The sounding of the 7th trumpet will take place in chapter 11:15-19 at the end of time.

2nd Peter 3:10–13– "But the day of the Lord will come as a thief in the night, in which the heavens will pass away with a great noise, and the elements will melt with fervent heat; both the earth and the works that are in it will be burned up. Therefore, since all these things will be dissolved, what manner of persons ought you to be in holy conduct and godliness, Looking for and hastening the coming of the day of God, because of which the heavens will be dissolved, being on fire, and the elements will melt with fervent heat? Nevertheless we, look for new heavens and a new earth in which righteousness dwells."

Verses 8–11 "Then the voice, which I heard from heaven, spoke to me again and said, "Go, take the little book which is open in the hand of the' "angel who stands on the sea and on the earth. So I went to the angel and said to him, "Give me the little book. And he said to me, "Take and eat it; and it will make your stomach bitter, but it will be as sweet as honey in your mouth." Then I took the little book out of the angel's hand and ate it, and it was as sweet as honey in my mouth. But when I had eaten it, my stomach became bitter. And he said to me, "You must prophesy again about many peoples, nations, tongues, and kings."

The little book revealed the events of the mystery of God's plan for both the redeemed and the unrighteous. John ate the book, and it tasted sweet like honey. The little book was sweet because it contained messages of hope and victory for the church but it was sour in his stomach because the contents of the book revealed events of great tribulation during the end times. John learned that he would be prophesying, to many people all over the earth. The book of Revelation contains the words of the prophecy revealing the mystery of the destiny of the whole creation during the final judgment of God.

The judgments of God during the end times will come one at a time over a period of a few years. People who are still alive after each judgment will have an opportunity to repent and accept Christ. Daniel wrote that Michael, the great angel who is the protector of God's people, would come to earth to help the church. Daniel prophesied that the dead will be resurrected, and everyone whose name is written in the book of life will be delivered. Daniel 12:3–Michael shall stand up, at that time, the great prince who stands watch over the sons of your people; There will be a time of trouble, Such as never was since there was a nation at that time. Your people shall be delivered, every one who is written in the book. Many of those who sleep in the dust of the earth will awake, some to eternal life, some to shame and everlasting contempt. Those who are wise will shine like the brightness of the firmament, and those who turn many to righteousness like the stars forever and ever. John was told that he must continue to prophesy about events involving many people of all nationalities and rulers.

Chapter 11: The Two Witnesses

Chapter 11 is the last chapter in section three and ends with the second coming of Christ at the end of time. It describes the great persecution against the church that will take place during the end times when the world is being controlled and devastated by Satan and the Lawless One (Antichrist) whom Paul wrote about in second Thessalonians. Chapter 11 begins by presenting a limited view of the end time when nations are at war, and the nation represented by the Lawless One (Antichrist) will have control and rule over a worldwide empire opposed to God and Christianity.

2nd Thessalonians 2:1–4–Now brothers, concerning the coming of our Lord Jesus Christ and our gathering together to him, we ask you, not to be soon shaken in mind or troubled either by spirit or by word, or by letter, as if from us, as though the day of Christ had come. Let no one deceive you by any means; for that day will not come unless the falling away comes first, and the man of sin is revealed, the son of perdition, who opposes and exalts himself above all that is called God or that is worshiped, so that he sits as God in the temple of God, showing that He is God.

The events that occur during the end times will not begin until after the man of sin who is called the Lawless One (Antichrist) rises up claiming to be God. He will rule over the whole earth for a little while. Satan and his demons will be the power behind the empire of the Lawless One (Antichrist). The lawless one (Antichrist) will persecute the church and attempt to turn everyone against the God of creation. Luke 21:8–11 "And He said: Take heed that you be not deceived. For many will come in My name saying I am He' and the time has drawn near.' 'Therefore do not go after them. But when you hear of wars and commotions, do not be terrified; for these things must come to pass first, but the end will not come immediately. Then He said to them, "Nation will rise against nation, and kingdom against kingdom. And there will be great earthquakes in various places, and famines and pestilences; and there will be fearful sights and great signs from heaven."

Chapter 11:1–2 "Then I was given a reed like a measuring rod. And the angel stood, saying, "Rise and measure the temple of God, the altar, and those who worship there. But leave out the court, which is outside the temple, and do not measure it, for it has been given to the Gentiles.

And they will tread the holy city underfoot for forty-two months." The Romans destroyed the Jewish temple in Jerusalem in A.D. 70, and the temple John writes about is symbolic of the church. The Holy Spirit dwells in every member of the church, the temple of God. The name Gentiles here represents those who are not members of the church.

Ephesians 2:19-22–Therefore, you are no longer strangers and foreigners, but fellow citizens with the saints and members of the household of God, built on the foundation of the apostles and the prophets, Jesus Christ Himself is the chief cornerstone, in whom the whole building, being fitted together, grows into a holy temple in the Lord, in whom you also are being built together for a dwelling place of God in the Spirit. Unbelievers will persecute the church, treading on the holy city. Holy city here metaphorically represents the church. John was told to measure the temple in heaven, the altar, and those who worship there. Measuring the temple, the altar, and the worshipers meant to count the number of members in the church.

The word altar means to sacrifice. Worshipers of God brought their animal sacrifices and offered them on the altar in the literal temple in Jerusalem. Since the death of Christ, God requires living sacrifices from the heart of the worshipers. All Christians are priests who offer sacrifices. Romans 12:1 "I beseech you therefore, brethren, by the mercies of God, that you present your bodies a living sacrifice, holy acceptable to God, which is your reasonable service." Verses 3–5 "And I will give power to my two witnesses, and they will prophesy one thousand two hundred and sixty days, clothed in sackcloth. "These are the two olive trees and the two lamp stands standing before the God of the earth. And if anyone wants to harm them, fire proceeds from their mouth and devours their enemies. And if anyone wants to harm them, he must be killed in this manner."

During the end time the church will have two witnesses who will prophesy, meaning they will speak for God. The witnesses will be in mourning, because of the persecution of the church. At the end time God will give miraculous power to witnesses to defend Christianity. God will protect the church with the witnesses, which is symbolized by fire proceeding from their mouth. The fire from their mouth could symbolize their ability to preach in a powerful way to turn people to obey Christ and also to reinforce the faith of the church. Fire could also mean powerful prayer that would be answered with miraculous action from God against their enemies. The 42 months is a figurative time, the same as 1260 days or three and one half years, the length of time for the end time.

Verse 6 "These have power to shut heaven, so that no rain falls in the days of their prophecy; and they have power over waters to turn them to blood, and to strike the earth with all plagues, as often as they desire." Zechariah prophesied about the end time before Christ came to earth and he saw a vision similar to what John wrote about. An angel told Zechariah that the lamp stand and the olive trees are symbols of the word of the Lord and the Holy Spirit of God. The word of God and the Holy Spirit are the two witnesses. Zechariah 4:1–6 "The angel who talked with me came back and wakened me, as a man who is wakened out of sleep.

And he said to me "What do you see?" So I said, "I am looking, and there is a lamp stand of solid gold with a bowl on top of it, and on the stand seven lamps with seven pipes to the seven lamps.' "Two olive trees are by it, one at the right of the bowl and the other at its left." So I answered and spoke to the angel who talked with me saying, "What are these my Lord?" Then the angel who talked with me answered and said to me, "Do you not know what these are?" And I said "No, my Lord." So he answered me and said to me, "This is the word to Zerubbabel: Not by might nor by power, but by My Spirit says the Lord of hosts."

The Holy Spirit and the word of God at the end time will be reminiscent of the prophets of Israel as they used the inspiration of the Holy Spirit to proclaim God's word. The security of the church will not depend on the church members or their power but on the power of the Lord. The testimony of the word of God is not by the might and power of the one who testifies but by the Spirit of God. The Holy Spirit and the word of God will protect the church during the end time. Those who testify for God and righteousness will be preaching the word of God and prayer to defend the church and God will answer their prayers.

Verses 7–8 "When they finish their testimony, the beast that ascends out of the bottomless pit will make war against them, overcome them, and kill them. And their dead bodies will lie in the street of the great city, which spiritually is called Sodom and Egypt, where also our Lord was crucified." Satan is the beast from the Abyss (bottomless pit). When those who testify for God have completed their testimony, Satan and the demons will be out of the bottomless pit, and they will attack those who are witnesses for the word and kill them. Satan will put an end to the witnessing for a time. There may be any number of people proclaiming the word of God at that time. The number two is most likely a symbolic number for all those who are proclaiming the word. According to verses 5 and 6, the witnesses will have great power. Their power comes from God when the church prays for help but Satan will temporarily prevent the proclamation of the Holy Spirit inspired word of God by killing the witnesses.

No one, not even Satan can literally kill the Holy Spirit and the word of God, but Satan can cause the death of those who proclaim the word of God and cause the witnessing to cease for a while. The news of the death of the two witnesses will be a time of celebration for Satan and those who follow him. The dead bodies of the witnesses will lie in the street of the great city that is identified figuratively as Sodom and Egypt. The dead bodies symbolically represent those who were witnessing. Sodom and Egypt are symbolic examples of the great evil that will exist on earth during the end times. Both Sodom and Egypt were known for their gross immorality and all kinds of evil and wickedness symbolizing the type of people at the end of time. The bodies of the witnesses will not receive a decent burial; their bodies will be left on the street in a world that is opposed to God. People of the world will look at the bodies lying in the street, but no one will bury them. The people in an anti-God world full of evil will celebrate the death of the two witnesses.

Verses 9–10 "Then those from the peoples, tribes, tongues, and nations will see their dead bodies, three-and-a-half days, and not allow their dead bodies to be put into graves. And those who dwell on the earth will rejoice over them, make merry, and send gifts to one another, because these two prophets tormented those who dwell on the earth.' The two prophets who proclaimed the word of God had tormented the unrighteous with their preaching, and they were killed.

Verses 11–14 "Now after the three-and-a-half days the breath of life from God entered them, and they stood on their feet, and great fear fell on those who saw them. And they heard a loud voice from heaven saying to them, "Come up here. And they ascended to heaven in a cloud, and their enemies saw them. In the same hour there was a great earthquake, and a tenth of the city fell.' "In the earthquake seven thousand people were killed, and the rest were afraid and gave glory to the God of heaven. The second woe is past. Behold the third woe is coming quickly." Three and a half days figuratively represents the length of time the bodies of God's witnesses lay dead in the street. Then a voice from heaven calls them to come up here, strongly suggesting that those who were witnesses for the word of God become martyrs.

Christians who die during the great tribulation of the end time will also become martyrs. The resurrection of the witnesses is a miraculous sign for all to see the saving power of God. Then there will be a terrible earthquake, and a tenth of the evil population of the world will die as a result of the great earthquake, which is a sign of God's great wrath against Satan and the unrighteous for harming His witnesses.

The Seventh Trumpet

Verses 15–19 "Then the seventh angel sounded: And there were loud voices in heaven saying, "The kingdoms of this world have become the kingdoms of our Lord and of His Christ, and He shall reign forever and ever! And the twenty-four elders who sat before God on their thrones fell on their faces and worshiped God saying: "We give you thanks, O Lord God Almighty, the One who is and who was and who is to come, because you have taken your great power and reigned. The nations were angry, and your wrath has come, and the time of the dead that they should be judged, and that You should reward your servants the prophets and the saints and those who fear your name, small and great, and should destroy those who destroy the earth. Then the temple of God was opened in heaven, and the ark of His covenant was seen in His temple, And there was lightning, noises, thunders, an earthquake, and great hail."

When the seventh and last angel blows his trumpet, it will be a sign that it is time for the mystery of God to be completed at the end of time. The third woe will take place and the full wrath of God will come upon all of those who refuse to accept Christ. Verse 15 is looking forward to and anticipating the second coming of Christ when the entire number of the redeemed will ascend to heaven and all of the kingdoms of men will be destroyed. Christ God and the church will reign forever in heaven. The population of heaven gives thanks to God in anticipation of God using His great power to complete the end of time when all the faithful people of God are rewarded. Then the temple of God is opened in heaven, and the ark of His covenant is seen in His temple (the redeemed church) a sign that God and Christ have used their great power to save the redeemed. And will destroy the unrighteous at the end of time.

The martyrs and the Ark of the Covenant are witnesses of the faithfulness of God and His word and His judgments. In the book of Daniel, an angel told Daniel that the events at the end will be for a time, times, and half a time: 3 and ½ years, 1260 days or 42 months the length of the end time. Christ will rescue his church from the wrath that will come upon the earth. When the angel blew his trumpet, John heard loud voices and saw a vision in heaven. He saw the Ark of the Covenant, the meeting place where the Lord reveals His will to His servants. John saw the coming judgment of God symbolized by lightning, thunder, an earthquake and a hailstorm. This is an indication that the coming wrath of God will be very severe. The power of God and Christ will have taken control of the nations on earth that were under the dominion of Satan and the Lawless one. The nations that are allied with Satan will be angry because of God's judgments. God will send a great earthquake to reveal himself to the people in an effort to make them repent before the final and total destruction of the earth. The survivors of the earthquake will be terrified, and some will turn to God, glorify Him, and repent because of the resurrection of the two witnesses and the earthquake.

The mystery of God will be accomplished, and those who are on earth at that time will understand the true meaning of John's message. There will be great distress upon the earth at the end time and end of time, because Satan, the Antichrist, and the Lawless One (Antichrist) will be on earth. God doesn't want anyone to perish; He wants everyone to have faith in Christ and repent of sin. God does everything he can to reach the hearts of people, even if He must use drastic and punishing measures to convince them. For more information about the Antichrist-Lawless One, read the second chapter of Paul's second letter to the church in Thessalonica and the twelfth chapter of Daniel. Daniel wrote that during the end times many people would be made pure. They will be made spotless and be refined because of the judgments of God that caused them to repent and obey the gospel.

Daniel prophesied that the dead will be resurrected, and everyone whose name is written in the book of life will be saved. After the resurrection of the dead God will judge the people on earth and reward His servants, the prophets, and all the faithful will ascend to heaven with Jesus and the angels.

After the faithful have been removed from the earth there will be great anguish for those who are left. The unbelievers and ungodly will have one last opportunity to repent during that time. The events in section 3 ends with events of the end time and the end of time. Section 4 reveals more end time events.

Section 4 Chapters 12 through 14

Section 4 begins with the birth of the church and ends with the second coming of Christ to reap the grapes of wrath at the end of time. The central theme of section 4 is the ultimate victory of Christ and the church over Satan and his evil forces. Chapters 12 through 14 portray a spiritual war between Christ and Satan featuring the beast out of the sea, the beast out of the earth, the false prophet, and the Lawless One (Antichrist). The focus is on the events of the end time and the end of time.

Chapter 12 is a Synopsis of the beginning of Christianity in the first century. Satan is cast out of heaven to earth. A Jewish woman named Mary from the nation of Israel named gives birth to the Messiah named Jesus. Jesus came to provide redemption for mankind from the guilt of sin. Satan called the dragon attempted to prevent Jesus from accomplishing God's plan of redemption. From the beginning of time Satan had the freedom to go back and forth between heaven and earth. Satan and his angels the demons persecuted the Jewish people living in the region where Mary lived in the first century. Satan knew God was sending the Messiah to earth and he was waiting for Christ to be born so he could kill him. Chapter 12:1–4 "Now a great sign appeared in heaven: a woman clothed with the sun, with the moon under her feet, and on her head a garland of twelve stars. Then, being with child, she cried out in labor and in pain to give birth.' "And another sign appeared in heaven: behold, a great, fiery red dragon having seven heads and ten horns, and seven diadems on his heads. His tail drew a third of the stars of heaven and threw them to the earth. And the dragon stood before the woman who was ready to give birth, to devour her child as soon as it was born.'

In the language of Revelation a sign is a person or an event that looks beyond itself and can represent more than one thing. The woman in verse 1 is a sign of the people belonging to God, first the nation of Israel, the Jewish nation and later in the first century the church, the people of God. Mary, the mother of Jesus, was an ordinary Jewish woman chosen by God to give birth to Jesus the Messiah, Who is the redeemer of mankind. After the church was established the woman represents the church, which is the kingdom of Christ on earth.

John saw a sign in heaven, an enemy of God, Christ and the church. The enemy was Satan the fiery red dragon who sent demons from heaven to earth to torment people. Satan is God's adversary and the enemy of God's people. The Jews who remained faithful to God had been waiting for the coming of the Messiah for hundreds of years. Satan was waiting for the Messiah so he could kill Him while he was still an infant and prevent Christ from establishing redemption. Verse 5 "She bore a male Child who was to rule all nations with a rod of iron, and her Child was caught up to God and His throne." Mary the Jewish woman bore Jesus the Christ child who would provide redemption and eventually rule all unrighteous nations with a rod of iron. Christ came as a Messiah to die on the cross and redeem mankind from the guilt of sin and to establish His spiritual kingdom the church. Jesus the Son of Mary was caught up to the throne of God in heaven after His death, burial and resurrection. Jesus will return to earth at the end of time and will rule all nations with a rod of iron. Rule with a rod of iron means to punish the unrighteous nations.

When Satan was on earth Christ was born, He conducted His ministry of redemption, died on the cross, ascended to heaven and assumed all authority in heaven and on earth. Satan and his demons are cast into the Abyss affording the opportunity for the establishment and growth of the kingdom of God, which is the church. God can imprison and releases Satan from the Abyss anytime He chooses to. The kingdom of Christ on earth was established during the first century. John the Baptist told the people in the first century to repent because the kingdom was at hand Mt 3:2. Jesus said in Luke 11:20 that the kingdom has come upon you.

Christ will not return to earth to set up an earthly kingdom, the kingdom is here now. When Christ returns to earth He will gather up the church and the church will be given a place in a new heaven and a new earth. The kingdom later called the church was formally established in the first century. Christ reigns; over His kingdom the church now and has reigned since the church was established. Verse 6 "Then the woman fled into the wilderness where she had a place prepared by God that they should feed her there one thousand two hundred and sixty days." In this section John Moves from events of the first century after the establishment of the church to events of the end time lasting 1260 days the length of the end time. During the end time Satan and the demons will be released from the Abyss and cause great tribulation on earth and persecute the church. The, woman in verse 6 represents the church that will be attacked by the evil forces of Satan at the end time and will go into the wilderness where she will be safe. The wilderness represents a condition of safety the church is protected by God and she can worship God without being killed. Jesus will return at the end of time to reward the church with eternal life. Satan and the demons will be destroyed and Christ will punish the unrighteous nations with a rod of iron.

Verses 7–9 "And war broke out in heaven: Michael and his angels fought with the dragon; and the dragon and his angels fought, but they did not prevail, nor was a place found for them in heaven any longer. So the great dragon was cast out, that serpent of old, called the Devil and Satan, who deceives the whole world; he was cast to the earth, and his angels were cast out with him." Verses 7 through 9 explain why Satan and his angels were cast out of heaven and were on earth during the life and ministry of Christ. There was a war in heaven between the Arch Angel Michael and his angels with Satan and his angels called demons. Michael is the protector of God's people and Michael and his angels prevailed over Satan and the demons and they were cast out of heaven. Satan and the demons were cast out of heaven at the beginning of the Christian age and they attempted to prevent Christ from fulfilling His mission to provide redemption. Satan and his demons were banned from that part of heaven forever.

Verses 10–11 "Then I heard a loud voice saying in heaven, "Now salvation, and strength, and the kingdom of our God, and the power of His Christ have come, for the accuser of our brethren who accused them before our God day and night has been cast down. And they overcame him by the blood of the Lamb and by the word of their testimony, and they did not love their lives to the death." John hears a voice from heaven saying Satan had been cast down referring to throwing Satan and his angels out of heaven. This was a victory for Christ and the church because Satan and his angels were no longer in heaven fighting against God's plan of redemption. Satan and his angels attempted to thwart God's plan of redemption on earth after they were thrown out of heaven but Christ sacrificed His life and guaranteed redemption.

Verses 12–17 "Therefore rejoice, O heavens, and you who dwell in them! Woe to the inhabitants of the earth and the sea! For the devil has come down to you, having great wrath, because he knows that he has a short time. But the woman was given two wings of a great eagle, that she might fly into the wilderness to her place, where she is nourished for a time and times and half a time from the presence of the serpent.' "So the serpent spewed water out of his mouth like a flood after the woman that he might cause her to be carried away by the flood. But the earth helped the woman, and the earth opened its mouth and swallowed up the flood, which the dragon had spewed out of his mouth.' The dragon was enraged with the woman, and he went to make war with the rest of her offspring who keep the commandments of God and have the testimony of Jesus Christ." Spewed water like a flood is figurative language that describes Satan's attempt to destroy the church like a flood destroys anything in its path. Satan was not able to destroy the church in the first century and he will not be able to destroy the church at the end time, because God and the earth will help the church. The earth may refer to those who are not Christians but will sympathize with the church and will help her escape from the wrath of Satan. Sometime after the church was established Satan was imprisoned in a place in the heavens called the Abyss and bottomless pit. Later during the end time Satan will be free to roam the earth again and he will persecute the church.

Chapter 13:1–4 "Then I stood on the sand of the sea. And I saw a beast rising up out of the sea, having seven heads and ten horns, and on his horns ten crowns, and on his heads a blasphemous name. "Now the beast I saw was like a leopard, his feet were like the feet of a bear, and his mouth like the mouth of a lion." The dragon gave him his power, his throne and great authority. And I saw one of his heads as if it had been mortally wounded, and his deadly wound was healed. And all the world marveled and followed the beast. So they worshiped the dragon who gave authority to the beast; and they worshiped the beast, saying "Who is like the beast? Who is able to make war with him?'

Chapter 12 took us to the end time when Satan and his demons will be on the earth. Chapter 13 describes some of the events that will take place during the 1260 days (three and one half years or 42 months) of the end time. John saw a beast coming out of the sea. The beast is a symbol of a powerful world empire that comes from among the world of unrighteous humanity. The beast John saw was like a leopard, bear, and lion. Beasts are used in scripture to represent world empires. In the 7th chapter of the book of Daniel, Daniel saw a vision of four beasts that represented the Babylonian, Persian, Greek, and Roman empires. Beasts represent evil world empires, because they like beasts are powerful and viscous without any regard for their victims. Satan accomplishes his evil through human agencies such as nations and empires, and he spreads deception and evil among the people.

The empire that is represented by the beast will be an evil empire ruled by an unrighteous individual from among the unrighteous people on earth that Paul called the man of sin and the Lawless One (Antichrist). The world empire of the Lawless One (antichrist) will be a powerful empire that controls several smaller nations. Satan will be the power that creates and controls the empire during the end time when he is out of the Abyss. The beast John saw had seven heads and ten horns with crowns. The heads, horns, and crowns are symbols of rulers and authorities under the control of a great power and authority like an evil world empire. Paul wrote about the Lawless One (Antichrist) in his second letter to the church in Thessalonica.

2nd Thessalonians 2:1–4 "Now brethren, concerning the coming of our Lord Jesus Christ and our gathering together to Him, we ask you, not to be soon shaken in mind or troubled, either by spirit or by word or by letter, as if from us, as though the day of Christ had come. Let no one deceive you by any means; for that day will not come unless the falling away comes first, and the man of sin is revealed, the son of perdition, who opposes and exalts himself above all that is called God or that is worshiped, so that he sits as God in the temple of God, showing himself that he is God."

Satan will be let out of the Abyss at the end time, and Satan will give power to the beast the Lawless One (antichrist) and he will declare that he is God, and many people will worship him. Some will fall away from a belief in the true God at that time. 2nd Thessalonians 2:5–8 "Do you not remember that when I was still with you I told you these things? And now you know what is restraining, that he may be revealed in his own time. For the mystery of lawlessness is already at work; only He who now restrains will do so until He is taken out of the way. And then the lawless one will be revealed, whom the Lord will consume with the breath of His mouth and destroy with the brightness of His coming.' The lawlessness is already at work refers to the descendants of a people that already existed but would not gain their power until the end time. Paul said the second coming of Christ was being restrained now because he will not return until after the coming of the Lawless One (Antichrist). At the time Paul wrote the letters to the church in Thessalonica the second coming of Christ was being restrained by God. God will prevent Christ's second coming until He is ready for Him to return at the end of time after the Lawless One (antichrist) has wielded his power and influence throughout the earth at the end time.

2nd Thessalonians 2:9 "The coming of the lawless one is according to the working of Satan, with all power, signs and lying wonders, and with all unrighteous deception among those who perish, because they did not receive the love of the truth that they might be saved. And for this reason God will send them strong delusion that they should believe the lie that they all may be condemned who did not believe the truth but had pleasure in unrighteousness."

Satan will be let out of the Abyss, then the beast of the sea Paul called the Lawless One (antichrist) will come into power. Satan is the one who gives him his power. The people of the earth will be deceived by the great power Satan gives the Lawless One (Antichrist) and their demonstration of great power will deceive the people on earth. Verses 5-10– "And he was given a mouth speaking great things and blasphemies, and he was given authority to continue for forty-two months.

Then he opened his mouth in blasphemy against God, to blaspheme His name, His tabernacle, and those who dwell in heaven. It was granted to him to make war with the saints and to overcome them. And authority was given him over every tribe, tongue and nation. All who dwell on the earth will worship him, whose names have not been written in the Book of Life of the Lamb slain from the foundation of the world. If anyone has an ear, let him hear. He who leads into captivity, he who kills with the sword must be killed with the sword. Here is the patience and the faith of the saints.

The Lawless One (antichrist) will claim to be God, and he will speak against God and worship Satan. Lawlessness has always existed since the Garden of Eden when Satan first deceived Adam and Eve but there will be extreme wickedness during the end time. Satan was free in the beginning to roam heaven and earth, but God had him thrown into the abyss. Satan will come out of the abyss when God lets him out at the end time to torment the people on earth. Satan will then take control of the people of the earth except for the members of the church. God will allow the Lawless One (Antichrist) to go to war with the church. The church will survive during the end time, because the Church will have God's protection.

God has a two-fold reason to allow the events of the end time. One is a last resort to cause unrighteous people to repent and accept Christ and the second reason is to punish the unrighteous that will not repent. The mystery of the type of lawlessness that will exist during the end time was already at work symbolically by the Roman Empire when John wrote. There were already men in Rome who claimed to be God and demanded their subjects to worship them.

Satan and the Lawless One (antichrist) will blaspheme God's name and attempt to turn the population of the world against God and Christ. There will be a great rebellion on earth against

God, Christ, and the church at that time. All of the world, except those who choose to obey God and confess faith in Christ, will marvel at the beast and will worship Satan.

"Then I saw another beast coming up out of the earth, and he had two horns like a lamb and spoke like a dragon. And he exercises all the authority of the first beast in his presence, and causes the earth and those who dwell in it to worship the first beast whose deadly wound was healed.' The beast out of the earth will already be on earth and he will have an evil nature like the beast out of the sea. He will claim to be a true prophet. The beast out of the earth will join the Lawless One (antichrist). The antichrist will accept the beast out of the earth and allow him to have authority, because he will have the power to create false miracles. He will claim to be a true prophet, but he will be a false prophet. His two horns represent his power and authority. The false prophet will be a demon that prophesies for the Lawless One (Antichrist) that claims to be God.

"And I saw three unclean spirits like frogs coming out of the mouth of the dragon, out of the mouth of the beast, and out of the mouth of the false prophet." Revelation 16:13– The beast out of the earth is a demon that is allied with Satan, and he speaks with lies and deceit. He will appear to be religious and have the nature of a gentle harmless person, but he will be a demon that supports the Lawless One. He speaks like Satan the dragon, because he is controlled and supported by Satan. During His ministry, Jesus warned His disciples that there would be false prophets. Jesus said, "Watch out for false prophets, for they come to you in sheep's clothing, but on the inside they are ferocious wolves." The false prophet will promote the worship of the beast with false miracles, signs, and wonders and, he will have extraordinary power to deceive the people of the world.

Verses 13–15"He performs great signs, so that he even makes fire come down from heaven on the earth in the sight of men. And he deceives those who dwell on the earth by those signs which he was granted to do in the sight of the beast, telling those who dwell on the earth to make an image to the beast who was wounded by the sword and lived.

He was granted power to give breath to the image of the beast that the image of the beast should both speak and cause as many as would not worship the image of the beast to be killed." The signs the false prophet performs will look so real that people will be deceived and believe the Lawless one is God. One of the false miracles of the false prophet and the Lawless One (Antichrist) will be to claim that the Lawless One was wounded and was dead, and the false prophet brought him back to life. Anyone who would not believe the lie and not worship the beast would be killed.

Verses 16–18 "He causes all, both small and great, rich and poor, free and slave, to receive a mark on their right hand or on their foreheads, and that no one may buy or sell except one who has the mark or the name of the beast, or the number of his name. Here is wisdom. Let him who has understanding calculate the number of the beast, for it is the number of a man. His number is 666." The Lawless One (antichrist) and the false prophet will require everyone be identified as a loyal follower of the Lawless One. People will be identified by a mark on their forehead or right hand. Since we are reading from a source of figurative language we cannot know for sure ahead of time what the mark is or the name of the beast or the number of his name. To have the mark of the beast means to be loyal to the beast and worship him. The beast identifies his followers with the mark so everyone can see that they belong to the beast. What the mark looks like is not important everyone that is living during the end time will know the significance of the mark when they see it.

Revelation 14:9–10 "Then a third angel followed them saying with a loud voice, "if anyone worships the beast and his image, and receives his mark on his forehead or on his hand, he himself shall also drink of the wrath of God, which is poured out full strength into the cup of His indignation." The angel warned that if anyone followed the beast and received his mark, they would be punished by the wrath of God. The church and the people of the world will not be able to ignore or defeat the power of the beast. Only Christ, at the end of time, will be able to destroy Satan, the Lawless One (antichrist) and the false prophet.

The end time will be a time that tests the faith of everyone on the earth. Speaking figuratively, God will give Satan and the beast forty-two months to deceive the people and persecute the church. This is the same length of time predicted by the prophet Daniel for the trampling of the holy city (the church) and for the ministry of the two witnesses in chapter 11.

Daniel 12-7– I heard the man clothed in linen, he was above the waters of the river, he held up his right hand and his left hand to heaven, and swore by Him who lives forever, that it shall be for a time, times, and half a time; when the power of the holy people has been completely shattered, all these things shall be finished. The man clothed in linen represents either Gabriel or Michael who swore before God that the tribulation at the end time would last for a time, times and half a time, which is 1260 days, three and one half years or 42 months. After the end time the beast and the false prophet will be destroyed in a lake of burning sulfur at the end of time.

The Lamb and The One Hundred Forty-four Thousand

Chapter 14 is the last chapter in section 4. John begins the chapter by writing about the earliest days of Christianity, then he gradually merges into the end times with a scene of Christ and the redeemed singing a new song; a song of victory for Christ and the redeemed. Three angels will make a public declaration of the gospel. An angel flies in the midst of heaven preaching the gospel to the people on earth encouraging them to obey the gospel, because the time for the final judgment of God had come. Another angel proclaims that Babylon, the symbol of evil had fallen. A third angel warns the people on earth that they will suffer the wrath of God if they continue to worship the beast until the end of time and Christ returns to earth with His angels, and they destroy all unrighteousness.

Revelation 14:1–5 "Then I looked and behold, a Lamb standing on Mount Zion, and with Him one hundred and forty-four thousand, having His Father's name written on their foreheads. And I heard a voice from heaven, like the voice of many waters, and like the voice of loud thunder.' "And I heard the sound of harpists playing their harps.

They sang as it were a new song before the throne, before the four living creatures, and the elders; and no one could learn that song except the hundred and forty-four thousand who were redeemed from the earth.' "These are the ones who were not defiled with women, for they are virgins. These are the ones who follow the Lamb wherever he goes. These were redeemed from among men, being first fruits to God and to the Lamb. And in their mouth was found no deceit, for they are without fault before the throne of God."

Christ is the Lamb and the one hundred and forty four thousand represent the redeemed in heaven, and they are identified as God's people. God's name is written on their forehead, because they belong to Him. These are the faithful that remained true to God. Mt Zion is symbolic of the temple that was built on Mt Zion in Jerusalem figuratively representing God's people, the church. Name written on the forehead is symbolic of God's knowledge of everyone that belongs to Him. The temple was the place where God met with His people. In Revelation the temple figuratively represents the church, God's redeemed people in heaven. There were many redeemed who were already in heaven from both covenants when John wrote. The martyrs and all of the redeemed were represented figuratively as one hundred and forty four thousand.

John heard a loud sound like the sound of many waters and loud thunder. The sound came from the temple in heaven from the voices of the redeemed. The redeemed are the only ones who can learn and sing a new song. The song is new to them, because it had not been sung before. It was a song of complete victory over Satan and the forces of evil. The expression were not defiled with women means they were not idolaters; they had remained true to God and Christ. The Lamb and the 144,000 figuratively represent all of the redeemed in heaven during the end time, a short time before the end of time when their fellow brothers and sisters in Christ would join them. In the interim, the gospel would continue to be preached. Verses 6–8 "Then I saw another angel flying in the midst of heaven, having the everlasting gospel to preach to those who dwell on the earth—to every nation, tribe, tongue, and people—saying with a loud voice, "Fear God and give glory to Him, for the hour of His judgment has come; and worship Him who made heaven and earth, the sea and springs of water."

And another angel followed saying, "Babylon is fallen, is fallen, that great city, because she has made all nations drink of the wine of the wrath of her fornication."

When Christ returns to earth, many of the unrighteous will still be on earth, and an angel will be preaching the gospel warning the unrighteous of the coming of God's judgment. Babylon is used as a symbol for evil and the angels are declaring that now is the time all evil will be destroyed, including Satan the empire of the Lawless One (Antichrist), the beast out of the earth, and all of the unrighteous people left on earth.

Verses 9–13 "Then a third angel followed them, saying with a loud voice, "If anyone worships the beast and his image, and receives his mark on his forehead or on his hand, he himself shall also drink of the wine of the wrath of God, which is poured out full strength into the cup of His indignation. He shall be tormented with fire and brimstone in the presence of the holy angels and in the presence of the Lamb. And the smoke of their torment ascends forever and ever; and they have no rest day or night, who worship the beast and his image, and whoever receives the mark of his name. Here is the patience of the saints; here are those who keep the commandments of God and the faith of Jesus. Then I heard a voice from heaven saying to me, "Write: Blessed are the dead who die in the Lord from now on." "Yes," says the Spirit that they may rest from their labors, and their works follow them."

At the end of time, Christ will come and reap the earth. Everyone will see the coming of Christ and the angels will be with Him. Reaping the earth represents judging all people and rewarding the righteous and destroying the unrighteous. Everyone has been warned not to follow the evil and unrighteous examples of Babylon. The saints are told to be patient, and if they are killed, they will find rest with God. The saints have a place of paradise waiting for them in a new heaven. The unrighteous will suffer, and they will be tormented forever if they do not repent and obey the gospel.

Luke 21:25–28 "And there will be signs in the sun, in the moon and in the stars; and on the earth distress of nations, with perplexity, the sea and the waves roaring.

Men's hearts failing them from fear and the expectation of those things, which are coming on the earth, for the powers of the heavens will be shaken. Then they will see the Son of Man coming in a cloud with power and great glory. Now when these things begin to happen, look up and lift up your heads, because your redemption draws near."

Verses 14–16 "Then I looked, and behold, a white cloud, and on the cloud sat One like the Son of Man, having on His head a golden crown, and in His hand a sharp sickle. And another angel came out of the temple, crying with a loud voice to Him who sat on the cloud, "Thrust in Your sickle and reap, for the time has come for You to reap, for the harvest of the earth is ripe." So he who sat on the cloud thrust in His sickle on the earth and the earth was reaped."

The crown is a sign of the King of Kings and a symbol of His authority to fulfill the wrath of God at the end of time. The sickle represents the destruction of the unrighteous people on the earth. The earth will be ripe for reaping, because the people have become so evil that God would not wait any longer, and He will send Christ and the angels to reap the earth.

Verses 17–18 "Then another angel came out of the temple that is in heaven, he also having a sharp sickle. And another angel come out from the altar, who had power over fire, and he cried with a loud cry to him who had the sharp sickle saying, "Thrust in your sharp sickle and gather the clusters of the vine of the earth, for her grapes are fully ripe.' "So the angel thrust his sickle into the earth and gathered the vine of the earth, and threw it into the great winepress of the wrath of God. And the winepress was trampled outside the city, and blood came out of the winepress up to the horses' bridles, for one thousand six hundred furlongs." John's visions give a figurative view of the execution of God's wrath poured out on the unrighteous by Christ and the angels at the end of time. Section 4 ends with events of the end of time. In section 5, more events of the end time will take place beginning with chapter 15. Section 5 ends with chapter 16 when the 7th bowl of wrath is poured out.

Chapters 15-16 Bowl Judgments

Chapter 15 introduces the bowl judgments that will be poured out during the end time. John begins chapter 15 with a vision in heaven of seven angels who have the seven last plagues that will come upon the earth during the end time. They are seven bowls of God's wrath, one bowl for each angel. Pouring out the bowls of wrath reveals the final judgments that come when the end time becomes the end of time. When the seventh angel completes delivering God's wrath against the unrighteous, the judgment of God is completed. John saw those who had remained faithful to Christ during the end time. They hadn't worshiped the beast or any image of the beast, and they were in heaven. They had become martyrs. The sea of glass is a place for worship that is in front of God's throne. All of those who gained a victory over the beast were standing on the sea of glass waiting for the trumpet blasts to signal the angels to act, and they sang the song of victory like the song that Moses sang when the Israelites were delivered from Egypt. When the seventh bowl is poured out, the islands and mountains disappear. Great hail falls upon the earth. The statement will rule them with a rod of iron symbolize the destruction with force against the unrighteous from the bowls of wrath at the end of time.

Chapter 15:1–8 "Then I saw another sign in heaven, great and marvelous: seven angels having the seven last plagues, for in them the wrath of God is complete. "And I saw something like a sea of glass mingled with fire, and those who have the victory over the beast, over his image and over his mark and over the number of his name, standing on the sea of glass, having harps of God. They sang the song of Moses, the servant of God, and the song of the Lamb, saying: Great and marvelous are Your works, Lord God Almighty! Just and true are your ways, O King of the saints! Who shall not fear You, O Lord, and glorify Your name? For You alone are holy. For all nations shall come and worship before You, For Your judgments have been manifested.'

After these things I looked, and behold, the temple of the tabernacle of the testimony in heaven was opened. And out of the temple came the seven angels having the seven plagues, clothed in pure bright linen, and having their chests girded with golden bands.

"Then one of the four living creatures gave to the seven Angels seven golden bowls full of the wrath of God who lives forever and ever. The temple was filled with smoke from the glory of God and from His power, and no one was able to enter the temple till the seven plagues of the seven angels were completed." Angels will be instrumental in carrying out the last plagues of God's wrath on a world of unrighteous people. John sees the redeemed in heaven they had been victorious over Satan and the unrighteous. They were in heaven where they would be safe from the plagues and the beast. They were the martyrs who died because they would not deny Christ, and they were redeemed.

When the redeemed sing the song of victory, the song will praise God as the Almighty King of the saints, the Only Holy and Righteous One. John saw the temple of the tabernacle of the testimony, and it was opened. (A testimony is a statement used for evidence or proof.). In the Old Testament, the tabernacle in the wilderness and the temple in Jerusalem were testimonials for God and the places where God met with His people. During the Christian dispensation the church is the temple of God, and the church meets with God spiritually in the hearts of Christians producing praise, prayer, worship, and song. John saw seven angels with the seven final plagues of God's wrath come from the midst of the redeemed.

The angels were dressed in clothes that symbolized righteousness. God will be righteous in taking action against Satan, the false prophet, the beast, and the ungodly people on earth. The angels each received a bowl of God's wrath from one of the living creatures in heaven. The temple was filled with smoke so that no one could enter, symbolizing the protection of the church, which is God's temple. The pouring out of the bowls of wrath will not harm the church.

God's Bowls of Wrath Poured on The Earth

First Bowl — Loathsome Sores

Chapter 16:1–2 "Then I heard a loud voice from the temple saying to the seven angels, "Go and pour out the bowls of the wrath of God on the earth."2 So the first went and poured out his bowl upon the earth, and a foul and loathsome sore came upon the men who had the mark of the beast and those who worshiped his image.'

Second Bowl Verse 3 "Then the second angel poured out his bowl on the sea, and it became blood as of a dead man; and every living creature in the sea died."

Third Bowl — Waters Turn to Blood

Verses 4–7 "Then the third angel poured out his bowl on the rivers and springs of water, and they became blood. And I heard the angels of the waters saying: "You are righteous, O Lord, The One who is and who was and who is to be, because you have judged these things. "For they have shed the blood of saints and prophets. And you have given them blood to drink. For it is their just due. And I heard another from the altar saying, "Even so, Lord God Almighty, true and righteous are your judgments."

Fourth Bowl — Men are Scorched

Verse 8–9 "Then the fourth angel poured out his bowl on the sun, and power was given to him to scorch men with fire. And men were scorched with great heat, and they blasphemed the name of God who has power over these plagues; and they did not repent and give Him glory."

Fifth Bowl — Darkness and Pain

Verses 10–11 "Then the fifth angel poured out his bowl on the throne of the beast, and his kingdom became full of darkness; and they gnawed their tongues because of the pain. They blasphemed the God of heaven because of their pains and their sores, and did not repent of their deeds."

Sixth Bowl — Euphrates Dried Up

Verse 12–16 "Then the sixth angel poured out his bowl on the great river Euphrates, and its water was dried up, so that the way of the kings from the east might be prepared. And I saw three unclean spirits like frogs coming out of the mouth of the dragon, out of the mouth of the beast, and out of the mouth of the false prophet.

For they are spirits of demons, performing signs, which go out to the kings of the earth and of the whole world, to gather them to the battle of that great day of God Almighty. "Behold, I am coming as a thief. Blessed is he who watches and keeps his garments, lest he walk naked and they see his shame." And they gathered them together to the place called in Hebrew, Armageddon."

Seventh Bowl — Earth Utterly Shaken

Verse 17–21 "Then the seventh angel poured out his bowl into the air, and a loud voice came out of the temple of heaven, from the throne saying, "It is done! "And there were noises and thunder and lightning; and there was a great earthquake, such a mighty and great earthquake as had not occurred since men were on the earth. Now the great city was divided into three parts, and the cities of the nations fell. And great Babylon was remembered before God, to give her the cup of the wine of the fierceness of His wrath.' 20 Then every island fled away, and the mountains were not found. 21 And great hail from heaven fell upon men, each hailstone about the weight of a talent. Men blasphemed God because of the plague of the hail, since that plague was exceedingly great."

The loud voice to begin the bowl judgments came from the authority of God. God's judgment against the earth will be completed when the last bowl is poured out at the end time. No one can enter the temple (the church) until after the angels have completed their mission. When the mission is complete, the three angels in chapter 14 have the everlasting gospel to preach on earth to all people telling them to fear God and give him glory, for the hour of His judgment has come. This will be the last chance for those who are still living to obey the gospel. Once the process of the bowl judgments starts, it will not be interrupted. No one can prevent God from completing the plan He had from the beginning to punish the unrighteous and reward the righteous with a new heaven and a new earth.

John still looking into heaven heard a voice coming from the temple telling the seven angels with the bowls of wrath to go ahead and pour out the bowls on the earth. The first angel will pour out his bowl when the end time is close to merging into the end of time.

There is not a sharply defined beginning and ending of the separation between the end time and the beginning of the end of time. There is no exact length of time prescribed for the end of time but it will take place quickly once it begins. Before the actual destruction of the earth by fire, there will be a period of great suffering for the unrighteous and those who worship the Lawless One. The angels preaching the gospel of Christ are trying to persuade the unrighteous to accept and obey Christ before the day of the end of time, because there will not be another chance (chapter 14:6-11). Satan and the demons will have been released from the Abyss to persecute and torture the people on earth. Satan and the demons will remain on the earth until they are destroyed at the second coming of Christ; they will be on the earth during the bowl judgments.

When the first angel pours out his bowl, sores will break out on the people who are identified with the mark of the beast. The sores will cause great pain in one last effort to make the unrighteous repent. The sores are not meant to kill but are a sign that God's wrath is beginning. The bowls are poured out one at a time to inflict maximum suffering, and the lapse of time between pouring out each bowl will give people an opportunity to repent. The second and third bowls are poured out, and they affect the sea and the sources of fresh water. Every creature in the sea dies. The term sea is used metaphorically to represent the sea of unrighteous humanity on earth that will die when the second angel pours out his bowl. The statement blood to drink means many people will die during the end times. Life can no longer be sustained in the sea or on the portion of land that was affected by the first three bowls. People cannot survive without water.

The angel who will be responsible for damaging the water will praise God for his righteous judgment. The angels will proclaim that God is righteous in everything He does. The heat of the sun will scorch the unrighteous, but they will not repent. Instead they will blaspheme God. Suffering is intended to help people realize their need for God and repent, but some people will blame God and curse Him. In chapter 1 of Romans, Paul writes about the guilt of mankind and God's wrath against unrighteousness. Romans 1:18–21 "For the wrath of God is revealed from heaven against all ungodliness and unrighteousness of men, who suppress the truth in unrighteousness, because what may be known of God is manifest in them, for God has shown it to them.

For since the creation of the world His invisible attributes are clearly seen, being understood by the things that are made, even His eternal power and Godhead, so that they are without excuse, because, although they knew God they did not glorify Him as God, nor were thankful, but became futile in their thoughts, and their foolish hearts were darkened."

2nd Thessalonians 1:3–10– We thank God always for you brethren, because your faith grows exceedingly, and the love of everyone of you all abounds toward each other, so that we ourselves boast of you among the churches of God for your patience and faith in all your persecutions and tribulations that you endure, which is manifest evidence of the righteous judgment of God, that you may be counted worthy of the kingdom of God, for which you also suffer. It is a righteous thing with God to repay with tribulation those who trouble you, and give you who are troubled rest with us when the Lord Jesus is revealed from heaven with His mighty angels, in flaming fire taking vengeance on those who do not know God, and on those who do not obey the gospel of our Lord Jesus Christ.

The tribulation and persecution that Christians endure comes from the actions of the unrighteous, but faithful Christians do not deny their faith in God and Christ. When God repays the unrighteous with tribulation, it is a righteous punishment. The manifestations of God have existed from the beginning of time and there is no excuse for anyone to ignore God and Christ and God's redeeming plan. God could end everything on earth within a moment during the end time but instead He punishes in measured sections of time to encourage repentance so people will obey the gospel.

Those who die from God's wrath will be evil, ungodly people who deserve to die. John heard another voice confirming what the angel said. "Even so, Lord God Almighty, true and righteous are your judgments." (Revelation 16:7.) The voice came from the altar, and could have been from

229

the saints who were under the altar. God's judgments will be just, because the evil people who suffer from his judgments are like those who killed his saints, prophets, and apostles. They will be receiving what they deserve.

The fourth bowl affects the heavenly bodies, and when the fourth bowl is poured out on the sun, it will cause intense heat that will scorch people, and they will curse God.

The depravity of people at the end time is evidenced by the fact that no amount of suffering keeps them from cursing God. The judgments of God will be terrible, but the people who are scorched by the sun will be of the worst kind. They will be those who speak evil of God and refuse to repent even after being warned over and over again. The fifth angel pours out his bowl of God's wrath on the kingdom of the beast, and it becomes full of darkness. The unrighteous will blaspheme God because of the pain and the sores, but they still will not repent. The Euphrates River dries up when the sixth angel pours out his bowl. The demons perform miraculous signs to stir up the unrighteous people against God. The seventh angel pours out his bowl of wrath fulfilling God's wrath against Satan, the demons, and the unrighteous people on earth. God doesn't pour out his wrath on those who are righteous. The angel will make a direct hit on the beast, which figuratively is the evil empire of the Lawless One, the false prophet and Satan.

Chapter 8: 13, an angel flew through heaven and in a loud voice he said, "Woe, woe, woe to the inhabitants of the earth, because of the remaining blasts of the trumpets of the three angels who are about to sound." The woes were to be announced by the fifth sixth, and seventh trumpet blast. Woe means great grief, trouble, and distress. The forces of God will attack the beast and his followers, but they will stubbornly refuse to repent, and the sixth angel will pour out another bowl of God's wrath. The sixth bowl of wrath involves warfare between the forces of God, Christ, and the angels against Satan, the demons, the empire of the Lawless One (Antichrist), and the false prophet at the end of time.

The forces of evil will gather together for a final battle before they are destroyed. John writes about the last and final battle against evil symbolized as Babylon the Great, the mother of evil. Babylon figuratively represents all evil regardless of time. The ancient city of Babylon situated on the banks of the Euphrates was an enemy of God's people at one time. The Euphrates River in ancient times was the place where the enemies of God's people gathered to invade Israel. The Euphrates River is used figuratively to represent the location of the last and final battle (Armageddon) against all evil on earth.

The word Armageddon is found nowhere outside the Bible and it is mentioned only once in Revelation 16:16.

The word Armageddon symbolizes Christ's war against the forces of evil at the end of time. The kings of the earth, Satan and the demons will unite with the lawless one to war against God in the battle of Armageddon on the great day of God Almighty. The place of the battle of Armageddon is symbolic, so it doesn't matter where the battle is located. We do know what the outcome will be, because it has already been decided. God and the church will be victorious and that will be the day when the forces of God destroy all evil on the earth, a great day for God Almighty and the church.

Christians who have remained faithful will be blessed and will not be harmed, but the unrighteous will suffer from the judgments sent by God. The term it is done means God's final act of judgment will be completed when the seventh bowl is poured out ending the plagues. The result of pouring out the seventh bowl is recorded in Revelation 16:18-21. When Christ said He was coming as a thief, He meant that no one knows the time when the Lord will come until they see Him coming in the clouds. Verses 18 through 21 describe the great battle when Christ returns.

When the seventh angel blows his trumpet, God's mysterious plan will be completed. The fifth, sixth, and seventh bowls have been poured out by the angels symbolizing the battle of Armageddon, the last battle between good and evil. Section 6–Chapters 17 through 19In chapter 16, God remembered Ancient Babylon and her great evil, and the seventh bowl of God's wrath was poured out. The evil Empire of the Lawless One (Antichrist) is like Ancient Babylon. Babylon was a type of evil. Types refer to a person or thing having the characteristics of a kind, class, or group. Anti-types are copies of an earlier type. Ancient Babylon is a type and the Roman Empire and the empire of the Lawless One (Antichrist) are anti types of the evil demonstrated by Ancient Babylon.

Chapter 17 God's wrath is directed against Babylon and her antitypes. Babylon the symbol of all kinds of evil is described as a prostitute, the mother of harlots and the sinful abominations of the earth. Chapter 18 portrays the fall of Babylon the Great. During the end of time Christ will return and will destroy the antitype of Babylon, the Empire of the Lawless One (Antichrist).

God will destroy all traces of her evil. Chapter 19 portrays the Second coming of Christ with the angels at the end of time to strike down the evil nations symbolized by the phrase 'He Himself will rule them with a rod of Iron.'

Revelation mentions, types and anti-types and features Ancient Babylon in order to describe what the empire of the Lawless one (Antichrist) and the morals and attitudes of people will be like during the end times. The world Empire of Babylon is called the great harlot, therefore the Empire of the Lawless One (Antichrist) at the end time will be a great harlot that corrupts the morals of many people symbolized by sitting on many waters. Waters is figurative for people. The greater part of the population of the earth will be under the control of The Lawless One (Antichrist) who will be under the control of Satan.

Chapter 17 — Great Harlot Sits On Many Waters

Chapter 17: 1–6 "Then one of the seven angels who had the seven bowls came and talked with me saying to me, "Come, I will show you the judgment of the great harlot who sits on many waters, with whom the kings of the earth committed fornication, and the inhabitants of the earth were made drunk with the wine of her fornication. So he carried me away in the Spirit into the wilderness. And I saw a woman sitting on a scarlet beast that was full of names of blasphemy, having seven heads and ten horns. The woman was arrayed in purple and scarlet, and adorned with gold and precious stones and pearls, having in her hand a golden cup full of abominations and the filthiness of her fornication. And on her forehead a name was written:

MYSTERY, BABYLON THE GREAT, THE MOTHER OF HARLOTS AND OF THE ABOMINATIONS OF THE EARTH. I saw the woman, drunk with the blood of the saints and with the blood of the martyrs of Jesus. And when I saw her, I marveled with great amazement." The woman on the scarlet beast first represents Ancient Babylon, then Rome, and finally the Empire of the Lawless One (Antichrist) near the end of time who will be guilty of every kind of evil and is yet to come. Verses 7–8 "But the angel said to me, "Why did you marvel?

I will tell you the mystery of the woman and of the beast that carries her, which has the seven heads and the ten horns. The beast that you saw was, and is not, and will ascend out of the bottomless pit and go to perdition. And those who dwell on the earth will marvel, whose names are not written in the Book of Life from the foundation of the world, when they see the beast that was, and is not, and yet is." The Empire of the Lawless One (Antichrist) is represented as a woman. The beast that carried and supported the woman is Satan. Satan supported Ancient Babylon, then the Roman Empire, and at the end time Satan will support the Lawless One (Antichrist). The evil empires are represented by a woman the beast that carries them is Satan. The term beast is used to represent Satan the false prophet and the evil empires. The seven horns and ten heads represent the great power of empires like the worldwide Empire of the Lawless One (Antichrist).

Satan is the power behind the empires called beasts and the beast that John saw in his vision. Satan was at one time in heaven, then was on earth, then was cast into the Abyss, and is not now on earth. Ancient Babylon was the first beast. The Roman Empire was the second beast and the Empire of the Lawless One will be the third and last beast. The beast that John saw was Satan that controlled the Babylonian Empire, and the Roman Empire

Verses 9–14 "Here is the mind which has wisdom: The seven heads are seven mountains on which the woman sits. There are also seven kings. Five have fallen, one is, and the other has not yet come. And when he comes, he must continue a short time. The beast that was, and is not, is himself also the eighth, and is of the seven, and is going to perdition." "The ten horns which you saw are ten kings who have received no kingdom as yet, but they receive authority for one hour as kings with the beast. These are of one mind, and they will give their power and authority to the beast.' These will make war with the Lamb, and the Lamb will' "overcome them, for He is Lord of lords and King of kings; and those who are with Him are called, chosen, and faithful."

The woman in verses 9 and 10 is the Roman Empire that was supported by Satan. Rome, the capital of the Roman Empire, was built on seven hills. At the time John wrote, he and other Christians would recognize that the Empire of the Lawless One (Antichrist) would be an anti type of the Roman Empire. The seven kings were those who once ruled the Roman Empire.

Five kings were in the past, one was ruling when John wrote, and there was one more to come. The one to come will be the Lawless One (Antichrist) who will be an anti-type of the evil rulers of the Roman Empire. The empire of the Lawless One (Antichrist) is the harlot that was yet to come.

The beast that was represents Ancient Babylon and the Roman Empire as a harlot. The Roman Empire was, is not now, but is coming back as the Lawless One (Antichrist), an anti-type of the Roman Empire. Ten kings who have not yet received a kingdom will be allied with the Lawless One (Antichrist) for a very short time and war against Christ. Christ will be victorious. The ten kingdoms will be kingdoms in existence when the Lawless One is in power. The kings that were allied with the Lawless one will, in time, come to hate the Lawless One (Antichrist), and they will make her desolate and naked, eat her flesh, and burn her with fire, because God will turn them against her. The nations on earth that turned against the Antichrist will help the church.

Verses 15–18 "Then he said to me, "The waters which you saw, where the harlot sits, are people, multitudes, nations, and tongues. And the ten horns that you saw on the beast, these hate the harlot, make her desolate and naked, eat her flesh and burn her with fire. For God has put it into their hearts to fulfill His purpose, to be of one mind, and to give their kingdom to the beast, until the words of God are fulfilled. And the woman whom you saw is that great city which reigns over the kings of the earth." Chapter 18 John describes the destruction of the Lawless One (Antichrist) and the attitudes of the people who loved her in her beginning and will still love her at the end.

God Summons His People to Come Out of Babylon

In chapter eighteen John saw an angel coming from heaven with great authority. He was a mighty angel with a loud voice that cried out, "Babylon the Great has fallen." Babylon the Great fell many years earlier, but John is speaking of the anti-type of Babylon, the Empire of the Lawless One (Antichrist) at the end time. Ancient Babylon was destroyed because of her evil ways and her persecution of God's people. Ancient Rome fell for the same reason, and the empire of the Lawless One (Antichrist) is destined to fall as well at the end of time.

The Angel saw the destruction of the empire of the Lawless One (Antichrist) at the end of time ahead of time so he could warn God's people. God warns his people to come out of Babylon before it is too late. The expression come out of Babylon means to come out of the sin caused by Satan and the Lawless One. The destruction of the evil forces symbolized by Babylon of the past, present, and future will be exposed to God's wrath at the end of time. The anti-type forces of evil will receive a double punishment. The empire of the Lawless One will receive back double all of the anguish, grief and tribulation she was guilty of imposing on God's people and the people of the earth. God's people will be glad to see the great evil empire punished, but the rulers of the earth and those that profited from her, especially the greedy, will mourn because of the loss of wealth and luxury. They will be terrified when they learn of her punishment knowing that they must face the judgment of God. Those who profit from evil are those who become wealthy from the guilt of the seven sins God hates.

Proverbs 6:12–19 "A worthless person a wicked man walks with a perverse mouth. He winks with his eyes he shuffles his feet he points with his fingers. Perversity is in his heart he devises evil continually.' "He sows discord therefore his calamity shall come suddenly. Suddenly he shall be broken without remedy.' "These six things the Lord hates, Yes seven are an abomination to Him; A proud look, A lying tongue, Hands that shed innocent blood, a heart that devises wicked plans, Feet that are swift in running to evil, a false witness who speaks lies, and the one who sows discord among brethren."

The fall of Babylon the Great

John saw a mighty angel come down from heaven, probably Michael who came down to protect God's people. The angel shouted with a loud voice to all of the nations of earth who are guilty of her evil deeds. Chapter 18 pictures the great evil that will exist on earth at the end time and declares that it will be destroyed. Chapter 18:1–5 "After these things I saw another angel coming down from heaven, having great authority, and the earth was illuminated with his glory.

And he cried mightily with a loud voice saying, "Babylon the great is fallen, is fallen, and has become a dwelling place of demons, a prison for every foul spirit, and a cage for every unclean and hated bird! For all the nations have drunk of the wine of the wrath of her fornication, the kings of the earth have committed fornication with her, and the merchants of the earth have become rich through the abundance of her luxury. And I heard another voice from heaven saying, "Come out of her, my people, lest you share in her sins, and lest you receive of her plagues. For her sins have reached to heaven, and God has remembered her iniquities."

Verses 6-8 "Render to her just as she rendered to you, and repay her double according to her works; in the cup, which she has mixed, mix double for her. In the measure that she glorified herself and lived luxuriously, in the same measure give her torment and sorrow; for she says in her heart, 'I sit as queen, and am no widow, and will not see sorrow.' Therefore her plagues will come in one day—death and mourning and famine. And she will be utterly burned with fire, for strong is the Lord God who judges her.'

God will repay all evil at the end of time with a judgment of fire. Verses 9–20 "The kings of the earth who committed fornication and lived luxuriously with her will weep and lament for her, when they see the smoke of her burning, standing at a distance for fear of her torment saying, "Alas, alas, that great city Babylon, that mighty city! For in one hour your judgment has come.' And the merchants of the earth will weep and mourn over her, for no one buys their merchandise anymore: Merchandise of gold and silver, precious stones and pearls, fine linen and purple, silk and scarlet, every kind of citron wood, every king of object of ivory, every kind of object of most precious wood, bronze, iron, and marble; and cinnamon and incense, fragrant oil and frankincense, wine and oil, fine flour and wheat, cattle and sheep, horses and chariots, and bodies and souls of men. The fruit that your soul longed for has gone from you, and all the things which are rich and splendid have gone from you, and you shall find them no more at all. The merchants of these things, who became rich by her, will stand at a distance for fear of her torment, weeping and wailing, and saying, 'Alas, alas, that great city that was clothed in fine linen, purple, and scarlet, and adorned with gold and precious stones and pearls!"

"For in one hour such great riches came to nothing. Every shipmaster, all who travel by ship, sailors, and as many as trade on the sea, stood at a distance and cried out when they saw the smoke of her burning saying, 'What is like this great city. They threw dust on their heads and cried out, weeping and wailing and saying, 'Alas, alas, that great city, in which all who had ships on the sea became rich by her wealth! For in one hour she is made desolate.' "Rejoice over her, O heaven, and you holy apostles and prophets, for God has avenged you on her!" The fall of the Empire of the Lawless One (Antichrist) will be become desolate within one hour.

Verses 21–24 "Then a mighty angel took up a stone like a great millstone and threw it into the sea saying, "Thus with violence the great city Babylon shall be thrown down, and shall not be found anymore. The sound of harpists, musicians, flutists, and trumpeters shall not be heard in you anymore. No craftsman of any craft shall be found in you anymore, and the sound of a millstone shall not be heard in you anymore. The light of a lamp shall not shine in you anymore, and the voice of bridegroom and bride shall not be heard in you anymore. For your merchants were the great men of the earth, for by your sorcery all the nations were deceived. And in her was found the blood of prophets and saints, and of all who were slain on the earth."

Before her destruction the empire will have confidence that nothing will ever be able to harm her, but the plagues from the wrath of God will overtake her, and she will be destroyed by fire from the mighty judgment of God. The people of earth, who made money by doing business with her because of greed one of the sins God hates, will mourn when they see her destruction. In John states that her destruction will be a time of rejoicing for Christians, including the apostles and prophets, because of the way she treated God's people. John saw a symbolic description of the death of all the evil forces that were anti-types of Babylon the Great at the end of time, the unbelievers and those who were evil. A powerful angel picked up an enormous boulder, threw it into the sea, and stated aloud, "With the same violence the great city of Babylon will be thrown down and will never be found again."

Heaven Celebrates Babylon's Defeat

Chapter 19:1–3 "After these things I heard a loud voice of a great multitude in heaven, saying, "Alleluia! Salvation and glory and honor and power belong to the Lord our God! For true and righteous are His judgments, because He has judged the great harlot who corrupted the earth with her fornication; and He has avenged on her the blood of His servants shed by her." Again they said, "Alleluia! Her smoke rises up forever and ever!"

Babylon, the great harlot, symbolizes the epitome of all kinds of evil. After her fall, the inhabitants of heaven will celebrate her destruction. Alleluia! For the Lord God Omnipotent reigns! Let us be glad and rejoice and give Him glory, for the marriage of the Lamb has come, and His wife has made herself ready." And to her it was granted to be arrayed in fine linen, clean and bright, for the fine linen is the righteous acts of the saints.' Now I saw heaven. Then he said to me, "Write: Blessed are those who are called to the marriage supper of the Lamb!'" And he said to me, "These are the true sayings of God." And I fell at his feet to worship him. But he said to me, "See that you do not do that! I am your fellow servant, and of your brethren who have the testimony of Jesus. Worship God! For the testimony of Jesus is the spirit of prophecy." John heard them say, "The wedding of the Lamb has come, and his bride is ready." Christ is the bridegroom, and the faithful church is the bride. The time for the wedding of Christ and the church comes when Christ returns at the end of time. The church that remains faithful will be waiting for the bridegroom and the new heaven and new earth.

Christ on a White Horse–End of Time

Verses 11–16 "Now I saw heaven opened, and behold, a white horse. And He who sat on him was called Faithful and True, and in righteousness He judges and makes war. His eyes were like a flame of fire, and on His head were many crowns. He had a name written that no one knew except Himself. He was clothed with a robe dipped in blood, and His name is called The Word of God.

And the armies in heaven, clothed in fine linen, white and clean, followed Him on white horses. Now out of His mouth goes a sharp sword, that with it He should strike the nations. And He Himself will rule them with a rod of iron. He Himself treads the winepress of the fierceness and wrath of Almighty God. And He has on His robe and on His thigh a name written: KING OF KINGS AND LORD OF LORDS." John looks into heaven, he saw a rider on a white horse. The rider was named Faithful and True. Christ is the rider on the white horse. White is a symbol for righteousness, and Christ and the white horse both symbolize righteousness and justice. Christ had crowns on his head, signifying that he is a ruler with authority. Christ is Sovereign over heaven and earth. He has all authority and power. Christ had on a bloody robe, and he was called The Word of God. The bloody robes symbolized the death and destruction of the unrighteous. The angels from heaven will follow Christ, dressed in white robes and riding on white horses. They are His army. Everything that John saw indicated a great battle on earth that would involve great bloodshed. Christ and his army of angels are going to strike down the nations. There will be a sharp sword in the mouth of Christ, a symbol of the word of God, which gives Him authority to punish the nations of ungodly people, and on His thigh will be written: KING OF KINGS AND LORD OF LORDS."

The Beast and His Armies Defeated

Verses 17–21 "Then I saw an angel standing in the sun; and he cried with a loud voice, saying to all the birds that fly in the midst of heaven, "Come and gather together for the supper of the great God, that you may eat the flesh of kings, the flesh of captains, the flesh of mighty men, the flesh of horses and of those who sit on them, and the flesh of all people, free and slave, both small and great.' "And I saw the beast, the kings of the earth, and their armies, gathered together to make war against Him who sat on the horse and against His army. Then the beast was captured, and with him the false prophet who worked signs in his presence, by which he deceived those who received the mark of the beast and those who worshiped his image.' "These two were cast alive into the lake of fire burning with brimstone. And the rest were killed with the sword, which proceeded from the mouth of Him who sat on the horse. And all the birds were filled with their flesh."

Christians are invited to the wedding supper of the Lamb. When Paul wrote the second letter to the church in Corinth, he told the members that he promised them one husband. Christ is that husband the church will be presented to Christ as a pure virgin bride. The church is united with Christ spiritually now, but at the end of time the church will be with Christ in person. At the end of time, Christ and all of the faithful will come and the church will take her place in the new heaven and the new earth. John was about to worship the angel that revealed these events to him, but the angel would not let him. God and Christ are the only ones who are worthy to receive worship.

Section 7 Chapters 20-22

Chapter 20:1-3 Christ will deal with Satan and the judgment at the end of time. "Then I saw an angel coming down from heaven, having the key to the bottomless pit and a great chain in his hand. He laid hold of the dragon, that serpent of old, who is the Devil and Satan, and bound him for a thousand years; and he cast him into the bottomless pit, and shut him up, and set a seal on him, so that he should deceive the nations no more till the thousand years were finished. But after these things he must be released for a little while."

The first three verses of chapter 20 begin with the first century when Satan was put in the Abyss. Chapter 20 ends with the great judgment of God at the end of time. The thousand years that Satan was bound in the Abyss is called the millennium, a figurative term denoting the period of time from the first century to the second coming of Christ. The exact length of that time is literally unknown by anyone but God. Satan was put in the Abyss where he is now, but at the end time near the end of the millennium, he will be released and will begin his reign of terror on the earth against the church until he is destroyed at the end of time. 1st Corinthians 15:20–28–Christ rises from the dead, He becomes the first fruits of those who have died. Death came by man and by man also came the resurrection of the dead. For as in Adam all die, even so in Christ all will be made alive. But each one in his own order: Christ first, afterward those who are Christ's at His coming. Then the end comes and Christ delivers the kingdom to God the Father. He puts an end to all rule and all authority and power. For He must reign until He has put all His enemies under His feet except God the Father. Now when all things are made subject to Him, then the Son Himself will also be subject to Him who put all things under Him that God may be all in all.

Christ reigns during the Christian dispensation, and all Christians reign with Christ. At the end of time Christ will deliver the church to God and the rule of Christ will end.

Romans 5:17–18 "For if by the one man's offense death reigned through the one, much more those who receive abundance of grace and of the gift of righteousness will reign in life through the One, Jesus Christ." Reign means to exist or to prevail. Christians will live on earth until Christ returns and they will prevail over death in the resurrection. Christ, the King of Kings reign over the church on earth now until the time of His return, then He will deliver the church to God in heaven. The Bible does not mention a kingdom existing for one thousand years. The one thousand years, also called the millennium, is figurative language meaning a long period of time of which the literal length is not known. Christ began His millennial reign when He ascended to heaven and sat down at the right hand of God.

Matthew 28:18–20 "And Jesus came and spoke to them, saying, "All authority has been given to me in heaven and on earth. Go therefore and make disciples of all the nations, baptizing them in the name of the Father and of the Son and of the Holy Spirit." Verses 4–6 "And I saw thrones and they sat on them, and judgment was committed to them. Then I saw the souls of those who had been beheaded for their witness to Jesus and for the word of God, who had not worshiped the beast or his image, and had not received his mark on their foreheads or on their hands.' "And they lived and reigned with Christ for a thousand years. But the rest of the dead did not live again until the thousand years were finished. This is the first resurrection. Blessed and holy is he who has part in the first resurrection. Over such the second death has no power, but they shall be priests of God and of Christ, and shall reign with Him a thousand years."

The thrones John saw were in heaven, and those on the thrones were martyrs who were given authority to judge. The spirits of the martyrs go directly to heaven at the time of their death. There have been many martyrs since the death of Christ, and there will be many more before the end of time including those who refuse to worship the beast during the end time. The martyrs live and reign with Christ in heaven during the millennium, but the other dead must wait until the end of time to be resurrected. Christians only die once and will be resurrected at the end of time with a glorious body and will go to heaven. At the end of time the unrighteous will be resurrected and judged, then they will experience a second death in the lake of fire.

Verses 7–10 "Now when the thousand years have expired, Satan will be released from his prison and will go out to deceive the nations which are in the four corners of the earth, Gog and Magog, to gather them together to battle, whose number is as the sand of the sea.' "They went up on the breadth of the earth and surrounded the camp of the saints and the beloved city. And fire came down from God out of heaven and devoured them. The Devil who deceived them was cast into the lake of fire and brimstone where the beast and the false prophet are. And they will be tormented day and night forever and ever."

During the end time Satan and the demons will be released from the bottomless pit and go out over the earth to deceive the leaders of the nations turning them against God, Christ, and the Church. That is the time when the Lawless One (Antichrist) led by Satan will be in power and the time when the great battle takes place, the battle called of Armageddon in chapter 16. All of the nations will be gathered together in a rebellion against God. The nations are symbolized as Gog and Magog, and their number will be too great to count. Gog and Magog were common rabbinical titles for the nations in rebellion against the Lord. (Notes from NKJV) The nations will surround the church, symbolized as the Great City of God. The battle will be brief, because fire will come down from heaven and destroy the great army led by Satan. Then Satan and the demons will be cast into a lake of fire where the beast and the false prophet will have been thrown.

2nd Peter 3:10–13 "But the day of the Lord will come as a thief in the night, in which the heavens will pass away with a great noise, and the elements will melt with fervent heat; both earth and the works that are in it will be burned up. Therefore since all these things will be dissolved, what manner of persons ought you to be in holy conduct and godliness, looking for and hastening the coming day of God, because of which of which the heavens will be dissolved, being on fire, and the elements will melt with fervent heat? Nevertheless we according to His promise, look for new heavens and a new earth in which righteousness dwells."

Judgment of the Great White Throne

Verses 11–15 "Then I saw a great white throne and Him who sat on it, from whose face the earth and the heaven fled away. And there was found no place for them. And I saw the dead, small and great, standing before God, and books were opened.' "And another book was opened, which is the Book of Life. And the dead were judged according to their works, by the things, which were written in the books. The sea gave up the dead who were in it, and Death and Hades delivered up the dead who were in them. And they were judged, each one according to his works. Then death and Hades were cast into the lake of fire. This is the second death. And anyone not found written in the Book of Life was cast into the lake of fire."

The great white throne symbolizes God's throne in heaven where He judges all creation and determines their fate based on their righteousness or unrighteousness. Everyone who has ever existed is subjected to the judgment of God. The books symbolize the knowledge of God concerning the life and works of every individual, including those who were in Hades and those who die before the great judgment. The dead will be resurrected and stand before God's judgment. Everyone will be judged except for the martyrs already in heaven. The unrighteous people of all times will be cast into the lake of fire, and the righteous will go to a new heaven and new earth that has been prepared for them by God. Those who failed to become righteous through faith in Christ will be cast into the lake of fire and experience a second death. During the early days of the church, some Christians did not believe there would be a resurrection. In the 15th chapter of 1st Corinthians, Paul taught about the resurrection of the dead at the end of time.

1st Corinthians 15:33–34 "Awake to righteousness, and do not sin; for some do not have the knowledge of God. I speak this to your shame." 1st Corinthians 15:40–44 "There are also celestial bodies and terrestrial bodies; but the glory of the celestial is one, and the glory of the terrestrial is another. There is one glory of the sun, another glory of the moon, and another glory of the stars; for one star differs from another star in glory. So also is the resurrection of the dead.' "The body is sown in corruption, it is raised in incorruption. It is sown in dishonor it is raised in glory. It is sown in weakness it is raised in power. It is sown a natural body it is raised a spiritual body. There is a natural body, and there is a spiritual body."

1st Corinthians 15:50-57– This I say brethren, flesh and blood cannot inherit the kingdom of God; nor does corruption inherit incorruption. I tell you a mystery: We shall not all die, but we shall all be changed—in a moment, in the twinkling of an eye, at the sounding of the last trumpet last trumpet. The trumpet will sound, and the dead will be raised incorruptible, and we shall be changed. For the corruptible has put on incorruption, and this mortal has put on immortality, then shall be brought to pass the saying that is written: "Death is swallowed up in victory." "O Death where is your sting? O Hades, where is your victory?" The sting of death is sin, and the strength of sin is the law. But thanks be to God, who gives us the victory through our Lord Jesus Christ."

The New Heaven and the New Earth

Chapter 21:1-21–John saw a new heaven and a new earth, for the first heaven and the first earth had passed away and there was no more sea. Then John, saw the holy city, New Jerusalem, coming down out of heaven from God, prepared as a bride adorned for her husband. And I heard a loud voice from heaven saying, the tabernacle of God is with men, and He will dwell with them, and they shall be His people. God Himself will be with them and be their God. And God will wipe away every tear from their eyes; there shall be no more death, nor sorrow, nor crying. There shall be on more pain, for the former things have passed away. Then He who sat on the throne said, "Behold, I make all things new."

And He said to me, "Write, for these words are true and faithful. And He said to me, "It is done! I am the Alpha and the Omega, the Beginning and the End. I will give of the fountain of the water of life freely to him who thirsts.' "He who overcomes shall inherit all things, and I will be his God and he shall be My son. But the cowardly, unbelieving, abominable, murderers, sexually immoral, sorcerers, idolaters, and all liars shall have their part in the lake which burns with fire and brimstone, which is the second death. Then one of the seven angels who had the seven bowls filled with the seven last plagues came to me and talked with me, saying, "Come, I will show you the bride, the Lamb's wife. And he carried me away in the Spirit to a great and high mountain, and showed me the great city, the Holy Jerusalem, descending out of heaven from God, having the glory of God.' "Her light was like a most precious stone, like a jasper stone, clear as crystal.' "Also she had a great and high wall with twelve gates, and twelve angels at the gates, and names written on them, which are the names of the twelve tribes of the children of Israel: three gates on the east, three gates on the north, three gates on the south, and three gates on the west.'

"Now the wall of the city had twelve foundations, and on them were the names of the twelve apostles of the Lamb. And he who talked with me had a gold reed to measure the city, its gates, and its wall. The city is laid out as a square; its length is as great as its breadth.

And he measured the city with the reed; twelve thousand furlongs. Its length, breadth, and height are equal.' "Then he measured its wall: one hundred and forth-four cubits, according to the measure of a man, that is, of an angel. The construction of its wall was of jasper; and the city was pure gold, like clear glass.

The foundations of the wall of the city were adorned with all kinds of precious stones:' "The first foundation was jasper, the second sapphire, the third chalcedone, the fourth emerald, the fifth sardonyx, the sixth sardius, the seventh chrysolite, the eighth beryl, the ninth topaz, the tenth chrysoprase, the eleventh jacinth, and the twelfth amethyst. The twelve gates were twelve pearls: each individual gate was of one pearl. And the street of the city was pure gold, like transparent glass."

John saw the Holy City, the New Jerusalem, which is the church, and it was coming down out of God's heaven. The Spirit brought a symbolic view of the church to John's mind — the redeemed church came into his view. The church looked like a bride beautifully dressed for her husband who is Christ. John saw the fulfillment of all of the prophet's writings and the gospel of Christ; the culmination of God's redeeming plan. John heard a voice saying, the tabernacle of God is with men, and He will live with them, and they will be His people. God Himself will be their God. God will wipe away every tear from their eyes and there shall be no more death, no sorrow, or crying. There shall be no more pain, for the former things have passed away. Then He who sat on the throne said, Behold, I make all things new. And He said to me, "Write, for these words are true and faithful." And He said to me, "It is done." The church will live in a new heaven and new earth with God and Christ for all eternity. The people will be God's people in heaven.